D0224888

Gilles Deleuze

and the
Theater
of
Philosophy

DISCARDED

Gilles Deleuze

and the
Theater
of
Philosophy

EDITED BY CONSTANTIN V. BOUNDAS
& DOROTHEA OLKOWSKI

ROUTLEDGE New York · London

COLLEGE OF THE SEQUOIAS
LIBRARY

Published in 1994 by

Routledge
29 West 35th Street
New York, NY 10001

Published in Great Britain by

Routledge
11 New Fetter Lane
London EC4P 4EE

Copyright© 1994 by Routledge

Copyright acknowledgments

Alain Badiou, "Gilles Deleuze, The Fold: Leibniz and the Baroque," translated from *Annuaire Philosophique, 1988–89* by permission of *Editions du Seuil:* Copyright 1988 by *Editions du Seuil.*

Gilles Deleuze, "Begaya-t-il" ("He Stuttered . . . ") was first published in 1993 by Les Edition De Minuit.

Elizabeth Grosz, "A Thousand Tiny Sexes" was first published in TOPOI, 1993, vol. 12/2 (Kluwer Academic Publishers).

Marie-Claire Ropars-Wuilleumier, "The Cinema, Reader of Gilles Deleuze," reprinted from *Camera Obscura: A Journal of Feminism and Film Theory,* September 1989, No. 18 by permission of *Camera Obscura:* Copyright *Camera Obscura,* 1988.

All rights reserved. No part of this book may be reprinted or reproduced or utilized in any form or by an electronic, mechanical or other means, now known or hereafter invented, including photocopying and recording or in any information storage or retrieval system, without permission in writing from the publishers.

Library of Congress Cataloging-in-Publication Data

Deleuze and the theater of philosophy / edited by Constantin V. Boundas and
    Dorothea Olkowski.
       p.   cm.
    ISBN 0-415-90504-4 (cloth). — ISBN 0-415-90505-2 (pbk.)
     1. Deleuze, Gilles. 2. Philosophy, Modern—20th century. 3. Aesthetics, Modern —
20th century. I. Boundas, Constantin V. II. Olkowski, Dorothea.
B2430.D454D45 1993
194—dc20   92-41492
                                                                    CIP

British Library Cataloging-in-Publication Data

Deleuze and the Theater of Philosophy
    I. Boundas, Constantin V. II. Olkowski, Dorothea
    801.092

    ISBN 0-415-90504-4

British Library Cataloging-in-Publication Data

Deleuze and the Theater of Philosophy
    I. Boundas, Constantin V. II. Olkowski, Dorothea
    801.092

    ISBN 0-415-90505-2

For Choi Ke Ryang

For Max and Kurt

Contents

IV The Question of Becoming-Woman

V Minor Languages and Nomad Arts

VI Lines of Flight

Acknowledgments

SHAPING THIS VOLUME has taken several years, many hours, and much patience, not just on the part of the editors, but also on the part of the many individuals who participated in the effort and share the commitment to Deleuze's work. All of the contributors to the volume have labored to produce essays that reflect the complex and timely concerns addressed by Deleuze and, for this, we, the editors wish to thank each of them. We particularly thank Gilles Deleuze for the moving essay which leads off this collection. In addition, there are the individuals who helped us carry out the labor of producing this volume, especially Lee Duren and Marg Tully, and who also earned our thanks. Our families extended much good will toward us, encouraging us and giving us the understanding needed to carry out our task, and we are grateful for their support. We wish also to acknowledge the generous support of the Canadian Social Science and Humanities Research Council which made possible the 1992 Trent University Deleuze Conference—the dress rehearsal of the production displayed in this volume. Finally, we wish to thank especially Maureen MacGrogan, our editor at Routledge, and her assistant Katherine Lieber for their constancy, good humor, and kindness in the face of what must have seemed like constant delays and changes in this book.

1

Editors' Introduction

Constantin V. Boundas and Dorothea Olkowski

> From an always nomadic and anarchical difference to the unavoidably excessive and displaced sign of recurrence, a lightning storm was produced which will, one day, be given the name of Deleuze: new thought is possible; thought is again possible . . . genital thought, intensive thought, affirmative thought, acategorical thought—each of these an unrecognizable face, a mask we have never seen before; differences we had no reason to expect, but which nevertheless lead to the return, as masks of their masks, of Plato, Duns Scotus, Spinoza, Leibniz, Kant, and all other philosophers. This is not philosophy as thought, but as theatre . . .
>
> —Michel Foucault, *Theatrum Philosophicum*[1]

FROM DELEUZE'S EARLY WORK on Hume, Masoch, and Nietzsche to his later collaborations with radical psychoanalyst Félix Guattari, Deleuze's thought *is* startling—a lightning storm for thinkers like those who have contributed to this volume of critical essays. But in what sense are Deleuze's works of philosophy theater? For one, these works are marked by the constant invention of conceptual characters: the inquirer, the judge, the friend, and the rival are such conceptual characters invented and put on stage by Deleuze. They are not meant to resemble the philosophers (Hume, Kant, Plato) whose work they stage. But they are meant to assist in the arrival of a new image of thought. Unlike Platonism, which determines the question of the Idea in the form "What is F?," Deleuze brings Ideas closer to accidents and argues that they can be determined only with questions like "Who?," "How?," "How many?," "When and where?," that is, with questions that plot their true spatiotemporal coordinates.[2]

If, as Deleuze says, philosophy is the activity that traces a prephilosophical plane of immanence (reason), invents prophilosophical characters (imagi-

1

nation), and creates philosophical concepts (understanding), it is with the invention of the conceptual characters that the creation of concepts and the tracing of the processes that form the plane of immanence begins in earnest.[3] It is through "dramatization" that the virtual Idea is incarnated and actualized (Deleuze 1967, p. 96).[4] Without it, the concept would never be divided and specified. Pure spatiotemporal dynamisms have the power to dramatize concepts because they are the ones that incarnate and actualize Ideas: "There is a drama beneath every logos" (p. 101).

Deleuze makes it clear that this drama is taking the place of the Kantian schema. It constitutes "a strange theatre made up of pure determinations, agitating space and time, acting directly on the soul, having larvae as actors—a theatre for which Artaud has chosen the expression 'theatre of cruelty'" (p. 95)—all this, of course, provided that the conceptual character is not mistaken for the philosopher's representative. "The philosopher is the envelope of his main character, and of all the other characters who are the real subjects of his philosophy" (Deleuze 1991, p. 62). If then Deleuze's philosophy is a theater, as Foucault thought, it is most certainly a minor theater. Only a minor theater can address the sense in which Deleuze's work always opens up an area of inquiry that had been thought to be completely exhausted and long since abandoned by philosophy or, at least, by any novel inquiry. Only a minor theater can retrace these abandoned philosophies so as to transform each one so completely that it is barely recognizable and bears no resemblance to the old exhausted ideas.

The present collection of essays—the first, we believe, in any language—is intended as a tribute to Deleuze. One, of course, does not pay Deleuze a tribute by canonizing his texts or by fencing them in with commentaries and annotations. This is the reason why we solicited essays that would be like gusts of fresh air from the outside. We tried to trade off the search for hidden signifieds for a better understanding of how Deleuze's texts work. We wanted to trace the diagram of the series that make up his work, instead of "representing" it or blurring its lines altogether, making it totally unrecognizable. The essays that we included enact a variety of research styles and ambitions. American, Canadian, French, and Australian scholars, fairly well distributed among philosophers, literary theorists, sociologists, and women's studies specialists came together to form the diverging, yet resonant, series that made this volume possible. Deleuze, with his usual grace, responded to our intrusive request for participation with his never before published essay "Begaya-t-il," which we decided to place at the beginning of the collection, in order to avoid creating the impression that this essay in any sense stands for the customary "response" to one's critics. In the beginning was the stuttering, and the stuttering was of the outside. *Stutterer, thinker of the outside*—what better way is there for registering the passage of a philosopher?

Delimiting even the six areas that constitute this volume was, for us, the editors, an arduous task. Although our six chosen "themes" resonate throughout Deleuze's writings, these themes (difference and repetition, subjectivity, desire and the overturning of Platonism, becoming-woman, minor languages and nomad thought, and lines of flight) are not developed *thematically* in any sense by Deleuze himself. Deleuze's nomadic thought cannot give way to thematic organization because so much of what Deleuze thinks and writes has to do with the overturning of all familiar themes and of thematization itself.

The first section of our collection consists of two essays that analyze and discuss the Deleuzian themes of difference, sameness, and singularity. Todd May's essay, "Difference and Unity in Gilles Deleuze," attempts to disentangle Deleuze from the nets of a total affirmation of alterity and anarchism. Redescribing this affirmation, May argues that Deleuze cannot coherently maintain the primacy of difference over unity without lapsing into the kind of transcendentalism that his entire philosophy was poised to denounce, reducing language to unintelligible verbiage, or letting the very surfaces upon which thought is supposed to happen break up into a host of unrelated molecules. "Difference," May writes, "must be thought of alongside unity, or not at all!" May does not deny that there is a tendency in Deleuze's thought toward pure difference and its resounding affirmation, but he is struck by what he takes to be the presence in it of an opposite tendency that makes Deleuze appeal constantly throughout his work to writers whose work is "unitary and monistic" (Scotus, Spinoza, Bergson). In order to resolve this "tension," May finds it necessary, first, to ponder over the role that Deleuze assigns to philosophy (the creation of concepts), in order to decide subsequently what a typical Deleuzian philosophical claim looks like, given that the primary task of philosophy is normative. Philosophy, on this reading, is a practice that can be evaluated only on the basis of the effects that it brings about, and this evaluation can have no recourse to any transcendental standpoint. From such considerations about the nature of philosophy, May concludes that the correct approach to the Deleuzian concept of difference is the investigation of how it functions, and not of how one can ground its metaphysical priority. Difference, he concludes, functions as a concept that resists transcendence in all its forms. Positive in maintaining the irreducibility and contingency of singularity, and disruptive in resisting all principles of unification, Deleuze's difference, according to May, is not mobilized against unity, but only against those transcendental principles of unification that preclude difference and relegate it to the status of the negative. With Deleuze, May finds in Spinoza's expressionism the best guarantor of the compossibilty of difference and unity, provided that, as in Spinoza, expressionism is put in the service of univocity. In the figure of the rhizome, May reads the univocity of being, that is, "the affirmation neither of difference nor of unity but of the surface which is the intertwining of the two."

Deleuze's choice and affirmation of alterity requires the creation of new concepts, and our inclusion of Alain Badiou's essay—a long meditation on *Le pli: Leibniz et le baroque*—is dictated by the fact that it explores in an exemplary fashion the function and resonances of such a concept. From a position proximate to, and yet distant from Deleuze's own, Badiou discusses the concept of the fold and finds it to be an antiextensional concept of the multiple, an antidialectical concept of the event, and an anti-Cartesian concept of the subject. According to Badiou, the cross of metaphysics has been the impossible choice between the animal and the number. Against this background, Deleuze's fold, a figure of the multiple anchored in an anti-set-theoretical ontology, a continuist horror of vacuum, and an organicist vision, opts without hesitation for the animal. Deleuze's multiple, argues Badiou, "is a *living tissue* which folds and unfolds as if under the effect of its organic expandings and contractings, in perfect opposition to the Cartesian concept of extension which is punctual and regulated by the shock." The fold is the triumph of the wave over the particle. Badiou realizes, of course, that such an organicist vision of the multiple puts the singular at risk. This is why he reminds us that singularities and events are not, for Deleuze, points of rupture, but rather "what singularizes continuity in each one of its local folds." The event is an immanent activity against the "dark" background of a preexisting world; it is a creation, a novelty, that is thinkable only inside the interiority of a continuum. It follows, argues Badiou, that the multiple and the concept (the multiple and the one) are not opposed to each other, since the multiple exists by the concept and is warranted by the universality of continuity; but, at the same time, the multiple is the condition of the possibility of concepts. As for Deleuze's organicism, Badiou adds, it is not built around the Leibnizian compossibility of worlds, but rather around Nietzsche's (and Mallarmé's) resonant and vibrant diverging series.

In the sequence, Badiou's essay assimilates the Deleuzian fold to the concept of a subject that is neither Cartesian (reflection, cogito) nor Husserlian (focus, relation to, intentionality) nor Lacanian (eclipse). The articulation of this concept of the subject requires the outside to be thought as the exact inversion of the inside, the world as a texture of the intimate, and the macroscopic as the torsion of the microscopic. For Badiou, the advantages of such a concept are obvious: the subject emerges as multiple series, a veritable unfolding of predicates, and not as a substance; it is a point of view from which there is a truth, and an "objectless subject," since it frees knowledge from all relations to objects. Badiou's essay concludes with an extremely nuanced and yet thorough critique of Deleuze's "ontological choice"—a critique based on his own alternative choice, focusing on number, set theory, and the admission of the vacuum. We leave it to the reader to assess the advantages and disadvantages of this choice over Deleuze's.

For the second section of our collection, we chose two essays that promise to initiate discussion concerning the role and function that subjectivity has in the writings of Deleuze. We think that the North American reception of the poststructuralist "death of man," or "death of the subject," thematics and rhetoric has not been adequately discussed. The Deleuzian inflections of the problem and our assemblage aim at filling this deplorable lacuna.

Peter Canning's essay, "The Crack of Time and the Ideal Game," returns to the questions of multiplicity, time as the multiplicity of the eternal return, and subject as the kind of multiplicity that one finds suspended over the crack of time. His essay is itself a multiplicity, successfully preventing its own forms of expression and content from sedimenting around any one unifying principle, rhythm, or theme. Deleuze's multiplicity, argues Canning, is not the One turning into many, but rather an assemblage that changes dimensions and mutates constantly, according to its own lines of flight. Real time has nothing to do with the passing present; it starts when the present stops: it affects itself not with itself, but with becoming, and emerges as pretime from the crack between times. Repetition is the power of the rhythmic idea that produces differences, intensities, and disparities as its own excess. As the repetition of the future, it has nothing to do with the return to the past, which is accomplished in memory. It begins with metamorphosis and forgetting—*Chaosmos*, the between of chaos and order where structures form and dissolve—and has its own rhythms that account for the intensities and originary differences produced by repetition. Canning argues for the proviso that repetition is not to be seen as the function of the subject, because the subject is the result of the rhythm that creates and selects the intensive traits and the directional components of the plane of immanence. Under these circumstances, is it still possible to speak about the subject? Canning does not address this question directly, but he does speak, nonetheless, of the subject as an intervention and interval. The subject, for Canning, who echoes the Deleuze of *Foucault,* is the splitting between the virtual (Idea-multiplicity) and the actual (individual-multiplicity), and the folding of the one upon the other. The human subject is a being suspended over the caesura of time.

Constantin V. Boundas's essay makes the claim that a powerful theory of subjectivity can be teased out from Deleuze's texts, provided that the processes of serialization and subject formation were to be explored together. Boundas proposes to read Deleuze the way Deleuze reads others, that is, according to the series he creates, the ways in which these series converge and become compossible, and the means by which they diverge and begin to resonate together. The author's proposal is made in the context of recent discussions attempting to elucidate subjectivity in terms of narrativity, but it stays clear of the phenomenological and hermeneutic postulate of the unity of the self or the assumed coherence of lived-time consciousness. Deleuze, for whom narrativization is serialization and for whom the conjunctive linkages among series are subordinated to their disjunctive resonances, is able to provide us with a theory of subject formation liberated from old phenomenological trappings. For this purpose, Boundas spreads Deleuze's contributions to a theory of subjectivity across several series, each one of which he identifies by means of the question/problem that the series helps to introduce: the *Hume series* (how does the mind become a subject?), the *Bergson series* (how can a static ontological genesis of the subject be worked out beginning with prepersonal and preindividual singularities and events?), the *Leibniz series* (how can there be a notion of individuality that is neither a mere deduction from the concept "subject"—in which case it would be contradictory—nor a mere figure of an individuality deprived of concept— in which case it would be absurd and ineffable?), the *Nietzsche-Foucault series* (how can a dynamic genesis of subjectivity be given, with the subject as the fold and the internalization of outside forces, without giving in to a philosophy of interiority?), the *Michel Tournier series* (how is the field of subjectivity affected by the presence or absence of the other?), and the *Nietzsche-Klossowski series* (how is it possible to think the subject in terms of inclusive disjunctions and simultaneously affirmed incompossible worlds?). Boundas then goes on to show that the formation of the subject, in Deleuze, is indissolubly linked with the question of the becoming world. In fact, the series listed here would have run along their own lines of flight without ever permitting the construction of planes of consistency, were it not for Deleuze's concepts *chaosmos (= chaos + cosmos)* and "cracked I" (= *Je fêlé*), which in their capacity as portmanteau words circulate among the series and make possible the inclusive, disjunctive affirmation of all of them at once. It is *chaosmos,* that is, the becoming-world, that posits the constitution of the subject as a task, and *chaosmos* again that guarantees that the constituted subject will not emerge as a substantive *hypokeimenon,* but rather as an always already "cracked I."

Sections three through six of our volume make a turn, not just in the direction of *chaosmos,* but toward becomings, insofar as they articulate desiring production, minoritarian groups and their discourses, nomadic distributions, and lines of flight, and insofar as becoming is no longer the simple reversal of Platonism. In "Theatrum Philosophicum," Foucault had asked, "What philosophy has not tried to overturn Platonism?" (p. 166). In the history of philosophy, the overturn of Platonism has always meant nihilism: the necessity of embracing nothingness as well as the nullity of all values, even the highest. Understood in these terms, all philosophy subsequent to Plato might be nothing more than anti-Platonism. However, there is another way to take measure of this limit: active destruction of everything that is passive in oneself. As Deleuze writes, "Destruction becomes active to the extent that the negative is transmuted and converted into affirmative power: the 'eternal joy of becoming.'"[5] Such a strategy amounts to accounting for a philosophy in terms of its "Platonic differential, an element absent in Platonism but present in other philosophies" (Foucault 1977, p. 166). Indeed, the question of a differential at the origin is fundamental to any Deleuzian encounter with philosophy. But the organization of this difference is also a key factor in Deleuze's work.

Foucault points to Deleuze's articulation of Plato's "delicate sorting operation which precedes the discovery of essence, because it necessitates the world of essences in its separation of false simulacra from the multitude of appearances" (p. 167). It is the process of division that enables Plato to discover true being, establish its *identity,* separate it once and for all from all impostors, which are "reduced to nonexistence" by the mere presence of the Idea (p. 167). Deleuze sees Plato's philosophy organized in accordance with two dimensions: (1) that of limited and measured things including the establishment of "presents" and of "subjects" with a certain size at a certain moment or "present"; and, opposed to this, in fact, subsisting beneath it, (2) pure becoming without measure, escaping the present, thus escaping identity and making past and future coincide.[6] Deleuze's philosophy is organized not as a simple reversal of impostors and true being, but as an element of the Platonic differential, the pure becoming that is a divergence from the Platonic series.

With this, Deleuze leads us to the surface where it is not possible either to signify or to denote. That is, if we are looking for language and sense, we will find it only at the surface, between the Platonic heights of signifiers (Ideas) and the depths of designation (of bodies). On the surface there are only pure events, and it is on the surface that Deleuze locates language, and not only language, but all regimes of signs: cinema, painting, literature, social organizations, cultural life. Without significations and designations, whatever takes place between these two realms can only be wholly contingent, thus wholly singular. Independent of Ideas, which will actualize them, and bodies, in which they are manifested, events are the expressed or expressible of bodies. It is these considerations that are addressed variously in the remainder of this collection.

Partly in response to what she takes to be a current misreading of Deleuze's working out of desire and partly as an exploration of issues centering on the body assemblage in Deleuze, Dorothea Olkowski has written "Nietzsche's Dice Throw: Tragedy, Nihilism, and the Body without Organs." Olkowski begins with Deleuze's discussion of the body in *Nietzsche and Philosophy*. What stands out in this discussion, according to Olkowski, is Deleuze's insistence that the 'body' is no medium and does not designate a substance, rather, "it expresses the relationship between forces," and "it becomes . . . semiological, a question of different regimes of signs." Olkowski discovers that Nietzsche's conception of the body remains coded by a certain image of the body as force. Not even the Heraclitean image of forces prevents Nietzsche from inscribing the name of the Greek hero on the qualities of force. Olkowski goes on to argue that such inscription does not take place with regard to the Deleuzian body assemblage. In *Différence et répétition*, Deleuze has certainly left behind the image of the Greek hero. What is at stake there, she notes, is the ontological proposition that "Being is univocal." Being is univocal, but it is "said" of difference itself. Such metaphysical flux is the Nietzschean dicethrow wherein the relation between forces (body assemblages) is subject to chance. This, then, is the meaning of "tragedy" in Nietzsche's work. "Every body is nothing but the arbitrary relation of force with force; every body, every difference between forces . . . is chance and nothing but chance." Not only does this make existence radically innocent and just, but also it releases it from any specific purpose or end. Thus when Deleuze reads Nietzsche's claim that forces affirm or deny, he *does not read this oppositionally*, nor does he read it with the Greek heroic inscription Nietzsche gave it; rather, it is a question of the action and reaction of forces, of body assemblages.

With this, the essay turns to the question of how active body assemblages become reactive. The answer Deleuze provides, says Olkowski, is Law. "Law, by separating active force from what it can do, leads to nihilism." For Deleuze, desire, which *experiments* with forces, is the limit of a power in that "every body extends its power as far as it is able"; so a limit is nothing but the point from which a force deploys all its power. Such a deployment is measured not by Law but by a *nomadic nomos,* which is without property, enclosure, or measure and distributed in a space without precise limits so as to make possible experimentation, wandering distribution, and even delirium. Olkowski concludes by noting that in this context, the Nietzschean question of "how one becomes what one is" brings forth the body assemblage, and with it the inquiry: What forces have taken hold of each series and struggle for domination? Given Nietzsche's insight that base evaluations dominate Western culture, the only possible solution to this is total nihilism. Deleuze, Olkowski believes, ever aware of Nietzsche's cultural inscriptions, turns instead to the "real," and "Deleuze's reading of Nietzsche," she states, "is part of a line of flight that eventually commits him to that aspect of the body assemblage which is called the Body without Organs, what remains when all is taken away, when the dice are thrown and only enough organism is kept for it to reform each day." For, she concludes, the removal of codes and inscriptions leaves nothing to interpret; there is only the real.

Concluding this section is Paul Patton's essay, "Anti-Platonism and Art," which is directed specifically to the overthrow of Platonism in Deleuze's writing. Overturning Platonism, Patton writes, is part of a larger task in *Différence et répétition*; that task is a critique of representation. In turn, such a critique, even while overturning Platonism, nonetheless, conserves certain aspects of Plato's thought. Such is Deleuze's larger strategy—to develop the neglected aspects of major thinkers, which themselves constitute "minor traditions." Patton notes that for Plato, difference is only understood as the comparison between Ideas and their copies, which are similar to the Ideas themselves; in other words, in terms of Plato's foundations of representation. But simultaneously, the ensuing ordered hierarchy of representation is threatened by mimicry: the production of semblances and the mere imitation of appearances. Patton points out that while a philosopher like Jacques Derrida sees the reproduction of the real (Ideas) on a continuum with the reproduction of appearances (simulacra), Deleuze finds no possible common ground between the two. The distinction Deleuze finds here, Patton insists, is between figures (copies), which internally and spiritually resemble what they reproduce (Forms), and those "simulacra" that resemble only superficially. Simulacra are so different from copies that they internalize dissimilarity.

The purpose of this distinction, according to Patton, is purely moral. Hence, to overturn Platonism is to deny the primacy of originals over copies to the benefit of the simulacra and to the detriment of representation, which is ultimately denied legitimacy. What then are the consequences of the denial of representation? Patton answers this by turning to an examination of contemporary art. In the work of Andy Warhol, for example, he finds that art is made to be simulation, the production of an "effect of resemblance by means of difference," and not even the reproduction of an appearance. Difference, then, becomes the primary relation, and "'[a]rt does not imitate . . . because it repeats.'" Warhol's "serial" works, for example, deliberately draw attention to the reproductions of newspaper or publicity photographs, which they reproduce. By repeating these images, Warhol is engaged in the production of difference insofar as "simulation is a matter of displaced or disguised repetition. The moral issue in these works is the loss of hierarchy and privilege in a world of simulacra. Without a hierarchy of representation guiding one's encounter with the work of art, it becomes possible to make sense of a work of art not only in terms of its conceptual framework, but also as "'an encounter, a passion.'" Here Deleuze's minor theater comes into full play. Any nonrepresentational conception "embraces precisely that power of poetry which rendered it most dangerous in Plato's eyes," and this, Patton makes clear, is an encounter that is possible, not only with regard to art, but with regard to all thought.

Section four extends these lines of thought to Deleuze's articulation of the practices of minoritarian groups. This aspect of his thought has been of particular interest to feminists insofar as Deleuze (along with Guattari) maintains, in *A Thousand Plateaus*,[7] that of all processes "the becoming-woman of everything, the whole," which is never a representation, imitation, or conformation to a model of any sort, is the key to all other becomings. Luce Irigaray and Alice Jardine are preeminent among feminists who have addressed this with some concern. Jardine has asked if it is not the case that "to the extent that women must 'become woman' first . . . might that not mean that she must also be the *first* to disappear . . . There would remain only her simulacrum: a female figure caught in a whirling sea of male configurations . . . necessary only for *his* metamorphosis?"[8]

Ever mindful of these words, Rosi Braidotti, in her essay, "Towards a New Nomadism, Feminist Deleuzian Tracks, or: Metaphysics and Metabolism," seeks to both meet these criticisms and to extend them in the depth of her own research on feminist political practice and feminist discursive, methodological, and epistemological premises: in short, the political practice of sexual difference insofar as it intersects with the Deleuzian project. Given this, the question of the moment for feminist thinkers is, according to Braidotti, how to reconcile historicity and, so, agency with "the political will to change, which entails the (unconscious) desire for the new, which, as Deleuze teaches, implies the construction of new desiring subjects." For Braidotti, "women's desire to become," as opposed to their will-to-have, which produced an objectification of the subject, is what is at stake in articulating new definitions of female subjectivity that seek to express women's structural need to posit themselves as female subjects, as corporeal and sexed beings. Such a move requires that thought start with the body and with subjectivity rooted in a body, the site of physical, symbolic, and material overlappings. It is then a site of differences rather than a universal, ungendered, knowing subject. "[T]his puts a great deal of emphasis on the question of how to rethink alterity and otherness . . . so as to allow differences to create a bond, i.e., a political contract among women, so as to affect lasting political changes." In this project, Braidotti argues, feminists can profit from the inclusion of the Deleuzian project of transforming the image of thinking as well as that of the subject. In fact, Deleuze's vision of thought and subjectivity as an intensive, multiple, and discontinuous process has much to offer feminists willing to look at it concretely.

For Deleuze, notes Braidotti, the body is not a natural biological materiality; it is the play of forces (affects) and a surface of intensities: mobile and transitory. This is of great help to the feminist attempt to deessentialize the body and sexuality. Given the absence of any interiority in this thought of the body, thinking is the process whereby a multiplicity of impersonal forces establish connections with one another. Such an image undermines both Lacan's negative vision of desire and psychoanalysis's metaphysics of the unconscious. Instead, for Deleuze, the unconscious is a process of "displacement and production," desire and affirmation. This conception has the advantage of replacing the traditional (allegedly neutral) writer/reader coupling in philosophy with writers and readers in an "intensive mode," and who act as "transformers" and "processors" of intellectual energies and extratextual experiences.

Eschewing the polarizations and "ex-communications" of feminist debate, Braidotti hopes to bring Deleuze's "rhizomatics" into feminist practice. However, this cannot be done blindly or without addressing the concerns of materialist feminists like Luce Irigaray, Judith Butler, Monique Wittig, and Donna Haraway. Braidotti argues that "one cannot deconstruct a subjectivity one has never been fully granted control over." And yet— insofar as 'woman' has been excluded from masculine systems of representation, she is unrepresentable; she is the site of "an-other system of representation." Braidotti thinks that Butler is saying the same thing when she writes that "Deleuze's post-Lacanian reading of the subject as a libidinal entity, in constant displacement in language, situates desire not only as a positive force, but also as the point of vanishing of the willful, conscious self." In the work of Haraway, more than any other contemporary feminist, Braidotti discovers the Deleuzian impetus at work. Like Deleuze, she finds that Haraway is interested in rethinking the "unity" of the human subject without resorting to humanism, dualism, or the divine. Haraway's image of the cyborg, like Deleuze's machinic couplings and Body without Organs, is a figure of "inter-relationality, receptivity, and global communication that deliberately blurs categorical distinctions." Still, Braidotti concludes her essay with a warning that the new "nomadism" she advocates is not simply a question of willful practice (a position, of course, that Deleuze never takes). It requires working through our historical condition, in particular, the mass of images, concepts, and representations of women, before women can hope to emerge into difference and, especially, into the difference that is becoming-woman.

Like Braidotti, Elizabeth Grosz takes up "feminist suspicions" concerning Deleuze's rhizomatics and becoming-woman. In "A Thousand Tiny Sexes: Feminism and Rhizomatics," Grosz voices the concern expressed by Jardine that "'becoming-woman,' desiring machines, and other similar concepts are merely excuses for male forms of appropriation of whatever is radical and threatening about women's movements." Grosz takes it upon herself to determine whether or not such reservations and suspicions are warranted, and to determine whether rhizomatics is simply the future (as Braidotti implies), or whether it provides a "powerful ally and theoretical resource for feminist challenges" to philosophy now. For one, Grosz points to the over-throw of Platonism, and along with this, the "displacement of the centrality and pervasiveness of the structure of binary logic." Grosz recognizes that for Deleuze and Guattari, "metaphysical identities and theoretical models" are repositioned. The insight operating here is that, rather than being ultimate and global phenomena, such identities and models are merely the "effects or consequences of processes of sedimentation." What she reveals at work in Deleuze and Guattari is not only a new image of philosophy, but a way to look at the entire history of philosophy that does not mire contemporary thinkers in the residue of absolute interpretations and systems out of which new images could never be forthcoming. The provisionality of such "align-ments"—though "deeply implicated in regimes of oppression and social subordination," especially with regard to women—nevertheless guarantees that such oppression and subordination can be "problematized" and even rendered "anachronistic." Thus, Grosz has seen clearly how Braidotti's reser-vations are met and answered by Deleuze and Guattari.

Grosz goes on to locate various conjunctions between key feminist notions and those of Deleuze and Guattari. Most common among these is the conceptualization of a difference that is in no way subordinated to iden-tity or the same, and which makes way for the being of becoming and a radical form of multiplicity defined by the outside: "the abstract line, the line of flight, or deterritorialization." Along with this arises a notion of polit-ical struggle that is decentered, molecular, multiple, diversified, and only provisionally aligned in temporary and nonhierarchical networks.

Following this line of thought, the "body" is a discontinuous and non-totalized series of processes, organs, flows, energies, corporeal substances and incorporeal events, intensities and durations, a body of affects, not will, yet defined by what it can do. This makes way for the sense of desire as affirmative, immanent, positive, and productive, a desire which "forges connections, creates relations, produces machinic alignments." Finally, Grosz finds that this articulation of the body, inspired by a Spinozist frame of reference "resurrect[s] the question of the centrality of ethics, of the encounter with otherness," in ways not unrelated to feminist rethinking of the relations between dominant and subordinated groups, oppressor and oppressed. Given Deleuze and Guattari's conception of the body, ethics distances itself from the "rampant moralism underlying ecological and environmental politics, which also stresses interrelations, but does so in a necessarily prescriptive and judgmental fashion," ultimately, subordinating them to some hierarchical and totalizing order.

Grosz remains troubled by Deleuze and Guattari's use of "the most notoriously phallic and misogynist writers" to exemplify fields of becoming, and by the dubious privileging of women's bodies when becoming could have been less conspicuously articulated in terms of some "asubjective and asignifying becoming." This is why, she concludes, as long as they are able to see in "becoming-woman" only a stage in the movement of microscopic and fragmenting processes, feminists may yet view Deleuze and Guattari with suspicion.

The fifth section of our volume puts together three essays that deal with the question of "minor" languages and "nomad" arts. Derrida's theory of the deconstructive efficacy of language and the practice that this theory entails are already well-entrenched in our intellectual landscape. But Deleuze's (and Guattari's) "minor deconstructive" approaches to language and literature are more timidly involved in the context of our local discussions. Réda Bensmaia's and Dana Polan's essays have, therefore, been selected to remedy this deficiency.

Bensmaia has often and with subtlety written on minor literature.[9] In the essay included in this volume, "On the Concept of Minor Literature: From Kafka to Kateb Yacine," after a brief characterization of minor literature and its function, and after devoting some time to defending Deleuze and Guattari against misreadings and misappropriations of their writings on this subject, he assesses the potential of minor literature through an appeal to the work of the Algerian writer and theater producer, Kateb Yacine. For Bensmaia, the strength of Deleuze and Guattari's notion of minor literature lies in their demonstration that minorization is not the problem only of immigrants, marginals, and minorities. It is the problem of all those who seek to open "the question of 'literature' to the forces and the differences (of class, race, language, or gender) that run through it." Moreover, Bensmaia argues, being a minor writer, from Deleuze and Guattari's perspective, is not a matter of an aesthetic choice made by a subject transparent to itself, but rather of the response to the exigencies of an existential situation. Minor literatures are characterized by the search for a language that could conjugate the lines of flight of the minority with the lines of flight of the majority in such a way that the combination could precipitate the minorization of the majority itself. Minor literatures are, therefore, political in the sense that the individual is always an arrangement whose function depends on its connections with other "machines." As such, minor literatures refer to a collectivity that is virtual (and real), albeit not yet actual. Bensmaia shows his subtle appreciation of Deleuze and Guattari when he states that minor literatures exist because peoples, races, and cultures have been reduced to silence. As the practical manifestation of this (absent) voice, minor literatures cannot adequately be thought as the products of our transgressive and anarchic (anti-Oedipal) thrust, as Louis Renza has tried to do.[10] They are not mere alternatives to the existing canon, on the way to establish their own canon. On this issue, Bensmaia quotes with approval David Lloyd, for whom the fact that the literary canon is not imposed today as a necessary and sufficient system of values is due, not only to the fact that literature has changed but also to the fact that institutions that used to shore it up are now in the process of disintegration.[11] We leave it to the reader to savor Bensmaia's discussion of minor literature in the context of Yacine's productions.

It is worth recalling here that in *Différence et répétition,* Deleuze argued that the idea, in order to be grasped, requires a chain reaction of plateaus of intensity that can only start with sensible encounters. Only the violence of the *sentiendum* stands a chance to bring about the resonance and the compossibility of Ideas. In 1981, Deleuze decided to face this violence seriously, choosing the paintings of the British artist Francis Bacon.[12] Struck by the powerful tensions that run through these paintings (tension between figuration and defiguration; between unsettling, convulsive forces and an emerging balance; between motion and rest; contraction and expansion; destruction and creation) Deleuze concluded that their function is "to produce resemblances with nonresembling means." The violence of sensation tormenting Bacon's canvases trades off representation for the exploration of a world never before seen, and yet strangely familiar and near.

Dana Polan's essay reads Deleuze's *Francis Bacon: Logique de la sensation* as a "pedagogy of the image," undertaken for the sake of a painterly practice that deforms the world in order to make it visible again. "How to make visible forces that are invisible?" is the question with which Bacon struggles and on account of which Deleuze makes him the object of his meditation, in his attempt to build a general logic of sensation. Deleuze, according to Polan, chooses Bacon as the painter who defigures representation in search of a sensation that would give itself, in itself and for itself. This search constitutes a major revision of the kind of subjectivity that underwrites phenomenology. In Bacon, subjectivity is broken up, traversed by intensities, and hystericized. Deleuze suggests that sensation emerges in the encounter between a perceiving subject and the disintegrating figure of the painting. Bacon's practice, indebted to the Gothic tradition, is directed against the organic representation of classical art, but also against the kind of abstraction that moves toward geometric form. In between the two, Deleuze, according to Polan, focuses his attention on Bacon's modulation and gradation of significations, and on the slow meltings away of the body as the exemplary form of painting this modulation. In search of modulation, Bacon pursues the special project of undoing the face, and of rediscovering the head beneath the face. None of this would be possible, if sensation were a mere representation of the interaction of an eye and an object. But sensation is the response not to a form, but rather to a force, and Bacon's paintings aim at the capture of force. Since a force must itself exist on a body for there to be sensation, force is the necessary condition of sensation, provided, of course, that sensation is not asked to represent the force. Deleuze calls the logic of sensation that he finds in Bacon "haptic," in order to designate its ability to surpass simultaneously eye and hand into a singular logic of sensation—not of sensations. Sensations are extensive and contiguous, whereas sensation is intensive. In Polan's view, Deleuze's book on Bacon deserves high marks for its acute awareness of the problems generated by the attempt to speak in one medium about the practices of another; thus Polan particularly appreciates Deleuze's concern to overcome the verbal/visual dichotomy by making use of intensely imagistic and tableauesque language.

It is important to notice what Deleuze *never* does in his discussion of nomad arts. Deleuze is not visiting the artist's studio for themes and symbols capable of recharging dull senses and slumbering thought. In this sense, it is instructive to contrast Marcuse's *Eros and Civilization,* for instance, with Deleuze's writings on nomad art. *Eros and Civilization* witnesses, melancholically, the advancing colonization of all life activities by the performance principle; laments its dehumanizing and commodifying effects; and gratefully zeros in on the marginalized arts, which, because of their marginality, have preserved the dreams of the pleasure principle and the means (thematic and symbolic) to emancipation. But for Deleuze nomadism is the ability to be displaced in a certain way, transversally or diagonally across all life activities—that is, an ability we encounter on all levels and in all territories. Hence, the laboratories of the artists are entered, by Deleuze, not for emancipatory potentials exclusively their own, but for the sake of a "confirmation of aparallel evolutions." In laboratories of research adjacent to one another, the painter, the cinematographer, the philosopher, and the scientist experiment with their own materials. Sometimes the porousness of the walls of the laboratories permit us to see that we have all been working with the same problems. But more often, an outside, which is the outside of all these laboratories, asserts itself, allowing an unstable, resonant communication, without wiping out the differences or the discordance of the "regional" concerns.[13]

It is because it speaks convincingly about aparallel evolutions that Marie-Claire Ropars-Wuilleumier's essay, "The Cinema, Reader of Gilles Deleuze," is included in this volume. It is faithful to Deleuze's warning: "[a] theory of cinema is not 'about' cinema but about the concepts that cinema gives rise to and which are themselves related to other concepts corresponding to other practices." Far from shutting himself within cinematic space, Deleuze asks cinema to intervene as accelerator of reflection. His cinematophilia, according to Ropars-Wuilleumier, is due to his perception of the aparallel evolution of world and cinema. His reflection on the seventh art is an attempt to show that cinema corroborates Bergson's pluralistic vision and that it makes possible the intuition of *durée* according to spatial and temporal flows that are no longer static surfaces or immobile points. Despite Bergson's skepticism, Deleuze's cinema has made possible our ascent to the nonhuman or superhuman moving images-*durées*. "Like the world," writes Ropars-Wuilleumier, "the cinema is Bergsonian . . . because it reactivates the concept of duration . . . [M]atter (which is image-movement) changes into memory (thus into image-time)." Or again, like the world, the cinema is Nietzschean, because in both "the circular becoming of time precipitates . . . short circuits, bifurcations, and detours, and irrational divisions where the notion of intensity is substituted for that of truth."

The author is convinced that Deleuze-Bergson's world can be conceived on the basis of the cinematic model, because cinema helps us recognize the world: Deleuze finds a kind of "catholicity" in cinema, a kind of universality that accepts, arranges, and reconciles everything inside an open-ended whole. The plane of consistency, therefore, which allows differences to resonate together without dulling their edges, is being modeled in and on the cinema. In fact, Ropars-Wuilleumier suggests that there is a conciliation, in cinema, that would make it possible to "negotiate[ ] an exchange between the image and the real." Such a conciliation, she argues, takes place in the realm of belief (rather than certitude): there is an adumbration of redemption with the "wholeness of the aesthetic . . . responding to the nothingness of the ethical."

In Ropars-Wuilleumier's opinion, Deleuze's preoccupation with cinema highlights his preoccupation with the prelinguistic, that is, with a material that bears, without expressing, everything "prior to all processes of signification." Deleuze's choice of Peirce against Metz makes this preoccupation very clear: it marks the yielding to the appeal of sight, and to the asignifying and asyntactic plentitude of the image against all operations of a signifying nature. The two volumes on cinema and, in fact, the way in which they are written, testify, according to the author, to Deleuze's desire to break "with the empire of the sign and with the exact coincidence of signifier and signified." Much more than in any of his other books, Deleuze seems now ready to borrow the completed analyses of other researchers, and despite his unfailing recognition of his debts, to mix and match them until they become fully inscribed in his own system of thought, as if he wants in this sort of inscription to cause viewpoints, hypotheses, and ideas to shed their initial sense and origin, and to circulate rhizomatically. But in the last analysis, Ropars-Wuilleumier observes, the reconciliation of Peirce's classificatory logic with Nietzschean displacing strategies is not an easy task. In fact, according to the author, to the extent that Deleuze leans heavily on Peirce for his analysis of classical cinema (in *Cinema 1*), and then on Nietzsche for his discussions of modern cinema (in *Cinema 2*), "the foundations of the first volume tumble down in the second." It is certainly the case that Deleuze describes an aesthetic and historical break that, around 1950, separates a cinema marked by a temporality based on the movement of action and the linearity of narration (organic cinema) from a cinema whose time is built on serialization, repetition, and discontinuity (crystalline cinema). But in Ropars-Wuilleumier's reading, Deleuze allows the two temporalities to coexist, without accounting for the contradiction between them or coping with the aporias that the contradiction generates.

The final section of our collection, "Lines of Flight," consists of two exemplary essays that take the work of Deleuze as their starting point and engage in lines of flight, movements of "deterritorialization" and "destratification," the dismantling of organic hierarchies and organisms.

Jean-Clet Martin's "Cartography of the Year 1000, Variations on *A Thousand Plateaus*," brilliantly works out the parameters of monastic space in Romanesque architecture. Within this configuration, Martin discovers experimentation: the dome is being developed and a new space is opening, a space of overlap, incompatibilities, proliferations, heterogeneities, and change. Such a space is a patchwork where "the rules of distribution and dispersion change nature, without any law or superior principle capable of legislating and extending its homogeneous jurisdiction over them." Romanesque architecture is a matter, then, not of a theorem, but of a "problem" that can receive a variety of solutions whose outlines can be diagramed. Thus, in monastic art, one finds a singular and eccentric choice, the giving up of wooden frames for stone, a choice not separable from the agitations in Europe in the year 1000 A.D. "[P]eregrinations and crusades determine changes of itineraries, halts, and deviations, which are related to technical innovations; they also determine mutations of forms that participate in the same movement of deterritorialization." Simply put, the need to house travelers opens the monastery.

Thus, Gothic art demands more light and attaches itself to the psalmodic model with its fluid outline and variable flow of acoustic singularities in nonmeasured musical time—the kyrielle: tonic accents repeated in unequal intervals creating unequal and heterogeneous points. It is here, argues Martin, that Deleuze's philosophy comes alive. Monastic art is not the offspring of the royal science of geometry, but the art of a problem, a proto-geometric choice "following heterogeneous bifurcations of the lines of material forces" such as those found in the proliferation of unclassifiable animal forms and subject to the forces of the material used. Insofar as the material is like a vein animated from the inside, matter and energy are in continual variation and even the artist must follow their plan. This intermediate zone between matter and form is the site of "creative dicethrows," which release their singularities in all possible directions—countless, diverging arabesques.

Within the social field of monastic art, Martin locates spreading, smooth space in the holy relics that challenge organized, striated space and its hierarchies of similarities, analogies, categories, resemblances, and identities. The relics deploy a plane of consistency around a function that cuts across the irreducible and incommensurate objects which are accounted for primarily in terms of pragmatics and semantics, not linguistics. These relics are expressed inside sign regimes marked by a particular proper name—the name of a saint—though with frightful, incorporeal effects. Such sign regimes, however, are everywhere. The despotic sign regime of the pope is successful in its drive to make Rome the center of holy places, and the pope the despotic center of significance, the site of absolute unity. Such unity is completely feasible insofar as the people see that "a God who dies on the Cross is not a sign of powerlessness." Instead, the message is that there are "plenty of other dreadful, atrocious, and eternal sufferings" available to those who might resist. Not surprisingly, this regime invents the face of the tortured, and blocks every line of flight and deterritorialization, except the negative, the heretical—the scapegoat whose deviation is always already inscribed within the despotic sign regime.

Yet, this is not to say that there is not a mixture of semiotics operating here. There are at least three intersecting lines that guarantee the formation of ever-new assemblages. There is a line of deterritorialization from which emerges the hordes and packs of pilgrims and crusaders producing architectural, scientific, and political mutations. The despotic regime of the church is itself carried along this vector, deterritorialized, and barbarized, while the passional system of relics and saints' names migrates in all directions. Meanwhile, the "pontifical and imperial language begins to stutter," as the invaders begin to speak a vulgar form of Latin, minorizing the very language of church power, and the hordes continue the production of relics marked with the names of saints. What remains of this project, for Martin, is to develop the ethical, juridical, and political thresholds of monastic and Gothic space, to cleanse them of constraining theorems, and to constitute them as "problems." Such a move will enable continuous deviation on the "trajectories of a nomadic philosophy."

It is certainly on these nomadic trajectories that the work of Alphonso Lingis falls. His essay, "The Society of Dismembered Body Parts," begins by citing social contract theory's organic image of society as an integrated hierarchy of terms defined by function, and as individuals integrated as functions of an organism. But Lingis's purpose here is to dismiss such conceptions of the society and its body in favor of the "libidinal body of the primary process," the "anorganic-orgasmic body" derived from a structuralist model of interchangeable terms, a body that guides what Deleuze and Guattari have to say about society.

What is the anorganic body? Take, for example, the infant body, writes Lingis. It "closes its orifices, curls up upon itself, closes its eyes and ears to outside fluxes, makes itself an anorganic plenum, a 'body without organs,'" a state of "primary catatonia." The body of the infant does not consist of organs that lead to the inner functional body. Rather, they are themselves productive, as Freud had already noted, functioning "polymorphously perversely to extend pleasure surfaces." Such surfaces, however, are not a closed plenum. Vital systems are coded and the anorganic plenum is the site of inscription, as is the social system, the "socius." Lingis refers to the three kinds of codings that Deleuze and Guattari cite. The socius is determined as the body of the earth in nomadic society, the body of the despot in imperial society, and the body of capital in capitalist society.

In savage, hunter-gatherer societies, the earth is the Body without Organs, the undivided plenum to which humans' organs are attached. As such, humans are not separated from the earth and experience their own bodies not as individual wholes, but as attached to the earth. Social interaction, rather than being a case of rights and responsibilities, is a matter of initiation, of being marked as belonging in some way to the earth. Membership in the society is "attachment to the earth," organs are "attached to the full body of the earth." And such attachments, Lingis informs us, are a matter of couplings: couplings of voice with hearing (there are over 700 languages among hunter-gatherers in New Guinea), hand with surfaces of inscription (hand craft and the immediate imitation of physical skills), and eye with pain (the excitement, even jubilation, at the spectacle of pain). When savage society is transformed and incorporated into sedentary and imperial societies whose organs converge on the body of a despot that has been detached from the earth, barbarian society arises. The hand is coupled onto the voice and the voice coupled with hearing by means of graphics (the signs of spoken words necessary for legislation, accounting, tax collecting, state monopoly, imperial justice, historiography), while the eye is uncoupled from the vision of pain. "[T]he eye no longer winces when it sees the mark . . . it does not see the incision, the wound, it passes lightly over the page." The eye becomes the passive receptor of abstract patterns. Lingis's analysis evokes Martin's exposition of the Kyrielle and the pontifical power that pursued it: "Now the voice no longer resonates, chants, invokes, calls forth; one hears only the voice of the law." And to make sense of this voice, one must subject oneself to the law.

If you were able to listen, Lingis continues, to the voices of the Quechua people without knowing their language or anything about "imperial society," what you would hear is the vocalizing of their togetherness. But as soon as you know that they are speaking about drug deals with Colombians, hearing is transformed, incorporated into the "codings of imperial society," an international code established in "Washington and Bonn and Tokyo." Now, these voices mean "crime," while you, listening, mean "tourist," an observer of the empire. The only possible resistance is to speak the language of the imperial code against itself: words lose consistency, become nonsensical, and turn against their own order. Thus the question, for Lingis, seems to be how not to speak the law of imperial discourse; how, instead, to speak the language of becoming-minor, even if your own language is English, German, or Japanese.

Yet capitalism, insofar as it subordinates the body of the entire productive enterprise (including the limbs and members of others) to the "integral body of the individual," responds primarily with privatization. Capitalist privatization is the removal of organs from the social field, "decoding their couplings with their immediate objects, and making their flows of substance and energies abstract." As a result, we "individuals" have substituted for the real pleasures of the body the imaginary or symbolic pleasures of meaning. Lingis complains that "[i]n our societies the flows for pubescent semen and blood are decoded, deterritorialized, privatized: it is supposed to take place behind locked doors at night." Individual privacy, then, is constituted around such privatized organs and flows, and Marx's "integral man" is nothing but a moment in capitalist coding. While Lingis seems to lament the loss of primitive public territorializations of the body, he nonetheless recognizes that Deleuze and Guattari do not seek primitive coding but, rather, seek even greater deterritorialization and decoding, freeing organs for ever more diverse couplings, and in this too, he finds much to lament.

With Martin and Lingis, our volume passes through the primitive territorial machine, the imperial despotic machine, and the capitalist machine, and the image of a theater of philosophy gives way to that of rhizomatic mapping, minoritarian becomings, packs, waves, intensities, and lines of flight. As editors, we have a sense that this is not simply possible, but necessary, given the new image of thought, the creation of concepts, and the mapping of processes that form the plane of immanence that we predicted at the beginning of this introduction. The "theater of cruelty" is cruel insofar as even the concept of the theater has been discarded in the very moment of its articulation. Just as, in the Deleuzian process, life is continuously phased out for something new, so philosophy as theater is phased out in the face of new modes of thought, new deterritorializations, destabilizations, and becomings that also cannot be stopped.

Notes

1. Michel Foucault, "Theatrum Philosophicum," *Language, Counter-Memory, Practice,* trans. Donald F. Bouchard and Sherry Simon (Ithaca: Cornell University Press, 1977).

2. Gilles Deleuze, "La Methode de dramatisation," *Bulletin de la Société Française de Philosophie,* 61.3 (1967).

3. Gilles Deleuze and Félix Guattari, *Qu'est-ce que la philosophie?* (Paris: Editions de Minuit, 1991), p. 74.

4. See also Gilles Deleuze, *Différence et répétition* (Paris: Presses Universitaires de France, 1968), pp. 276–285.

5. Gilles Deleuze, *Nietzsche and Philosophy,* trans. Hugh Tomlinson (New York: Columbia University Press, 1983), p. 174.

6. Gilles Deleuze, *The Logic of Sense,* trans. Mark Lester with Charles Stivale, ed. Constantin V. Boundas (New York: Columbia University Press, 1990), p. 1.

7. Gilles Deleuze and Félix Guattari, *A Thousand Plateaus: Capitalism and Schizophrenia,* vol. 2 (Minneapolis: University of Minnesota Press, 1987; orig. published in 1980).

8. Alice Jardine, "Woman in Limbo: Deleuze and His Br(others), *Substance* 44/45 (1984): 46–59, p. 54.

9. See Réda Bensmaia, "L'effect-Kafka," *Lendemains,* no. 53 (1989): 63–71; "Un philosophe au cinema," *Magazine Littéraire,* no. 257 (1988): 57–59.

10. Louis Renza, *"A White Heron" and the Question of Minor Literature* (Madison: University of Wisconsin Press, 1984).

11. David Lloyd, *Nationalism and Minor Literature: James Clarence Mangan and the Emergence of Irish Cultural Nationalism* (Berkeley: University of California Press, 1987).

12. Gilles Deleuze, *Francis Bacon: Logique de la sensation,* 2 vols. (Paris: Editions de la Différence, 1987).

13. See Constantin V. Boundas, "Editor's Introduction," *The Deleuze Reader,* Constantin V. Boundas, ed. (New York: Columbia University Press, 1993), esp. pp. 1–3.

2

He Stuttered

Gilles Deleuze

PEOPLE LIKE TO SAY that poor novelists experience the need to alternate their
dialogic markers and to replace "he said" with "he murmured," "he stum-
bled," "he sobbed," "he sneezed," "he cried," or "he stuttered"—all of them
being expressions that mark different voice modulations. It seems, in fact,
that the writer, faced with such modulations, has only two possibilities:
either to do it[1] (as did Balzac, who used to make Father Grandet stutter,
whenever the latter said anything at all, and Nucingen speak in a distorting
patois—cases in which Balzac's pleasure is easily felt); or else to say it
without doing it, and to be satisfied with a mere indication that the reader
will have to actualize: this is the case with characters who always whisper
with a voice that *must* be a scarcely audible murmur. Melville's Isabelle has
a voice that is little more than a whisper, and the angelic Billy Budd does not
stir without us having to reconstitute his stutter; Gregor, in Kafka's *Metamorphosis,* warbles more than he speaks, but this again is according to the
testimony of others.

It seems, however, that there is a third possibility: the performative. This
is what happens when the stuttering no longer affects preexisting words,
but, rather, itself ushers in the words that it affects; in this case, the words
do not exist independently of the stutter, which selects and links them
together. It is no longer the individual who stutters in his speech, it is the
writer who *stutters in the language system* (*langue*): he causes language as
such to stutter. We are faced here with an affective and intensive language
(*langage*) and not with an affection of the speaker. Such a poetic undertaking seems to be very different from the previous cases, but it is perhaps
less different from the second case than is usually thought. The fact is that
in the cases where the writer is satisfied with a merely external marker,
leaving the form of expression intact ("he stuttered . . . "), we understand
the efficacy of this operation poorly unless a corresponding form of content,

an atmospheric quality, or a milieu functioning as the conductor of discourse brings together the quaver, the whisper, the stutter, the tremolo, or the vibrato and imparts upon words the resonance of the affect under consideration. We are able to witness this in the best writers like Melville, where the humming of forests and caves, the silence of the house, and the presence of the guitar bear witness to Isabelle's whispers and to her soft, "foreign intonations." Kafka confirms Gregor's warbling through the trembling of his paws and the oscillations of his body. As for Masoch, he doubles the stuttering of his characters through the heavy suspenses of the boudoir, the buzzing of the village, and the vibrations of the steppe. The affects of the language system are here the objects of an actualization that is indirect and yet still close to what is happening directly when there are no longer any characters other than the words themselves.

> What did my family want to say? I do not know. It was stuttering since birth, and yet it had something to say. Upon me and many of my contemporaries the stuttering of birth weighs heavily. We learned to mumble—not to speak—and it was only after paying attention to the increasing noise of the century, and after we got whitened by the foam of its crest, that we acquired a language.[2]

Make the language system stutter—is it possible without confusing it with speech? Everything depends on the way in which language is thought: if we extract it like a homogeneous system in equilibrium, or near equilibrium, and we define it by means of constant terms and relations, it is evident that the disequilibriums and variations can only affect speech (nonpertinent variations of the intonation type). But if the system appears to be in perpetual disequilibrium, if the system bifurcates—and has terms each one of which traverses a zone of continuous variation—language itself will begin to vibrate and to stutter, and will not be confused with speech, which always assumes only one variable position among others and follows only one direction. Language merges with speech only in the case of a very special speech, a poetic speech realizing all the power of bifurcation and variation, of heterogenesis and modulation that characterize language. For example, the linguist Guillaume considers every term of the language system not as a constant in relation to other terms, but as a series of differential positions or points of view upon a dynamism that can be specified: the indefinite article "a" covers the entire zone of variation generated by the movement of particularization, and the definite article "the" covers the entire zone generated by the movement of generalization.[3] We are faced here with stuttering, since every position of "a" or of "the" constitutes a vibration. Language quivers in all its limbs, and we discover at this point the principle of a poetic understanding of language itself: it is as if language were carving a line to stretch—both abstract and infinitely varied.

This is then how the question is posed, even with respect to pure science: can we make any progress without entering those regions that lie far from the equilibrium? Keynes caused political economy to advance because he submitted it to a situation of "boom" and not to an equilibrium. This is the only way to introduce desire into various fields. How about placing language in a state of boom, close to a state of bust? We admire Dante for having "listened to the stutterers," and for having "studied all the mistakes of elocution," not only in order to assemble discursive effects, but rather in order to undertake a vast phonetic, lexical, and even syntactic creation.[4]

This is not a matter of bilingualism or multilingualism. It is possible to think in two languages, blending, with constant transitions from the one to the other: they are no less homogeneous systems in a state of equilibrium; their blending is accomplished in speech. But the great authors do not proceed in this manner, even though Kafka is a Czech writing in German, and Beckett an Irishman (often) writing in French. They do not mix two languages together, not even a minor language and a major language, although many of them have made their linkage to minorities the sign of their vocation. Rather, what they do is invent a *minor use* for the major language within which they express themselves completely: they *minorize* language, as in music, where the minor mode refers to dynamic combinations in a state of perpetual disequilibrium. They are big by virtue of minorization: they cause language to flee, they make it run along a witch's course, they place it endlessly in a state of disequilibrium, they cause it to bifurcate and to vary in each one of its terms, according to a ceaseless modulation.

All this goes beyond the possibilities of speech and attains the power of a language system—and even of language. This means that a great writer is always like a stranger in the language in which he expresses himself, even if this is his mother tongue. In the last analysis, he finds his strength in a silent and unknown minority that belongs only to him. He is a foreigner in his own language: he does not mix another language with his, he shapes and sculpts a foreign language that does not preexist *within* his own language. "The beautiful books are written in a sort of foreign language."[5] The point is to make language itself cry, to make it stutter, mumble, or whisper. What better compliment is there than the one of a critic saying of *Seven Pillars of Wisdom* that it is not written in English. Lawrence made English stumble in order to draw out of it the melodies and the visions of Arabia. And Kleist? What kind of language was he awakening in the depths of German by means of grins, slips of tongue, grinding of teeth, inarticulate sounds, elongated connections, brutal speeding up and slowing down, risking always to provoke Goethe's horror—Goethe, the most important representative of the major language—and reaching for strange goals, petrified visions, and vertiginous melodies?[6]

Language is subject to a double process of choices to be made and sequences to be established: disjunctions or selection of similars; connection or sequel of combinables. As long as language is considered as a system in a state of equilibrium, disjunctions will necessarily be exclusive (we do not say "passion," "ration," "nation" all at once, we must choose) and connections progressive (we do not combine a word with its elements with the gearshift in the neutral or by alternating between drive and reverse). But away from the state of equilibrium, *disjunctions become included and inclusive and connections become reflexive* on the basis of a rolling gait that affects the process of language and no longer the flow of discourse. Each word is now divided, but it is divided in itself (fat-cat fatalist-catalyst); and it is also combined, but combined with itself (gate-rogate-abrogate). It is as if the entire language had begun to roll from left to right, and to toss from back to front: *the two stutterings*. Gherasim Luca's speech is extremely poetic because he makes the stutter an affect of language instead of an affection of speech. The entire language runs and varies in order to liberate an ultimate sound block, a single gasp reaching the cry "I love you passionately . . . "

> *Passione nez passionnem je*
> *je t'ai je t'aime je*
> *je je jet je t'ai jetez*
> *je t'aime passionnem t'aime.*[7]

Luca the Romanian, Beckett the Irishman. It is Beckett who perfected the art of the inclusive disjunction; this art no longer chooses but rather affirms the disjointed terms in their distance and, without limiting or excluding one disjunct by means of another, it criss-crosses and runs through the entire gamut of possibilities. Notice, for example, in *Watt*, the way in which Knott puts on his shoes, moves about in his room, or changes his furniture.[8] It is true that these affirmative disjunctions, more often than not in Beckett, refer to the air and the gait of his characters: an indescribable way to walk, by rolling and tossing. The transfer from the form of the expression to the form of the content has been completed. But we can equally well bring about the reverse transition, if we suppose that people speak as they walk or stumble: the one is no less a movement than the other, they both transcend speech toward language, and the organism transcends itself toward a body without organs. We find confirmation of this in one of Beckett's poems that deals specifically with the connections of language and turns stuttering to the poetic or linguistic strength par excellence.[9] Beckett's method differs from Luca's and is the following: he places himself in the middle of the sentence, he makes the sentence grow from the middle, adding one particle to another (*que de ce, ce ceci-ci, loin la là-bas à peine quoi*) in order to direct the course of a block of a single, expiring gasp (*voulais croire entrevoir quoi . . .*). Creative stuttering is what makes language grow from the middle, like grass; it is what makes language a rhizome instead of a tree, what puts language in a state of perpetual disequilibrium: *Ill Seen, Ill Said* (content and expression). Fine words have never been the characteristic or the concern of great writers.

There are many ways to grow from the middle and to stutter. Péguy does not necessarily operate with asignifying particles, but rather with highly signifying terms; he operates with substantives each one of which defines a zone of variation; the latter reaches the neighborhood of another substantive, which, in turn, determines another zone (*Mater purissima, castissima, inviolata, Virgo potens, clemens, fidelis*). Péguy's retakes give words a vertical thickness and make them resume the "irresumable" without end. With Péguy, stuttering fits language so well that it leaves the words intact, complete and normal, but it makes use of them as if they were themselves the disjointed and decomposed members of a superhuman stuttering. Péguy is like a frustrated stutterer. In the case of Roussel, we have a different procedure again, because his stuttering does not affect particles or complete terms, but it affects propositions, perpetually inserted in the middle of a sentence, each one of them again inserted in the one before, according to a proliferating system of parentheses: often we have up to five parentheses one inside the other so that "[w]ith each additional increase this internal development couldn't fail to overwhelm the language it enriched. The invention of each verse was the destruction of the whole and stipulated its reconstruction."[10]

We are, therefore, talking about a ramified variation of the language system. Each state of a variable is a position on a crest line which bifurcates and prolongs itself in other lines. It is a syntactic line, whereby syntax is constituted by means of the curves, links, bends, and deviations of this dynamic line as it passes by positions with a double perspective on disjunctions and on connections. It is no longer the formal or superficial syntax that presides over the equilibrium of language, but a syntax in the process of becoming, a veritable creation of a syntax that gives birth to a foreign language within language and a grammar of disequilibrium. But in this sense syntax is inseparable from an end, it tends toward a limit that is no longer syntactic or grammatical, even if, from a formal point of view, it still seems to be: take, for example, Luca's formula, "I love you passionately," which explodes like a cry at the end of long stuttering series (or Bartleby's "I would prefer not to," which has absorbed all previous variations, or

Cummings's "he danced his did," which is freed from variations that are supposed to be merely virtual). Such expressions are considered to be inarticulate words, blocks of a single breath. This final limit sheds all grammatical appearances and bursts forth in its brute state in Artaud's gasp-words: Artaud's deviant syntax, to the extent that it wants to take by force the French language, finds the destination of its own tension in these gasps or pure intensities that mark the limits of language. Sometimes all this happens in different books: in the case of Céline, *Le Voyage au bout de la nuit* puts the native tongue in a state of disequilibrium; *Mort à credit* develops the new syntax according to affective variations; whereas *Guignol's Band* finds the ultimate goal, that is, the exclamatory sentences and suspensions that do away with all syntax to the advantage of a pure dance of words. Nevertheless, the two aspects can be correlated: the tensor and the limit, tension inside language and the limit of language.

The two aspects are realized according to an infinity of tonalities, but always together: a limit of language subtending the entire language system, and a line of variation or subtended modulation that brings the language system to this limit. And just as the new language is not external to the language system, the asyntactic limit is not external to language either: it is *the outside* of language, not outside of it. It is a painting or a piece of music, but a music of words, a painting with words, a silence within words, as if words were not disgorging their content—a grandiose vision or a sublime audition. The words paint and sing, but only at the limit of the path that they trace through their divisions and combinations. Words keep silent. The sister's violin takes over Gregor's warbling, and the guitar reflects (on) Isabelle's whisper; the melody of a singing bird about to die drowns out the stuttering of Billy Budd, the sweet "barbarian." It is when the language system overstrains itself that it begins to stutter, to murmur, or to mumble; then the entire language reaches the limit that sketches the outside and confronts silence. When the language system is so much strained, language suffers a pressure that delivers it to silence. Style—the foreign language system inside language—is made by these two operations; or shall we rather speak, with Proust, of a nonstyle, that is, of "elements of a style to come which do not yet exist"? Style is the parsimony of language.[11] Face to face, or face to back, to cause language to stutter, and at the same time to bring language to its limit, to its outside, and to its silence—all this will be like the boom and the bust.

—*Translated by Constantin V. Boundas*

Notes

1. [Translator's note.] These two possibilities facing the writer, as well as the third introduced in the next paragraph, allude to the French translation of J. L. Austin's *How to Do Things With Words* as *Quand dire c'est faire.*

2. Ossip Mandelstam, *Le Bruit du temps* (Lausanne: L'age d'homme, 1983), p. 77.

3. Cf. Gustave Guillaume, *Foundations for a Science of Language,* trans. W. Hirtle and J. Hewson (Philadelphia: Benjamins, 1984). Not only articles in general, or verbs in general, have dynamisms and zones of variation, but also each particular verb, and each particular substantive.

4. Ossip Mandelstam, *Entretien sur Dante* (Geneva: Dogana, 1989), p. 8.

5. Marcel Proust, *Contre Sainte-Beuve, on Art and Literature: 1856–1919,* trans. Sylvia Townsend Warner (New York: Meridian, 1958).

6. Pierre Blanchaud is one of the rare translators of Kleist who correctly raised the problem of style; see Heinrich von Kleist, *Le Duel* (Paris: Presses-Pocket, 1985). This problem can be extended to all translations of great writers: it is obvious that translation is treason if it takes as its model the norms of equilibrium of the standard language to which the translation is made.

7. This is Luca's most famous poem, "Passionément" *Le chant de la carpe* (Paris: J. Corti, 1986).

8. See François Martel, "Jeux formels dans Watt," *Poétique* 10 (1972).

9. Samuel Beckett, "Comment dire" *Poemes* (Minuit).

10. On this procedure of *Nouvelle impressions d'Afrique,* see Michel Foucault, *Death and the Labyrinth: The World of Raymond Roussel* (New York: Doubleday, 1986), pp. 129–30.

11. On the problem of style, his relationship with the language system, and these two aspects, see Giorgio Passerone, *La linea astratta: Pragmatico dello stile* (Milano: Edizioni Angelo Guerini, 1991).

I. Difference and Repetition

3.

Difference and Unity
in Gilles Deleuze

Todd May

> How could there be a "play of the Same" if alterity itself was not already *in* the Same, with a meaning of inclusion doubtless betrayed by the word *in*?
>
> —Jacques Derrida, *Writing and Difference*

IT IS ONE OF THE IRONIES of Gilles Deleuze's thought that although it counts itself as a rigorous thought of difference, it often uses for its models philosophers whose own work has been considered tightly unitary or monistic. Deleuze's studies on Spinoza, Bergson, and even Kant, for instance, cannot be considered external to the heart of the Deleuzian project; indeed, it can be argued that those studies constitute its very heart. The thinker who wrote "difference is behind everything, but behind difference there is nothing"[1] is also the thinker who praises Scotus and Spinoza for discovering the univocity of being, and especially the latter for revealing it as "an object of pure affirmation."[2] How is it that the thinker of multiplicities, of haecceities, disjunctions, and irreducible intersecting series, is also the thinker of the univocity of being and untranscendable planes of immanence?

It is the argument of this paper that such juxtapositions of unity and difference are not accidental, but are indeed the requirements of Deleuze's thought. Indeed, these juxtapositions are symptoms of a concomitance so necessary that it will not be overstating the case to claim that, in the end, Deleuze is not a thinker of difference at all, if by that is meant that he is a thinker who should be read as considering difference to be privileged over unity. The claim here is not that Deleuze understands himself as anything other than a thinker of difference; in fact, there are numerous instances in which he seems to consider himself exactly that. Instead, I will try to make the case that he cannot coherently be a thinker of difference. In that sense, this text can be considered a deconstruction, if by that term we mean that we are to find the suppressed term of a binary opposition (unity) internal to the possibility of privileging the other term (difference). I will also argue, though, that Deleuze need not be a thinker who privileges difference at the expense of unity. He can commend to us a way of thinking that values difference and that allows him to engage in the multifarious experiments into thinking with difference that have been his legacy without having to go beyond what he can reasonably allow himself with respect to claims about the status of difference.

The attempt to assess Deleuze's claims about difference cannot proceed, however, in a traditional philosophical fashion. We cannot merely ask ourselves what his claims are, and then proceed to evaluate them. This is because Deleuze's conception of what it is to do philosophy, and thus what it is to make a philosophical claim, are hardly straightforward. When it seems in his texts that Deleuze is making a claim about the way things are, most often he is not—and he does not take himself to be—telling us about the way things are. Instead, he is offering us a way of looking at things. Thus, in order to begin to assess the Deleuzian claims of difference, it will be necessary to understand what it is to be a Deleuzian claim; that is, it will be necessary to understand what Deleuze is doing when he does philosophy. It will be seen here that Foucault's suggestive remark that *Anti-Oedipus* is "a book of ethics"[3] is in fact a fitting epigram for the entirety of Deleuze's corpus.

Only when we have understood Deleuze's conception of philosophy can we proceed to inquire about the place of the concept of difference in Deleuze's work, and from there to an understanding of the necessary chiasm of difference and unity that urges itself upon, although never definitively establishes itself within, Deleuze's texts. Here the touchstone will be Spinoza, the thinker of unity most often referred to—and referred to as such—in Deleuze's articulation of his position regarding unity. Finally, we can show what Deleuze can and cannot claim for difference within his own work, and indicate briefly why the strictures we set upon it should not be deeply troubling for his project, but only for certain realizations of it.

For Deleuze, the project of philosophy is one of creating, arranging, and rearranging perspectives; it is, as he puts it, "the discipline that consists in *creating* concepts."[4] To engage in philosophy is to develop a perspective, by means of concepts, within which or by means of which a world begins to appear to us. Such has been Deleuze's position from his first extended text, his book on Hume, in which he writes:

. . . a philosophical theory is an elaborately developed question, and nothing else; by itself and in itself, it is not the resolution to a problem, but the elaboration, *to the very end*, of the necessary implications of a formulated question. It shows us what things are, or what things should be, on the assumption that the question is good and rigorous.[5]

This tells us much about what Deleuze thinks philosophy is not, but less about what he thinks it is. Philosophy is not the attempt, as Quine would have it, "to limn the world"; it is not the discipline that tries to "get things right," in the sense that it would offer an account of how things are that would be able to replace numerous other accounts. To conceive philosophy as a project of truth is, in Deleuze's view, to misconceive it. "Philosophy does not consist in knowledge, and it is not truth which inspires philosophy, but rather categories like the interesting, the remarkable or the important which decide its success or failure."[6] Although he does not tell us why philosophy ought not to be concerned with truth, his positive articulation of philosophy's task leaves little doubt that the reason is ethical rather than metaphysical or epistemological. It is not for the reason that there is no truth that philosophy ought not to be concerned with it (and it is a superficial reading that finds Deleuze engaged in a self-defeating denial of truth); rather, it is that philosophy ought to be about something else: specifically, about creating concepts.

In Deleuze's recent collaboration with Félix Guattari on the nature of philosophy, he articulates three central and intertwined characteristics that concepts possess. First, a concept is defined by its intersections with other concepts, both in its field and in surrounding fields. This is an idea that Deleuze speaks of elsewhere when he writes that "philosophical theory is itself a practice, as much as its objects. . . . It is a practice of concepts, and it must be judged in the light of other practices with which it interferes."[7] Second, a concept is defined by the unity it articulates among its constituent parts. This is called by Deleuze and Guattari the "consistence" of the concept.[8] It occurs when heterogeneous elements are brought together into a whole that is at once distinct and inseparable from those composing elements. Last, a concept is "an intensive trait, an intensive arrangement which must be taken as neither general nor particular but as a pure and simple singularity."[9] By this, we must understand the concept as a productive force that reverberates across a conceptual field, creating effects as it passes through and by the elements and other concepts of that field.

A concept, then, is not a representation in any classical sense. Rather, it is a point in a field—or, to use Deleuze's term, on a "plane"—that is at once logical, political, and aesthetic. It is evaluated not by the degree of its truth or the accuracy of its reference, but by the effects it creates within and outside of the plane on which it finds itself. The concept, write Deleuze and Guattari, "does not have *reference*: it is autoreferential, it poses itself and its object at the same time that it is created."[10] Thus philosophy, as the creation of concepts, is to be conceived less as articulation or demonstration than as operation. Philosophy brings together or introduces new points onto the planes with which it is involved, and by this means either rearranges a plane, articulates a new plane, or forces an intersection of that plane with others. To evaluate a philosophy, then, is to gauge its operation, to understand the effects that it introduces, rather than to assess its truth.

There is another part of philosophy's operation to which we shall return later but which must be introduced now. "Philosophy is a constructivism, and its constructivism possesses two complementary aspects which differ in nature: creating concepts and tracing a plane."[11] As Deleuze and Guattari note, the plane traced by the concepts that create it is not reducible to those concepts. Rather, the concepts outline a plane that must be conceived as an open whole (which is not to say a totality[12]): a whole in the sense that there is a relatedness among the concepts that exist on or within it, open in the sense that those concepts do not exhaust the plane but leave room for development and retracing. Deleuze calls the planes that are traced by philosophy "planes of immanence" in order to indicate that there is no source beneath or beyond the plane that can be considered its hidden principle. Unlike traditional views of philosophy, then, Deleuze's view rejects all forms of transcendence as descriptions of the nature or goal of philosophical work. In fact, first among the illusions that characterize philosophy's account of itself is "the illusion of transcendence."[13]

An illustration of the plane of immanence is offered in Spinoza's philosophy of the univocity of being. "What is involved," Deleuze writes, "is the laying out of a *common plane of immanence* on which all minds, all bodies, and all individuals are situated."[14] Spinoza's concepts do not exhaust the plane of immanence of which they seek to be the principles; nevertheless, taken together they constitute its geometry. In fact, for Deleuze the famous "geometrical method" of the *Ethics* is nothing other than the geometry of a plane of immanence.

Given this reading of the philosophical project, Deleuze's claim that it is a "practice" becomes clear. Philosophy is a practice whose operations are to be evaluated by the effects that they give rise to. Thus we can see both that there is a place for truth in philosophy—although it is a secondary, derivative place—and that the primary task of philosophy is normative. The place of truth on this reading lies in the assessment of effects. If a philosophy is to be evaluated on the basis of its effects, there must be some agreement as to what those effects are. This does not mean that there is an objective fact of the matter outside of all planes of discourse; what analytic philosophers call realism is not a commitment of this approach. Rather, if two people are to agree on an evaluation, they must also agree on what effects a philosophy has had, that is, on what has happened as a result of the concepts it has created.

This agreement, however, is only a means to the end of evaluating a philosophical practice. As Deleuze and Guattari note, such evaluation must itself be immanent in some sense:

> We do not have the least reason to think that the modes of existence need transcendental values which would compare, select, and decide which among them is "better" than another. On the contrary, there are only immanent criteria, and one possibility of life is valued in itself by the movements it traces and the intensities it creates on a plane of immanence.[15]

The sense of immanence that Deleuze seeks for evaluation, however, remains ambiguous, between two possibilities. The rejection of transcendental values can be read either as a rejection of all evaluation outside the specific plane of immanence on which the concepts are being created; or it can be read as a rejection of moral realism, of the idea that ethical evaluation is anchored in a moral reality divorced from all planes of immanence. It is important, although I believe unpalatable for Deleuze, that the rejection be of the second sort. To reject the possibility of the evaluation of a philosophy outside of the plane that it traces is to lapse into an aestheticism that allows for the possibility of a barbaric set of philosophical commitments that cannot be called such because to do so would constitute an evaluation lying outside the plane of immanence on which those concepts are traced. However, it is both coherent and plausible to claim that the very concept of barbarism lies on its own plane of immanence without which we would be able neither to understand nor to utilize it. This latter possibility, a more or less anti-Platonic one, although far more modest in scope, seems both necessary and undamaging for Deleuze's approach to philosophical evaluation.

The concept of "life" that Deleuze invokes periodically in his writings reflects his ambiguity about evaluation. When he writes, for instance, that "[t]here is, then, a philosophy of 'life' in Spinoza; it consists precisely in denouncing all that separates us from life, all these transcendent values that are turned against life, these values that are tied to the conditions and illusions of consciousness"[16], Deleuze utilizes the concept of life both as a term—albeit nascent—within Spinoza's philosophy through which it affirms itself and as a value by which the entire philosophy is judged. The concept of life, then, is, for Deleuze, always partially transcendent to the plane to which it is being applied; although this does not mean that it is transcendent to all planes, but instead that it is irreducible to the plane of application. Thus, when Deleuze claims that for Spinoza "Ethics, which is to say a typology of immanent modes of existence, replaces Morality, which always refers existence to transcendent values,"[17] we must understand the term "immanent" as referring broadly to all planes of discourse and "transcendent" as referring to the outside of all planes of discourse.[18]

Such a move privileges normative planes in relation to other planes by making them the axes around which evaluation revolves. This, however, is precisely the Deleuzian view of philosophy, which sees philosophy as a creation rather than reflection, and theory as a practice rather than a pure speculation.[19] If his concept of life brings evaluation closer to the planes that are being evaluated, it does not dispense altogether with a move outside those planes, as indeed it cannot without being committed to the endorsement of many values that Deleuze's philosophy has constituted a ceaseless struggle against. All of this, however, is not meant to claim that nonnormative planes are reducible in any sense to normative ones (a point whose importance will become clear below), but rather to insist on the general importance of normative planes in Deleuze's view of philosophical practice.[20]

Philosophy, then, is a project of creation, of bringing into being concepts that define new perspectives. It is primarily a normative endeavor, a discipline whose effects are to be judged normatively.[21] And it is within this context that we need to assess the role of Deleuze's concept of difference and the claims made for it in his work.

Deleuze, of course, privileges difference. The claims he makes on its behalf are both ethical and metaphysical, and in most cases the ethical and the metaphysical claims are entwined. Throughout his philosophy, he has tried to yoke a metaphysics of difference with an ethics of experimenting with difference in a way that can leave one uncertain where the metaphysical claims leave off and the ethical ones begin. In *Différence et répétition*, for example, Deleuze claims that "in its essence, difference is the object of affirmation, affirmation itself. In its essence, affirmation is itself difference."[22] Here the nature of affirmation and difference and the evaluation of each are indistinguishable. One wants to ask here, is Deleuze claiming that we ought to affirm difference because that is what difference is—it is affirmation? Assuming we could make sense of this claim, it would seem to run perilously close to a naturalist fallacy. On the other hand, is Deleuze claiming that when we affirm, we are always affirming difference? If so, then the normative force that Deleuze would seem to want for this claim is lost.

In fact, Deleuze is making neither of these claims. When Deleuze privileges difference, he is engaging in the practice he calls philosophy. He is creating a concept that he hopes will help shape a perspective from which we see things in a new way. His metaphysical claims are not claims about the way things are; rather, they are the structure of a new perspective. And his ethical claims—which are indeed ethical claims—are the articulation of a framework for thinking about other practices when one has taken up the perspective created by the concepts of a given metaphysics. What we must ask, then, regarding the concept of difference is not whether difference indeed does possess some sort of metaphysical priority, but how such a concept is meant to function, what effects it is designed to have. Concepts are like texts, we must treat them thus: "We will never ask what a book means, as a signified or a signifier; we will not look for anything to understand in it. We will ask what it functions with, in connection with what other things it does or does not transmit intensities, in which other multiplicities its own are inserted and metamorphosed, and with what bodies without organs it makes its own converge."[23]

The function of the concept of difference is at once to attack the unifying forces that have abounded in philosophical discourse and to substitute for such forces a new perspective by means of which one can continue to think philosophically. "It is necessary that a system is constituted on the basis of two or three series, each series being identified by the differences between the terms which compose it."[24] Systems should not be thought of as unities, but rather as compositions of series, each of which is itself defined on the basis of difference. The thought of such difference at the level of compositions of series Deleuze calls "singularities." Thus, in *The Logic of Sense*, if we are to consider meaning as a product of sense (and whether we should do so Deleuze calls "an economic or strategic question"[25]), and if sense is composed by the two heterogeneous series of words and things, then words and things are composed of prepersonal, preindividual singularities:

> What is neither individual nor personal are, on the contrary, emissions of singularities insofar as they occur on an unconscious surface and possess a mobile, immanent principle of auto-unification through a *nomadic distribution*, radically distinct from fixed and sedentary distributions as conditions of the syntheses of consciousness. Singularities are the true transcendental events, and Ferlinghetti calls them "the fourth person singular."[26]

Thus Deleuze asks us to think of difference as constitutive all the way down, and of unity as a product of the play of difference.

But if difference is to be thought of as constitutive, this is in order to rid philosophy not of unities, but of unifying forces or principles that either preclude difference or relegate it to a negative phenomenon. After all, Deleuze sees philosophical discourse, and indeed all discourse, as a process of *both* deterritorializing and reterritorializing. Therefore, it is not the fact of unities that fossilizes the creation of concepts, but the necessity that attaches to unifying principles, principles that dictate a necessary structure of concepts or an unsurpassable perspective. In this sense, Deleuze's notion of difference is distinct from Derrida's notion of *différance*. The latter involves an inevitable play of presence and absence, a specific economy of the two, which, although issuing in any number of philosophical possibilities, nevertheless governs them with a certain type of logic that is necessary to all discourse. Deleuze grants both that the intersection of different series may determine a specific structure, and that neither the structure nor the intersecting series that produced it are subject to alteration by a being in virtue of that being possessing a "free will." None of this implies, however, that there is a guiding principle that underlies structures and that would thus be a unifying force determining them. This is why Deleuze cites the Stoical distinction between destiny and necessity:[27] the former is subject to slippages of contingency of which the latter is incapable.

The concept of difference, then, is both positive and disruptive: positive in taking series (as well as singularities, desire, active forces, rhizomatic stems, etc.) as irreducible, contingent, constituting forces; disruptive in resisting all accounts of these constituting forces that would bring them under the sway of a unifying principle that would make them—or the phenomena they constitute—merely derivations from or reflections of one true world or source. These two characteristics converge on what may be called the essential role of the concept of difference: to resist transcendence in all of its forms.

As noted earlier, the "illusion of transcendence" is the primary philosophical illusion. That illusion consists in the idea that there is some unifying principle—or small set of principles—outside the planes on which discourse—and other practices—take place that gives them their order and their sense, and that the task of philosophy is to discover that principle or that set of principles. The history of philosophy is replete with such principles, from Forms to God to the cogito to language to *différance*. To recognize difference in its Deleuzian form is to reject the illusion of transcendence, and to philosophize from the surfaces rather than from the depths or the height of transcendence. "The idea of positive distance belongs to topology and to the surface. It excludes all depth and all elevation, which would restore the negative and identity."[28] To think in terms of difference is to affirm surfaces, which can only occur when one ceases trying to take those surfaces as derivative from or secondary to something lying outside of them, and begins to see them as constitutions of series, etc. that come to form them and that, in some sense, they are. And in this sense, the concept of difference is inextricable from the project of philosophy; for if philosophy is to remain a practice of creation, it cannot be bound to a transcendence that would stultify it. Philosophy is a practice of difference, which is at once an art of surfaces. "The philosopher is no longer the being of the caves, nor Plato's soul or bird, but rather the animal which is on a level with the surface—a tick or a louse."[29]

The question remains, however, of the relationship of surfaces to their constituting series, forces, desire, etc. If difference is taken as our sole guiding concept, then it seems difficult to understand how there could be planes or surfaces at all. By what principle or for what reason do we call one collocation of points a series, or one or several sets of series the articulation of a plane, if pure difference is our only guiding concept? On the other hand, how are surfaces to be introduced without their becoming a reduction of difference, without their becoming a new principle of transcendence? It would seem that any priniciple of unity that could be invoked to explain surfaces would have to be transcendent, at least to the difference it balances. It is at this level of questioning that Spinoza's thought of the univocity of being becomes crucial.

"The philosophy of immanence appears from all viewpoints as the theory of unitary Being, equal Being, common and univocal Being."[30] This claim, which applies equally to both Spinoza and Deleuze, must be understood if we are to see how a Deleuzian philosophy of surfaces and differences is to be coherent. What must be kept sight of is that Deleuze's concept of difference is essentially an antitranscendental one; he is trying to preserve the integrity of surfaces of difference from any reduction to a unifying principle lying outside all planes of immanence.

The attraction of Spinoza for Deleuze lies precisely in the fact that, for Spinoza, there can be no transcendental principle of explanation precisely because there can be no transcendence. There is no outside from which a source (whether that source be a metaphysical one or merely an explanans[31]) could come to exercise sway. The philosophical problem Spinoza sets himself is one of developing a perspective within which the antitranscendental position can be coherently realized. For Deleuze, the central concept—concept in accordance with Deleuze's use of the term—is "expression." Expression is the relation among substance, attributes, essences, and modes that allows each of these elements to be conceived as distinct from, and yet part of, the others:

[T]he idea of expression accounts for the real activity of the participated, and for the possibility of participation. It is in the idea of expression that the new principle of immanence asserts itself. Expression appears as the unity of the multiple, as the complication of the multiple, and as the explication of the One.[32]

Expression is Spinoza's concept, then, for characterizing the relationship among the traditional concepts of the philosophical discipline of his time. Although the term itself is introduced by Scotus, it achieves maturity only with Spinoza, for whom it is not merely a neutral description of being, but at the same time a revealing of being as an object of affirmation.[33] It is this concept that, by substituting itself for emanation and by displacing all forms of dualism, introduces into philosophy the antitranscendental notion of the univocity of being. "What is expressed has no existence outside its expressions; each expression is, as it were, the existence of what is expressed."[34]

The concept of expression comprises three related aspects: explication, involvement, and complication.[35] Explication is an evolution; attributes explicate substance in the sense of being evolutions of substance. By evolution, however, we must understand not a chronological development, but rather a logical one. As Deleuze notes elsewhere in a discussion of the relationship of substance's production, "God in understanding his own essence produces an infinity of things, which result from it *as properties result from a definition*."[36] Attributes thus explicate substance; and in explicating it they necessarily involve it. Attributes, as logical rather than chronological evolutions of substance, involve substance in a fashion similar to the way the conclusion of a syllogism involves its premises. Given this relationship of evolution and involvement, complication also follows. "Precisely because the two concepts are not opposed to one another, they imply a principle of synthesis: *complicatio*."[37] There are distinctions to be drawn among the attributes of substance, and those distinctions are real, but they are not numerical; the multiple is part of—indeed, *is*—the one, as the one is the multiple.

Expression, then, is a concept that removes the possibility of transcendence from the philosophical field of Spinoza's time. Throughout all its expressions, being remains univocal. It must be seen at once, however, that to be univocal is not to be identical:

The significance of Spinozism seems to me this: it asserts immanence as a principle and frees expression from any subordination to emanative or exemplary causality. *Expression itself no longer emanates, no longer resembles anything*. And such a result can be obtained only within a perspective of univocity.[38]

What univocity implies is not that everything is the same, or that there is a principle of the same underlying everything, but, instead, precisely the opposite. With univocity comes difference, difference for the first time taken seriously in itself.

If there is nothing outside of the surface, if all there is is surface, then what characterizes the surface is inescapable, unsurpassable. There is no looking elsewhere in order to discover or understand our world or our worlds.[39] This thought, at once Spinozist and Nietzschean, returns us to the complexity and irreducibility that characterize surfaces, but does so with the affirmation that such complexity and such irreducibility are precisely *the characteristics of a surface*. Differences do not float ethereally as pure singularities, in the manner that Deleuze would sometimes have it. In such a state they would be nothing, not even differences. Deleuzian difference can arise as such only in relationship to surfaces, which are nontranscendable, only on the basis of an ontological univocity. And it is in this way that difference can be both posited and affirmed. It is posited as the result of a perspective—that is, a creation of concepts—that denies transcendence and returns us to surfaces and their differences. It is affirmed because those surfaces and differences are seen no longer merely as derivative from or parasitical upon a unifying transcendent source or principle.

Such a result is in keeping with Deleuze's view of the philosophical project as the normative endeavor of creating concepts. At another level, however, it is also in keeping with the necessity of his own philosophical creation. In order to develop the perspective that has been emerging here, Deleuze has had to create, not a number of distinct and unrelated philosophical concepts, but rather a surface composed of different but related concepts: concepts such as difference, expression, surface, and univocity. The perspective itself is at once the creation of concepts and the tracing of a plane of immanence that is distinct from the concepts populating that plane. The plane is the unity of different concepts, but not in the sense of being their product. Instead it is a unity without which these concepts would not be the concepts they are; indeed, they would not be concepts at all. Alternatively, without the differential nature of the concepts, there would be no plane. At this level—and at all levels—a perspective is not the product of difference but the product coequally of unity and difference.

This dual necessity, the necessity of unity and difference in the formation of any perspective, is the horizon within which Deleuze's and Guattari's notion of the rhizome must be understood. The rhizome is a testimony neither to pure difference nor to pure unity. Unlike the arboreal perspective the authors eschew, which is the embodiment of the transcendental project of reducibility to a unifying principle, the rhizome is reducible neither to some central point that forms its source or place of nourishment, nor to the stems that shoot out from it. The rhizome is a play of the unity of its stems and their difference, and it is only because of this play that it offers a view of difference as a positive rather than negative phenomenon. The rhizome, in short, is the univocity of being, a univocity that, rightly understood, is the affirmation neither of difference, nor of unity, but of the surface that is the intertwining of the two. In this sense, we must understand Deleuze himself to be practicing the geometrical art inaugurated by Spinoza when he writes that:

> Spinoza thinks that the definition of God as he gives it is a real definition. By a proof of the reality of the definition must be understood a veritable generation of the object defined. This is the sense of the first propositions of the *Ethics: they are not hypothetical, but genetic.*[40]

This necessity of Deleuze's thought means that we can no longer consider him to be a thinker of difference, if by that we intend that he is a thinker who privileges difference. Rather, we must come to consider Deleuze to be a holist, in the Wittgensteinian sense.[41] By this, we mean that philosophical perspectives, viewed in a Deleuzian fashion, must be considered neither as realizations of a single driving principle by which our world can be explained—that is, as the will to truth—nor as a product of pure difference upon which unities are created as secondary phenomena. The antitranscendental path that Deleuze has trodden requires him to reject the primacy of difference at the same moment that he rejects the primacy of unity. As the latter reduces all difference to the tired repetition of a received pattern of discourse, the former renders all discourse impossible.

Deleuze, it seems, recognized this requirement on his thought in many places throughout his work. However, he wanted to circumvent it at crucial moments as well, in order to give the privilege to difference. There is, then, at the core of his thought a tension that he is never entirely able to move beyond. We must turn in the last section to that tension, in order to sketch out the limits of Deleuze's claims, and to show where he fell prey to the temptation to surpass them.

There are two places in Deleuze's thought where the tension between his recognition of the inseparability of unity and difference and his temptation to privilege difference raise questions that threaten the coherence of his thought. The first place is in his critique of representation, the second—already briefly noted—is in his positing of singularities at the base of metaphysics. We will address each of these in turn.

The critique of representation is bound to Deleuze's critique of resemblance and unifying principles. Representation is the practice in which the prejudices of the primacy of identity have become sedimented, where differences are either reduced, marginalized, or denied altogether. Moreover, in being the site upon which identity comes to dominate difference, it is, as well, the place where Nietzsche's "all the names of history" are frozen into a single one (itself called an "identity") and where the fluid and contingent nature of the philosophical project is forced to unify itself into a single and precise set of defensible claims oriented toward truth rather than remaining a plane of concepts oriented toward creation. Thus the task of a philosophical project that would reassert the irreducibility of difference must also involve the subversion of the representationalist practice of language:

> Representation allows the world of difference to escape . . . [i]nfinite representation is inseparable from a law which renders it possible: the form of the concept as an identity-form, which constitutes sometimes the in-itself of representation (A is A), sometimes the for-itself of representation (I=I). The prefix "re-" in the word representation signifies this conceptual form of the identical which subordinates differences.[42]

This subversion, although its effects appear throughout Deleuze's texts,[43] is performed in the most sustained fashion in *The Logic of Sense*.

The concept of sense when introduced (an introduction that, as noted above, Deleuze made for reasons that are "economic or strategic" rather than epistemic[44]) attempts to demonstrate that linguistic meaning is founded not upon a representationalist relationship between words and the world, but rather upon a play of words and world that itself escapes representation. Sense "is exactly the boundary between propositions and things."[45] It is thus incorporeal, escaping the possibility of being brought into representation by virtue of escaping the very categories of being upon which representation is founded. In fact, "we cannot say that sense exists, but rather that it inheres or subsists."[46] Meaning is founded on this sense, this happening or event of sense, rather than upon any correspondence between words and the world. "What renders language possible is the event insofar as the event is confused neither with the proposition which expresses it, nor with the state of the one who pronounces it, nor with the state of affairs denoted by the proposition . . . The event occurring in a state of affairs and the sense inhering in a proposition are the same entity."[47] Moreover, sense itself is founded on nonsense, which, as Deleuze notes, is not an absence of sense but rather a play of different series of singularities.

Such an analysis of sense reflects the tension in Deleuze's thought between a desire to give primacy to difference, here embodied in the event of sense, and a recognition of the inseparability of unity and difference by the attempt to preserve unity—but as a second-order phenomenon composed of differences. Here, however, as elsewhere, where the primacy is given to difference the thought becomes incoherent. When the identity of representationalist theories of language is rejected in favor of its opposite, difference embodied in the concept of sense, then it is discourse itself that is abandoned. If meaning were merely the product of difference, there would be no meaning, only noises unrelated to each other. In order for meaning to occur, identity must exist within difference, or better, each must exist within the other. To speak with Saussure, if language is a system of differences, it is not only difference but system as well; and system carries within it the thought of identity. To put the matter baldly, a thought of pure difference is not a thought at all.

Deleuze's problem here is that he has cast the issue in terms of a binary opposition between the primacy of identity and that of difference. However, as the concept of the plane of immanence testifies, unity is not equivalent to a transcendent reducibility. Here the unity—that of linguistic identity—can occur on the plane of immanence, as long as the conception of language as a strict correspondence between words and world is abandoned. Such an abandonment, which is the abandonment of transcendence at the level of linguistic meaning, does not imply the rejection of identity, but rather a rejection of its subsumption under a transcendental principle. The project of an account of meaning, then, would be to construct a narrative about meaning that relied neither upon a principle of identity nor upon the subversion of such a principle.[48]

In the course of the discussion of meaning, another set of terms arise that constitute the second tension of Deleuze's thought regarding unity and difference. These are terms that vary throughout Deleuze's corpus, but occupy similar roles in each case. The term used above is "singularities," but "haecceities"[49] and perhaps "constituents"[50] perform the same functions. For Deleuze, it is these concepts which are invoked in order to name the primary differential components whose collocation traces a plane of immanence. It is by means of these concepts, then, that the primacy of difference emerges in Deleuzian philosophy. These concepts, which are, strictly speaking, placeholders for what lies beneath all qualities, which compose but do not themselves have qualities, are the positive differences that subtend all unities. For Deleuze, they exist—or better, subsist—beneath sense, language, concepts, bodies, consciousness, in short beneath all phenomena of experience. They are unexplained explainers, in that they must be brought into play if we are to offer an account of the world that gives primacy to difference, but precisely because there is a primacy of difference that lies beneath linguistic practice, they themselves escape all accounting.

It should be clear at this point that such a strategic move is bound to fail. To posit a concept whose function is to give primacy to difference is to violate the necessary chiasmic relationship between unity and difference. Such a positing betrays the univocity of being by merely inverting the picture of a philosophy that would give primacy to identity; in doing so it renders incomprehensible the concept of surfaces without which transcendence cannot coherently be denied. Only a philosophy that finds difference on the surface rather than in a source beneath or beyond it—even when that source eventually becomes the constitution of the surface—can articulate a role for difference that possesses both coherence and normative power. In allowing a place, often a constitutive place, for positive differences that are not themselves already differences of a surface, Deleuze allows his thought to lean exclusively on one half of the intertwining that is necessary in order to prevent his fragile project from collapsing.[51]

Of the tensions cited here, neither Deleuze's antirepresentationalism nor his privileging of differential elements are necessary or inextricable aspects of his thought. What Deleuze's reliance on Spinoza—and I believe his equally important reliance on Bergson—demonstrates is a recognition (if at times a concealed one) that a thought of difference cannot give primacy to difference. The fact that Deleuze sees himself as creating concepts rather than offering metaphysical truth-claims does not exempt him from the problem of the primacy of difference, because the dilemma of such a primacy is that it either renders the thought incoherent or returns to the transcendence it sought to avoid. The Deleuze we must bear in mind when we read him is the rhizomatic Deleuze, the Spinozist Deleuze, the Deleuze of surfaces of difference, and not the Deleuze of singularities or haecceities. There can be no thought that takes difference seriously—and indeed we live in an age that desperately needs a thought that does so—that can avoid the unity that attaches itself to such a project of thought. Difference, in short, must be thought alongside unity, or not at all.

Notes

I would like to thank Bruce Baugh, Constantin Boundas, and especially Dorothea Olkowski for comments on an earlier version of this paper.

1. Gilles Deleuze, *Différence et répétition* (Paris: Presses Universitaire de France, 1968), p. 80. Translations from this text and *Qu'est-ce que la philosophie?* are my own; all others are from the translations cited below.

2. *Différence et répétition*, p. 58. See pp. 52–61 for a discussion of Scotus and Spinoza on the univocity of being. See also Gilles Deleuze, *Expressionism in Philosophy: Spinoza,* trans. Martin Joughin (New York: Zone Books, 1990), esp. Chapter 3.

3. Gilles Deleuze and Félix Guattari, *Capitalism and Schizophrenia,* vol. 1, *Anti-Oedipus,* trans. R. Hurley, M. Seem, and H. R. Lane (New York: The Viking Press, 1977; orig. pub. 1972), p. xiii.

4. Gilles Deleuze, *Qu'est-ce que la philosophie?* (Paris: Les Editions de Minuit, 1991) p. 10.

5. Gilles Deleuze, *Empiricism and Subjectivity: An Essay on Hume's Theory of Human Nature,* trans. Constantin V. Boundas (New York: Columbia University Press, 1991; orig. pub. 1953), p. 106.

6. *Qu'est-ce que la philosophie?,* p. 80.

7. Gilles Deleuze, *Cinema 2: The Time-Image,* trans. Hugh Tomlinson and Robert Galeta (Minneapolis: University of Minnesota Press, 1989; orig. pub. 1985), p. 280.

8. *Qu'est-ce que la philosophie?,* p. 25.

9. *Ibid,* p. 25.

10. *Ibid,* p. 27.

11. *Ibid,* p. 38.

12. See below, note 41.

13. *Qu'est-ce que la philosophie?,* p. 50.

14. Gilles Deleuze, *Spinoza: Practical Philosophy,* trans. Robert Hurley (San Francisco: City Lights Books, 1988; orig. pub. 1981), p. 122.

15. *Quest-ce que la philosophie?,* p. 72.

16. *Spinoza,* p. 26. Cf. the continuation of the quote cited in the footnote above: "A mode of existence is good or bad, noble or vulgar, full or empty, independent of the Good and the Evil, and of all transcendent values: there is never any other criterion than the tenor of existence, the intensification of life" (*Qu'est-ce que la philosophie?,* p. 72).

17. *Spinoza,* p. 22. See also *Expressionism in Philosophy: Spinoza,* where Deleuze says of the *Ethics* that "*A method of explanation by immanent modes of existence* thus replaces the recourse to transcendent values. The question is in each case: Does, say, this feeling, increase our power of action or not? Does it help us come into full possession of that power?" (p. 269). This assessment fails to address the question of which powers are to be increased and which diminished, a question that he answers by means of the concept of life.

18. This discussion has avoided the question of whether we ought to consider Deleuze as holding that there is more than one plane of immanence at a given time. There is a tension in his thought around this question; for instance, in the Spinoza texts we discuss below, he seems to identify the univocity of being with the plane of immanence. However, in some later discussions, e.g., *Qu'est-ce que la philosophie?*, he seems to believe that there can be many at the same time. The truth may be, as he indicates on pp. 51–52 of the latter text, that the answer is a matter of interpretation. In any case, nothing in the current discussion hinges on it; ethical evaluation can be another plane, or at another place on the same plane. Its importance remains central.

19. It is not entirely clear that Deleuze would always ratify the distinction that has been drawn here between the ethical and the metaphysical. In fact, in some of his passages regarding naturalism, it seems that his philosophy moves toward effacing this distinction. However, both the drift of his philosophy, especially in his latest collaboration with Félix Guattari, and the incoherence of the alternative render this most fruitful way to interpret Deleuze's conception of the philosophical project. The incoherence would devolve upon the attempt to engage in a metaphysics that posits a realm inaccessible to thought and proceeds to tell us what it is like.

20. For more on the concept of life in Deleuze's thought, see my "The Politics of Life in the Thought of Gilles Deleuze", *SubStance* 66, 1991, pp. 24–35.

21. Thus his focus upon values and evaluation in his text on Nietzsche. "Nietzsche's most general project is the introduction of the concepts of sense and value into philosophy" (*Nietzsche and Philosophy*, trans. Hugh Tomlinson [New York: Columbia University Press, 1983; orig. pub. 1962], p. 1).

22. *Différence et répétition*, p. 74.

23. Gilles Deleuze and Félix Guattari, *A Thousand Plateaus: Capitalism and Schizophrenia, vol. 2* (Minneapolis: University of Minnesota Press, 1987; orig. pub. 1980), p. 4.

24. *Différence et répétition*, p. 154.

25. *The Logic of Sense* (New York: Columbia University Press, 1990; orig. pub. 1969), p. 17.

26. *The Logic of Sense*, pp. 102–3.

27. *Ibid*, p. 6.

28. *Ibid*, p. 173.

29. *Ibid*, p. 133.

30. *Expressionism in Philosophy*, p. 167.

31. The difference here is immaterial, because, as Spinoza notes throughout the *Ethics*, there is an indifference between being and being conceived. Cf., e.g., Part 1, definitions 1–3 and 5.

32. *Expressionism in Philosophy*, p. 176.

33. For a brief history of the concept of the univocity of being, see *Différence et répétition*, pp. 57–61. There, in fact, Deleuze cites Nietzsche as the crowning moment of the thought of the univocity of being, whose concept of the eternal return overcomes the problem that "the Spinozist substance appears to be independent of its modes, and the modes dependent on substance as if on another thing"(p. 59): in a word, a residual transcendence. Deleuze seems to have revised this assessment since then.

34. *Expressionism in Philosophy*, p. 42.

35. Cf. *ibid*, pp. 15–16.

36. *Ibid*, p. 100.

37. *Ibid*, p. 16.

38. *Ibid*, p. 180.

39. For a political development of this thought, see Antonio Negri's book—much admired by Deleuze—*The Savage Anomaly: The Power of Spinoza's Metaphysics and Politics*, trans. Michael Hardt (Minneapolis: University of Minnesota Press, 1991; orig. pub. 1981). Although Negri finds the crux of this thought in the third and fourth books of the *Ethics*, the development articulated here suggests that it is equally characteristic of the earlier books.

40. *Expressionism in Philosophy*, p. 79.

41. For Wittgensteinian holists, for example Wilfrid Sellars, Robert Brandom, and at moments Richard Rorty, a linguistic or epistemic whole is characterized not by its closure, but rather by the fact that for any element to have a meaning, there must be other elements to which it refers. This does not imply that those elements form a closed totality. Rather, since both language and knowledge are practices that are engaged with and by other practices, closure is impossible. This is the significance of Wittgenstein's claim that "the end [of epistemic questioning] is not an ungrounded presupposition: it is an ungrounded way of acting." *On Certainty*, trans. Denis Paul and G. E. M. Anscombe; G. E. M. Anscombe and G. H. von Wright, eds. (New York: Harper and Row, 1969), p. 17e. For Wittgenstein's epistemic holism, see *On Certainty* generally; his linguistic holism is contained in *Philosophical Investigations*, trans. G. E. M. Anscombe (Oxford: Blackwell, 1953).

42. *Différence et répétition*, p. 79.

43. Cf., for example, *Anti-Oedipus* ("The whole of desiring-*production* is crushed, subjected to the requirements of *representation*, and to the dreary games of what is representative and represented in representation" [p. 54]).

44. See above, note 23.

45. *The Logic of Sense*, p. 22.

46. *Ibid*, p. 21.

47. *Ibid*, p. 182.

48. Although the outline of such an account would be well beyond the scope of this paper, the works of Ludwig Wittgenstein, Wilfrid Sellars, and recently Robert Brandom go a long way in this direction.

49. Cf., e.g., *A Thousand Plateaus*, pp. 260–265, and *Dialogues*, trans. Hugh Tomlinson and Barbara Habberjam (New York: Columbia University Press, 1987; orig. pub. 1977), pp. 92–93.

50. This is the term—*composantes*—Deleuze uses in discussing the parts that make of a concept in *Qu'est-ce que la philosophie?*, e.g. pp. 25–26.

51. On the interpretation of Deleuze offered here, one might wonder what becomes of his notion of "intensities." Intensities should not be thought of as transcendent constitutive singularities, but as both produced and producing. Intensities arise when two or more planes of immanence come into contact, and often either force changes on those planes or become part of the site of a new, emerging plane.

4

Gilles Deleuze,
The Fold: Leibniz and the Baroque[1]
Alain Badiou

THERE IS A BOOK that proposes a concept (that of the fold). The concept is seized within its history, varied within the fields of its application, ramified by its consequences. It is furthermore distributed in accordance with the *description* of the site where it is thought[2] and the *narration* of its uses. It is recorded as a law of the place, and of what takes place. It is *what it is about*. These are the last words of the last page: "What always matters is folding, unfolding, refolding" (p. 189).

An attentive and discerning exposition of Leibniz, leaving unexplored not even the most subtle detail, might serve as a vector to Deleuze's conceptual proposition. The next to last statement of the book is: "We remain Leibnizian" (p. 189). What is important finally is not Leibniz, but that, compelled to folding, unfolding, and refolding, we moderns remain Leibnizian.

This raises the question as to what is meant by "remain."

We might here open an academic discussion on Deleuze's exactitude as historian (an exemplary and subtle exactitude: he is a perfect reader). We might again oppose a wily, nominalist Leibniz, a shrewd eclectic, to the exquisitely profound and mobile Leibniz of Deleuze's paradigm. Or work our way through the details of the text. Or simply treat it as a genealogical quarrel.

But all this aside. This rare, admirable book offers us a vision and a conception of *our* world. We must address it as one philosopher to another: for its intellectual beatitude, the pure pleasure of its style, the interlacing of writing and thought, the fold of the concept and the nonconcept.

Nonetheless, a discussion is necessary, but it will be a very difficult one in that it must begin with a debate on discord; on the *being* of discord. Because for Deleuze, as for Leibniz, it is not to be found between true and false, but between possible and possible. Leibniz justified this by something of a divine measure (the principle of the best). Deleuze, not at all. Our world, that of an

COLLEGE OF THE SEQUOIAS
LIBRARY

"enlarged chromatism," is an identical scene "where Sextus both rapes *and* does not rape Lucretia" (p. 112). A discord is the "and" of the concord. To perceive the harmony of this, we need only stay within the musical comparison of "unresolved discords."

If we wish to maintain the vigilant tension of the philosophic *disputatio*, we have no choice but follow the thread of the central concept, even if it means abandoning Deleuze's equanimous sinuosity. It is absolutely necessary to unfold the fold, to force it into some immortal unfold.

We shall operate within the yoke of a triplet, a triple loosening of the lasso Deleuze uses to capture us.

The fold is first of all an *antiextensional* concept of the multiple, a representation of the multiple as a labyrinthine complexity, directly qualitative and irreducible to any elementary composition whatever.

The fold is yet again an *antidialectic* concept of the event, or of singularity. It is an operator that permits thought and individuation to "level" each other.

The fold is finally an *anti-Cartesian* (or anti-Lacanian) concept of the subject, a "communicating" figure of absolute interiority, equivalent to the world, of which it is a point of view. Or again: the fold allows us to conceive of an enunciation without "enouncement,"[3] or of knowledge without an object. The world as such will no longer be the fantasy of the All, but the pertinent hallucination of the inside as pure outside.

All these *antis* are put forth with moderation, the marvelous and captious moderation of Deleuze's expository style. Forever asserting, forever refining. Dividing unto infinity in order to lead division itself astray. Enchanting the multiple, seducing the One, solidifying the implausible, citing the incongruous. But we shall stop here. Stop short.

I. The Multiple, Organicity

It is not by abruptly imposing an order that we might hope to overcome the Deleuzian dodge. An example: We need to read no further than twenty lines before coming across this: "The multiple is not what has many subsets, but also what can be folded in many ways" (p. 5). One is immediately tempted to make an objection: to begin with, a multiple is not composed of its *subsets*, but of its *elements*. Furthermore, the *thought* of a fold is its spread-as-multiple, its reduction to elementary belonging, even though the thought of a knot is given in its algebraic group. Finally, how can "what is folded many ways" be *exposed* to the folding, topologized into innumerable folds, if it was not innumerable to begin with in its pure multiple-being, its Cantorian being, its cardinality, indifferent to any fold, because containing within itself the being of the fold, as a multiple *without qualities*?

But what is the value of this punctuation in terms, or parameters, of Leibniz-Deleuze? He is challenging a set-theory ontology of elements and belonging, and there is in that a classical line of *disputatio* on the one and the multiple. Leibniz-Deleuze's thesis is that the point, or element, cannot have the value of a unit of matter: "The unit of matter, the smallest element of the labyrinth, is the fold, not the point" (p. 9). There is thus a constant ambivalence between the "belonging" (of an element) and the "inclusion" (of a subset). Leibniz-Deleuze's ontology apprehends the multiple as a *point-subset*, that is, as an extension (an unfold) or a contraction (a fold), with neither atom nor vacuum. This is diametrically opposed to a resolute "set-theory ontology," which *weaves out of the vacuum* the greatest complexities, and *reduces to pure belonging* the most entangled topologies.

And yet, this line of examination is hardly established before it is unfolded and complicated. Deleuze-Leibniz's ruse is to leave uncovered no pair of oppositions, to be overtaken or taken over by no dialectic scheme. What can be said of the point, the element? We know that Leibniz-Deleuze distinguishes between three kinds: the material or physical point-fold, which is "elastic or plastic"; the mathematical point, which is both pure convention (as representing the end of the line) and "site, focus, locus—locus of the conjunction of the curve vectors"; and finally the metaphysical point, the mind, or subject, which occupies the point of view or position that the mathematical point designates at the conjunction of the point-folds. So that, Deleuze concludes, you must distinguish "the point of inflection, the point of position, the point of inclusion" (p. 32). But he also concludes, as we have just seen, that it is impossible to think of them separately, each supposing the determination of the other two. What figure of the multiple "in itself" can be opposed, without appearing foolish, to this ramified evasion of the point under the sign of the fold?

Philosophy, according to Deleuze, is not an inference, but rather a *narration*. What he says about the baroque (p. 174) can be applied admirably to his own style of thought: "the description takes the place of the object, the concept becomes narrative, and the subject [becomes] point of view or subject of the enunciation." You will then not find a case of the multiple, but a description of its figures, and, even more so, of the constant passage from one figure to another; you will not find a concept of the multiple, but the narration of its being-as-world, in the sense that Deleuze says very rightly that Leibniz's philosophy is the "signature of the world" and not the "symbol of a cosmos" (p. 174); and neither will you find a theory of the subject, but an attentiveness to, a registering of the point of view that every subject can be resolved into and which is itself the term of a series that is likely to be divergent or without reason.

Thus, when Deleuze credits Leibniz with a "new relation between the one and the multiple" (p. 173), it is principally for what is diagonal, subverted, indistinct in this relation, in as much as "in the subjective sense" (and so the monadic), "there must also be multiplicity of the one and unity of the multiple." Finally, the "relation" One/Multiple is untied and undone to form the quasi relations One/One and Multiple/Multiple. These quasi relations, all subsumed under the concept-without-concept of fold, the One-as-fold, reversal of the Multiple-as-fold, are dealt with by description (which is what the theme of the baroque is used for), narration (the world as a game), or enunciating position (Deleuze neither refutes nor argues, he states). They can neither be deduced, nor thought within the fidelity of any axiomatic lineage or any primitive decision. Their function is to avoid distinction, opposition, fatal binarity. The maxim of their use is the chiaroscuro, which for Leibniz-Deleuze is the *tincture of the idea*: "in the same way the clear plunges into the obscure and never ceases plunging into it; it is chiaroscuro by nature, development of the obscure, it is *more or less* clear as revealed by the sensible" (p. 120).

The method is typical of Leibniz, Bergson, and Deleuze. It marks a position of hostility (subjective or enunciating) with respect to the ideal theme of the clear, which we find from Plato (the Idea-as-sun) to Descartes (the clear Idea), and which is also the metaphor of a concept of the Multiple that demands that the elements composing it can be exposed, by right, to thought in full light of the distinctiveness of their belonging. Leibniz-Bergson-Deleuze does not say that it is the obscure that predominates. He does not meet the debate head-on. No, he shades. Nuance is here the antidialectic operator par excellence. Nuance will be used to *dissolve* the latent opposition, one of whose terms the clear magnifies. Continuity can then be established locally as an exchange of values at each real point, so that the couple clear/obscure can no longer be separated, and even less brought under a hierarchical scheme, except at the price of a global abstraction. This abstraction is itself foreign to the life of the world.

If the thought of the Multiple put forth by Deleuze-Leibniz is so fleeting, if it is the narration, devoid both of gap and outside, of the folds and unfolds of the world, this is because it is neither in opposition to an other thought, nor set up on the outskirts of an other. Its aim is rather to *insepa-rate itself from all thoughts*, to multiply *within* the multiple all possible thoughts of the multiple. For "the really distinct is not necessarily either separated or separable," and "nothing is separable or separated, but every-thing conspires" (p. 75).

This vision of the world as an intricate, folded, and inseparable totality such that any distinction is simply a local operation, this "modern" conviction that the multiple cannot even be discerned as multiple, but only "activated" as fold, this culture of the divergence (in the serial sense), which compossibilizes the most radical heterogeneities, this "opening" without counterpart ("a world of captures rather than enclosures" [p. 111]): all this is what founds Deleuze's fraternal and profound relationship to Leibniz. The multiple as a large animal made up of animals, the organic respiration inherent to one's own organicity, the multiple as *living tissue,* which folds as if under the effect of its organic expandings and contractings, in perfect contradiction with the Cartesian concept of extension as punctual and regulated by the shock: Deleuze's philosophy is the capture of a life that is both total and divergent. No wonder he pays tribute to Leibniz, who upholds, more than any other philosopher, "the assertion of one sole and same world, and of the infinite difference and variety found in this world" (p. 78). No wonder he defends this audacity, "baroque" par excellence: "a texturology which is evidence of a generalized organicism, or of the presence of organisms everywhere" (p. 155).

In fact, there have never been but two schemes, or paradigms, of the Multiple: the mathematic and the organicist, Plato or Aristotle. Opposing the fold to the set, or Leibniz to Descartes, reanimates the organicist scheme. Deleuze-Leibniz does not omit remarking that it must be separated from the mathematic scheme: "in Mathematics, it is individuation which constitutes a specification; this is not so with physical things or organic bodies" (p. 87).

The animal or the number? This is the cross of metaphysics, and the greatness of Deleuze-Leibniz, metaphysician of the divergent world of modernity, is to choose without hesitation for the animal. After all, "it is not only animal psychology, but animal monadology which is essential to Leibniz's system" (p. 146).

The real question underlying this is that of singularity: where and how does the singular meet up with the concept? What is the paradigm of such an encounter? If Deleuze likes the Stoics, Leibniz, or Whitehead, and if he does not much like Plato, Descartes, or Hegel, it is because, in the first series, the principle of individuation occupies a strategic place, which it is denied in the second. The "Leibnizian revolution" is greeted with rare stylistic enthusiasm in Deleuze's supple narration, as the "wedding of concept and singularity" (p. 91).

But to begin with, what is singular? In my opinion, it is this question that dominates throughout Deleuze's book, and it is as a *spokesman for the singular* that Leibniz is summoned. He who has sharpened thought on the grindstone of the infinity of occurrences, inflections, species, and individuals.

II. The Event, Singularity

The chapter "What is an event?" occupies the center of the book (pp. 103–112) and is more about Whitehead than Leibniz. But in both what precedes and what follows, the category of event is central, because it supports, envelopes, dynamizes the category of singularity. Deleuze-Leibniz considers the world as "a series of inflections or events: it is a pure *transmission of singularities*" (p. 81).

Once again, the question central to the thought of the event attributed by Deleuze to Leibniz-Whitehead is intriguing and provoking. We quote: "What are the conditions of an event if everything is to be event?" (p. 103).

The temptation is great to counter with this: if "everything is event," how can the event be distinguished from the *fact*, from what-happens-in-the-world according to its law of presentation? Shouldn't we rather ask: "What are the conditions of an event for *almost nothing* to be event?" Is what is presented really singular just as being presented? It can be argued just as reasonably that the course of the world in general displays nothing but generality.

How then can Leibniz-Whitehead-Deleuze extract from the organicist scheme of the Multiple a theory of the singular-*as-event*, when event means: everything that happens, in as much as everything happens?

This enigma can be expressed simply: while we often understand "event" as the singularity of a rupture, Leibniz-Whitehead-Deleuze understands it as *what singularizes continuity in each of its local folds*. But on the other hand, for Leibniz-Whitehead-Deleuze, "event" nonetheless designates the origin, always singular, or local, of a truth (a concept), or what Deleuze formulates as the "subordination of the true to the singular and the remarkable" (p. 121). Thus the event is both omnipresent and creative, structural and extraordinary.

As a result, the series of notions related to the event are continually disseminated and contracted into the same point. Take three examples.

1. From the moment Leibniz-Deleuze thinks[4] the event as an immanent inflection of the continuous, he must simultaneously suppose it is from the *point of this immanence* that we speak of the event (never "before," nor "from outside"); and yet, that an essential preexistence, that of the global law of the world, *must* elude us if we are to speak of it: "Leibniz's philosophy . . . requires this ideal preexistence of the world . . . this mute and shadowy part of the event. We can only speak of the event when we are already at one with the mind which expresses it and the body which accomplishes it, but we could not speak of it at all without this part which is subtracted from it" (p. 142).

This image of the "mute and shadowy part of the event" is admirable and adequate. Yet, we can see that what is excessive—shadowy—in the event for Leibniz-Deleuze is *the All that preexists it.* This is because in an organicist ontology of the Multiple, the event is like a spontaneous gesture over a dark *background* of an enveloping and global animality. Deleuze explains that there are two aspects to Leibniz's "mannerism," and that this mannerism opposes him to Cartesian classicism: "The first is the spontaneity of the manners which is opposed to the essentiality of the attribute. The second is the omnipresence of the dark background which is opposed to the clarity of the form, and without which the manners would have no place to emerge from" (p. 76).

For Leibniz-Deleuze, the preexistence of the world as a "dark background" designates the event as *manner,* and this is coherent with the organicity of the Multiple. According to this conception it is a combination of immanence and excessive infinity which authorizes us to "speak of" an event. Thinking the event, or making a concept of the singular, always requires that a commitment and a substraction be conjoined, the world (or the situation) and the infinite.

2. The most highly dense chapter of Deleuze's book, and in my opinion the most accomplished, is chapter 4, which deals with "sufficient reason." Why is it that Deleuze is particularly skillful and (faithful) in this passage? Because the version he gives of the principle as "the identity of the event and the predicate" (p. 55), which is even better summarized when he states: "Everything has a concept!," is in reality the maxim of his own genius, the axiom without which he would be discouraged from philosophizing.

Once again, Deleuzian determination is assembled to blur an established dialectic through the play of nuances: this principle of reason allows him to superimpose at each point nominalism and universalism. Here we find the most profound of Deleuze's programs of thought:

> For the Nominalists, only individuals exist, concepts being only well regu-
> lated words; for the Universalists, the concept can be infinitely specified,
> the individual only referring to accidental or extra-conceptual determina-
> tions. But for Leibniz, it is both true that the individual exists *and* that this
> is in virtue of the power of the concept: monad or mind. Thus this power
> of the concept (to become subject) does not consist in infinitely specifying
> a genre, but in condensing and prolonging singularities. These are not
> generalities, but events, drops of events. (p. 86)

We grant that the couple universalism/nominalism must be subverted. But can it be to the extent of the "monadic" statement: "Everything has a concept"?

In fact, Deleuze *reverses* the implicit axiom common to nominalism and universalism, an axiom that says that nothing *of the Multiple* has a concept.

For the nominalist, the Multiple exists, while the concept, and so the One, is nothing but language; for the universalist, the One exists in accordance with the concept, and the Multiple is inessential. Leibniz-Deleuze says: the Multiple exists by concept, or: the Multiple exists *in the One.* This is precisely the function of the monad: to extract the one from within the Multiple so that there may be a concept of this multiple. This will establish a fertile equivocity between "to be an element of," or "belong to," ontological categories, and "to possess a property," "have a certain predicate," categories of knowledge. Deleuze expresses this precisely: "Finally, a monad has as its property, not an abstract attribute . . . but other monads" (p. 148).

At this point thought is submitted to the most extreme tension:

—either the Multiple is pure multiple of multiples, and there is no One from which it can be held that "everything has a concept";

—or the Multiple "possesses" properties, and this cannot be only in the name of its elements, or its subordinate multiples: there must be conceptual inherence, and therefore essences.

Deleuze congratulates G. Tarde for having spotted in Leibniz a sort of substitution of having for being: the being of the monad is the sum, the nuanced, hierarchized, continuous inventory of what it "possesses": "what is new is having brought the analysis to bear on the species, the degrees, the relations and variables of possession, making of it the content or the development of the notion of Being" (p. 147).

Of course, Deleuze knows that "possession," "having," "belonging" are metaphorical operations here. But the analysis of being within the register of having (or domination) allows him to *slip* concepts into the web of the Multiple without having to take a clear position on the question of the One. The problem is even greater for Deleuze than for Leibniz, because for the latter there is a total language, an integrating series of all multiplicities, God. At this stopping point, dissemination, through default of the One, necessarily makes a fiction of the concept (just as the crucial concept of vanishing quantity, or the infinitely small, is a fiction for Leibniz).

A solution probably does exist and Deleuze uses it *by segments.* It involves distinguishing the operations of knowledge (or *encyclopedic* concepts) from the operations of truth (or concepts *as events*). From the point of the situation, and so in "monadic" immanence, it is true that everything has an (encyclopedic) concept, but *nothing* is event (there are only facts). From the point of the event, *there will have been* a truth (of the situation) that is *locally* "forcible" as an encyclopedic concept, but globally indiscernible.

It is within this distinction that Deleuze-Leibniz discerns "two levels" of the thought of the world, the level of *actualization* (monads), and the level of *realization* (bodies)(p. 41). It might be said that, in infinity, the monadic dimension of a given thing proceeds with the verification-as-truth of what its corporeal dimension is the carrying out of. Or that the monad is a functor of truth, while bodies are encyclopedic arrangements. Particularly since actualization corresponds to the mathematical metaphor of an "infinitely inflected curve" (p. 136), and realization to "coordinates that determine extremes" (p. 136). The "open" transit of truth, in relation to the stability "in situation" of knowledge.

But *at the same time,* Deleuze tries to "sew back up" or fold one onto the other, the two levels thus discerned. To keep them apart, the event would have to break up *at some point* the "everything has a concept." There would have to be a break-down of meanings. But Leibniz-Deleuze thoroughly intends to establish that any apparent breakdown, any separate punctuality, is in fact a high-level ruse of continuity.

Deleuze is at his most brilliant when he is devoted to "repairing" the apparent gaps in Leibnizian logic.

The traditional objection to Leibniz is that his monadology prevents any thought of the relation. Deleuze shows that it is not the case. Leibniz "has done nothing but think the relation" (p. 72). In passing he produces this stupefying definition of a relation: "the unity of the non-relation with a matter structured by the couple: the whole and its parts" (p. 62), which subjugates and persuades—except that, in mathematical ontology, the whole and its parts would have to be replaced by the multiple and the vacuum.

There seems to be an unsustainable contradiction between the principle of sufficient reason (which requires that everything possess a concept and the requisites of its activity, thus binding everything to everything else) and the principle of indiscernibles (which claims there is no real being identical to an other, thus unbinding everything from everything else). Deleuze gives an immediate response: no, the connection of reasons and the interruption of indiscernibles only engender the best flux, a higher type of continuity: "The principle of indiscernibles establishes cuts; but the cuts are not gaps or ruptures in the continuity. On the contrary, they redistribute continuity in such a way that there is no gap, that is, in the 'best' way" (p. 88). It is for the same reason that "we cannot know *where the sensible finishes and the intelligible begins*" (p. 88). It is clear that the universality of events is also the universality of continuities for Deleuze-Leibniz. Or we can say that for Leibniz-Deleuze, "everything happens" means nothing is interrupted, and *therefore* everything has a concept, that of its inclusion in continuity, as an inflection-as-cut, or fold.

3. What a joy to see Deleuze mention Mallarmé so naturally, as a poet-thinker, and to feel he places him among the greatest!

On page 43, Deleuze calls him "a great baroque poet." Why? Because "the fold . . . is Mallarmé's most important operatory act." And he mentions the fan, "fold upon fold," the leaves of the book as "folds of thought" . . . the fold in "unity which gives rise to being multiplicity which gives rise to inclusion, collectivity become consistent" (p. 43).

This topology of the fold is descriptively unchallengeable. Pushed to its logical consequences, it brings Deleuze to write: "The book, as fold of the event."

On page 90, Mallarmé is evoked once more, in the company of Nietzsche, as a "revelation of a world-as-thought, which emits a throw of dice." The throw of dice, Deleuze says, "is the power to assert chance, to think all chance, which is certainly not principle, but the absence of all principle. He thus renders to absence or nothingness what escapes chance and pretends to elude it by limiting it in principle." Deleuze's aim is clear: show that beyond the Leibnizian baroque there is our world, where a gamble "causes the incompossibles to enter into the same shattered world" (p. 90).

It is paradoxical to summon Mallarmé in service of such an aim, but I shall come back to that. This paradoxical reference permits us, however, to understand why the list of thinkers of the event according to Deleuze (the Stoics, Leibniz, Whitehead . . .) is only made up of names that could just as well be cited for their *opposition* to any concept of the event: declared adversaries of the vacuum, of the clinamen, of chance, of disjunctive separation, of the radical break, of the idea, in short, of everything that opens onto thinking the event as rupture, and to begin with what has neither inside nor connection: a separated vacuum.

Fundamentally, "event" means just the contrary for Deleuze: an immanent activity over a background of totality, a creation, a novelty certainly, but thinkable within the interiority of the continuous. *Un élan vital.* Or a complex of extensions, intensities, singularities, which is both punctually reflected and accomplished in a flux (p. 109). "Event" names a predicate-as-gesture of the world: "predicates or events" Leibniz says. "Event" is only the pertinence for language of the subject-verb-complement system, as opposed to the essentialist and eternitarian judgment of attribution, with which Plato or Descartes are reproached. "*Leibnizian inclusion reposes on a subject-verb-complement schema, which has resisted since antiquity the schema of attribution: a baroque grammar, where the predicate is above all relation and event, not attribute*" (p. 71).

Deleuze maintains immanence, excludes interruption or caesura, and only moves the qualification (or concept) of the judgment of attribution (and so of the One-as-being) to the active schema, which subjectivizes and complements.

This is because Deleuze-Leibniz, deprived of the vacuum, wants to read the "what happens" in the flesh of the full, in the intimacy of the fold. The last key to what he says is thus: interiority.

III. The Subject, Interiority

Deleuze intends to follow Leibniz in his most paradoxical undertaking: establish the monad as "absolute interiority" and go on to the most rigorous analysis possible of the relations of exteriority (or possession), in particular the relation between mind and body. Treating the outside as an exact reversion, or "membrane," of the inside, reading the world as a texture of the intimate, thinking the macroscopic (or the molar) as a torsion of the microscopic (or the molecular): these are undoubtedly the operations that constitute the true effectiveness of the concept of Fold. For example: "the unilaterality of the monad implies as its condition of enclosure, a torsion of the world, an infinite fold, which can only unfold, according to the condition, by restoring the other side, not as exterior to the monad, but as the exterior or the outside *of* its own interiority: a wall, a supple and adhesive membrane, coextensive with the entire inside" (p. 149). We can see that with the fold, Deleuze is searching for a figure of interiority (or of the subject) that is *neither* reflection (or the cogito), *nor* the relation-to, the focus (or intentionality), *nor* the pure empty point (or eclipse). Neither Descartes, nor Husserl, nor Lacan. Absolute interiority, *but* "reversed" in such a way that it disposes of a relation to the All, of a "primitive non-localized relation which bound the absolute interior" (p. 149). Leibniz calls this primitive relation, which folds the absolute interiority onto the total exterior, the *vinculum*, and it is what allows the monadic interior to subordinate, or illuminate, the "exterior" monads, without having to "cross over" the boundaries of its interiority.

The analysis of the axial concept of vinculum proposed by Deleuze, in the light of the fold, is pure wonder (all of chapter 8). His intelligence is visibly excited by the challenge, by the tracking down of an entirely new piste: a subject *directly* articulating the classical closure of the reflexive subject (but without reflexive clarity) and the baroque porosity of the empiricist subject (but without mechanical passivity). An intimacy spread over the entire world, a mind folded everywhere within the body: what a happy surprise! This is how Deleuze recapitulates the requisites:

1) *Each* individual monad possesses *one* body from which it is inseparable;
2) each possesses a body in as much as it is the constant subject of the

vinculum attached to it (*its* vinculum); 3) the variables of the vinculum are the monads taken as a mass; 4) this mass of monads cannot be separated from an infinity of material parts, to which they belong; 5) these material parts make up the organic part of *one* body, of which the vinculum, considered in relation to the variables, assures the specific unity; 6) *this* body is the one that belongs to the individual monad, it is *its* body, in that it already disposes of individual unity, thanks to the vinculum, now considered in relation to the constant (p. 152).

This conception of the subject as interiority whose own exterior forms a primitive link to the infinite Multiple or the world has three principal effects.

First, it releases knowledge from any relation to an "object." Knowledge operates through the summoning up of immanent perceptions, as an interior "membrane" effect, a subsumption or domination, of multiplicities taken "as a mass." Knowing is unfolding an interior complexity. In this sense, Leibniz-Deleuze is in agreement with what I have called the contemporary question of an "objectless subject": "I always unfold between two folds, and if perceiving is unfolding, I always perceive within the folds. *Any perception is hallucinatory, because perception has no object*" (p. 125).

Second, Deleuze-Leibniz's conception makes of the subject a series, or an unfolding of predicates, and not a substance, or a pure empty reflexive point, whether it be as an eclipse or as the transcendental correlate of an object = x. Leibniz-Deleuze's subject is *directly multiple*, and this is its strength. For example: "Everything real is a subject whose predicate is a character submitted to a series, the set of predicates being the relation between the limits of these series" (p. 64). And Deleuze adds: "we must avoid confusing the limit and the subject," which is far from being a simple statement of Leibnizian orthodoxy: contemporary humanism, what is called "the rights of man," is literally poisoned by an unexpressed conception of the subject as limit. But the subject is in fact, at most, what provides multiple supports for the relation of several serial limits.

Third, Leibniz-Deleuze's conception makes of the subject the point (of view) from which there is a truth, a *function of truth*. Not the source, or the constituent, or the guarantee of truth, but the point of view from which the truth is. Interiority is above all the occupation of such a point (of view). The vinculum is also the ordering of the cases of truth.

Deleuze is perfectly right in showing that if "relativism" is involved, it does not affect the truth. For it is not the truth which varies according to, or with, the point of view (the subject, the monad, interiority). It is the fact that *truth is variation* which demands that it can be so only *for* a point (of view): "This is not a variation of the truth from subject to subject, but the condition under which the truth of a variation appears to the subject" (p. 27).

This conception of the truth as "varying" (or undergoing a process) does demand that it always be ordered at one point, or from case to case. The true is only manifest in the movement that examines the variation that it is: "the point of view is *the power to order cases* in each domain of variation, a condition for the manifestation of the true" (p. 30).

The problem is undoubtedly that these considerations remain linked to an "inseparated" vision of the event, and *therefore of points (of view)*. Deleuze points this out with his customary perspicacity: "of course there is no vacuum between two points of view" (p. 28). But this absence of a vacuum introduces a complete continuity between the points of view. The result is that the continuity, which depends on the whole, is opposed to the singularity of the variation. But a truth could very well be, on the contrary, the becoming-varied. And because this becoming is separated from any other by emptiness, a truth is a trajectory *left to chance.* This is what neither Leibniz nor Deleuze can consent to in the end, because ontological organicism forecloses the vacuum, according to the law (or desire, it is the same thing) of the Great Animal Totality.

IV. Nature and Truth

The extreme amplitude of Deleuze's philosophic project contrasts with the modesty and accessibility of his prose. Deleuze is a great philosopher. He wants and he creates a real quantity of philosophic greatness.

Nature is the paradigm of this greatness. Deleuze wants and creates a philosophy "of" nature, or rather a philosophy as nature. This can be understood as a *description in thought of the life of the world,* such that the life thus described might include, as one of its living gestures, the description itself.

I do not use lightly the word *life.* The concepts of flux, desire, fold, are captors of life, descriptive traps that thought sets for the living world and the present world. Deleuze likes the baroque, those for whom "the principles of reason are actual cries: All is not fish, but there are fish everywhere . . . The living is not universal, but ubiquitous" (p. 14).

A concept must undergo the trial of its biological evaluation, or its evaluation by biology. So for the fold: "What is essential is that the two conceptions (epigenesis and preformation) have in common their conception of the organism as an original fold, folding or creasing (and never will biology relinquish this determination of the living, as can be witnessed today in the fundamental pleating of globular proteins)" (p. 15).

The question of the body, of the specific mode through which thought is affected by the body, is essential for Deleuze. The fold is an adequate image of the incomprehensible tie between thought and body. The entire third part, which concludes Deleuze's book, is entitled "Having a body." We read there that "[the fold] also passes between mind and body, but after having already passed between the inorganic and the organic for the bodies, and the monad 'species' for the minds. It is an extremely sinuous fold, a zigzag, a primitive unlocalizable link" (p. 162).

When Deleuze mentions "modern mathematicians," he is of course talking about Thom or Mandelbrot, or of those who (outside of being great mathematicians in their own fields) have attempted the morphological and descriptive projection of a model based on certain mathematical concepts onto geological, organic, social, or other empirical data. Mathematics is only touched on or mentioned in as much as it claims to be included without mediation in a natural phenomenology (pp. 22–23).

Nor do I use lightly the term *description*. We saw that Deleuze requires the style of thought implicit in description and narration, in opposition to the essentialist argument or dialectic development. Deleuze lets thought roam through the labyrinth of the world; he lays down marks and lays out threads, sets mental traps for beasts and shadows. Monadology or nomadology: he proposes this literal permutation himself. He likes the question to be indirect and local, the mirror to be tinted. He likes there to be a tight-woven screen that forces us to squint to perceive the outline of being. The aim is to sharpen perception, to make hypothetical assurances move about and stray.

When you read Deleuze, you never know exactly who is speaking, nor who assures what is said, or declares himself to be certain of it. Is it Leibniz? Deleuze? The well-intentioned reader? The passing artist? The (really inspired) matrix Deleuze gives of Henry James's novels is an allegory of the detours of his own philosophic work: "*That which* I am talking of and *which* you are thinking of too, do you agree to say *it* of *him*, providing we know what can be expected from *her* in relation to *it* and we can also agree on which is *he* and which is *she*?" (p. 30). This is what I call a description *for thought*. What is important here is not so much to decide (on him, her, that which, etc.), but to be led to the point of capture or of focus where these determinations define a figure, a gesture, or an occurrence.

If Deleuze were less prudent, or more direct, he might have chanced vast and culminated descriptions in the style of Plato's *Timaeus*, Descartes' *Monde*, Hegel's *Philosophy of Nature*, or Bergson's *Creative Evolution*. This is a tradition. But he suggests, rather, the vain possibility (or the contemporary impossibility) of these attempts. He suggests this while presenting the concepts, the operations, the "formatives." The fold might be most important of all (after difference, repetition, desire, flux, the molecular and the molar, the image, movement, etc.). Deleuze submits it to us through partial descriptions, as that which possibly *describes* a great description, a general capture of the life of the world, which will never be accomplished.

V. Five Punctuations

The author of these lines has made *the other ontological choice*, that of subtraction, of the empty set and the matheme. Belonging and inclusion play for him the role Deleuze attributes to the fold and the world.

However, the word "event" signifies for both of us an edge, or border, of Being, such that the True is assigned to its singularity. For Deleuze as well as for myself, truth is neither adequation nor structure. It is an infinite process, which has its origin randomly *in a point.*

The result is a strange mixture of infinitesimal proximity and infinite distance. I shall only give here a few examples, which will also serve as a contrasting reexposition of Deleuze's thought.

1. The Event

That there be excess (indifferently shadow or light) in the occurrence of the event, that it be creative, I agree. But my distribution of this excess is opposed to Deleuze's, who finds it in the inexhaustible fullness of the world.

For me, it is not from the world, even ideally, that the event gets its inexhaustible reserve, its silent (or indiscernible) excess, but *from its not being attached to it,* from its being separated, interrupted, or—as Mallarmé would say—"pure." And it is, on the contrary, what *afterward* is named by minds or accomplished in bodies that brings about the global or ideal situation in the world of the event (a suspended effect, that I call a truth). The excess of the event is never related to the situation as an organic "dark background," but as a multiple, so that the event *is not counted for one by it.* The result is that its silent or subtracted part is an infinity *to come,* a postexistence that will bring back to the world the pure separated point of the supplement produced by the event, under the laborious and unachievable form of an infinite inclusion. Where Deleuze sees a "manner" of being, I say that the worldly postexistence of a truth signals the event as *separation,* and this is coherent with the mathematicity of the multiple (but effectively is not so if we suppose its organicity).

"Event" means: there is some One, in the absence of continuity, in the suspension of significations, and *thus* there are some truths, which are chance trajectories subtracted—by fidelity to this supernumerary One— from the encyclopedia of the concept.

2. Essence, Relation, All

In his war against essences, Deleuze promotes the active form of the verb, the operation of the complement, and sets this "dynamism"—opposed to the judgment of attribution—against the inexhaustible activity of the All.

But is the relational primate of the verb over the attributed adjective sufficient to save the singularity, to free us of essences? Must not the event rather be subtracted from any relation *just as* from any attribute, from the doing of the verb *just as* from the being of the copulative? Can the taking-place of the event support being in continuity, or in intermittence, between the subject of the verb and its complement?

The great All annuls just as surely the local gesture of singularity, as the transcendent essence crushes individuation. Singularity demands that the separating distance be absolute and thus that the vacuum be a *point* of Being. It can support the internal preexistence, neither of the One (essence), nor of the All (world).

3. Mallarmé

Although descriptively exact, the phenomenology of the fold cannot be used to think what is crucial to Mallarmé's poem. It is only the secondary moment, a local passing through, a descriptive stasis. If it is the case for Mallarmé that the world is folds, a folding, an unfolding, the aim of the poem is never the world-as-fan or the widowed stone. What must be counterposed to the fold is the stellar point, the cold fire, which places the fold in absence and eternalizes that which, being precisely "pure notion," counts no fold. Who can believe that the man of the "calm block," of the constellation "cold with forgetfulness and disuse," of the "cold gems," of the severed head of Saint Jean, of Midnight, etc. has taken on the task of "folding, unfolding, refolding"? The "operatory act" essential to Mallarmé is that of detaching, of separating, of the transcendent occurrence of the pure point, of the Idea that eliminates all chance, in short, it is the contrary of the fold, which metaphorizes obstacle and intricacy. The poem is the *scissor* of the fold.

The book is not "the fold of the event," it is the pure notion of the event as singularity, or the poetic isolation of *what is absent from any event.* More generally, Mallarmé cannot be used for Deleuze's aim (to certify the divergence of the series of the world, to enjoin us to fold, unfold, refold), for the following reasons:

1. Chance is not the *absence* of any principle, but "the *negation* of any principle," and this "nuance" separates Mallarmé from Deleuze by the entire distance that brings him closer to Hegel.

2. Chance, as a figure of the negative, is the principal support of a dialectic ("The infinite is the result of chance, which you have denied") and not of a gamble (in the Nietzschean sense).

3. Chance is the *autoaccomplishment* of its Idea, in any act in which it is at stake, so that it is an affirmative, delimited power, and not at all a correlation of the world (the term "world-as-thought" is totally inadequate).

4. The accomplishment, by thought, of chance, which is also the pure thought of the event, does not give rise to "imcompossibles" or whimsical chaos, but to "a constellation," an isolated Idea, whose scheme is a number ("the only number which cannot be an other"). It is a question of matching the Hegelian dialectic and the Platonic intelligible.

5. The question is not to reduce to nothingness whatever is opposed to chance, but to get rid of nothingness so that the transcendent stellar isolation, which symbolizes the absolute separation of the event, might emerge. Mallarmé's key concept, which is certainly not the fold, might just be purity. And his central maxim, the conclusion of *Igitur:* "Nothingness gone, the castle of purity remains."

4. The Ruin of the Category of Object

One of Deleuze's strong points is to have thought with Leibniz an objectless knowledge. The ruin of the category of object is a major process of philosophic modernity. And yet, Pascal would say, Deleuze's strong point only holds "up to a certain point." Caught up in the twists and turns of the All and the denial of the vacuum, Deleuze assigns the absence of object to (monadic) interiority. But the lack of object is a result of truth's being a process of making holes in what constitutes knowledge, rather than a process of unfolding. And also of the subject's being the differential of the perforating path, rather than the One of the primitive tie to worldly multiplicities. Deleuze seems in fact to keep, if not the object, at least the *traces of objectivity*, in as much as he keeps the couple activity/passivity (or fold/unfold) at the center of the problem of knowledge. And he is forced to keep it there, because his doctrine of the Multiple is organicist, or vitalist. In a mathematized conception, the genericity (or the hole) of the True implies neither activity nor passivity, but rather *paths* and *encounters*.

5. The Subject

Deleuze is a thousand times right to think the subject as "relation-as-multiple," or as a "relation of limits," and not as simple limit (which would reduce it to the subject of humanism).

However, we cannot avoid formally distinguishing the subject as multiple configuration, from other "relations of limits," which are constantly being inscribed in some situation or other. I have proposed a criterion for this, which is the *finite* fragment: a subject is a finite difference in the process of a truth. It is clear that in Leibniz what we have is on the contrary an interiority—one whose vinculum subordinates *infinite* multiplicities. Deleuze's subject, the subject-as-fold, has as its numeric formula 1/∞, which is the formula for the monad, even if its clear part is 1/n (p. 178). It articulates the One with the infinite. My conviction is rather that *any finite formula* expresses a subject, if it is the local differential of a procedure of truth. We would then be referred to the characteristic numbers of these procedures, and of their types. In any case, the formula 1/∞ certainly brings us within the toils of the subject, the paradigm of which is God, or the One-as-infinite. This is the point where the One makes up for its excessive absence in the analysis of the event: if the event is reduced to the fact, if "everything is event," *then* it is the Subject who must take on both the One and the infinite. Leibniz-Deleuze cannot escape this rule.

In face of which, pure interiority must be abandoned, even if it is reversed to coextensive exteriority, in favor of the local differential of chance, which has neither interior nor exterior, being the matching up of a finitude and a language (a language which "forces" the infinite of the variation of the subject-as-point from its finite becoming-varied). There is still too much substance in Leibniz-Deleuze's subject, too much concave folding. There is only the point, and the name.

In Conclusion

Deleuze cumulates the possibilities of a "descriptive *mathesis*," whose performances he tests locally, without engaging its systematic value.

But can and must philosophy remain within the immanence of a description of the life of the world? An other road, which it is true must relinquish the world, is that of the salvation of truths. It is subtractive and active, while Deleuze's is presentifying and diverting. To the fold it opposes the motionless intricacy of the empty set. To the flux, the stellar separation of the event. To description, inference, and axiom. To the gamble, to the experiment, it opposes the organization of fidelities. To creative continuity, it opposes the founding break. And finally, it does not join together, but separates, or opposes, the operations of life and the actions of truth.

Is it Deleuze or Leibniz who assumes the following: "The mind is a principle of life by its presence and not by its action. *Strength is presence and not action*" (p. 162)? In any case, this is the concentration of everything from which philosophy, in my opinion, must preserve us. It should be possible to say: "A truth is the principle of a subject, by the empty set whose action it supports. A truth is action and not presence."

Unfathomable proximity, within what bears the name "philosophy," of its intimate other, of its internal adversary, of its royal misappropriation. Deleuze is right on one point: we cannot cut ourselves off from it without perishing. But should we merely content ourselves with it convivially, we shall nonetheless perish, but by it.

—*Translated by Thelma Sowley*

Notes

1. Gilles Deleuze, *The Fold: Leibniz and the Baroque,* trans. Tom Conley (Minneapolis: University of Minnesota Press, 1992). Originally published in French as *Le Pli: Leibniz et le baroque* (Paris: Les Édition de Minuit, 1988). All page references in this essay refer to the French volume.

2. "[S]on site de pensée": "Pensée" can (and in French philosophical language often does) have a more verbal and creative sense than "thought" in English. I think the ambiguous noun/past participle of *thought* in "the site where it is thought" captures something of this. For other occurrences of "thought," e.g., "the thought of the event," the reader will sometimes want to force the English toward this more creative sense.   —*Translator*

3. For *enouncement*, I follow Ann Banfield's translation in J. C. Milner's *For the Love of Language* (New York: Macmillan, 1990), p. 77. She authorizes her translation from Beckett's in *The Unnameable*: "Suppositions are equally vain. It's enough to enounce them, to regret having spoken . . . ," *Three Novels by Samuel Beckett* (New York: Grove Press, 1955), p. 375   —*Translator*

4. And not "thinks of the event." "Penser" has here a creative sense ("creates by his thought a new concept of the event"), somewhat parallel to the difference between "conceives" and "conceives of." I have preferred, throughout my translation, keeping the relatively strange construction with "think" in English to avoid other confusions that can arise from the difference in French between "pense l'évènement" and "conçoit l'évènement" as well as between "pensée" and "concept."   —*Translator*

II. Subjectivity

5.

The Crack of Time and the Ideal Game

Peter Canning

I. Why a Multiplicity

DELEUZE DEFINES PHILOSOPHY as a "theory of multiplicities that refer to no subject as preliminary unity,"[1] but why—if a multiplicity is not a subject, nor unity of object "referred" to a subject, what is the relation? Kant defined the subject as "transcendental unity of apperception," but from a multiplicity the One always has to be subtracted, making it a purely dimensional, or rather directional and eventful, formation of variable (and fractional) dimensions.[2] A human-multiplicity *consists* in changing dimensions, mutating all the time. It increases dimensions with every connection, combination, or *agencement*, every "synthesis" it makes, by assembling the dimensions it persists in changing. So an *agencement* (assemblage) is an "increase in the dimensions of a multiplicity that necessarily changes in nature as it expands its connections" (Deleuze and Guattari 1987, p. 8, cf. 21). An event-multiplicity may, according to the Leibnizian reading of the real (God's eye or the Monad), be described by a tensor through which its complete predicate or lifeline is included in its individual notion. But this complete predicate does not exist, however it may insist by way of the virtual and multiple Idea it actualizes by *differenciation*.[3] We may say, following Leibniz, that the complete idea exists in the mind of god, but for us to find it we must search for it, invent, create, or assemble it, and so subtract its given presupposition as "our" "nature" changes. Always subtract one, precisely the One that would lock in the overcoding command program and transcend all other dimensions and directions.

So much for the infinite individual "analytic" monad; but how can I withdraw the transcendental subject of synthetic finitude? Don't I need it to synthesize the unity of "my manifold" (multi-pli), the event of my polymorphous existence? Perhaps, since we are programmed to imagine we can't do without, can't live without that unity, which is nevertheless everywhere lacking (transcendent), but in any event the unity of composition of a multiplicity (inventing its plan of consistency) can be had only by subtracting the specious One-over-All dimension of Identity bound to its rigid designator (limitative or exclusive use of Proper Name): to inform an informal "flat [or plane] multiplicity" (Deleuze and Guattari 1987, passim) of n–1 dimensions. Are we not giving up the indispensable operation of transcendental unification of our world by subjective synthesis? By denying identity don't we essentially open the world to anarchy and schizophrenia?[4] Rather, to the "real inorganization" of desiring assemblages.[5] In fact, *the* One (the Signifier of the missing One) can never really overcode or transcend the multiple, because when it does increase or change dimensions (through a *pointe de déterritorialisation*), a multiplicity mutates, it "undergoes metamorphosis, changes in nature" (Deleuze and Guattari 1987, p. 21).[6] The immanence of a unifying force consists in its potential ubiquity throughout the multiple system (transcendental field) of which it is a nomadic presence.

Multiplicities are dimensional events, our dimensions are drawn by directional vectors, tensions, or tendencies, "directions in motion" (p. 21) urging and driving assemblages to face the chaos, the supreme music, and turn us into something, always something else, other than the one intended. These happenings form tensors or "lines of flight" emerging from points of deterritorialization, the hazards and risks one takes to break out of a habitual mold and to *become*, to modulate. The *pointes* or emergences involve changes of plan, direction, or plane of the multidimensional, introducing mutant lines and new figures into the assemblage—for example, to alter the normal sequence of one's movements, habitual pattern of behavior, rhythm of speech, accent, tone, or attitude, to throw open the itinerary or hour of a regular excursion, thus encountering a new situation and doubling oneself with another of whose existence I had no Idea because it did not make me until now . . . A vector of deterritorialization (tensor: spacetime diagram—Spatium-Aion, depth of field-time—describing a roaming vector modulating forms, assembling connections) opens a new dimension (periodic function) by drawing out and stretching the coordinates of an assemblage according to shifting force relations in the field or plane of encounter.[7] An assemblage is defined by its lines of escape rather than by fixed coordinates or rules of structure, because the "thing" (event) as tensor-multiplicity is of time or between-time and can express itself for the time being only by offering itself to immanent mutation (variation) as its ownmost potential. "The line of flight is part of the rhizome" (Deleuze and Guattari 1987, p. 9) or multiplicity, which it transforms or relays—"translates"—to another dimension; so the dimensional is a static consideration of the dynamic or directional (tensor). And the *pointe*, while it is breaking out, thus defines from its outside edge (becoming) the assemblage as "increase in dimensions" of the changing multiplicity. Human being, language, or society; book or brain, event or concept—these are formations of mutability including alteration (line of flight), variation of component lines, within their definition, because they are beings of becoming, tensors whose "properties are independent of the chosen system" of spatiotemporal coordinates—and of axioms. Thus, a language is a tensor-matrix in a multiplicity of dialects, isotopic wave-fronts emitting (included) divergent budding singularities (idiolects) in a semiotic rhizome-tissue. An "atypical expression" is a language-event that alters the syntax or usage-pattern of the matrix, responding to historical actualities and preparing them by fabulating. The semiotic tensor varies expressive forms and combines them with metamorphic content forms in a *compositif*. But content and expression become, in their folding together, distinct, indiscernible, a semiotic double (matter-function) that "causes language to tend toward the limit of its elements, forms, or notions, toward a near side or a beyond of language. The tensor effects a kind of transitivization of the phrase, causing the last term to react upon the preceding term back through the entire chain" (Deleuze and Guattari 1987, p. 99)—retroaction of flight or invention as new dimension.

Our language is regulated by ordering words and slogans and phrases, which propagate in waves, but *and* is the password, "tensor for all of language," the traveling semiotic point-fold connecting the thought of any topic in the language-rhizome to any other—or to some time to come—breaking out and circling back to a new conjunction (encounter) in the transverse spacetime of the "book" or life under perpetual reconstruction.

Every line of escape or *pointe* potentially folds back upon its rhizome-multiplicity to become one of its dimensions; that is, the being's indetermination coupled with its memory, its "virtuality," enables any movement to become periodic and repeatable, thus a component-dimension of its pattern of existence. This holds for any event affected with "life" or with the capacity of a memory of acts.

A human, considered topologically or geometrodynamically, consists in affect-multiplicities or waves of emotions, bands of intensities varying to form neighborhood zones and shifting alliances, polymorphous assemblies: assemblages differentiate qualitatively each time we change connections with people or animals, vegetables or things, techniques . . . society as manifold of complying and refractive "social forces," all implicated with each other and complicated in the same Natura or Multiple City. Social beings can be defined by their "involutionary" potential, Body without Organs, the way they fold back into past times and futures with each other, multiplying through their immanent horizon, Idea, or n-dimensional plane (n–1, discounting the transcendental subject). *The line of flight is part of the rhizome.* The BwO is the variable interval of death within lifetime, antimetric, always undoing and redoing the habit of measures: "the interval is substance" (Deleuze and Guattari 1987, p. 478). It acts from within the period or cycle of regular transformations, which accomplishes and maintains the structure, "substance," or essence of a being in its identity (repetition of component transformations). It is rhythm, "the link between truly active moments" (p. 313); in a key text, Deleuze-Guattari (quoting Bachelard) affirms the incommensurability of the rhythmic plane between assemblages and abstract machine(s), the actual variations and the virtual variability potential. We realize we are approaching the limit of the subject when we can "comprehend" the concept only by introducing the incomprehensible—Death, BwO, *forgetting*, escape-outside—within our theory of consciousness and memory. Rhythm plays the role of forgetting—the virtual or potential action—in relation to the memory of metric time, its measure.

The "laws" of a society or group or language or individual character (ethos), considered in their becoming, are defined by variation, mutation—how they come apart and go together again, informing new composites, new assemblages, the way they "change nature with every division" or connection. A connection is thus never just "another one," never defined numerically, it is always qualitative or durational. The radical Bergsonian continuum, *durée* as qualitative multiplicity, is not divisible for it is itself a cut or *pointe*, a line of becoming. When it does divide, or division happens, the continuum changes its nature, mutating into another essence or "species" (bifurcation). A duration is an incommensurable span of internally regular time across which the "substance" (BwO) travels as it reemerges. When a genetic-transformational "character" (or group—but every subject is already a group) gives up or takes on a habit, a behavior, cops an attitude, it changes nature. Characters are like languages in that variety is their idea and essence. Every true being is, in this way, a simulacrum.[8]

Deleuze follows Kant, Bergson, and Leibniz in creating an ever varying concept of time, a play of syntheses culminating in a Nietzschean outcome. But isn't Nietzsche the philosopher of eternal recurrence, and isn't that the end of time altogether, "nothing new under the sun"? Deleuze constantly warns against confusing "his," Deleuze-Nietzsche's, notion of eternal return with the "cyclic hypothesis" supposedly entertained by the Greeks and eclipsed by the modern linear theory of time. In fact, it is Kant who sprang time from hinging upon movement, more precisely upon the periodicity of a cyclic movement of reference, a model and standard measure for time. The "relation" of time to movement is ultimately as complex as theoretical physics itself, which must deal with the problem in its way, quantum mechanically or geometrodynamically. But it is in cosmological, biological, and especially semiotic domains that the theory of time is thrown altogether "out of joint," off of its hinges on periodic movement. In effect, nothing can ever begin as a function of movement, for movement itself is powerless to begin at any certain time—whence the continuing potential of Lucretian-Epicurian fluid dynamics, the *incerto tempore* of the clinamen, the smallest deviation from linearity into the elementary vortex, and, too, of the Kantian definition of time as *self-affection*, time as "subject," which has dominated the theory of the pragmatic subject since Kant, especially through Heidegger's interpretation.[9] A living being, even more, a human subject-multiplicity assemblage is not *in* preexisting empty time or space, it *creates* the spatiotemporal milieu, which it expresses like a spider exuding a web.

What happens when time gets thrown off its dependency on movement and into "deregulation"? Deleuze's answer reveals one of the secrets of his method, which is to carry and push an idea to its extreme consequences; out of a rigorous sense of play, certainly, but also in pursuit of raw truths that his predecessors did not care to expose (that is, create). Kant determined time as "order, set, and series"[10] of pure singularities (events), which enter into strange relation with each other in mutual determination. The *order* of time is defined by a *static synthesis* in which time-without-movement freezes into place, or rather, crystallizes into its pure and empty form (Aion), past-(present)-future—but where the present is determined to disappear into the absolute interval splitting past *and* future whence it reappears as an event, emerging in the image of an action "adequate to the whole of time," a "set" or ensemble not closed, nor bounded, but determined in the image of the split or "caesura" itself (Deleuze 1968, p. 120). The "whole of time" is (in) the interval, the cut. Now the crack or split (*fêlure*) is the simple effect of a static ordering, a self-relation whereby "I affect myself" in the emptiness of an absolute (in)determination or "abandonment" to freedom.[11] Past/future, the order of time means "this purely formal distribution of the unequal as a function of a caesura"—unequal because time no longer makes ends meet in the cyclic return of the end to the beginning, rebeginning at the end: time ceases to rhyme (Deleuze 1968, p. 120). It is "the form of the most radical change, but the form of change does not change"—mutability can drive a body mad with freedom. But "having abjured its empirical content," this empty form remains to be determined in its transcendental "content" by the action—while the action consists or insists in doubling the caesura, in becoming capable of the crack one already is becoming, "an event unique and formidable," such as "taking time off its hinges, making the sun blast, jumping headfirst into the volcano, killing god or the Father" (p. 120). Or "Anti-Oedipus" (to kill the complex)—to release the singularities of desire from their signifying chains. The action is a symbol that "gathers the caesura, the before and the after" into an "ensemble of time" in its constituent disparity, its internal difference (dy/dx or t/c). The caesura extends into a before- and after-image of itself becoming, a time-series that "operates the distribution" of the lines and surfaces of time on either side of the fissure. The past is defined as the action's being "too much for me," I can't take it, I'm not up to it (even if it has already happened). The present is the gaping, sheer metamorphosis of a changing nature, shifting dimensions and becoming equal to the unequal (to the task), a Nietzschean or Dionysian release wherein "all it was becomes 'thus I willed it, thus I shall will it'" (Zarathustra) and all hatred of the past, all "responsibility" dissolves into an event, a turning point without equal in any history (the becoming of history prior to actual eventuation). The past as "repetition by default" has prepared this transformation, "metamorphosis in the present" (Deleuze 1968, p. 121). This begins the new Game, "schizophrenic" reconstruction of a world in ruins, with a throw or drawing of singularities, to link back, from out over the abyss, to unconscious renaissance (the third synthesis, eternal return).

This has something to do with writing and composition. In effect, the Deleuzian synthesis (the future beginning in "disjunction," "eternal return") prepares a new image of thought and of the concept. Where movement stops, where time stops moving, "passing," there it starts to *become*. The passing present gives a false image of "real time" as succession—as though the real of time could ever be clocked and captured by letting the camera run. Real time has nothing to do with the passing present, it starts when the present stops and we are thrust into the interior, the Milieu.[12] Let us call Brain or Rhizome this kind of inside-time (inside is the fold of outside) that affects itself, not with itself (time), but with becoming, a pretime emerging from the crack between times. "It is no longer time which is between two instants [as with Bergson], it is the event which is a between-time [*entre-temps*, 'meanwhile, meantime']: the between-time is not of the eternal, but it is not (of) time either, it is (of) becoming . . . it coexists with the instant or the time of accident . . . in the strange indifference of an intellectual intuition. *All the between-times superimpose themselves*, while the times succeed each other."[13] The "meantime" of becoming comes strictly *between* the time of the event's occurrence, of actualization in a state of things. It does not itself occur or "happen" (*se passer*) but comes between time, not just between the times that pass and follow each other, but *between time and itself*, within itself, as the outside (future) within ourselves, our "subject" as time.[14]

It is not that time comes to a halt; only the movement stops or becomes "aberrant" (Deleuze 1985, passim) where time begins: in eternal return (the "being of becoming"). For the image of self-affection means self-affection by "one's own" image in a crystal medium, but the image is an Other, a virtual self or I that affects itself as me (in me), according to the Rimbaldian formula, "I is an Other." This virtual-actual circuitry, or I-me loop of automatism forms the primordial image of time, even recurring to approximate the traditional notion of substance, *causa sui.* They say that "nothing can come of nothing": then the "cause of itself" is absurd—no less than Freedom or time's affection of itself by the transcendental Other, free automaton, or desiring machine. It forms the originary nonsense from which sense proceeds.[15] Deleuze-Guattari insists the strings of the marionette or the body of the actor are not connected to the will of the puppeteer or actor or author, but to the second order automaton of the human body-brain rhizome (Deleuze and Guattari 1987, p. 8). From virtual to actual and back, in the ever-renewing feedback loop of self-motivation, self-communication, self- . . . (the Other), the regime of the crystal engages its subject in a pure order of succession in which past and present, present and future, become distinct but indiscernible; past and future begin to revolve and "turn about the different," the *dispars* or simulacrum, "the symbol itself, that is, the sign in as much as it interiorizes the conditions of its own repetition." The present ceases to be determined as substance and duration ("the identity of things is dissolved") as it hinges or "seizes upon the disparity" between times that it takes as its "unit of measure, that is, always a difference of difference as immediate element" (Deleuze 1968, pp. 92–94). The sign-image we are (becoming), the Double. Rhythm.

This difference "of" immediacy "with" itself "in" time forms the smallest internal circuit between the self and itself, "a perpetual *Se-distinguer* [Self-distinguishing]" (Deleuze 1985, p. 109), as in the mirror or the mime, "*ici devançant, là remémorant, au futur, au passé, sous une apparence fausse de présent.*"[16] It is a mere nothing in terms of metric time, the slightest disparity, which consists in being aware of an internal, intervallic vacuum, outside-in, future-past just arriving, just departing, which it is the task of philosophy to diagram in concepts gathered and selected, recombining and returning, the thing's self-created concept of its own event, thinking image as simulacrum self-diverging, overflying time (*survol*).

The crystal may begin as a simple mirror image, which starts a short-circuit recoiling into the vortex of its being, uncoiling back to where expanding strata of the past are superimposed in continuous layers, folding each over into the next, a brain-rhizome-affect-percept-concept continuum with "one single side whatever the number of its dimensions, which remains co-present to all its determinations . . . runs through them at infinite speed" and maintains "a state of overflight without difference, at ground or earth level, self-overflight [*auto-survol*] which no abyss, no fold or hiatus escapes" (Deleuze and Guattari 1991, p. 198). With the rhizome, Deleuze-Guattari has transformed and subverted Bergson's memory-perception cone, the inverted spiraling pyramid of *Matter and Memory*. Of this image of time, Deleuze retains (in *L'image-temps*) the continuity of "sheets of past" with the "peaks [*pointes*] of present," implying that the cone is a vortical continuum; each sheet is a disk but also a winding stair continuing up and around in the "next" one, according to the Bergsonian formula of the flux, "interpenetration without succession." But de jure the loop of the present itself "contains all the past" in its "smallest circuit" (Deleuze 1985, p. 130), so the loop or circuit itself must practice a cross-section or cut a *transversal* through the entire past, through all the (apparently) "successive" layers (moving past and following each other according to the passage of presents). This diagonal line or cross-cutting plane is immanent to the whole of time, and yet it is not given; it must be created. And therefore it is precisely not made of "the" continuum, the same cone, but of a selection of sheets, planes, and points, which the philosopher-schizo-artist must assemble: "we constitute a continuum with fragments of different ages, we make use of transformations which operate between sheets to constitute a sheet of transformation" (Deleuze 1985, p. 161). This transverse operation occurs in reading or writing, the composition of the plane of immanence, but the plane sweeps across and transects all the past, gathers elements from the ages, and returns them to present their metamorphic configuration, a quasi-aleatory feedback loop, back from the void, "perhaps a constellation" (Mallarmé). The Deleuzian model of the history of philosophy, its use and abuse for life. The transformation sheet "invents a sort of transverse continuity or communication between several sheets, and weaves between them a set of nonlocalizable relations" (p. 161). This ensemble or set is "thought, the brain . . . the continuity which enrolls and unrolls them like so many lobes" in "superimposition," and even creates new lobes, "recreation of matter in the manner of styrene . . . the cerebral membrane where past and future, interior and exterior confront each other immediately, directly, without assignable distance" (p. 164). For time-life or Remembrain is a book made of one double-sided scrolling sheet in which the reader begins anywhere, connecting and condensing (dia)grammatical singularities, always sensing the meaning on the other side or between the lines, cutting through sedimental stratospheres of cosmic library dust. God the Monad-Lector is the ideal reader who hangs on the other side of time where he connotes all the eventual figures (*chiffres*) shaping and breaking on the crest of actuality.

Thus the real of time has nothing to do with the movement of the present that passes, *nor with anything given* in the form of intuition. It consists first in a past coexistent with the present and preexisting itself as present ("time consists in this splitting [*scission*]" (Deleuze 1985, p. 109); then in perpetually distinguishing itself into the indiscernible virtual (past-future) and actual (present) of the circuit or feedback loop in which I affect myself as an Other, the Subject; finally, in a rhizome-multiplicity, a neuronal labyrinth of virtual connections, synaptic disjunctions, and polyphrenic conjunctions, live assemblages eternally renewing and changing with every encounter, every singularity from the outside thus included in or as the form of cerebral time. Deleuze's answer to Kant, Lacan, and all dualisms is categorical, or rather, diagrammatical: everything, as Spinoza said, is double, at once thing and idea, "body and mind," although we ourselves have only "the idea of that which happens to our body, the idea of our body's affections." Each thing is double, virtual (idea) and actual (thing), though the complete and adequate idea exists only "in God."[17] Deleuze perhaps no longer believes in God (the refrain or *cri de guerre* of *Cinema II* is: "how can we believe in *this* world?") and yet, with Whitehead and Nietzsche, he insists still upon the immanence of the idea in "this world." Thus everything is doubled with itself in its becoming, its metamorphosis, of which the splitting of the human subject (*dédoublement*) is only the most developed figure. Deleuze does not wallow in the finitude of "castration" and "transcendence," because everything is becoming-idea, becoming-body, becoming-virtual, becoming-actual in a circuit without end or beginning, the new world-image of absolute immanence. It is we who become what is becoming and returning, for we, and everything in the universe, are at once thinking and being, idea and thing, united in the indiscernible image passing in and out of time between times. We may say that death is the other side of time, the virtual that actualizes itself in our "self"-consciousness and negativity (work), and which hollows our interiority. But beyond time and death ("a shallow stream") it is Becoming that, through death, reaches the Body without Organs between lives. "The BwO is the model of death" (Deleuze and Guattari 1983, p. 329), but also its virtual medium of "nonlocalizable connections" to life (p. 309), the region where death and rebirth become indiscernible in the dispersion of lives, "lottery drawings . . . depending on one another only by the order of the random drawings, and holding together only by the absence of a link" (p. 309). Death, the absolute outside, the unthought that forces us to think? Violence? Outside of any diagram, "the outside is always opening a future, with which nothing ends, because nothing has begun, but everything metamorphoses" (Deleuze 1986, p. 95). For Affect means transition on the plane.

It is true that Deleuze has attained the plane of immanence at the price of allowing the Object to disappear into its own double, its *description*, and the becoming of object and subject, into an absolute *narration*, the power of the false (Deleuze 1985, pp. 165–202). The circuit between indiscernibles draws a diagram that transects the time of the object and grasps it in its becoming, which thus merges with my own becoming.[18] The diagram—a concept developed by Deleuze-Foucault (by now we realize that Deleuze "himself" is double, "double-articulated" as they say somewhere)—is an image of the concept in "perpetual becoming" (Deleuze 1986, p. 91) on the plane. With the diagram we reach the throw of dice, the singularities, and the ideal game (see below). For the "drawing" of singularities, their distribution, comes always from outside, that is, from the future, from Thought ("for to think is to emit a throw of dice" [p. 93]) which breaks into our "clichés" precisely when habitual "schemata" break down (Deleuze 1985, p. 62ff). The diagram consists in the virtual matrix of its spontaneous transformations, its self-variations, the concept "prison" (for example) as quasi-immanent matrix of a "disciplinary diagram" composed of multiple variations: school, factory, hospital, camp, barracks . . . "concrete machines," "assemblages" actualizing the "immanent cause" or "abstract machine" of discipline.[19] Unlike the abstract possibility of classical thought, the Deleuze-Bergsonian virtual (diagram) results from a continual—even when interrupted—act of creation and thought, a "mental vision, almost a hallucination" (Deleuze 1985, p. 65): to create the concept, to think what must be thought through time and is precisely impossible to think, or to see what cannot be perceived (a becoming-imperceptible), to imagine the unimaginable, etc. (cf. Deleuze 1968, p. 182ff.). Into these direct images of time and thought, these diagrams of becoming, this Battle (Deleuze 1986, p. 129), subject and object merge and lose their boundaries; the world becomes its own image, "cinema," hallucination. Heidegger and, more recently, Christian Jambet have explored this region of the indiscernible under the name of Kant's "transcendental imagination."[20] Deleuze draws his own path through his preferred series of allies and doubles: Leibniz, Nietzsche, Bergson, Klossowski, Foucault, Guattari—always recreating the distinct indiscernible, the thing thought as two faces of a double-sided image (or a single-sided Möbius dyad); and furthermore, an entire world-multiplicity: not the multiplicity of different things in this world, but the multiplicity of worlds in a single thing or image in self-transformation according to the rules of thought or the ideal game, the regulative idea that has become the only thing(-hallucination), the only thought (-delirium), the imperative question whose self-regulations change with every move, every self, every emission of singularities gathered from the future and dispersed into an "other present" (Deleuze 1969, pp. 196, 78) in the passion of the subject, the metamorphosis of agency.

II. Rhythm as Differential Element (Repetition in Eternal Return)

In the beginning was the repetition, and that made all the difference. Intensity, "difference of intensity," begins to actualize the differential Idea, making a difference "by which the given is given as diverse" (Deleuze 1968, p. 286); while repetition "in the Idea, [which] runs through the varieties of relations and the distribution of singular points . . . is the power-potential [*puissance*] of difference and differentiation: whether it condenses the singularities, precipitates or slows down the times, or varies the spaces" (p. 284). Repetition is the power of the rhythmic Idea to produce a difference, an intensity, a "disparity" (p. 287) as its *excess* (the third time-synthesis begins in rhythm as repetition-variation). The "intensive system" induces a *simulacrum* (chaosmos)—"signal-sign system"—in which everything communicates through mutual difference and distance, "reciprocal determination," and every phenomenon is a "sign," which passes or "fulgurates" across "disparate orders" (p. 286, pp. 355–56). The virtual-actual (ideal-incarnate, -individual) complex forms two sides of a "Symbol": "an ideal half plunging into the virtual, and constituted by differential relations and corresponding singularities; an actual half constituted by qualities actualizing these relations, and by parts actualizing these singularities" (p. 358).

Can we continue to speak of a subject in such a case, the ideal I and the actual me? The subject began in "passive synthesis," the first form of repetition, which "withdraws" from itself the difference of spacetimes and intensities that would have caused it to divide and mutate into another. This is the synthesis of contraction, governing the present and constituting the production of a duration, from which, subtracting difference, we derive the permanence of an identity ("self-recognition" follows as the active reflection based on the prior passive synthesis). It makes the foundation of time. The second passive synthesis inaugurates the splitting of time, of the subject in self-affection by its own coexisting, preexisting past (the past is not a function of the present but is always contemporaneous with the present it "has been"). But what justifies positing the preexistence of a past that was never present, a time immemorial, beyond the active synthesis of memory, a forgetting coextensive with memory and prior to it, making of memory itself something passive and given by that which gives but is not itself given? The answer is the intensity at the origin, Spatium, the dark depth, and the Multiplicity (virtual Idea) which distributes itself—its singularities of thought—through all of time, "a Long thought" (Deleuze 1969, p. 76). The Idea that produces the intensity is the third synthesis, of productive repetition or rhythm.[21]

Where is the subject, is it still to come or already dissolved? Deleuze never gives up entirely on the subject concept, because of his demand for absolute

interiority ("internal multiplicity": Deleuze 1968, p. 237) or, rather, continuity, the continuum of the manifold with its cut—so that the subject is not
a void, but a cut, an intervention, or an *interval*. But the interval is the brain
itself ("the brain becomes subject": Deleuze and Guattari 1991, p. 198), fold
of the world, as in the moving image-novel of *St. Petersburg* by Biely, which
Deleuze cites in *Cinema II, L'image-temps*. Or the entire cerebral-nervous
system as interior milieu in topological contact with its own exterior,
according to Gilbert Simondon, whom Deleuze cites continually. The
Remembrane. We therefore determine the subject as the splitting between
virtual (Idea-multiplicity) and actual (individual-multiplicity) and the
folding of one upon the other, as in a categorical imperative, as well as the
genesis of the individual from the transcendental field of singularities in
their nomadic distribution (without identity or resemblance: cf. Deleuze
1969, pp. 124–142). For "the genesis [goes] . . . from the virtual to its actualization . . . from the differential elements and their ideal linkages to the
diverse real relations which constitute at each moment the actuality of
time" (Deleuze 1968, pp. 237–238). Finally, in the disjunctive-synthetic
moment of deindividuation, the subject reopens at a point of bifurcation,
"ambiguous sign of singularities . . . which stands for several of these [indi-
vidual, analytic] worlds, and at the limit for all, beyond their divergences
and the individuals who people them" (Deleuze 1969, p. 139). This "quasi
cause" opens the future and thus communicates with the origin of time and
world, will-to-power.[22]

> Repetition in the eternal return [tells itself] of the will to power . . . of its
> imperatives and its throws of the dice, and of the problems issuing from
> the act of throwing . . . reprise of pre-individual singularities . . . dissolu-
> tion of all prior identities. All origin is a singularity . . . a beginning on the
> horizontal line . . . where it prolongs itself [into a world]. But it is a re-
> beginning on the vertical line which condenses the singularities, where [the
> eternally disguised] repetition weaves itself, the line of affirmation of
> chance (Deleuze 1968, pp. 260–261).

The world thus disclosed by Deleuze-Leibniz-Bergson spirals to infinity at its
inverted base, which communicates directly, transversally with its *pointe* of
thought throwing and condensing singularities from actual to virtual and
back into time.[23]

How can we maintain the priority of the "will-to-power" or "imperative"
while dissolving the ego into a field of empiricities themselves going back
(*renvoi*) to transcendental singularities or differential elements, since this
transcendental field is not yet unified by the form of the I, "subject of enunciation" of the imperative? What are these elements? Are they the same as

intensities, differences of intensity? How are they "produced" by differential repetition or rhythm?

The ideal linkages (*liaisons*) of singularities are said to be "non-localizable" (Deleuze 1968, p. 237) because they are liaisons of time *between times*, the becoming or genesis of time, which is rhythm. When and where does everything begin? The abyss; but "chaos is not without directional components, which are its own ecstasies" (Deleuze and Guattari 1987, p. 313, translation modified), where it stands out, or points into order and sends out singularities to connect or "prolong themselves to the neighborhood of another singularity," forming time-series and multiple ensembles, dissipative structures hooking back into swirling chaos. A tangled tale. A milieu is defined by "periodic repetition of the component," constituting a "vibratory . . . block of space-time" (Deleuze and Guattari 1987, p. 313), a musical shape or coded dimension (code = "periodic repetition"); the codes are in "perpetual transcodage" or passage from one milieu to another, one dimension to another, as their lines change direction at a singularity or turning point (the Big Bang is also the event horizon or Singularity). "The milieus are open (in)to chaos . . . but the retort or riposte of milieus to chaos is rhythm" (p. 313, translation modified), and *in-between rhythm and chaos*, Chaosmos. This is where we are alive and transposed at all times ("the living being . . . passes constantly from one milieu to another") between "communicating" milieus. They communicate through the timeless chaos between them, with which they form a potential, a power gap, and in the rhythm between periodic times, "between two intermilieus," where the living being "changes direction" to create and shape a new component or dimension: a mutant form, or perhaps a malformation, *entre chien et loup*, anyway a monster (according to the norm or axiom). Rhythm is a tensor synchronizing multiple, overlapping coordinate (metric) systems it expresses through actualization-individuation but also conversely by sweeping all components into its potential. This holds for modulating tonal series and domains into a line of escape, which (part of the rhizome—to hazard an error in improvising) loops and folds back into the intense, nonextended chaosmic Spatium transforming each component, sending it into another dimension. For chaosmos is a membrane, or modulating *crible* (winnowing screen), facing chaos and countering with *nonlocalizable* rhythms and webs. These cannot be located in time or space, whose measure they originate or spring loose again. Aion, nonchronological time, in overflying itself (surface) condenses singularities to begin again. This Aion (lifetime) we are disjunctively continuing, immersed in strange waters of the afterlives.

The between chaos and order where quasi-stable elements take shape and dissipate, where we are still today constituting and dissolving our milieus and

abodes and patterns of existence, these "ecstasies" are the intensities or originary differences produced by repetition, in the third synthesis of time. We
saw that this synthesis of the future implied the metamorphosis of the
subject-agent. We can now begin to tell what this transformation involves.
First there is a receptivity to the violence of an encounter that forces one to
think and to create, to pose and solve problems, matters of life and death.
Whereas the past is defined by the complaint of insufficiency ("It's too much,
I can't"), the future is determined by an excess produced by repetition. The
world itself is such an excess or "reste" (Deleuze 1968, p. 286), an irrational
remainder after all calculations are done with.

Deleuze's reply to Kant, his "critical solution to the antinomy" of time—
the paradox of "preexistence": how can time begin with the first "event" or
singularity "in" a presupposed and preexistent time, etc.?—is this *disjunctive*
synthesis that replaces or remodels a prior empty time with an a priori
chronogenic and aionomorphic repetition "in the beginning." The agent/
thinker must undergo metamorphosis to become "equal" to the task of
thinking such a thought that "*transforms all of a sudden even the identity* of
the one to whom it reveals itself."[24] But metamorphosis means forgetting:
"isn't forgetting the source at the same time as the indispensible condition"
of a revelation that overcomes its agent and dissolves "all identities into
being"? Klossowski determines the "antinomy" in terms of forgetting and
memory, *oubli et anamnèse*, "supplemented" by a "will (to power)," as a
commanding paradox; what must be lived (again) of necessity ("for you will
have to relive and begin again"). The eternal return is an ontological
ontoethical imperative, a "necessity that must be willed"—a will to forgetting, to living, to being born: a paradox as old as Pythagoras, perhaps, or
beginning with Nietzsche-Klossowski: "for such an oblivion [*oubli*] will be
equal to a memory outside my own limits: and my present [*actuelle*]
consciousness has to have established itself in the forgetting of my other
possible identities."

Is forgetting not the *source* . . . of all time? Forgetting means mutation,
becoming; but "the being of becoming is returning" (refrain of Deleuze's
Nietzsche book): a necessity that must be willed. An ontoethical game: "to
affirm becoming and to affirm being of becoming," two moments of the
"game of becoming" in which "the being of becoming also plays the game
with itself; the aeon (time), says Heraclitus, is a child who plays . . . eternal
return . . . third term, identical to the two moments and valid for the whole."
We get carried into being, born to play the game "chaosmos."[25] Livable
cosmic milieus form by composing or synthesizing a periodic repetition of
the component, but remain open to chaos through the fault of time, the
crack where the future (power of the false, to change rules and shift metrics)

intercedes and the past (fixed lines of Truth) defaults, while sifting nodal lines reemerge disguised as waves wherever rhythm makes a riposte, to disjoin "rhythm-chaos" (Deleuze and Guattari 1987, pp. 311–313).

The human is a being suspended in a caesura of time, "the intrusion of an outside which hollows out the interval," cerebral-nervous milieu . . . interior? But "the interior presupposes a beginning and an end, an origin and a destination capable of coinciding, of making whole, the all. When there are only milieus and in-betweens" (Deleuze 1986, p. 93), when the caesura or the wavy crack of time takes over and overboards the interior, it forces one to think what cannot and must be thought . . . The mind or spirit or subject becomes affected with itself, but itself is outside, in the forgotten future; the subject has the form of time or self-affection, in that "time as subject . . . is memory," but "the 'absolute memory' which doubles the present, which redoubles the outside . . . is one with forgetting, since it is ceaselessly forgotten in order to be remade, redone" (Deleuze 1986, p. 115). Deleuze's book in memoriam of Foucault is also a treatise on oblivion and eternal return, mourning and memory, for if time as subject is defined as the "folding of the outside," implex which "makes every present pass into oblivion," it also "preserves the entire past in memory, forgetting or oblivion as the impossibility of returning, and memory as the necessity to begin again" (Deleuze 1986, p. 115). The actual and the virtual, memory and forgetting, "this" life and "all" the lives and souls in endless recirculation. When one side is present (actual) the other is absent (virtual), but both are inseparably real at the same time: to remember to live, to forget to die, or is it when I forget to live that I think of death? When indiscernibly the being begins to live, then it is "putting time outside, under the condition of the fold" (Deleuze 1986, p. 115).

Forgetting or oblivion, in its rhythmic alternation with remembering, is still too much the concern of a subject. We cannot determine repetition as the function of a subject, for the subject—as personality or even as concept—results from the rhythm that creates, that gathers and selects the intensive traits or directional components of chaos to synthesize a consistency and plane of immanence. The plane carries its concepts as "multiple waves," but the plane itself, "unique wave which enfolds and unfurls them," is made of "*diagrammatic traits*," "absolute directions" or *intuitions*. The plane is a connective tissue, diagram, or "abstract machine" of which concepts or events are the "concrete assemblages"; it is the "event horizon" or "reservoir" of event-concepts. The concepts are not yet actualizations of events in states of affairs, things, or bodies; they are "*intensive traits*" that may proceed to individuation in actual multiplicities, haecceities (Deleuze and Guattari 1991, pp. 38–42; cf. *A Thousand Plateaus*).

If an assemblage is an "increase in dimension" of a multiplicity that "changes its nature" and rules of formation, then the relation between dimension and direction comes into focus around the plane—or rather, the plane is the impossibility of "clear focus" for the concept or *agencement* in the anexact "neighborhood zones" or "thresholds of indiscernability" that define its "interior consistency" (Deleuze and Guattari 1991, p. 25). Topology of the concept: chiasmus or Möbius strip, its "interior" plane of consistency is distinct but indiscernible from its (exterior?) plane of immanence, a virtual section of chaos establishing a *Grund* in the *Abgrund*. *Who* establishes? It is still rhythm, perhaps the immanent "conceptual character" (Deleuze and Guattari 1991, pp. 60–81). For haecceities are characters, *personnages* in their incarnation-individuation, but everyone who ever lived or thought is a rhythm and sustains a tempo. Rhythm, then, makes a change in dimension (assemblage) on the plane of immanence continuous with the interior consistency of the subject-concept in its variations. Rhythm is the *crible* itself, the plane of planes, riposte to chaos, the virtual idea "of" repetition (compare Deleuze and Guattari 1991, p. 45, and Deleuze and Guattari 1987, pp. 311–313). It is the fluid milieu of thought and life ("for [thought] needs a milieu which moves in itself infinitely, the plane, the void, horizon": Deleuze and Guattari 1991, p. 38), the rhizome "without beginning or end" but only "a milieu through which it grows and overflows [*déborde*] (Deleuze and Guattari 1987, p. 21 translation modified). "Rhythm-chaos or the chaosmos" (Deleuze and Guattari 1987, p. 313) is the planing of the plane, the line of escape from chaos commutating with a virtual multiplicity of timelines, series of events, an idea—the *Inbegriff* of time.[26] The Idea is not the concept, it is the plane of immanence or *problematic horizon* of "everything that happens [*arrive*] or appears" (Deleuze 1969, p. 70). The horizon is the fold of thought or life coming back to itself from the source.

With the virtual Idea of the virtual concept . . . of becoming (on) the plane of immanence, Deleuze has shaped his finest creation, the Body without Organs. The BwO is the plane "substance" of which the intensities are the living concepts (cf. Deleuze and Guattari 1987, p. 153f.). But "the interval is substance (whence come rhythmic values)" (p. 478, translation modified); it is in its constitutive rhythm that the interval—musical brain, book, rhizome between—becomes or comes back, comes to, always another as the substance begins to turn upon the modes and identity "turns about the Different" (Deleuze 1968, pp. 59, 388); for intensity is the turning point, the singularity or change of interval which makes the "conformation of the inside space with outside space" (Deleuze and Guattari 1987, p. 418 translation modified)—interval as variation of substance. All is variation, "trajectory," *trajet* or trait; "the interval takes all" (p. 418).

We are playing with chaos, playing with fire, with water, with elementary "mad particles" (Deleuze and Guattari 1987, p. 40) on the plane of immanence; for the plane "is like a cut or section [*coupe*] of chaos, and acts like a sieve or screen [*crible*]," while in chaos there are no lasting "determinations" of things because "one does not appear without the other having already disappeared, and the one appears as vanishing when the other disappears in outline [*ébauche*, rough sketch]" (Deleuze and Guattari 1991, pp. 44–45; cf. Deleuze 1968, p. 96). The play of memory and forgetting, itself predetermined to forget itself and to begin again "ceaselessly weaving itself, gigantic shuttle" (Deleuze and Guattari 1991, p. 41)—chaos or immanence? Thinking or horizon? Matter or Idea?[27]

Chaos is the a priori of time, the inseparability, indiscernibility (limit) of memory and forgetting "in the infinite." It is the prior repetition, which "implies by rights a perfect independence of each presentation," where the harsh "rule of discontinuity or instantaneity" requires that "the one does not appear without the other having disappeared" (Deleuze 1968, p. 96). By the synthesis of contraction two "times" are linked into one "habit" or self, milieu or central nervous system. Then the self discovers the preexistence of pure empty time before creation, before the multiuniverse "self-caused" itself by chance or was given the chance by its nature or god. The *causa sui* is the absurd, self-causing agent described by Deleuze, characterized by "heterogeneous series of singularities which organize themselves into a system . . . provided with a potential energy [intensity] where differences distribute themselves between series" (Deleuze 1969, p. 125). It is the transcendental field-unconscious where singularities undergo or undertake "a process of self-unification" in this potential "energy of the pure event," of the virtual, unconscious Idea—doubled with (distinct, indiscernible) consciousness of itself ("consciousness . . . is the double . . . and each thing is consciousness because it possesses a double": Deleuze 1968, p. 284), Idea of Idea. For there is no thing without "its own" idea, no matter how confused (because too clear) or obscure (distinct) or complicated. At the limit, the membrane between them, the plane of immanence forms an idea of chaos, a rhythmic idea (chaos takes shape in the Idea of itself). The Idea is remembrane, the riddle, the *crible* ("the song is a kind of sketch of a . . . center in the heart of chaos . . . it jumps from chaos to the beginning of order . . . this involves an activity of selection, elimination and extraction . . . to borrow something from chaos through the filter or sieve [*crible*] of the space that's been drawn" (Deleuze and Guattari 1987, p. 311 translation modified). The *crible*, screen or filter, is the immanent plane cut or cross-section of chaos with variable grid, modular webbing, Chaosmic Communications Network. It is the potential from god-knows-where, *sponte sua,* the "thread . . . from which the spider descends" (Deleuze and Guattari 1991, p. 116). But god is dead(?) and the reason for that is . . . *repetition*. Thus repetition cannot be discerned before it begins to link up with another instance of itself in disguise or displacement (with a working memory), "a paradoxical element," which "makes the series resonate . . . in an aleatory point . . . in a single throw" for all throws (Deleuze 1969, p. 125). What is this *unique lancer* or "longest thought" in an interval shorter than time?

III. The Aionic (Ideal) Game

Repetition 0123 is of the chaos (disappearing apparition, oblivion), of self-linkage (the habit-of-living milieu), of contemporaneous preexistence (Memory) . . . and of the future (eternal return). The Idea is repetition, which produces intensity by varying its metric, which leaves memory behind, passes (back) through chaos, and reemerges from the crack of time (Ideas "swarm in the crack" and emerge from its rims, but the Idea also "interiorizes the crack and its inhabitants, its ants": Deleuze 1968, p. 220) through the filtering screen of remembrane. It is both inherence of the predicate in notion (monad) and absolute opening, the outside, because of its Möbius topology, Klein bottle or human being, inside-out, thinking itself ahead, leaving itself behind, encountering the "savage singularities" it draws and binds and strategically diagrams, the thinking line, folding point, "line of the outside" (Deleuze 1986, pp. 125–130). It is not a pretty sight, this (a)rhythmic-aleatory idea of infinite "chaoerrance" (Deleuze 1969, p. 305), that "terrible line that brews all the diagrams" (Deleuze 1986, p. 130). Homeless, pointless, without identity; absolute position without location ("in a sense, everything is everywhere at all times": Whitehead): it is utter nonsense, the pointless origin of all sense and sensibility. It is a jumping point, "leaping over itself" into a line (Klee; cf. Deleuze and Guattari 1987, pp. 311ff.), sweeping across itself onto a surface, folding its self-surface into a volume (cf. the Baker's transformation of Prigogine: Deleuze 1985) without ceasing to be a plane surface, the surface a line, the line a point, the point a fractalescent chaos.

It takes a leap of thought to make a connection, a resonance between two . . . series that did not exist until now. For example, to write connecting letters and echoing phrases; to draw connecting points, lines, planes, and volumes, resonating shapes and colors; to think connecting and reflecting thoughts into each other; to feel connecting intensities resonating in synesthesia; to imagine linking the source with the abyss, always making up shapes out of singularities of whatever nature, disappearing apparitions, protoplasmic powers. In chaosmos the splitting of the monad performs a disjunctive synthesis. Past and future become indiscernible as virtual and actual. In the realm of creation, of (non)sense, time the event has no predictable direction.[28] The monad is a nomad (Deleuze 1988, p. 189). Aion: time is a child playing . . . throwing singularities. On this earth which does not move, where movement stops, there time (*durée*, life) begins; and there is no entropy without potential, thus no "arrow of time" direction to the time becoming.

I can do no more here than sketch a description of the ideal game, the game of becoming (of returning). "Begin" with the formula of the Body without Organs: the interval is substance. The intervallic, interstitial substance synchronizes all the periods of the milieu components, their rates of synthesis, of transformation. All is metamorphosis, but substance is the enduring interval, lifetime, or Aion. Aion is the variable, nonmetric or "nonpulsed" (Deleuze and Guattari 1987, pp. 262, 267, 296, etc.) time of life "that has abandoned points, coordinates, and measure," "deterritorialized rhythmic block" that "no longer forms a localizable connection" *since it creates its own coordinates* (p. 296), that is, tensors, the tensor that it is—not having or referring to any subject or substance transcending the process of its self-prehension in the other; self-construction, drawing the diagram, the abstract machine. According to the ontology of Whitehead and Berkeley, all being is perception (prehension); and the object of perception is always the imperceptible, the noncategorizable (BwO): "Perception will no longer reside in the relation between a subject and an object, but rather in the movement serving as the limit of that relation, in the *period* associated with them. Perception will find itself confronting its own limit; it will be in among things, throughout its own proximity [*dans l'ensemble de son propre voisinage*], as the presence of one haecceity in another, the prehension of one by the other or the passage from one to the other" (Deleuze and Guattari 1987, p. 282, my emphasis, translation modified). But perception, prehension, is becoming, is metamorphosis, is being itself. Being, becoming, is the interval of substance, the returning or the repetition of component transformations, forever synchronizing periods and rhythms in the passage between milieus: Affect = Transition. To become is to jump into the middle or milieu where we are already (being born), in this zone of indiscernibility we are just now reconstructing (Deleuze and Guattari, cf. p. 293).

Music, as "deterritorialization of the voice," provides us with a "model" or rather, module of becoming, because the voice is territorialized by language and signification, the regimes of memory and discipline, but music is the art of forgetting, of changing memory and metric, of reaching the becoming of history prior to historification and measurement. *Desire directly invests the field of perception* (Deleuze and Guattari 1987, p. 284; cf. Jambet 1985, n. 17). Or painting as deterritorialization of figure, face, and image.

Anarchy means (etymologically) "without governing principle or foundation." In this sense the Deleuzian synthesis of disjunction is a rule of anarchism or (as he says) the system of "anarchy crowned." Anarchy rules, but what does this mean? It does not mean no rules, but, as we have seen, that the rules change with every move, every act of speech, every question or problem formation, every thought or drawing of the singularities. As in Sartre's "situational ethics"—but without even the form of consciousness or the regulative gaze to hold the game in check. What are we in for in the coming "Deleuzian era" that Foucault foretold? It is already here, in the encounter, the shape of our meeting with the outside-thought, the future.

Freud wrote a fabulous essay consummating the tradition of tradition, of principle, of the family. In "Dynamics of the Transference" he calmly lays out the coordinates and transmits a method of diagnosis and treatment of the typical neurotic haunted by familiar phantoms or "imagos." Every human being, he says, is a composite determined by a combination of destiny (*Daimon*) and chance encounter (*Tyche*). Destiny is comprised of genetic inheritance and symbolic tradition (which Lacan formally introduced into the equation), but what is chance, what is *Tyche*? *Tyche* is chance or fate, the singularity whose rules of composition (desire) must be reinvented with every move, every meeting with another being or with itself. Where then is the place of repetition? How can repetition "synthesize" the future?

The repetition of the future has nothing whatsoever to do with any return to the past or memory. It begins in the milieu of metamorphosis and forgetting—whence the past may certainly return, but as a component or trait of the disjunctive synthesis, of transformation, as an act or action of throwing time off its hinges, off its periodic cycle (try a simple Deleuze-Guattarian remedy for neurosis: dismount your dada, get off the complexes, throw up your childhood memories, blow out your fantasies, and get a clock that keeps "a whole assortment of times" [Deleuze and Guattari 1987, p. 271]). Aion is the name of the game, Igo I deal, Jeu Idéal. Repeat: it is not without rules . . . (not without rules, anarchy rules). Everything depends on the variation (concept) of the interval (subject-substance-multiplicity). Repetition governs the game, composition of the plane.

No foundation, on sky or on earth, the gaming tables? Not even below the earth (archeology, geology, biostratigraphy)? In the fold of the twins, heaven and earth, the third synthesis comes throwing the dice of time, brewing all the epochs and churning up epistemai, shuffling singularities for a new drawing of time: universal *effondement*.[29] All identities are dissolved, personal, individual components redistributed. The ethics of situation (a phrase Deleuze does not use and would perhaps refuse) commands affirmation of a world "constituted by divergent series (chaosmos) [of events 'incompossible' in the 'same' *identical* world], [where] the dice throw has replaced the game of Plenitude," the principle of the best of all possible worlds governed and selected by God's goodness and universal intuition. Time has radically entered altered being. If there is a God, there is no time (since He sees everything at all times displayed at once); but if time is real, there is no divine "intellectual intuition" *except on the plane of immanence* where the concept roams through its tensors at the speed of thought and folds back into chaos to drink from the source; and "the monad can no longer include the entire world as in a closed circle modifiable by projection, but opens itself onto a trajectory or expanding spiral that distances itself farther and farther from any center" (Deleuze 1988, p. 188). The ideal game is only this chaocacocosmos where everything returns repeat because there is no beginning or end of time, but only a mid milieu where I am writing you reading, reading you writing, if we well prehend each other in this mobile instance. For "the true subject of the eternal return is the intensity, the singularity . . . will to power as open intensity" in this virtual world where "each thing opens itself to the infinite of predicates through which it passes"—maximum communication!—"on condition that it lose its identity as concept and as ego or self" (Deleuze 1969, p. 344). For the Ego Idea governs the category of substance, inside and out; the One World Universe conditions the series of all causes; and God (Logic) monitors the distribution of exclusive identities (Deleuze 1969, p. 343). But in the system of Anarchist, "the anti-God determines the passage of each thing through all possible predicates" (Deleuze 1969, p. 344). This is what is happening, obscurely and distinctly now, in this indiscernible chaosmos of "history." The world becomes a Grand Canyon, the counter-ego a crack or a dissolving, dissipative structure, god becomes Dionysus, "divine dismemberment" (Deleuze 1969, p. 206), or Baphomet, "prince of modifications," and all the rest, ourselves, *mobile figures forming at the crest of waves.* For "this" world is the result of this series originating in that singularity, which will continue and prolong itself up to the next one.

Notes

1. "A Philosophical Concept," in *Who Comes after the Subject*, Eduardo Cadava, Peter Connor and Jean-Luc Nancy, eds. (New York: Routledge, 1991). Nietzsche already spoke of a *Subjekts-Vielheit* (subject-multiplicity) in *Beyond Good and Evil*, while for Kant the purpose of subjective synthesis was to combine the "manifold" (multiplicity) in intuition but also to unify it transcendentally.

2. "[A] fractional number of dimensions is the index of a properly directional space (with continuous variations in direction, and without tangent); what defines smooth space, then, is that it does not have a dimension higher than that which moves through it or is inscribed in it; in this sense it is a flat multiplicity, for example, a line that fills a plane without ceasing to be a line; space and that which occupies space tend to become identified, to have the same power . . . " Gilles Deleuze, *A Thousand Plateaus* (Minneapolis: University of Minnesota, 1987), p. 488.

3. Differentiation is the self-causing potential of the Idea, Aion and Spatium (dynamic space-time of Body without Organs), its self-differing into incompossible spacetimes and bodies, intensive particles and matter-functions, divergent series of singularities wherein alone it consists in itself (its plane of immanence), self-synthesizing in disjunction "a" multiple spirit-souffle of all series, "aleatory point of singular points"; while differenciation is the process of individuation—incarnation and presencing together in the same "compossible" world, the actual world. The idea-world or chaosmos complicates all series, virtual and actual. A virtual becomes possible to realize or actualize when an idea condenses into a concept, as the event is beginning to assemble its components by stepping out to self-encounter; perhaps it enfolds its virtue in the Idea from the absolute beginning beyond eternity, transcendental preexistence, or infratemporal a priori. This differential repetition (*t/c*) in virtual spacetime of preindividual, nonpersonal singularities (static series) or intensities (dynamic) forms the topic of *Différence et répétition* and *Logique du sens*. "Static" does not mean lacking directional displacement, it defines a temporal synthesis of indeterminacy (preparing the *concept* of time-direction) as prelude to Deleuzian synthesis: the infinite proliferation of incompossible series of timelines, lifelines, all included—or rather, "made and undone"—in "the same motley world . . . of captures rather than closures"; where even our "captures"—of knowledge and power, of desire, of information—"draw [us] outside" into an absolute future without foreknowledge or interiority, even in divine intellectual intuition. Gilles Deleuze and Félix Guattari, *Le pli: Leibniz et le Baroque*, (Paris: Minuit, 1988), p. 111. The *only* time *in this sense* is the future, the outside, chance, "emission of singularities" as in a Mallarmean constellation. But this outside (time) is our interiority. See note 12.

4. With a further right twist of his gadfly attitude, an antipsychiatrist like Thomas Szasz can go from exposing the "myth of mental illness" as a psychiatric invention or intervention to denouncing "schizophrenics" for simulating incompetence to stand trial and pretending to be disturbed when they commit atrocities, to avoid personal responsibility. *Insanity: The Idea and Its Consequences* (New York: Wiley, 1987).

5. Gilles Deleuze and Félix Guattari, *Anti-Oedipus* (Minneapolis: University of Minnesota Press, 1983), pp. 39, 309, et passim (quoting Lacan).

6. Ilya Prigogine and Isabelle Stengers, citing Whitehead ("the many become one and are increased by one"), comment: "no element of nature serves as permanent support of

changing relations, each draws its identity from its relations with the others . . . each existing [thing] unifies in the process of its genesis the multiplicity which constitutes the world, and adds to this multiplicity a supplementary set of relations." *La nouvelle alliance* (Paris: Gallimard, 1979), p. 112. In *A Thousand Plateaus* Deleuze and Guattari only subtract the one in order to relaunch the process of becoming or "genesis."

7. The tensor is an expression of force vectors as metadimensional: "Mathematical being, generalization of the vector, defined in a space of n dimensions by n^k components (k being the order of the tensor) and whose *properties are independent of the chosen system of coordinate axes. A vector is a tensor of order 1.*" *Petit Robert*, s. v. (my emphasis). Mandelbrot's constructions of fractional dimension seem to generate spontaneously "out of chaos" by nonlinear processes involving tensors. But Deleuze borrows and remodels the mathematical concept of tensor in order to define an essential activity of "self"-constructing forces, which perceive or "prehend" (Whitehead) other forces to compose a power field or desiring machine that varies its coordinates (changes nature and dimensions) with every "translation" (movement) it undertakes. Thus he has radicalized the concept of event as *change of nature*, Guattari's deterritorialization, to the degree that "every thought emits a throw of the dice" (Mallarmé), initiates a potential re-ordering of time.

8. This can be painful and go against the grain, "against nature." For example, an obsessional "structure" of tightly controlled ritual operations—as a function of what? All that tight webbing of regulations has the purpose of avoiding an encounter with the line of flight, which thus defines the obsessional behavior, apotropaic, phobic converse or "conversion," which negatively mimes the act it is avoiding. Or a society that defines itself by its "regimes of control" and becomes obsessed with internal or external enemies, subversion. To break out is to break down (according to the fundamental human or obsessional phantasm).

9. Martin Heidegger, *Kant and the Problem of Metaphysics,* trans. James S. Churchill (Bloomington: Indiana University Press, 1962; originally published in 1929). Deleuze's reading of Kant permeates his late-sixties work and the two volumes on cinema (especially the second); it is summed up rapidly and with extreme density in the 1983 preface to *Kant's Critical Philosophy.* Cf. Gilles Deleuze, *L'image-temps* (Paris: Minuit, 1985), p. 111: "[T]he actual is objective, but the virtual is the subjective . . . time itself, pure virtuality which splits and doubles itself into affecting and affected, 'the affection of self by self' as definition of time." On the virtual currency of Lucretian (meta)physics, see Michel Serres, *La naissance de la physique* (Paris: Minuit, 1977) and Ilya Prigogine and Isabelle Stengers, *La nouvelle alliance* (Paris: Gallimard, 1979).

10. Gilles Deleuze, *Différence et répétition* (Paris: Presses Universitaires de France, 1968), pp. 116ff.

11. "Once existence is no longer produced, nor deduced, but simply posed (this simplicity drives all our thought to madness) and once it is abandoned to this position and by it at the same time, it becomes necessary to think the freedom of this abandon." Jean-Luc Nancy, *L'expérience de la liberté* (Paris: Gallimard, 1988), p. 13.

12. "It is we who are internal to time . . . Time is not the interior in us, but just the opposite, the interiority in which we are, in which we move, live, and change" (*L'image-temps*, p. 110). It emerges from Deleuze's *Foucault* (Paris: Minuit, 1986) that the outside-future becoming "interiority" is deeper within ourselves than "our own" interiority as defined by habits, periods, programmed movements, consciousness, and memory (cf. *Différence et répétition*, pp. 96–115).

13. Gilles Deleuze and Félix Guattari, *Qu'est-ce que la philosophie?* (Paris: Minuit, 1991), p. 149, my emphasis.

14. "[T]he *order of time* [concerns] the coexistence of relations or the simultaneity of elements interior to time. The third [time-image or synthesis] concerns the *series of time*, which joins the before and the after in a becoming, instead of separating them: its paradox is to introduce an interval which lasts [*qui dure*] into the moment itself" (*L'image-temps*, p. 202).

15. Gilles Deleuze, *Logique du sens* (Paris: Minuit, 1969).

16. "Here out ahead, there remembering, in the future, in the past, under a false appearance of present," Stéphane Mallarmé, "Mimique," quoted in *Logique du sens*, p. 80.

17. Gilles Deleuze, *Spinoza: Practical Philosophy*, trans. Robert Hurley (Minneapolis: University of Minnesota Press, 1988), p. 86.

18. It is also true that the subject-concept emerging from the "new Hegel" of Henrich, Zizek, and Badiou is not without close affinities with Deleuze's absolute continuum of becoming (diagram), which replaces the subject-object schema. Deleuze's relations with "Hegel" and "Lacan" are too complex to summarize, but the difference seems to bear less on the process of unfolding the idea into any "figure" at any "moment" (cf. *Qu'est-ce que la philosophie*, p. 16) than on the construction of time-lines, which in Deleuze are in virtual coexistence within "incompossible worlds," all insisting always virtually now in this world, "remembering themselves" in the manner of Sheldrake's "morphic fields of resonance" and emerging in the manner of Prigogine's "dissipative structures." I think that this radical neo-Leibnizian simultaneity and panmathematical theory of negentropy would make little sense to Hegel, though the latter had already grasped the essential as concerns a theory of the subject-object indiscernible. See, e.g., the introduction to the *Phänomenologie des Geistes*. Deleuze's objections to the "negative transcendence" of desire determined as lack by castration are well known; nevertheless it was Lacan who initiated the critique of "Oedipus" and affirmed the "disappearing apparition" of a desire that is the only real.

19. The "informal diagram" consists in "force relations" drawn into a "map of density, intensity," "virtual, potential" relations between "fluent matter" and "diffuse function"; the concrete machines are "assemblages, devices or mechanisms [*agencements, dispositifs*]" effectuating the force relations of power through institutions (*Foucault*, p. 44ff). More generally, the abstract machine-diagram is the virtual side of the archival strata laid down in history or "the geology of morals"; the *agencements* actualize the "decisions" of the virtual machine, its "judgments," but all begin to mix and shuffle and communicate on the BwO, the synthesizer or abstract machine.

20. See Christian Jambet, *La logique des Orientaux* (Paris: Seuil, 1985), pp. 52–73.

21. The preceding paragraph refers to *Différence et répétition*, chapter 2 et passim, and to *A Thousand Plateaus*, plateau 11.

22. Kant defines the will as "a kind of cause" balancing between freedom and necessity, thus located not in time, but at the turning point or horizon of thought, of time and event (world-origin). Cf. the third Antinomy and the second Critique. Deleuze defines the Idea as "dialectical" (in *Différence et répétition*), but without the illusions of negation, opposition, resemblance, identity, or analogy in relation to "this" actual world. The Idea has nothing to do with logical possibility, everything to do with virtual reality. It is the Ideal Game, nomadic "self," singular encounter with "the unconscious of pure thought" (*Logique du sens*, p. 76), outside thought (the future origin of the world).

23. When the cosmologist assembles the differential equations governing the singularity, when Marcel thinks of his grandmother, when I imagine being with C., our thought and our emotion emit signs that cross the intermediary spacetime potential to "couple" and resonate with that other time, that other being, that originary difference of intensity, which thus comes back to us by a "forced movement . . . [that] overboards the base series" in a "return of greater amplitude." Cf. *Différence et répétition*, p. 154f. and Gilles Deleuze, *Proust et les signes* (Paris: Presses Universitaires de France, 1964–1976).

24. Pierre Klossowski, *Nietzsche et le cercle vicieux* (Paris: Mercure, 1969), pp. 93–95 (for this quote and the following).

25. Gilles Deleuze, *Nietzsche and Philosophy* (New York: Columbia University Press, 1983), p. 24, translation modified. To throw the dice is to affirm the chance combination, but the combination is already "the affirmation of necessity," "the number of destiny which brings the dice back. It is in this sense that the second moment of the game is also the two moments together or the player who equals the whole" (pp. 26–27). In playing dice with the past that sent us here we are replaying the present, throwing singularities back into a future that will have brought us to this quasi-aleatory, "Markov" point of linking back. "The singular points are on the die; the [ontological] questions are the dice themselves; the imperative is the act of throwing. Ideas are the problematic combinations that result"; while "questions express the relation of the problems with the imperatives they come from" (*Différence et répétition*, p. 255).

26. See Immanuel Kant, *The Critique of Pure Reason*, trans. Norman Kemp Smith (New York: St. Martin's Press, 1929), p. 185 on the schema of modality as the *Inbegriff*, "paragon" of time.

27. "Chaos chaoticizes, and undoes all consistency in the infinite. The problem of philosophy is to acquire a consistency without losing the infinite in which thought plunges" (*Qu'est-ce que la philosophie*, p. 45).

28. Deleuze cites the philosopher-mathematician Albert Lautmann:

> The geometric interpretation of the theory of differential equations shows us two absolutely distinct realities: there is a field of directions and the topological accidents that can arise in it, as for example the existence in the plane of *singular points to which no direction is attached*, and there are the integral curves with the form they take in the neighborhood of the singularities of the directional field (*Logique du sens*, p. 127 n.)

—i.e., the pullulating virtual self-differentiating point-folds, and the actual geometric figures they form in their elastic vicinity. But the self-shaping freedom-ego is itself the geometro-dynamic tensor ("aleatory-nomadic point of singular points") to be analyzed and synthesized. The only subject is the multiplicity: "The problem of the unconscious [has to do with] peopling, population" (*A Thousand Plateaus*, p. 30): multiple-cities swarming with "social Ideas" (*Différence et répétition*, pp. 240ff.) of crowds and gangs, the mob (*mobile vulgus*), riots and assemblies, packs or bundles of intensities, emotional turning points, the variable moods of neighborhoods (cf. *A Thousand Plateaus*, passim, and *Logique du sens*, p. 67).

29. A composite-word concept invented in *Différence et répétition* meaning the breakdown, "collapse" (*effondrement*), and "ex-foundation" of categorial schemes; the prelude or preface to their *brassage* (shuffling, brewing, mixing) and recomposition, mutation, or abandonment. For a condensed summary of Deleuze's "radical critique of the attributive [categorical] scheme" (*Leibniz et le Baroque*, p. 103), Kantian or Platonic, his invention of nomadic

"complexes of space and time," "phantastic notions" forming "conditions of real experience" for an immanent ethic-esthetics of "univocity"—in which perception becomes experimental and reality multiplies in technature ("each point of view is another city, the cities being joined only by their distance and resonating only across the divergence of their series, of their houses and streets" [*Logique du sens*, p. 203], of incompossible plans and schemes vying for effectuation in actuality)—see *Différence et répétition*, p. 364f.; *Logique du sens*, pp. 300ff.; *Leibniz et le Baroque*, pp. 103–112.

6

Deleuze: Serialization and Subject-Formation

Constantin V. Boundas

MANY CONNOISSEURS of the debates surrounding the lives and the deaths of the poststructuralist subject complain that the underdetermined content of the notion "subjectivity" often leaves the debate without a point. The jury is still out, trying to nail down the precise moment of the subject's ingress in the poststructuralist body, and voices are raised for the reprieve of the praxiological subject or for the memorial repetition of the postmessianic subject, which is "never yet p."[1] But was it ever clear that the poststructuralists had so unceremoniously ousted the subject from their discourse?

It will be foolish, of course, to deny that the death of a certain subject has really been wished for and that it has, perhaps, really taken place. Its death has been wished for in the wake of a certain deadly violence perpetrated against the Other,[2] and, because of this, the resurrection of another self and of an (otherwise) Other must understandably wait for the fulfillment of the critique of the Cartesian, Kantian, and Husserlian subject and for the unmasking of the fraudulent accreditation that the subject had received in classical and modern texts. All this is well known. But what the blurred, composite picture of the poststructuralists renders invisible is the fact that not everyone who wished the death of "the" subject and the advent of a new entity in its place did share the same motivation for the wish or the same vision for the new dawn.

Deleuze undoubtedly is among those who contributed decisively to the critical unmasking of old pretensions and to the hopeful invigilation for the arrival of the new. An important "theory of subjectivity" traverses his entire work, beginning with the essay on Hume and reaching impressive depth and precision with his essay on Leibniz. What is remarkable about this contribution is that it combines a radical critique of interiority with a stub-

99

born search for "an inside that lies deeper than any internal world."[3] In this sense, the search for the fold—"the inside as the operation of the outside" (Deleuze 1988, p. 96)—that Deleuze gallantly attributes to Foucault, is as much his own lifelong project and search as it was (for a more limited time span) his friend's.

In recent discussions, the hypothesis has been put forward that the structure of the subject can be elucidated through a better understanding of the structure of the narrative.[4] The resources of phenomenology and hermeneutics have been brought to bear upon this hypothesis with some promising results. But these results are of course not free from the integrative and coherentist presuppositions of the kind of tradition that phenomenology and hermeneutics tacitly assume. Gadamer and Ricoeur, it is true, have called for a perpetual, hermeneutic constitution and reconstitution of the self to follow the dispossession of the (naive or narcissistic) ego. I fail to see, however, what else this passage from the first to the second naivety—to speak like Ricoeur—entails, besides subjectivity reclaiming identity from the smoldering fires of difference. Neither the first nor the second naivety dispenses with the phenomenologist's belief that the life of the subject is given narrative structure by the subject itself "as it constructs a self who is then seen as the initiator of its actions and projects."[5] How would such a narrative structure help decide among competing narratives in those cases in which we strongly suspect that the narratee is the victim of self-deception, trapped in distorted communication, or systematically blinded by ideological prejudices? Traps and blindnesses of this kind affect the very *ideal* of the unity of the self that phenomenology and hermeneutics postulate as a zetetic principle. No such postulate can handle the fragmentation that affects the coherence of a personality or the multiple narratives that can be generated from the life of one individual. Why should a narrative strive after the coherence of the lived "inner-time" consciousness? Why not think of narratives that can accommodate, without compromise, fragmentation and multiplicity? The usual response to these questions is that the fragmentation of the subject brings about loss of meaning and the collapse of personality. But even if this were the case for the life of the self-constituting self, why would the frittering of (existential) meaning prevent the narrative biographer from making sense of her data? The standard edition of Freud's works is full of case studies (often in narrative form) of patients with shattered selves. It is very difficult indeed to privilege the sort of narrative that phenomenology and hermeneutics present as *the* narrative.

But if we turn to Deleuze, for whom narrativization is serialization, chances are that the yield may be instructive and helpful. For Deleuze, the process of narrativization is a veritable serialization, because it depends upon an originary disjunction governing the distribution of singular points along two, at least, diverging series. Since, in most narrative cases, the number of interacting series is greater than two, various conjunctive syntheses at work tend to establish bundles of series, which then begin to gravitate toward one or the other of the originary disjuncts.[6] Serialization, as Deleuze understands it, is zeugmatic, both in its form of expression and in its form of content. It is zeugmatic, first of all, with respect to the formation of a single series that, on the basis of connective syntheses, prolongs or extends a single line, placing singularities, contiguously, next to each other. It is zeugmatic also in the way in which, through conjunctive syntheses, bundles of series are grouped together. And finally, it is zeugmatic with respect to the *sui generis* operations of an originary, inclusive, disjunctive synthesis that places series in communication and in resonance with one another, the very moment that it separates one from the other.

Deleuze has always insisted that this last, disjunctive synthesis would not function without the very special intervention of an agent that he named "object = x"—a name calculated to displace Kant by endowing his text with the cipher of difference that it lacks. Being the simulacral effect of the originary disjunctive synthesis (founding and yet inaccessible), the object = x leaps from one series to another, "always absent from its place" and never totally landing or transferring itself to any one series; for, if it did, the result would be premature closure and an abrupt end of the narration.[7]

Now, my wager in this essay is that a powerful theory of subjectivity can be found in Deleuze's texts and that the zeugmatic arrangement of relevant segments of these texts—in other words, a serialization—may serve us well in the articulation of this theory. I am indeed convinced that the only way to assess correctly Deleuze's contributions to a theory of subjectivity is to read him the way he reads others: we must read him according to the series he creates, observe the ways in which these series converge and become compossible, and track down the ways in which they diverge and begin to resonate. A relentless vigilance is necessary in every step of such a reading. It will be a mistake, for example, to take each book of Deleuze for one series, and to try to establish compossibility or resonance among books. I do not doubt that the names of those that Deleuze reads and writes about stand for singular points (intensities), capable of generating series. In this sense, one could, with justification, speak of a Hume series, a Bergson series, a Leibniz series, etc. But none of these series is coextensive with the text or texts that bear the name of the thinker after whom a series has been named. Books and series do not coincide. This is why it would be better to talk about the "Hume-effect" series, the "Leibniz-effect" series, etc.

At any rate, provided that one takes adequate precautions, there is no harm in trying to spread Deleuze's contributions to a theory of subjectivity along several series, which could each be identified by means of the question/

problem that it helps to introduce. The Hume series: how does the mind become a subject?; the Bergson series: how can a static ontological genesis of the subject be worked out beginning with prepersonal and preindividual singularities and events?; the Leibniz series: how can there be a notion of individuality which is neither a mere deduction from the concept "subject"—in which case it would be contradictory—nor a mere figure of an individuality deprived of concept—in which case it would be absurd and ineffable?; the Nietzsche-Foucault series: how can a dynamic genesis of subjectivity be constructed, where the subject would be the fold and the internalization of outside forces, without succumbing to a philosophy of interiority?; the Nietzsche-Klossowski series: how is it possible to think the subject in terms of inclusive disjunctions and simultaneously affirmed incompossible worlds? These series would have run along their own lines of flight, without ever permitting the construction of any planes of consistency between them, were it not for Deleuze's concepts "chaosmos" (= chaos + cosmos) and "cracked I" (*Je fêlé*), which, in their capacity as portmanteau words, circulate among the series and make possible the inclusive, disjunctive affirmation of all of them at once (Deleuze 1990, p. 176).[8] It is chaosmos, that is to say, the becoming-world, that posits the constitution of the subject as a task, and chaosmos again that guarantees that the constituted subject will not emerge as a substantive *hupokeimenon* but rather as an always already "cracked I."

Before I go any further, though, I wish to make a few preliminary remarks. First of all, the effort to articulate a theory of subjectivity is not made easier by the multitude of terms with a family resemblance that are available to us and between which we move, as we talk, without respecting the important differences that separate one from the other. I am thinking about terms like "subject," "self," "I," "person," "particular," "individual," which do not all have the same meaning. In order, therefore, to keep things as crisp as possible I wish to indicate here that I follow the practice adopted by Manfred Frank.[9] I speak of "subject" or "the subject" whenever I refer to a particular subject, and when I do so, I understand that a person is a particular entity that can be deduced from the universal structure "Subject." I retain the term "individual" for a singular entity that cannot be deduced from the universal structure Subject. Occasionally, and in accordance with Deleuzian practice, I make use of the term "singular" or "singularity" in order to refer to preindividual and prepersonal elements that are indispensable for the constitution of individuals and persons. In other words, I side with Frank and Schleiermacher in thinking of personality as the mode of being of a particular entity, and of individuality as the mode of being of a singular entity. In the context of the ongoing debates surrounding subjectivity, this means that I side with Frank and Schleiermacher against Leibniz, because Leibniz's individuals are really particulars, to the extent that they are derived from the whole by means of a process of limitation. But, for Schleiermacher, the individual cannot be deduced from a concept, because it is the individual that provides the whole with its own concept. As Frank puts it, "it is the intervention of the individual that prevents the structure from ever coinciding with itself, and from ever being self-present" (Frank 1988, p. 93).

Despite the differences between the hypotactic, hermeneutic discourse of Schleiermacher and the paratactic serializations of Deleuze, the centrality of the notion of individuality without a concept is equally well marked in both. Neither Schleiermacher nor Deleuze think of the individual as the ineffable. As Bruce Baugh has pointed out in his reading of Deleuze, "the individual is not a bare particular, a 'this' like any other 'this,' but a singularity that has a determinate content in virtue of its actual genesis, that is, in virtue of the history of its coming to be."[10] If, in Baugh's words again, individuality is a function of individuating causal processes and the affair of intersecting series that bring it about, the actuality of the individual cannot fail to be the basis of the multiplicity that is the a priori condition of concepts, and the singularity of this actuality is a function of its historical genesis.

Now, these remarks presuppose an extended argument that I have not yet offered—the kind of argument that Deleuze entrusts, in segments, to his series. And it is to these series that I now turn my attention.

The Bergson Series

I name the series after Deleuze's long-standing commitment to Bergson, and to Bergson's skepticism about the alleged "apodeictic evidences" of consciousness that continue to feed phenomenological investigations. This series mobilizes segments of Deleuzian texts as different as *Bergsonism, Différence et répétition, The Logic of Sense,* and *Cinema 1* and *2*;[11] intersects with concerns about subjectivity of different textures generated by the reading of Leibniz, Nietzsche, Foucault, and Klossowski; and creates a frame for the discussion of individuality in the twin volumes of *Capitalism and Schizophrenia.* The Bergson series tends to be severe and uncompromising toward rival theories of subjectivity. But Deleuze is not severe or uncompromising only because of an allegiance to the (now) fashionable narratives decrying the plight of Others as the oppressed, suffering innocents and the unwilling victims of a neurotic, identitarian self. Not that Deleuze holds these narratives to be false, but, for him, these narratives often confuse empirical assessments and political vigilance with transcendental determinations and with the kind of vigilance that only an originary *epoché* can provide. *The Logic of Sense,* for example, warns against this confusion, in the clearest of terms:

"The error of all efforts to determine the transcendental as consciousness is that they think of the transcendental in the image of, and in the resemblance to, that which it is supposed to ground . . . [But] the transcendental field is no more individual than personal, and no more general than universal" (p.99).

An early text of Deleuze on Hume, which clearly belongs to the Bergson series, had already argued that the subject is not given, and that the mind, before it becomes subject, is, in fact, a set of singularities.[12] That early text had already made the subject a task to be fulfilled (Deleuze 1990, p. 105). In its later segments, the Bergson series assumed the responsibility for the fulfillment of this task and strove to articulate a veritable "static ontological genesis" of the subject. It was *Différence et répétition* that set up the parameters within which this static genesis had to be worked out. In this work, Deleuze shows how unwise it is to entrust the philosophy of difference to the impure data of the conscious, perceptual field. Such a field, he argues, may provide us with the concept in search of an idea but can never mobilize the idea in search of a concept. In the name, therefore, of his "new image of thought," Deleuze prepares for the reduction of the conscious, perceptual field and argues that this reduction is the only gesture capable of setting up the investigation of a world that he now calls "non-human" or "pre-human." It is this world that will function in his texts as the real transcendental ground of visibilities, statements, and fields of interiority.

From this early text down to the latest, motivating the entire Bergson series and governing the selection and the articulation of its segments, is the desire to displace consciousness and its function of casting light upon things, in order to restore to things their pure phosphorescence. Beyond the evidence of consciousness, the Bergson series will discover singularities and events, that is, the intensive magnitudes, out of which the human world, with individuals and subjects populating it, must be constituted. Unlike metaphysics and transcendental philosophy, which tend to think of singularities as being already encompassed by the form of a self or of a person, Deleuze looks for the singular that is neither individual nor personal. Only such impersonal and preindividual, "nomadic" singularities can be allowed to function as the building blocks of the transcendental field. This is the task of the genealogist: to begin with events and singularities and to account for the constitution of a world of things on this basis alone (Deleuze 1968, pp. 173ff). Events and singularities have, therefore, priority over things, and the error of the traditional duplication of the empirical in the transcendental is that it leaves us with things that are recognizable, instead of allowing us to savor the radical contingency of differences in their multiple repetitions.

All this, of course, reads like a research project with several unknowns in it. One must find out first of all what a singularity is. What is the being of the singular? What are the atoms and the building blocks of the transcendental field? Deleuze's ingenious answer—*the singular is the event*—redirects these questions: What is an event? What is the being of an event?

Crucial on the way to answering these questions is the sharp distinction that Deleuze makes between events and states of affairs in his repetition of the Stoic deconstructive reading of Plato's ontology (Deleuze 1990, pp. 109–17). For the Stoic Deleuze, states of affairs are accidents (in the Aristotelian sense) that affect bodies or are caused by bodies. A line of ontological difference runs between, on one hand, bodies and their relations (qualities, states of affairs, their mixtures) and, on the other hand, "incorporeal events." Bodies and their mixtures are actual, they exist in the present, and they causally affect other bodies and other mixtures. But they also cause "incorporeal" events, which are virtual—albeit real. These events exhibit toward bodies and their mixture a *quasi-causal efficacy*, they elude the present, although they are responsible for making it pass, and they simultaneously affirm the future and the past. They do not preexist bodies or states of affairs—they insist or subsist. As a result, the only two modes of insistence of the incorporeal event that is virtual are the being-past or the being-future.

The event, in other words, as Deleuze understands it, is never what is happening in the present, but eternally that which has just happened and that which is about to happen. The best verbal mode, therefore, capable of referring to events is, in Deleuze's opinion, the infinitive. To green, to cut, to grow, to die, are the best designations possible for pure incorporeal events. Infinitives guarantee *specificity* and determinacy without imposing subjective or objective coordinates. They also guarantee *reversibility* between past and future, since by themselves they are atemporal matrices. Finally, they stand for a selection of forces, intensities, or acts—rather than for a display of substances and qualities.

The advantages of this Stoic/Deleuzian move are significant. Becoming (whether as becoming-world or as becoming-subject) in the name of which this entire philosophy is mobilized, cannot be constituted through a juxtaposition of "immobile segments." Participation in immobile segments has always been responsible for the hieratic and static world of Being. On the other hand, forces seized *in actu*, liberated from substances that function as their support and vehicle, do seem better candidates for a diagrammatic mapping out of becoming: infinitives name forces that are neither active nor passive but both at once, since the quasi-causal function of the infinitive is always already reversible. It is important to notice that, by means of this Stoic conceptualization of the event, Deleuze is capable of assigning Being to bodies and their mixtures, and inherence, or "extra-Being," to pure events. The ontological difference between "to be" and "to insist" now controls the temptation to raise Being and presence to the plateau of the supreme ontological instance, as it subordinates Being to the unlimited and indefinite category of something in general (Deleuze 1990, pp. 148–53).[13]

The Leibniz Series

This series prolongs the previous one and resonates together with it. The problem that governs the selection and the articulation of the segments that make it up is this: How can there be a notion of individuality that is neither a mere deduction from (or specification of) the concept Subject (in which case the notion of individuality would be contradictory) *nor* a mere figure without a concept (in which case it would be absurd and ineffable)? This series involves, in a special way, texts like *Le Pli: Leibniz et le baroque* and *Foucault*. On the other hand, earlier writings like *Différence and répétition*, *Expressionism in Philosophy: Spinoza*,[14] and *The Logic of Sense* are not at all alien to the deployment of this series. By means of it, Deleuze brilliantly explores the resources of baroque mannerism—and equally so, Stoic and Whiteheadian strategies—in order to define the individual as a unique point of view upon the world. In fact, for Deleuze, individual and world are correlative notions. "The world is in the monad, and the monad is in the world" is Leibniz's statement, but it finds its Deleuzian resonance in *Le Pli* (Deleuze 1988, p. 68). The individual explicates and unfolds the world, which is implicated, included, and folded in it. The entire world series is "in" the individual, although only a segment of it gets to be expressed by the individual with any degree of clarity: this is the segment that coincides with the point of view on the world occupied by the individual.

This Deleuzian move gives the *in-der-Welt-sein* an interesting twist, in positing that an individual is always already inside a world understood as a circle of convergence; individuals and worlds are inseparable, because worlds may be formed and thought only in the vicinity of the individuals who occupy and fill them. One then begins to see how the Leibniz series will work out the details of the static genesis of subjectivity, which was envisaged for the first time seriously in the Bergson series: the point, we remember, was to show how individuals and worlds can be constituted against the background of the transcendental field, instead of being found (read: placed) ready-made in it. The Leibniz series will show that a singularity is extended analytically over a series of ordinary points until it reaches the territory or the vicinity of another singularity. A world is constituted, on the condition that several series converge. In other words, a world envelops a set of singularities selected through convergence, and the mechanism for its formation is conjunctive synthesis. Inside worlds, individuals are being constituted, as they select and envelop a finite number of the singularities available to them. It follows that the law of their synthesis is connection, that is, connection of singular points.

Starting, therefore, with singularities, Deleuze goes on to describe their actualization in a world and in the individuals who are parts of this world. To be actualized means to extend over a series of ordinary points: in other words, to be selected according to a rule of convergence, to be incarnated in a body; to become the state of this body, and to be renewed locally for the sake of limited new actualizations and extensions. Individuated worlds are formed only when series that depend on one singularity converge upon a series that depends on other singularities. Deleuze's fondness for Leibniz is located at this precise point: the "compossibility" of series is the indispensable condition for the "worlding" of worlds.

Now, even if this is an acceptable account of the constitution of the individual, Deleuze is aware that the self or the person is no less the product of a constitution and that, therefore, a static ontological genesis of it is also indispensable. With respect to persons or selves, the Leibniz series provides the following account: The individual is formed within a world that was understood as a *continuum* or as a circle of convergences. The person, as a knowing and acting subject, emerges when something is identified inside worlds that are incompossible, and across series that are divergent. In this case, the person as subject would exist vis-à-vis the world (*Welt*), whereas the living individual existed in her surrounding world (*Um-Welt*) and this world insisted in her. In the last analysis, Deleuze is prepared to admit that there is something = x common to all worlds. Consequently, the universal subject would be the becoming person that corresponds to something = x, common to all worlds, just as particular subjects would be the persons corresponding to a particular something = x, common to several, but not to all, worlds (Deleuze 1990, pp. 109–17).

Now, all this would be unintelligible if the world of the Leibniz series were an extended magnitude made up of *partes extra partes*, and the individual, a substance. But of course this is not the case. The world, according to Leibniz-Deleuze, is included in every individual as a predicate, and not as an attribute. We must recall here the role that *The Logic of Sense* assigned to attributes and predicates. Attributes express qualities and essences, whereas predicates stand for incorporeal events and form, by means of these, series of individuals and worlds (pp. 276–77). The air of paradox that surrounds Deleuze's account of the static ontological genesis of subjectivity finds here its legitimation. In a remarkably striking and challenging move, world and subject are turned into (intensive) events. "The world itself [writes Deleuze] is an event; being therefore an incorporeal [virtual] predicate, the world must be included in each subject as its ground. Each one draws from this ground the 'mannerisms' corresponding to his or her point of view [aspects]. The world is predication, the mannerisms, particular predicates, and the subject, that which goes from one predicate to the next, as from one aspect of the world to the next" (Deleuze 1988, p. 71).

The world of the Leibniz series is as fictional as the world of the earlier Hume series, and the subject, as delirious here as it was there. But the world is here fictional and the subject delirious in a special and new sense. When Deleuze says that the world exists only in the individuals expressing it, he adds immediately that it exists in them virtually. That which is virtual, though, for Deleuze-Leibniz and Bergson, is not the unreal or the merely possible. The virtual is the real that has not yet been actualized. To say, therefore, that the world is fictional is not to say that the world is not real. It is to say that the world does not have the extensional universality of a concept. The world, for Deleuze-Leibniz, is a metaphysical entity, a unique converging series, and a *veritable individual*. The world is a fiction, but its real constitutive powers are not at risk. It is the fiction of a concept, and yet a real individual in the process of constituting other real individuals.

It is around this point that the Leibniz series and the Bergson series encounter each other and strengthen Deleuze's resolve to reduce subject-formations to molecular singularities. But the transcendental reduction involved here is no more reductive than the famous phenomenological reductions used to be: the molecular singularity uncovered as the non-further-divisible unit of the transcendental field is not by itself sufficient to constitute anything at all. An entire theory of serialization, with the connective, conjunctive, and disjunctive operations at its disposal, must be deployed in order to account for molar, personal, and subjective arrangements. To say, therefore, as Deleuze does, that events/predicates are preindividual singularities and that the world is ontologically prior to the individuals expressing it, or to say, as he does, that the individual is the actualization of preindividual singularities, is half the story. The other half of the story is told in the series to which I now turn my attention and which I call the Nietzsche-Klossowski series.

The Nietzsche-Klossowski Series

This series is governed by the question "How can one think in terms of inclusive disjunctions or how can one simultaneously affirm incompossible worlds?" In the texts of Klossowski that give the series one half of its name, Deleuze admires "the dissolution of the Self [which] ceases to be a patho-

logical determination . . . [and] become[s] the mightiest power, rich in positive and salutary promises" (Deleuze 1990, p. 283). In Nietzsche's perspec-
tivism, which gives the series the other half of its name, Deleuze discovers a
"divergence which is no longer a principle of exclusion, and a disjunction, no
longer a means of separation. Incompossibility becomes now a means of
communication" (p. 174). Next to Nietzsche and Klossowski, Leibniz may
indeed have been the grand theorist of the event, but he never failed to be
also the grand advocate of god: the principle of sufficient reason, placed by
him in the service of the theological, reassuring discourse of the "best
possible World" subjected divergence and disjunction to a negative use. His
individual/points of view come to be and to form series only insofar as they
all converge upon the same town. But with Nietzsche and Klossowski,
diverging series become objects of simultaneous affirmation, insofar as their
divergence is affirmative and affirmed. "[A]nother town," says Deleuze,
"corresponds [now] to each point of view, each point of view is another
town, the towns are linked only by their distance and resonate only through
the divergence of their series, their houses and their streets" (p. 174).

The problem that this series raises concerns the conditions that must be
fulfilled in order for the disjunction to function as a synthetic operation,
making possible the connection of singularities and the conjunction of series.
It is *Différence et répétition*, *The Logic of Sense*, and *Capitalism and Schizophrenia*[15] that take up the problem of the conditions and, as we know, come
up with intriguing answers.

Accelerations and decelerations, leaps across molar thresholds, transversal
movements, aparallel evolutions, affirmations and negations, resonances and
rhythms—or, more simply, the sort of event that Badiou designates as "*what
singularizes continuity in each of its local folds*" (Badiou 1989, p. 168)—constitute the propelling forces of the becoming-compossible of series that diverge.
Deleuze's elaborate theory of repetition belongs here, where "each thing . . .
is unique, intrinsically different from every other thing," and where "similarity arises against the background of this '*disparité du fond*'"[16]

The Tournier Series

But often the itinerary of the Nietzsche-Klossowski series is felt to be more
ragged than it actually is when one follows it without adequate preparations.
Analogically (but only analogically) speaking, thinking the compossibility of
diverging series without any preparation is like attempting elaborate
phenomenological descriptions without the *ascesis* of the epoché. Hence, the
importance assumed by the Tournier series, which prolongs and deepens the

problematic of the Nietzsche-Klossowski series. I name it after Michel Tournier, whose book *Friday* Deleuze has made the object of a beautiful meditation.[17] In Deleuze's appropriation of the novel, *Friday* is an elegant description made by a "radical phenomenologist" of what an insular world would come to be like, were other people to disappear. With Tournier, Deleuze seeks the effects of the presence of other people in our everyday world, in order to conclude what Otherness is, and also what it would be like to live without other people.

Tournier's Robinson, on his desert island Speranza, initially alone, later on with Friday, is progressively "dehumanized," while his world is returned to its constitutional elements. Unlike the earlier Robinson of Daniel Dafoe, Tournier's Robinson is not bound to the recollection of origins from which only an accident separates him, but rather he is in the grips of a "futurist repetition," which drives him along with the inexorable necessity of a death drive. Instead of producing or reproducing, he deviates and becomes a pervert. This deviation/perversion/dehumanization of Robinson and the return of the island to its elements establish themselves irreversibly, as the gradual erasure, from Robinson's consciousness, of the structure of alterity moves inexorably toward its final stages. His prolonged isolation on the desert island sets in motion a slow process leading to the elimination of all traces of other people.

Why did Deleuze undertake this meditation? His choice of Tournier's fiction is dictated by his desire to test the hypothesis according to which the structure Other is equiprimordial with the structure subject, *only in the case* that it is from the very beginning endowed with individuality and personality. But then, instead of accepting complacently the ready-made, Deleuze asks that the constitution of the Other, no less than the constitutions of the individual and the person, be accounted for. In an important sense, therefore, the erasure of alterity explored by the Robinson hypothesis corresponds to the radicalization of the phenomenological intuition. If the reduction of the structure Other is, as Deleuze argues, *eo ipso* reduction of subjectivity, and if such a reduction does not cause the world to fritter away into nothingness, there must be ways to think this new domain, beyond the Other and beyond the self.

Let us pursue this line of thought for a little while longer. From the phenomenological point of view, that is, from the point of view that Deleuze provisionally adopts here, Other and self are strictly contemporaneous. But contemporaneity should not be taken to mean equiprimordiality. The phenomenological evidence that establishes contemporaneity between self and Other is (according to Deleuze) derivative; self and Other are not primordial, but rather constituted structures (Deleuze 1990, p. 301).

But what exactly is in the Other that we bracket? In the absence of others, Deleuze observes, objects entering Robinson's field of perception hit him without pity like projectiles. A brutal opposition between light and darkness, with no transitions to protect the eye, marks the spot that the retreating others leave unoccupied. The soft margins and the cushions that these others provided are now out of play. Speranza, the island, having turned into a world of absolute distances and unbearable repetitions, displays a meanness that no longer can be assigned to the inhumanity of other people. Foreclosure of the Other discloses a world of necessity, where the virtual and the possible can no more find a firm foothold. The elements that, in the presence of others, sedimented and stratified, made up Speranza, are now liberated and volatilized, and Robinson begins to lose his personological and subjective coordinates, as if haunted by a powerful—and yet un-Freudian—death drive. And without the others, Robinson's desire is for the first time really restored to him; separated from its object, desire is spared its former obligatory detour through sexuality and finds its telos, perfection, and completeness within itself: it becomes a veritable nonhuman desire. Speranza's becoming-Other parallels the becoming-Other of Robinson, and a new structure—Deleuze calls it the structure of perversity—emerges for the first time. This new structure corresponds to the world without others—the world with the Other foreclosed (pp. 303–304).

It is the absence of the Other that helps release the double of a world until then captive and enveloped inside the Other. The double is not emerging as a replica, but rather marks the rising to the surface of liberated elements. Robinson finally understands that the "Other is the grand leveler, and consequently that the destructuration of the Other is not a disorganization of the world, but an upright organization, as opposed to the old recumbent organization" (pp. 312–313). Yesterday's dreaded simulacra emerge into the light of the surface as friendly phantasms. "Initially, [Robinson] experienced the loss of others as a fundamental disorder of the world . . . But he discovers (slowly) that it is the Other who disturbs the world" (p. 31). What is then this Other that has the ability to disturb the World?

The Other, concludes Deleuze, is not inside the field of perception, one structure only among others (it is not the paradoxical instance of a subject that can be my object). *The Other* is the structure that conditions the entire field of perception, along with its functioning, and renders possible *ab initio* the constitution and application of the categories of subject and object. "It is not the ego [writes Deleuze] but the Other as structure which renders perception possible" (Deleuze 1991, p. 309). Inhabiting the transitions from one object to another, relativizing distances and differences, and assembling a background from which forms surge forth and fall back in harmony, the Other renders perception possible, because it spatializes (forms, unforms, or coordinates spaces) and temporalizes. Without this, perception would not be possible.

Notice that "perception" has retained in the texts of Deleuze its lived, phenomenological resonance, and that the Other has been implicated as the condition *sine qua non* for the kind of perception that opens itself up to the phenomenological gaze. But as the story unvelops, instead of being firmly and irreducibly rooted in the natural evidences of the phenomenological intuition, the Other must go, and along with it, the privileges given to phenomenology and to the kind of perception that sustains it. Of course, for all this to happen, the Other must, first, be depersonalized and desubjectified. If the function of the Other, as Deleuze argues, is coextensive with the smooth operation of the entire perceptual field, it is because the Other is the expression *of a possible world*. Its absence, therefore, would bring about the collapse of the possible and the triumph of the necessary. And given Deleuze's decision to make self and Other contemporaneous, the foreclosure of the Other brings along with it inevitably the foreclosure of the self.

We are now ready to take stock of the segments of the Tournier series. In fact, this series is made up of two subseries. One of them has the Other, as the structure of a possible world, or more simply, as the structure of the possible, sustaining the reality of the self. In a sense, self and Other are here deployed along the axis of the possible, the contingent, or the axis of the play of mirrors. The second subseries, the one of the liberated elements, singularities, events, intensities, and inclusive disjunctions, is called "virtual." It is the series of the simulacrum in the process of becoming-phantasm. It is the *imaginary* and *phantasmatic* series.[18]

We recall that the Bergson series sharply distinguished between the possible and the virtual: the possible is not real, it is the realizable; whereas the virtual (being already real) is the actualizable. In the Tournier series, the reduction of the possible allows, for the first time, the emergence of the virtual. Since the subseries of the possible is made of segments of personality and subjectivity, it is the reduction of subjectivity that allows the manifestation of the subseries of the phantasm. There are displacements at work here that we must not overlook. The reality of the self, in the first subseries, cannot be maintained without the possibility of the Other, which occupies the same series. The real slides toward the possible, and the possible feeds the real. But the self is *not* the realization of the possible Other. The Other lives as a permanent possibility in the interstices between selves, but it goes no further. As for the virtual of the second line, its reality is guaranteed, but not its completeness. The virtual, according to Deleuze, its reality notwithstanding, finds its completeness in its becoming-actual—

in its actualization. The real suffers from a limitation: it cannot be without the possible. The virtual suffers from an incompleteness: it seeks its completeness in its actualization.

But the actualizations of the virtual (the phantasm, the event, the singular) initiate the intensive constitutions of the individual. There would be no self and no Other without the virtual. There would be no possible or actual without the phantasmatic virtual. In other words, the second subseries sends us over, once again, to the first. Persons and subjects are the extensions of intensities, the dilations of contractions, and the domestications of differences. The subseries are then repeated without end, because of an instability internal to them and a lack of equilibrium. They repeat themselves, thanks to an agent of repetition that circulates between them, places them in communication, and makes them vibrate, without ever eliminating the disjunctive duality that characterizes them. This agent of repetition is the virtual energy of the phantasmatic series whose disjunctive potential always already exceeds the noematic content of the real, the possible, and the actual. According to Deleuze, it can be designated equally well by the expressions "chaosmos" and "cracked I," both chosen to remind us that becoming-world and becoming-subject are never-ending tasks of constructing and deconstructing identities.

The Nietzsche-Foucault Series

Finally, one last series—the Nietzsche-Foucault series—seems to be designed to make all the others move. The Leibniz series gives us the building blocks for the static ontological genesis of the subject. The Nietzsche-Klossowski series displays the extensive and intensive rules governing the synthesis of these blocks. The Nietzsche-Foucault series sketches, for the first time, the segments and the lines of a dynamic genesis of the subject. It mobilizes texts like *Foucault, Le Pli, Capitalism and Schizophrenia*, but also *Nietzsche and Philosophy*,[19] *Spinoza, Practical Philosophy*,[20] and, once more, *The Logic of Sense*. The subject is now introduced as the result of a process of folding and as an internalization of an outside that no folding can ever exhaust. The outcome, in Deleuze's words, is the constitution of "an inside that lies deeper than any internal world."

None of the series that we studied until this point has within itself the reason for the serialization (subject-formation): no clear reason has been given as to why—beginning with singularities and events—individuals, persons, and subjects come to be formed as they do. The Tournier supplement to the Nietzsche-Klossowski series provides a powerful description of the intensive reduction of the possible for the sake of the virtual, but not a clear motivation for undertaking it. It is the Nietzsche-Foucault series that attempts to make good these deficiencies, building around the rich notions of *fold* and *outside*, the dynamic genesis of the subject.

The space between preindividual singularities and the full-fledged subject is here filled with forces that, once bent and folded, complicate the outside inside a fold—a term that Deleuze borrows from Foucault and uses to designate the subject. Inaugurated by the Greeks, this series marks the captivation of outside forces and invents the subject "as a derivative or as the product of 'subjectivation'" (Deleuze 1988, p. 101). When the Greeks decided that the mastery of others must go through the mastery of oneself, the folding of outside forces by means of a series of practical exercises was already on its way.

We should note that Deleuze does not entrust the bending and folding responsible for the dynamic genesis of the subject to any agent who would ride the waves of the conflicting forces, and perhaps intentionally give them sense and direction. Such an agent, according to his view, would be redundant in the context of intersecting forces, for which spontaneity and receptivity are essential characteristics. "Force," says Deleuze, "is what belongs to the outside, since it is essentially a relation between other forces: it is inseparable in itself from the power to affect other forces (spontaneity) and to be affected by others (receptivity)" (pp. 100–101). It is the individual who causes the outside to fold, thereby endowing itself with subjectivity, as it bends and folds the outside. The subject of the Nietzsche-Foucault series emerges dynamically as the "relation which a force has with itself," or as the "affect of self on self" (Deleuze 1991, p. 101).

We should also note that the outside, in this series, maintains its ontological priority. "It is never the other," writes Deleuze, "who is a double in the doubling process, it is a self that lives me as the double of the other . . . [T]he primacy can(not) be reversed: The inside will always be the doubling of the outside" (Deleuze 1991, pp. 98, 99). It follows that, in the Nietzsche-Foucault series, the fold that names the absolute interiority of the subject cannot be conceived on the model of an oppositional relation between a substantive subject bent upon itself and an external world. Nor is the inwardness of this subject the mere reflection of an outside: the fold is never a mere reflection. Rather, Deleuze's outside is the irrecuperable and inexhaustible source of negentropic energy and of capture-resisting subjectivity. As such, and here Monique Scheepers is right, it has, in the segments of the Nietzsche-Foucault series, a clear political significance.[21]

The outside is not another site, but rather an off-site that erodes and dissolves all other sites. Its logic, therefore, is like the logic of difference, provided that the latter is understood in its transcendental, and not in its empirical, dimension: instead of difference between x and y, we must now conceive the difference of x from itself. Like the structure of supplementarity whose logic it follows, the outside is never exhausted; every attempt to capture it generates an excess or a supplement, which in turn feeds anew the flows of deterritorialization and releases new lines of flight. As Pascal Levoyer and Philippe Encrenaz have recently argued, the outside is Deleuze-Leibniz's virtual that is always more than the actual; it is the virtual that haunts the actual and, as it haunts it, makes it flow and change.[22] A Heideggerian *es gibt* bestows upon forces the role of both the subject and the object of forming and unforming processes. This same *es gibt* permits Deleuze to endorse Foucault's claims about the primacy of resistances: "There will always be a relation to oneself which resists codes and powers; the relation to oneself is even one of the origins of these points of resistance" (Deleuze 1988, p. 103). To the extent that the subject, for Deleuze, is the result of the folding of the outside, that is, of bending forces and making them relate to one another, the subject is the individual who, through practice and discipline, has become the site of a bent force, that is, the folded inside of an outside.

Notes

1. Calvin O. Schrag, for instance, has argued for the reprieve of the praxiological subject, and John Fekete complained about the eclipse of the critical memory of a subject which is "never yet p." See C. O. Schrag, *Communicative Praxis and the Space of Subjectivity* (Bloomington: Indiana University Press, 1986), esp. part 2. See also Fekete, *The Structural Allegory: Reconstructive Encounters with the New French Thought* (Minneapolis: University of Minnesota Press, 1984), p. xviii.

2. For a gathering of dissonant voices on this violence and the possibilities of containing it, see *Who Comes after the Subject?*, Eduardo Cadava, Peter Connor and Jean-Luc Nancy, eds. (New York: Routledge, 1991).

3. Gilles Deleuze, *Foucault*, trans. Sean Hand (Minneapolis: University of Minnesota Press, 1988), p. 96.

4. See, for example, David Carr, *Time, Narrative and History* (Bloomington: Indiana University Press, 1986), passim. See also his "Narrative and the Real World," *Theory*, no. 15 (1986): pp. 118–31.

5. Richard Holmes and Mano Daniel, "Biography and Anti-Narrativism: Sartre's Flaubert," unpublished ms. of a lecture given to the Ontario Philosophical Society Meetings, Trent University, October 26, 1991.

6. On series and the formation of series, see Gilles Deleuze, *The Logic of Sense*, trans. Mark Lester with Charles Stivale, Constantin V. Boundas, ed. (New York: Columbia University Press, 1990), pp. 36–47. See also Michel Pierssens, "L'appareil seriel," *La Critique générative* (Paris: Seghers, 1973), pp. 265–85.

7. Deleuze's debt to Lacan at this point is obvious and always acknowledged. See *The Logic of Sense*, pp. 42–47.

8. For a discussion of portmanteau words see *The Logic of Sense*, pp. 42–47.

9. Manfred Frank, *Die Unhintergehbarkeit von Individualität* (Frankfurt a. M.: Suhrkamp, 1986). I consulted the French translation of this text, *L'ultime raison du sujet*, trans. Veronique Zanetti (Le Mejan: Acte Sud, 1988).

10. Bruce Baugh, "Deleuze and Transcendental Empiricism," *Man and World*, vol. 25, no. 2 (1992).

11. *Bergsonism*, trans. Hugh Tomlinson and Barbara Habberjam (New York: Zone Books, 1988); *Différence and répétition* (Paris: Presses Universitaires de France, 1968); *Cinema 1: The Movement-Image*, trans. Hugh Tomlinson and Barbara Habberjam (Minneapolis: University of Minnesota Press, 1986); *Cinema 2: The Time-Image*, trans. Hugh Tomlinson and Robert Galeta (London: Athlone, 1989).

12. See Gilles Deleuze, *Empiricism and Subjectivity: An Essay on Hume's Theory of Human Nature*, trans. with an introduction by Constantin V. Boundas (New York: Columbia University Press, 1991).

13. See also, Gilles Deleuze, *Le Pli: Leibniz et le baroque* (Paris: Éditions de Minuit, 1988), part 2, sec. 6. For a discussion of Deleuze's theory of the event see Alain Badiou, "Gilles Deleuze, Le Pli: Leibniz et le baroque," *Annuaire Philosophique 1988–89* (Paris: Seuil, 1989), pp. 161–84. In English, trans. Constantin V. Boundas, "Le Pli: Leibniz and the Baroque," chapter 4 in this volume, pp. 51–69.

14. Gilles Deleuze, *Expressionism in Philosophy: Spinoza*, trans. Martin Joughin (New York: Zone Books, 1990).

15. Gilles Deleuze and Félix Guattari, *Capitalism and Schizophrenia*, vol. 1, *Anti-Oedipus*, trans. Robert Hurley, Mark Seem, Helen R. Lane (New York: Viking Press, 1977); *Capitalism and Schizophrenia*, vol. 2, *A Thousand Plateaus*, trans. Brian Massumi (Minneapolis: University of Minnesota Press, 1987).

16. J. Hillis Miller, *Fiction and Repetition: Seven English Novels* (Cambridge: Harvard University Press, 1982), p. 6.

17. See "Michel Tournier and the World Without Others" in *The Logic of Sense*, pp. 301–321. Originally published as "Une théorie d'autri" (Michel Tournier), *Critique*, vol. 23 (1967): pp. 503–525.

18. For a discussion of the phantasm, see *The Logic of Sense*, pp. 210–16.

19. Gilles Deleuze, *Nietzsche and Philosophy*, trans. Hugh Tomlinson (New York: Columbia University Press, 1983).

20. Gilles Deleuze, *Spinoza, Practical Philosophy*, trans. Robert Hurley (San Francisco: City Lights, 1988).

21. Monique Scheepers, "Subjektivität und Politik," *Lendemains*, no. 53 (1989): pp. 30–34.

22. Pascal Levoyer and Philippe Encrenaz, "Politique de Deleuze," *Lendemains*, no. 53 (1989): pp. 35–47.

III. Desire and the Overturning of Platonism

7

Nietzsche's Dice Throw: Tragedy, Nihilism, and the Body without Organs

Dorothea Olkowski

> Ultimately, no one can extract from things, books included, more than
> he already knows.
>
> —Friedrich Nietzsche, *Ecce Homo*

THIS PAPER IS BOTH a tangent and a collision in relation to my current interest in Deleuze's work. It is a tangent insofar as I began by questioning that assemblage in Deleuze's work that might be called the "body," but the tangent led me here to this detour into Nietzsche. Awakened from a relatively uncritical position by Elizabeth Grosz's paper *A Thousand Tiny Sexes* (included in this volume, pp. 187–210), which discusses feminist concerns with Deleuze-Guattari's notion of the body, I finally asked in what sense the body-assemblage as construed by Deleuze-Guattari might be gendered male, or might carry the inscription of Deleuze-Guattari themselves. It seemed to me that if Deleuze and Deleuze-Guattari's body-assemblage were inscribed with either their own names or with the name of some other male philosopher (Nietzsche, for example), this would have vast reverberations for their rethinking of desire as well.

In investigating the body, it became clear to me that I had to go back to Deleuze's work on Nietzsche. This was the collision. I have long avoided Nietzsche. In fact, I have for years found Nietzsche unreadable. The parody of woman as Truth, the male hysterical notion of Will to Power, Nietzsche's invention of the Greeks and Greek philosophy, and Pierre Klossowski's acknowledgment that in spite of or even because of the fragmented text, Nietzsche's own voice and values are everywhere in his writing—all this left me uncomfortable with Nietzsche, even Deleuze's Nietzsche. To complicate matters, I found myself in disagreement on several key issues with Judith Butler's essay on Deleuze's notion of desire (which I had turned to in hope of some clarification).[1] While admiring Butler's historical placement of Nietzschean desire, I cannot, as she does, find any dialectic at work in Deleuze's reading of Nietzschean force; nor could I agree with her interpretation of force as some sort of naturalistic, organic eros. Yet, given my concern about the possibility of a gendered inscription on the body-assemblage and my interest in philosophical approaches to the body in general, I began this paper, a paper which I believe can only be prefaced with Nietzsche's claim from *Ecce Homo* that no one can extract from things more than she already knows.

In *Nietzsche and Philosophy*, Deleuze raises this important question about what the body is: "We do not define it by saying that it is a field of forces, a nutrient medium fought over by a plurality of forces. For, in fact, there is no medium, no field of forces or battle. There is no quantity of reality, all reality is a quantity of force."[2] The body is not a medium and does not designate substance: it expresses the relationship between forces. The term "body" does not simply refer, for Deleuze, to the psychophysiological bodies of human beings. Bodies may be chemical, biological, social, or political, and the distinction between these modes is not ontological. If anything, it becomes for Deleuze (with Guattari) semiological, a question of different regimes of signs. Ultimately then, the "body" is too general a term for Deleuze-Guattari. "Body" is too easily taken to be a thing, final, finished, and fully formed. But if the body is not a thing, but multiple, implicated in a multiplicity of elements in a variety of possible sign systems, then the sense of "body" can only be articulated in terms of each system of signs, semiotics informed by pragmatics. For Nietzsche, this takes place on the level of evaluations.

Active Force and Nietzsche's Creation and Critique

Nietzschean evaluations are not simply values; they are the ways of being, the modes of existence of those who evaluate. "So," writes Deleuze, "we have the beliefs, feelings and thoughts we deserve given our way of being or style of life" (Deleuze 1983, p. 1). Attention to the origins of values signifies precisely the differential element of their origin—which, for Nietzsche, is the distance and difference between high and low, noble and base. Nietzsche writes:

> [T]he judgement "good" did not originate with those to whom goodness was shown. Rather, it was "the good" themselves, that is to say, the noble, the powerful, high-stationed and high-minded who felt and established

themselves and their actions as good, that is, of the first rank, in *contradistinction* to all the low, low-minded, common and plebeian (emphasis added).[3]

As noble and powerful, the high-minded called themselves "good." In so doing they created "good" as a value. Looking around at the common and lowly, the high-minded and powerful called them "base," thereby signifying a critique of all that is common and plebeian. When evaluations are carried out in this manner, on the basis of a noble way of life, they carry the value "good." Deleuze does not concur with Nietzsche's valuations, rather he draws the conclusion that such evaluations are both critical and creative, both *ethical and aesthetic*; they constitute an active difference at the origin and so are active. It is, perhaps, the avoidance of Nietzsche's judgments and the insistence on both the ethical and the aesthetic dimensions of Nietzsche's thought that distinguish Deleuze's reading of the Nietzschean texts, and which serve as loci for much of Deleuze's rethinking of philosophy. There is, writes Deleuze, an "aesthetic form of joy" instituted as affirmation and creation, and not as the passive sensation of Kantian aesthetics. Of equal if not greater importance, there is an "ethic of joy" instituted through evaluating the origin and genesis of a value. Both of these active practices are involved in the Greek concept of the tragic, both contribute to the affirmation of life without justifying or redeeming it (Deleuze 1983, pp. 17, 18).

Difference at the origin, as constituted by Nietzschean affirmation and evaluation, may account for the fact that not all evaluations actually are the result of what Deleuze calls an active force; most evaluations, in fact, can be traced back to revenge and are the result of a base way of living— reaction. How is it possible that in the history of the West, what Deleuze calls *reactive* forces have dominated the process of evaluation? The answer requires a careful look at the singular history of a thing; for the history of a thing (including that of a body) is the succession of forces that take hold of it, as well as the *struggle* between those forces for possession of it (Deleuze 1983, p. 3). Nietzsche points to how we miss the history of a thing in the face of its uses.

> But purposes and utilities are only signs that a will to power has become master of something less powerful and imposed upon it the character of a function; and the entire history of a "thing," an organ, a custom can in this way be a continuous sign-chain of ever new interpretations and adaptations (Nietzsche 1969, II, 12; p. 77).

Given this, given the history, the succession of independent processes of subduing forces, resistances, reactions, and counteractions, "[t]he form [of a thing] is fluid, but the 'meaning' is even more so" (Nietzsche 1969, p. 78). Only a genuine critique (active ethics) makes it possible to investigate the forces that take hold of something. Such a critique was never carried out until Nietzsche did so. "In Kant, critique was not able to discover the truly active instance which would have been capable of carrying it through . . . it never makes us overcome the reactive forces which are expressed in man, self-consciousness, reason, morality, and religion" (Deleuze 1983, p. 89). Deleuze claims that rather than carrying out a critique of knowledge (reason), morality, and religion, Kant simply justifies them because he *believes* in the reigning system of values. Kant's critique of pure reason is carried out by reason, but from the outside, from a traditional transcendental point of view, the point of view of conditions that are prior and external to the conditioned. Kant never provides an account of the genesis of reason, understanding, and its categories. Kant never asks the questions: Who wants this kind of reason? What will wills such a reason? What is the history of this reason? What forces dominate it? Such questions are fundamental to Nietzsche's genetic and plastic principles, which "give an account of the sense and value of beliefs, interpretations and evaluations" (Deleuze 1983, p. 93); while in Kant's critique, reigning values are simply subjectivized, rather than evaluated, heading off, blocking the creation of new values.

With this assessment, Deleuze pursues themes that will be central to *Anti-Oedipus*. Like a theologian, declare Deleuze and Nietzsche, Kant installs the priest and the legislator *in us*, a move that in no way eliminates the positions of subject and object, noumenon and phenomenon, priest and believer, a move that, in fact, serves only to justify current knowledge, morality, and religion, "When we stop obeying God, the State, our parents, reason appears and persuades us to continue being docile because it says to us: it is you who are giving the orders" (Deleuze 1983, p. 92). This is why, according to Deleuze, thought must think against reason and oppose reason, and thinkers must oppose all reasonable beings (Deleuze 1983, p. 93). Becoming a genealogist, the philosopher no longer affirms and incorporates existing values; she creates new ones; she is the philosopher of the future, Nietzsche's "relatively superhuman type,"[4] whom Nietzsche also describes as "man, insofar as he wants to be gone beyond, overcome"—insofar as he is overcome in the creation of a different way of feeling, another sensibility—or, as Deleuze writes, "the overcome, overtaken man" (Deleuze 1983, p. 94). Thinking against reason and becoming a genealogist require new principles that enable "man" to be gone beyond. To carry out this project, Nietzsche relies on the notion of force.

"Force," as Deleuze defines it, "is the appropriation, domination and exploitation of a quantity of reality" (Deleuze 1983, p. 3). Forces are quantitative and qualitative; the difference in quantity between two forces is a "differential" element, a quantitative element of *difference between* two forces, and it generates the qualitative element of a force, that is, the force as active or as reactive, for "[i]n a purely quantitative world, everything would be dead, stiff, motionless."[5] Thus, forces are constituted differentially, just as, for example, in Saussure, the sense of words in language are constituted differentially. But there is an important difference; in Saussure, the words make sense only insofar as they are differentiated from one another in relations of negativity. This will not be the case for the Nietzschean conception of force as Deleuze sees it.

The absence of dialectical negativity in the relationship between forces is extremely important for Deleuze, and this is certainly part of the attraction Nietzsche holds for him. Though critics of Deleuze's reading of Nietzsche have attempted to uncover hidden dialectics lurking among differences, this is an impossible move in terms of Deleuze's articulation of Nietzsche's ontology, aesthetics, and ethics. If the force that dominates does so, not by means of negation, but by affirming and enjoying its own difference from other forces, no negation is present. This is Nietzsche's empiricism: instead of negation, difference as affirmation and enjoyment. "Dialectic is labor," but "[Nietzsche's] empiricism is an enjoyment" (Deleuze 1983, p. 9); it is affirmation, a feeling of pleasure and power. The differential element, the relation to other forces, must always be present; no force can be quantitatively determined apart from its relation to other forces, yet each force is positive. This is, of course, essential to Deleuze's conception of desire. There are not two equal forces of any kind (whether physical or cultural), because such equality would, by eliminating the differential relation between forces, be the elimination of any determination of force (Deleuze 1983, p. 43). "Difference in quantity is, therefore, in one sense, the irreducible element of quantity" (that is, it generates quality); but then it is also necessarily the case that difference in quantity is "the element which is irreducible to quantity itself" (Deleuze 1983, p. 44). This strange remake of metaphysics bears repeating lest it be misread: *difference* in quantity is the element that is irreducible to quantity itself.

Heraclitus and Justice

For Nietzsche, of all philosophers, Heraclitus is the most innocent and most just thinker precisely because Heraclitus was able to think the difference in quantity that generates quality. In *Philosophy in the Tragic Age of the Greeks*, Nietzsche writes:

While Heraclitus' imagination was eyeing this never-ceasing motion of the cosmos, this "actuality," like a blissful spectator who is watching innumerable pairs of contestants wrestling in joyous combat and refereed by stern judges, a still greater intuition overtook him. He could no longer see the contesting pairs and their referees as separate; the judges themselves seemed to be striving in the contest and the contestants seemed to be judging them. Now, perceiving basically nothing but everlastingly sovereign justice itself, he dared proclaim: "The struggle of the many is pure justice itself! In fact, the one is the many. For what are all those qualities, in essence?"[6]

The answer that Heraclitus settles on, according to Nietzsche, is that qualities, not substances, are the game Zeus plays, the game of fire itself, since if everything is fire there is nothing opposite to it (Nietzsche 1987, pp. 58, 60). Even as it appears that opposite qualities diverge out of a single force, still "light and dark, bitter and sweet are attached to each other and interlocked at a given moment" (Nietzsche 1987, p. 54). And while one or the other may momentarily ascend, such ascendancy is not permanent; it is not the establishment of a stable substance; it is just one moment in an ongoing process. According to Nietzsche, *only a Greek* was capable of such an idea, and this is because it is modeled on the individual Greek's role in society:

> Just as the Greek individual fought as though he alone were right and an infinitely sure measure of judicial opinion were determining the trend of victory at any given moment, so the qualities wrestle with one another in accordance with inviolable laws and standards that are immanent in the struggle (Nietzsche 1987, p. 55).

There are two points to be made here: one, Heraclitus sees construction and destruction as innocent and this proves significant for Deleuze's philosophy of the flux; two, the name inscribed on noble and base evaluations, as well as on the Nietzschean terms *self-affirmative* and *passive* (as opposed to Deleuze's terms, *active* and *reactive*), is that of the Greek individual "fighting as though he alone were right": the Greek individual, knightly, aristocratic, with a privileged soul and with an "ease of mind" that quickly transforms itself into carelessness, remissness, frivolity; "man," that beast of prey; in short, the heroic Greek (Nietzsche 1969, I). Such a model is not inconsequential for Nietzsche, and it seems to me to be important to know if this heroic Greek is also inscribed in Deleuze's invocation of the notion of force and in the struggle of forces to dominate bodies.

In Nietzsche's reading of Heraclitus, only the limited human mind recognizes *hubris* in this struggle. No guilt, no injustice for Heraclitus; only a perception of diminished qualities. Guilt and injustice are like ice. Ice is not the opposite of fire, it is just a diminished warmth. For the fire god, there is no injustice. What calls new worlds into being is not *hubris* but the "self-renewing impulse to play" (Nietzsche 1987, p. 62). Certainly, in all life there is destruction, but such destruction, such satiety, is like a child throwing her toys away from time to time in order to start over. "In this world only play, play as artists and children engage in it, exhibits coming-to-be and passing away, structuring and destroying, without any moral additive, in forever equal innocence" (Nietzsche 1987, p. 62). Deleuze's comment on this point is only that "Heraclitus is the tragic thinker," for "[t]he problem of justice runs through his entire work" (Deleuze 1983, p. 23). Sharing in fire, in the logos, Heraclitus sees construction and destruction as innocent, as radically just. Such recognition constitutes tragic thought.

The Being of Becoming and the Dice Throw

In order to get a better sense of what is at stake for Deleuze in the treatment of force, I would like to turn to *Différence et répétition*[7], a text that seems to draw out, in a lengthy exposition, many of the themes approached in *Nietzsche and Philosophy*. Deleuze is careful here to leave behind the image of the Greek hero. From the point of view of *Différence et répétition*, there is no denying that what is at stake is the nature of the ontological proposition that "[b]eing is univocal . . . from Parmenides to Heidegger, it is the same voice which is repeated, in an echo which forms by itself alone the entire deployment of the univocal" (Deleuze 1968, p. 52). Being, however, is not a genus, and Deleuze replaces the Aristotelian model of judgment and the echo of being with a propositional model. The proposition expresses *meaning;* the *referent* expresses itself in the proposition. But propositions do not have the same "meaning" even though they have the same "referent," and such distinctions, notes Deleuze, though real, are neither numerical distinctions nor ontological distinctions: they are formal, qualitative (that is, *essential*, in the phenomenological sense), or semiological (Deleuze 1968, pp. 52–53). Why say this? Why say that formally distinct meanings are not themselves ontological, but that they relate to being, their "single, ontologically one, referent"? In a second crucial shift of Aristotle's metaphysics, Deleuze writes that being is not said in many ways; being is expressed "in one and the same sense" of each of its (numerically) distinct designates (*le designé*). So while the meaning of being is "ontologically" the same for each of its numerically distinct designates (being is the same for each designate), still "these differences do not have the same essence" they do not themselves have the same meaning (Deleuze 1968, p. 53). If it can be shown how it is possible for being to speak with a single voice, to be "said" of difference itself, then being is not equivocal; it is univocal, and being is said of differences, none of which have the same meaning.

How does Deleuze develop the notion that being is said of difference, of the differential element, and what contribution can this discussion make to clarifying the theory of force as the nondialectical differential element? Deleuze finds this metaphysics of flux in the Nietzschean image of the game of chance. Nietzsche's will to power is the differential element between quantities of force, and it is precisely this *difference* that constitutes forces in tension as active or reactive, that is, as qualities (Deleuze 1983, p. 50). Furthermore, the relation between forces is subject only to chance. Every body is nothing but the arbitrary relation of force with force; every body, every difference between forces, in Deleuze's terminology, and every "will to power" in Nietzsche's, is chance and nothing but chance (Deleuze 1983, p. 40). In this sense, existence must be understood, in Deleuze's reading of Nietzsche, as radically innocent and as just, a game of chance. Deleuze quotes from *Zarathustra*:

> [I]f ever I have played dice with the gods at their table, the earth, so that the earth trembled and broke open and streams of fire snorted forth:
>   for the earth is a table of the gods, and trembling with creative new words and the dice throws of the gods.[8]

If existence is a game of chance, then it is a serious game because it is also a game of the necessity of chance, a game played by gods with dice and the earth as their table. But that is not all.

> Above all things stands the heaven of chance, the heaven of innocence, the heaven of accident, the heaven of wantonness . . . you are to me a dance floor for divine chances, that you are to me a gods' table for divine dice and dicers! (Nietzsche 1961, p. 186.)

So, concludes Deleuze, chance is played out on two tables: on the earth and in the heavens, yet there is only a single dice throw at a time. Each single dice throw is played out on the earth—as the *affirmation of becoming*—and also in the heavens—as the *affirmation of the being of becoming*. Each dice throw affirms chance, but the numbers on the die affirm the *necessity* of chance as the being of becoming. The necessity of chance is precisely what constitutes its innocence and even wantonness; it releases all things from having a purpose. In this way, the necessity of chance in the dice throw is an affirmation, and force can only be understood as an affirmative and thoroughly nondialectical element. Only such an affirmation can actually lead to an ethic of joy, which heads off guilt and bad conscience. It is the only way to create chance and multiplicity (the being of becoming), that is, there is only *one* way to combine being and becoming so as to have innocence, necessity, and multiplicity instead of mere probability. Deleuze explains:

> Nietzsche identifies chance with multiplicity, with fragments, with parts, with chaos: the chaos of the dice that are shaken and then thrown . . . To abolish chance by holding it in the grip of causality and finality, to count on the repetition of throws rather than affirming chance, to anticipate a result instead of affirming necessity—these are all the operations of a bad player (Deleuze 1983, pp. 26, 27).

For the skilled dice player, there is an incommensurability between chance and cause; Nietzsche himself has stressed this: "We have absolutely no experience of a cause . . . We have combined our feeling of a will, our feeling of 'freedom,' our feeling of responsibility and our intention to perform an act, into the concept 'cause'" (Nietzsche 1968, p. 551). For the skilled player, the idea of a goal has been removed from the process, and, in spite of this, the player affirms the process, experiences every moment, every dice throw, as good and valuable, as pleasure (Nietzsche 1968, p. 36). But for lack of critique, we slip into playing badly, we forget that the interpretation of the qualities of forces and interpretation itself require critique.

Will to Power

Since will to power is the differential and genetic element, will to power is, for Nietzsche, what interprets; it "estimate[s] the quality of force that gives meaning to a given phenomenon, or event, and it measures the relation of the forces which are present" (Deleuze 1983, p. 53). And will to power evaluates. "The will-to-power as genealogical element is that from which senses derive their significance and values their value" (Deleuze 1983, p. 54):

> I emphasize this major point of historical method all the more because it is in fundamental opposition to the now prevalent instinct and taste which would rather be reconciled even to the absolute fortuitousness, even the mechanistic senselessness of all events than to the theory that in all events a *will to power* is operating (Nietzsche 1969, p. 78).

As such, each phenomenon is a "sign" or a "symptom" whose meaning is found only in an existing force, and, as Deleuze (perhaps generously) reads this in *Nietzsche and Philosophy*, "The whole of philosophy is nothing but a symptomatology, and a *semiology*. The sciences are a symptomatological and semiological system" (Deleuze 1983, p. 3). The symptoms they study are the "appropriation, domination, exploitation of a quantity of reality" by force (insofar as such quantities are force); each force is a "sense" (what metaphysics calls an appearance and science refers to as "cause") (Deleuze 1983, p. 3). Thus, for Deleuze, it is absurd to presume that something underlies sense or to claim that forces refer to a physics, when precisely these presuppositions of philosophy are the subject of Nietzsche's creative critique. Force is sense and insofar as forces in tension constitute bodies or phenomena, each phenomenon is a sign whose meaning is a force that must always be evaluated. In a sense, there is no "nature," or, at best, nature is a history, so that not only is desire semiotically (not linguistically) and culturally constructed, but all of nature is semiotically constructed, in "regimes of signs"[9]—or, as Nietzsche would have it, it is evaluated. History, desire, nature, all are constituted out of evaluations, which is, of course, another way of saying ethics—genuine critique.

If will to power is to interpret and evaluate the relation of forces and to determine them as noble or base, it must have its own qualities by means of which it can designate forces. These qualities are affirmation and denial. Deleuze also rereads these qualities, not in oppositional terms, and not in terms of the Greek hero, but as action and reaction: "On the one hand, it is clear that there is affirmation in every action and negation in every reaction. But, on the other hand, action and reaction are more like means, means or instruments of the will to power which affirms and denies, just as reactive forces are instruments of nihilism" (Deleuze 1983, p. 54). They are means in the profound sense that affirmation is the very act of becoming active and negation is the act of becoming reactive: "The signification of a sense consists in the quality of force which is expressed in a thing: is this force active or reactive and of what nuance? The value of value consists in the quality of the will to power expressed in the corresponding thing; is the will to power affirmative or negative and of what nuance?" (Deleuze 1983, pp. 54–55).

Since forces are purely quantitative, and their relations with other forces are purely chance, only the quality of will to power is subject to human interpretation. So Nietzsche, still using the model of the heroic Greek, asks of will to power in each case: Is it affirmative or negative? By which he means, is it creative or slavish? (Deleuze 1983, p. 205, n. 14). The signification of a sense and the value of a value can be derived or determined only in terms of the differential relations between forces, that is, in terms of quantity and quality, and they are not a function of some underlying principle, nor of some telos. No doubt this is part of Deleuze's claim in the very first chapter of this text that evaluation is both ethical and aesthetic, in the senses of critical and creative. Evaluations are not judgments based on knowledge, but ways of being. I repeat: "This is why we always have the beliefs, feelings, and thoughts that we deserve given our way of being or our style of life" (Deleuze 1983, p. 1). The body we have is the body we live—in this sense, the one we deserve.

Additionally, it appears that the negative is not entirely absent from Nietzsche's theory of force, but I cannot emphasize strongly enough that its role and status are entirely different here than they are within dialectic. At first, it appears as though the negative is located at the origin, in difference— in the difference between active and reactive forces, since it exists as a quality of will to power, as will willing negation, willing denial, rather than not willing at all. This reading is endorsed by Vincent Pecore, who claims, "Genealogy means 'origin' but also 'difference . . . in the origin'; and will to power is both the 'differential element' through which values, like signs, define themselves and a motive force behind the creation of values that is either active or reactive, affirmative or . . . dialectical."[10] And yet only active force, in complicity with affirmation, affirms difference. In Deleuze's rethinking of this, reactive force acts by *limiting* active force, restricting it in complicity with negativity and denial, and separating active force from what it can do (Deleuze 1983, p. 57).[11] So when Pecore says that the differential nature of will to power (both critical and creative) is dialectical at the origin—this reading succeeds only by separating will to power from what it can do (Pecore, p. 40). That is, he reads its critical aspect as a negative force that can somehow act negatively without dissolving into nihilism, and not as merely a diminished quality of active force. From Deleuze's perspective, it is Pecore's own reading that suffers from being reactive:

> This is why the origin itself, in one sense, includes an inverted self-image; seen from the side of reactive forces the differential and genealogical element appears upside down, difference has become negation, affirmation has become contradiction. An inverted image of the origin accompanies the origin; "yes" from the point of view of active forces becomes "no" from the point of view of reactive forces and affirmation of the self becomes negation of the other (Deleuze 1983, p. 56).[12]

Active forces are active by means of their self-affirmation. Reactive forces operate by denying the other, rather than by affirming themselves. Yet when active forces see themselves in the upside-down mirror of reactive forces, that is, when they are evaluated and interpreted from the perspective of reactive forces, their image is perverted into an image of evolution, like the Hegelian notion of contradiction. This is Deleuze's understanding of Nietzsche's critique of Hegel; Hegel's is a reactive thought, product of reactive forces, which *begin* by denying the *other*, by denying the difference at the origin, and by seeing active force as a derivative element that evolves out of originary reaction. The importance of this to Deleuze's thought about Nietzsche cannot be underestimated without missing the point of Deleuze's work in general.

Will to Power as Desire

The upside-down mirror of reactive forces has also contributed to a base interpretation of will to power by means of a base interpretation of desire. The relation between active and reactive force is the same relation as that between desire and law. Citing Plato's *Gorgias*, Deleuze comments on Plato's discussion with the sophist Callicles and introduces both the notion of desire and that of the law. Like Callicles, Deleuze seems to agree that whatever separates (active) force from what it can do is to be characterized as law, and it appears that Nietzsche himself endorses this:

> [L]egal conditions can never be other than *exceptional conditions*, since they constitute a partial restriction of the will of life, which is bent on power . . . A legal order thought of as sovereign and universal, not as a means in the struggle between power-complexes but as a means of *preventing* all struggle in general . . . would be a principle *hostile to life*, an agent of the dissolution and destruction of man, an attempt to assassinate the future of man, a sign of weariness, a secret path to nothingness (Nietzsche 1969, p. 76) .

Law, by separating active force from what it can do, leads to nihilism. The upside-down mirror image of reactive forces and negative will do precisely this. For Callicles, as for Nietzsche, says Deleuze, the weak cannot form a stronger force by banding together, rather, reactive forces can only stop active forces from doing what they do by confronting them with the upside-down image. Like Nietzsche, Callicles maintains that the slave does not cease to be a slave even when he is triumphant: "from the point of view of nature concrete force is that which goes to its ultimate consequences, to the limit of power or desire" (Deleuze 1983, p. 59) and which, consequently, has the strongest capacity for being affected; it can stand the most (Deleuze 1983, p. 62). The slave then, is a slave by reason of a weak capacity to be affected and to act. But Socrates, relying on a negative and dialectical notion, can only comprehend desire as an experienced pain followed by the experience of a pleasurable satisfaction—a reaction, property, or symptom of a reactive force. Whereas, for Deleuze, desire is the limit of a power in the sense that "every body extends its power as far as it is able" (Deleuze 1983, p. 206, n. 17).[13] Limit, in this sense, is "that point from which it [a force] deploys itself, and deploys all its power" such that "the smallest becomes the equal of the greatest as soon as it is no longer separated from that which it is capable of" (Deleuze 1968, p. 55). Nietzsche calls such desire *will to power*[14]—a desire that does not need to be interpreted. Deleuze drops this heroic expression and simply emphasizes that desire is what experiments with forces (Deleuze and Parnet 1987, p. 95).

In *Différence et répétition*, Deleuze creates anew the concept of law apart from the upside-down mirror. In Aristotle (and Plato), entities have different degrees of being, as if there were only so much being available for distribution. This occurs because "[t]here is a hierarchy which measures beings according to their limits, and according to their degree of proximity or distance in relation to a principle" (Deleuze 1968, p. 55). For Deleuze, such a measure of being is also a measure of power, a measure of law and the limits of law. Having rethought the Aristotelian notion of being, he proposes a different kind of law and measure for the "being which is said of difference." Such a measure is a "*nomadic nomos*, without property, enclosure or measure . . . an allocation of those who distribute *themselves* . . . in a space without precise limits" (Deleuze 1968, p. 54). The Aristotelian space of "being said in many ways" is a space that must be divided, shared, hierarchized in accordance with the above-stated principle of proximity to being-itself. The space of "being said of difference" is without this principle. It is characterized by Deleuze as a "wandering distribution," a "delirium" (without property, enclosure, or measure) free to fill up space and to leap beyond that limit (Deleuze 1968, pp. 54–55).

When force is separated from its power, from what it can do, it turns upon itself and denies itself in accordance with the law that divides and subtracts (takes power away). Of course, for Nietzsche, that law was originally the sphere of the active, strong, spontaneous, and aggressive warrior. Once the supreme power establishes law:

> [I]t treats violence and capricious acts . . . as offenses against the law . . . and thus leads the feelings of its subjects away from the direct injury caused by such offenses; and in the long run it thus attains the reverse of that which is desired by all revenge that is fastened exclusively to the viewpoint of the person injured: from now on the eye is trained to an ever more impersonal evaluation of the deed (Nietzsche 1969, p. 76).

In this way, through the intervention of law, that is, reactive negativity, active forces actually become reactive. The cure for this is nothingness.

It seems that it is also in this sense that Nietzsche differs fundamentally from Hegel. For although active and reactive forces are difference at the origin, their association with the quality of will to power, that is, with affirmation and negation, ultimately prevents their synthesis. Moreover, it is inappropriate to do what is so often done with the concept of power: to interpret it as the "object of a *representation*" as if "man . . . wants to see his superiority represented and recognized by others" (Deleuze 1983, p. 80). And this, in turn, presupposes the primacy of the identical and of negation over difference, which, in Nietzsche's inscription, is sought only by the sickly, those inhabitants of the "hospitals of culture":

> What do they really want? At least to *represent* justice, love, wisdom, supe-riority—that is the ambition of the "lowest," the sick . . . The will of the weak to represent *some* form of superiority, their instinct for devious paths to tyranny over the healthy—where can it not be discovered, this will to power of the weakest! (Nietzsche 1969, p. 123.)

This is simply another instance of the inverted mirror, whereby the sick represent themselves as superior by negating the healthy. The representation is necessary to the sickly because it stabilizes the world by providing an iden-tity that sidesteps the will to power as a shaping will: "The joy in shaping and reshaping—a primeval joy!" (Nietzsche 1968, p. 495). This is joy in becoming, which stands opposed to those weak sensations that are regarded not merely as alike, but are "sensed *as being the same*" (Nietzsche 1968, p. 506). As Deleuze makes clear from the beginning (even while disregarding the Nietzschean judgments "sickly" and "healthy"), a representation of power can only be a representation of an already existing power, a current state of affairs, insofar as representation is not a creative act of affirmation.

When a force becomes active it extends its power as far as it is able, as an *affirmation*. When a force becomes reactive, it does so as negative and nihilistic; its will to power is a will to nothingness, and not a will to dialectic (Deleuze 1983, p. 68). One example:

> Mankind itself is still ill with the effects of this priestly naiveté in medicine . . . the entire antisensualistic metaphysic of the priests that makes men indolent and overrefined . . . and finally the only-too-comprehensible satiety with all this, together with the radical cure for it *nothingness* (Nietzsche 1969, p. 32).

For this reason, according to Deleuze's reading of Nietzsche, it is not possible for reactive force to extend its power to its limit and to become more power-fully reactive. Because reactive forces are complicitous with negativity and denial, they can, through the will to nothingness, the ultimate extension of their force, only negate themselves! (Deleuze 1983, p. 70).[15] They negate their own reactive force. This "active negation" or "active nihilism" is the only way in which reactive forces become active. In other words, negation never negates active force and affirmation—it only separates them from its own power until, weakened, they become reactive. Nor can active affirmation become negative by extending its power to its limit. Given the complicity between active forces and affirmation, such a becoming only enhances the power of active forces. Rather, because of its complicity with negation, reactive force extends the full power of negation—the will to nothingness—to its limit at which point forces actively negate their own reactive negativity, finally becoming active. So Nietzsche writes concerning nihilism: "It reaches its maximum of relative strength as a violent force of destruction—as active nihilism" (Nietzsche 1968, p. 18). This cosmological or physical doctrine is, of course, and must be connected to an ethical and selective doctrine. Deleuze claims that philosophy serves neither church nor state, nor any power. If the job of philosophy is to expose all forms of thought, Deleuze is interested in how such powers dominate, that is, he is interested in the complicity—that mixture of baseness and stupidity—of victims and perpetrators (an interest that seems to also motivate *Anti-Oedipus*), as opposed to "freemen . . . who do not confuse the aims of culture with the benefit of the State, morality or religion" (Deleuze 1983, p. 106).

Untimely Philosophy: Nietzsche's Selective Ontology

Such an investigation is simultaneously and necessarily an investigation of the nature of time. If philosophy serves no power, philosophy is always against its time, a critique of the present world: thus untimely (*Unzeitge-masse*), active, a philosophy of the future. The role of memory in Nietzsche's texts comes to be understood, by Deleuze, as the province of reactive forces. Memory traces constitute the reactive unconscious, and these traces cannot be escaped once they have been received perceptually (Deleuze 1983, p. 112). However, "[t]his involves no mere passive inability to rid oneself of an impression . . . but an active *desire* not to rid oneself . . . Man must first of all have become calculable, regular, necessary, even in his own image of himself" (Nietzsche 1969, p. 58). Even though there is a steady stream of present excitations that should move a body on, still, a reactive consciousness develops to react to the flow of present conscious excitations. The old instincts, limited by law, unable to discharge themselves outwardly, "turn backward *against man himself.* Hostility, cruelty, joy in persecuting, in attacking, in change, in destruction—all this turned against the possessors of such instincts: that is the origin of the 'bad conscience'" (Nietzsche 1969, p. 85). As a result, "when reactive forces take conscious excitation as their object, then the corresponding reaction is itself acted," while keeping reactive traces in the unconscious (Deleuze 1983, p. 113). Thus, while the "origin, nature, and function" of consciousness must, nonetheless, be renewed, the flows of excitations that reactive consciousness reacts to (by taking them as its object) must keep coming; memory traces must not overflow consciousness or the activity of reactive forces will come to a halt.

What makes this possible is what Deleuze calls "the active super-conscious faculty of forgetting" (Deleuze 1983, p. 113):

> Forgetting is no mere *vis inertiae* as the superficial imagine; it is rather an active and in the strictest sense positive faculty of repression . . . so that it will be immediately obvious how there could be no happiness, no cheerfulness, no hope, no pride, no *present*, without forgetfulness (Nietzsche 1969, pp. 58–59).

But consciousness is the "weakest and most fallible organ" (Nietzsche 1969, p. 84), so forgetting, in its turn, is only functionally active. Reactive in its origins, forgetting must borrow its energy from reactive forces, so it is prone to failures: "excitation tends to get confused with its trace in the unconscious and conversely, reaction to traces rises into consciousness and overruns it" (Deleuze 1983, p. 114). With this, reactive forces cease to be acted. Denied any content to act with, active forces cease to act—they are *separated from what they can do*. With nothing to stop it, and with no renewal of conscious activity, the unconscious memory trace takes the place of the conscious excitation (Deleuze 1983, p. 114). Reaction prevails over action. This is the origin and genesis of *ressentiment*.

For the human being who suffers *ressentiment* neither action nor reaction is possible. So *ressentiment* is characterized by the inability to admire, respect, or love; passivity or whatever is nonacted; and the imputation of wrongs, distribution of responsibilities, and perpetual accusations (Deleuze 1983, pp. 117–118). As a result, the one who suffers from *ressentiment* can only give sense and value from the standpoint of the passive receiver who can neither act *nor even put reactive forces into play*. The passive receiver can only feel. This is why Nietzsche cautions that only someone who suffers *ressentiment* needs others who are evil so as to represent herself as good. And again, only from this point of view, what is evil is judged evil because it does not hold itself back (Deleuze 1983, p. 123). Nietzsche's strong heroes can never prevent themselves from acting—it is only the weak who simply cannot act because, in them, force is separated from what it can do. Yet from the passive point of view of the weak who cannot admire or respect the strong, the strong are evil because they should separate themselves from what they can do, yet they do not. Unlike active forces, reactive forces, in complicity with negation and denial cannot return, cannot be willed to return. Such a transmutation, of course, is not any sort of fundamental biological or physical process; it is tied to the *feeling* of power, which Nietzsche, in his earlier writing (Nietzsche 1968, p. 42), insisted upon. It is "a new way of feeling, thinking, and above all being (the Overman)" (Deleuze 1983, p. 71). This feeling is in no sense unable to respect, nor is it passive or looking for someone to blame; it is a feeling that is itself an active creation.

The Tragic

"Tragedy is a *tonic*" (Nietzsche 1968, p. 850); it is a tonic to *ressentiment*. Experiencing tragedy, what it can be in its highest form, is a question of forces, thus of quality. In its highest form, tragedy is a force that Nietzsche evaluates as affirmative and noble. Only when it is taken in this way can tragedy be a tonic to *ressentiment*. How are we to read Nietzsche in a way that does not reduce tragedy to a psychological experience like catharsis, or to a historical or personal destiny, an encounter with the gods?

To answer this question, I would like to take up again the theme of *ressentiment*. Deleuze defines *ressentiment* as an aspect of a principle upon which our entire psychology depends—that principle is nihilism, the motor and meaning of all history. All the categories of rational thought (identity, causality, and finality) presuppose a nihilistic interpretation of force as *ressentiment*. To think about tragedy as the tonic for such *ressentiment*, each of us needs to throw out a dice and to ask as Deleuze does, "What would a man [sic] without *ressentiment* be like?" (Deleuze 1983, p. 35). What would life be like without law as limit, without denial? This is a different question for each one who throws the dice.

Zarathustra claims that the past and present are his greatest burden because they have always been interpreted in terms of force as *ressentiment* and not with a dice.

> I should not know how to live, if I were not a seer of that which must come. A seer, a willer, a creator, a future itself and a bridge to the future— and alas, also like a cripple upon this bridge . . . To redeem the past and to transform every 'It was' into an 'I wanted it thus'—that alone do I call redemption (Nietzsche 1961, pp. 160–161).

The problem is that *ressentiment*, the imprisoned will, the "It was," fetters even the liberator. Zarathustra concludes that even while "The will is a creator," still, "[a]ll 'It was' *is* a fragment, a riddle, a dreadful chance—until the creative will says to it: 'But I willed it thus!'" (Nietzsche 1961, p. 163.) The creative will brings joy, and such joy, such pure and multiple positivity is, says Deleuze, what Nietzsche comes to mean by tragedy (Deleuze 1983, p. 36).

Everything gets referred to a force capable of interpreting it, and every force is referred to what it can do (Deleuze 1983, p. 22). And such affirmation affirms chance and the necessity of chance. There are no bets on probability here, no leaps of faith; Deleuze notes that Zarathustra opposes all such moves. Betting on probabilities contradicts the dice throw, or, better said, it eliminates the dice throw by reducing its sheer necessity to mere likelihood. Now I want to recall the epigraph with which I began this essay—the statement that no one can extract from things (books included) more than she already knows. Nietzsche continues this statement by noting that it is a question of experience: "For what one lacks access to from experience one will have no ear" (Nietzsche 1979, p. 70). Tragic thinking, in the sense of joyous and multiple affirmation, is a question, then, of experiences. It is this *existential* basis that distinguishes Nietzsche's tragic thought from any sort of idealism or dialectic. It is, I believe, this existential basis that Deleuze grasps while leaving behind the inscription of Greek heroics.

The question of tragedy becomes, for Deleuze, a question about what we have experienced, and how we have critiqued this experience. But with regard to the first point, what we have experienced is not enough. What is our mode of life?" is not an abstract question. What have I actually experienced? What values do I deserve given this? How do I evaluate? What interests do my evaluations promote? These are all important questions, concrete questions with individual as well as cultural implications. These are the questions presupposed by the dice throw. Do I affirm chance as necessity, or do I play for probability, thereby denying the necessity of chance and fleeing from the experience of the effects of my own ideas?

That said, it needs to be placed in the context of contemporary social life and its territorializations and deterritorializations. None of us is or will be Zarathustra. Still, we must be attuned to "how one becomes what one is" (Nietzsche 1979, p. 253), that is, how the forces that take hold of us struggle for domination. Since we cannot extract what we have not experienced, we tend to read what is interesting to us, what we understand given our own social and personal commitments. But Nietzsche says that we must think on our feet about what we experience, and we must provide ourselves with experiences of the dice throw if we are to think at all. Still, no one can "know" the Overman, know what it is. In a certain sense, we cannot even read Nietzsche's books and "know" them. No one, none of us understand Nietzsche. Each of us interprets from our own perspectives. Yet, the more perspectives we experiment with and live, presumably, the more of Nietzsche we can read, or, perhaps, the more irrelevant his texts become.

If tragedy is to overcome our pessimism, to throw dice and affirm each experience, tragedy is the tonic to pessimism. If, since the pre-Socratics, and especially since Socrates, we are all pessimists, because all our evaluations are part of a base way of life, the only cure for this, for Nietzsche, is complete nihilism. Partial or small affirmations do not interest Nietzsche—he even sees them as dangerously deceptive. So if we read Nietzsche, it is best if we read with *no interests at all*! This is the *nomadic nomos*, Heraclitean strife, justice, self-renewing creation. Nietzsche's iciness and coldness, living on high mountains, and his solitariness all have the effect of producing a complete and total nihilism—*no interests at all*. This strategy is necessary for Nietzsche because all our interests prior to complete nihilism are interests with a base evaluation; only complete nihilism can transmute/transvalue this base evaluation to something noble, bold, and forceful. Our evaluations after such transmutation will again be merely perspectives, but their point of view will then be affirmative and affirming. This is the importance of eternal return for Nietzsche. Only eternal return guarantees the move to complete nihilism. Tragedy is the means by which he makes this move.

Is this how Deleuze reads Nietzsche? Is there some sort of Deleuzian inscription operating? Deleuze does not deny the necessity of a transmutation of values. As I have indicated, this may even be his main point. But with regard to nihilism and Nietzsche's method for accomplishing it, Deleuze, I believe, remains aware of our contemporary cultural situatedness, and in his work another transmutation occurs. We are all committed to social and personal affiliations. We cannot go sit on top of a mountain; we cannot become icy. There are too many concerns below. So how are we to think the being of becoming in our situatedness? Deleuze's reading of Nietzsche is part of a line of flight that eventually commits him to that process of becoming that is called the Body without Organs, a process that he (with Guattari) finds in the writing of Antonin Artaud. This writing is not Nietzschean pronouncements. It is not poetry. It seems to be closer to something like "performance art" (which often grows out of actual experience). Closer, then, to tragedy than to any other historical art form, though I am unwilling to call up that ancient word "tragedy" to name our contemporary artistic inventions.

Nihilism, then, in the sense of active nihilism, reaches its maximum of relative strength in a violent force of destruction. For Artaud it is the body outside of socially organized, "genital" sexuality, as well as outside of the law, which castrates and makes impotent, which limits and turns back against "anything that has life or energy."[16] "I don't believe in father/ in mother,/ got no pappamummy" Artaud wails; "I Antonin Artaud, am my son,/ my father, my mother,/ myself" (Artaud 1965, pp. 247, 248). What remains is a crowd; a multiplicity; a pack in smooth, that is, unorganized and unstable, space; intensive matter; a *nomadic nomos*. Since, as Artaud claims, "there is nothing more useless than an organ,"[17] the Body without Organs is what remains when you take everything away: the organization of the body by law, Nietzsche's Greek evaluations, Deleuze-Guattari's own choices of literature and the psychoanalytic fantasy projections which constitute sexuality in contemporary culture. In a certain sense, then, Grosz is right to worry about the existence of personal inscriptions in the body assemblage. But Deleuze-Guattari also incite the removal of all such inscriptions. The removal of these inscriptions leaves nothing—no scene, no place, no support, no interests, nothing to interpret—only the real.[18]

Deleuze-Guattari acknowledge our situatedness in a particular sociopolitical environment when they point to the dangerous consequences of the disorder of the body. Active nihilism is dangerous; "You have to keep enough of the organism for it to reform each dawn," they warn (Deleuze and Guattari 1987, p. 160). Even while opening the body to connections and an assemblage of circuits, conjunctions, distributions of intensity, transmissions, stabilization and destabilization; nonetheless, drug addiction, alcoholism, paranoia, schizophrenia are all possible effects that must not be romanticized. So it is not surprising that what I have called active nihilism, the dissolution of the body under law (the organism), Artaud calls suicide.[19] "If I commit suicide, it will not be to destroy myself but to put myself back together again . . . I free myself from the conditioned reflexes of my organs" (Artaud 1965, p. 56). Suicide, Artaud continues, uproots; it uproots the law that has kept the body organized and makes a place for the Body without Organs.

And it is also not surprising that the Body without Organs is the field of immanence of desire, that is, desire not as lack or even as fulfillment, but desire as a process of production distributed intensively, consistently, without interruption: in short, a field of becomings (Deleuze and Guattari 1987, p. 154). Though Deleuze-Guattari have abandoned Nietzschean inscriptions in the creation of the Body without Organs, one Nietzschean prescription serves well here: experiment with caution. Lodge yourself on a stratum, observe Deleuze-Guattari; experiment with the opportunities it offers, the forces within that field; become a point of transmission; annihilate the genitally, socially, or politically stratified body; make yourself a Body without Organs.

Notes

1. Judith Butler, *Subjects of Desire. Hegelian Reflections in Twentieth Century France* (New York: Columbia University Press, 1987).

2. Gilles Deleuze, *Nietzsche and Philosophy*, trans. Hugh Tomlinson (New York: Columbia University Press, 1983), p. 39.

3. Friedrich Nietzsche, *On the Genealogy of Morals*, trans. Walter Kaufmann (New York: Vintage Books, 1969), Part I, Section 2, p. 26.

4. Friedrich Nietzsche, *Ecce Homo*, trans. R. J. Hollingdale, (New York: Penguin Books, 1979), p. 331.

5. Friedrich Nietzsche, *The Will to Power*, trans. Walter Kaufmann and R. J. Hollingdale (New York: Vintage Books, 1968), book 3, p. 564.

6. Friedrich Nietzsche, *Philosophy in the Tragic Age of the Greeks*, trans. Marianne Cowan (Washington, D.C.: Regnery Gateway, 1987), p. 57.

7. Gilles Deleuze, *Différence et répétition* (Paris: Presses Universitaires de France, 1968).

8. Friedrich Nietzsche, *Thus Spoke Zarathustra*, trans. R. J. Hollingdale (New York: Penguin Books, 1961), p. 245.

9. "Regimes of signs" is a term borrowed from Deleuze and Guattari's *A Thousand Plateaus. Capitalism and Schizophrenia*, trans. Brian Massumi (Minneapolis: University of Minnesota Press, 1987) and refers to semiotic mixtures of presignifying, countersignifying, postsignifying, and signifying elements, which constitute various types of social organization.

10. Vincent P. Pecore, "Deleuze's Nietzsche and Post-Structuralist Thought," *Sub-Stance*, vol. 14 (3), no. 48: p. 40.

11. This is the point, according to Deleuze, of sections of Nietzsche's *On the Genealogy of Morals*. For example, Nietzsche writes, "The active, aggressive, arrogant man is still a hundred steps closer to justice than the reactive man; for he has absolutely no need to take a false and prejudiced view of the object before him in the way the reactive man does and is bound to do. For that reason, the aggressive man, as the stronger, nobler, more courageous, has in fact also had at all times a *freer* eye, a *better* conscience on his side: conversely, one can see who has the invention of the 'bad conscience' on his conscience—the man of *ressentiment!*" (p. 75). This statement is part of an exposition on active and reactive justice that Deleuze takes to be the point of Nietzsche's work, in the sense that the question of affirmation is the question of existence that justifies through affirmation, as opposed to the reactive condemnation of existence.

12. At the "Greek" origin the noble man can "endure no other enemy than one in whom there is nothing to despise and *very much* to honor!" While, "[i]n contrast to this, picture 'The enemy' as the man of *ressentiment* conceives him—and here precisely is his deed, his creation: he has conceived 'the evil enemy,' 'the Evil One,' and this in fact is his basic concept, from which he then evolves, as an afterthought and pendant, a 'good one'—himself" (Nietzsche 1969, p. 39).

13. What Nietzsche writes in *The Will to Power* is, "There is no law: every power draws its ultimate consequence at every moment . . . A quantum of power is designated by the effect it produces and that which it resists" (Nietzsche 1968, p. 337).

14. Gilles Deleuze and Claire Parnet, *Dialogues*, trans. Hugh Tomlinson and Barbara Habberjam (New York: Columbia University Press, 1987), p. 91.

15. Nietzsche points to how once the belief in god, and an absolute moral order, "becomes untenable," "[n]ihilism appears at that point . . . One interpretation has collapsed; but because it was considered *the* interpretation it now seems as if there were no meaning at all in existence, as if everything were in vain." Such thinking leads, of course, to that most terrible thought: "existence as it is without meaning or aim, yet recurring inevitably without any finale of nothingness: '*the eternal recurrence*'" (Nietzsche 1968, p. 55).

16. Antonin Artaud, *Anthology* (San Francisco: City Lights Books, 1965), p. 111.

17. Antonin Artaud, *Selected Writings*, Susan Sontag, ed.; trans. Helen Weaver (New York: Farrar, Straus and Giroux, 1976), p. 571.

18. Gilles Deleuze and Félix Guattari, *Capitalism and Schizophrenia*, vol. 2, *A Thousand Plateaus*, trans. Brian Massumi (Minneapolis: University of Minnesota Press, 1987), p. 151.

19. These points were made by Lisa Franklin in an unpublished paper on Artaud and Deleuze-Guattari.

8

Anti-Platonism and Art

Paul Patton

MODERN ART HAS BEEN described as a succession of attempts to propose a definitive answer to the question, "What is art?" With the collapse of the representational ideal at the end of the nineteenth century, painters could no longer continue to refine their means of representing reality while remaining convinced that this was the task of painting alone. For many critics, the increasingly rapid succession of modern art movements, from fauvism and cubism through to pop, amounted to art's continuing investigation into its own nature. For some philosophers, modern philosophy follows a parallel course, offering up a succession of answers to the question, "What is thought?"[1] To the extent that philosophy itself is above all a reflection upon the nature of thought, this is a no less reflexive enterprise than modern art's concern with the nature of art. Moreover, as in the case of the successive styles of modern painting, different approaches to philosophy have tended to define themselves by what they reject. For many, the nature and task of modern philosophy has been defined in terms of the rejection of Platonism. However, it is not always the same Platonism that is envisaged, nor does rejection always take the same form in each case.

Deleuze is among those who have sought to develop a new conception of philosophy under the banner of "the overturning of Platonism." Moreover, he is one of those who has explicitly aligned his new conception of philosophy with the tendency of modern art: "The theory of thought is like painting: it needs that revolution which took art from representation to abstraction. This is the aim of a theory of thought without image" (Deleuze 1968, p. 354). The philosophical equivalent of abstract art, or imageless thought, would be a nonrepresentational conception of thought. Deleuze's own reflection upon the nature and task of philosophy, notably in *Différence et répétition*, is above all a critique of the persistent representationalism in philosophy. The aim of this paper is to explore the common ground between the abandonment of representation in painting and in philosophy, through an examination of Deleuze's remarks about Plato and modern art in the course of *Différence et répétition*. This discussion also raises the question of the nature of the Deleuzian "overturning" of Platonism. Since this involves inverting the hierarchy established by Plato between copies and simulacra, and since this reversal purports to abolish the very distinction in question, Deleuze's critical strategy with respect to Platonism appears similar to that of deconstruction. However, a comparison of the respective readings of Plato on this point by Deleuze and Derrida reveals that the similarities between them are more apparent than real.

In the visual arts in particular, the transition to modernity was precipitated by a crisis in and eventual abandonment of the representational theory of art. The search for aims other than the representation of appearances traversed a variety of alternatives, from the expression of feeling and emotion to the exploration of the formal possibilities of visual experience, before returning to a different version of the idea that visual art is essentially concerned with appearances. Much postmodernist art is explicitly concerned with the reproduction of appearances. The shock value in some cases derives from the fact that what is reproduced is the appearance of earlier artworks themselves. Artists such as Sherrie Levine rephotographed or repainted all or part of works by earlier artists. However, this is not just a return to the old ideal of art as representation, and not simply because it involves second-order representation, by reproducing appearances of appearances of reality. The crucial difference lies not in the objects depicted but in the conception of the artist's task: the reproduction of appearances rather than their representation. For production, at least in one of its senses, essentially involves the transformation of a raw material into a product. It is therefore inseparable from the creation or the institution of a difference where none existed before. The means of production, which include the artist's conceptual as well as physical materials and techniques, are the means by which this difference is created. By contrast, representation, at least in one of its senses, essentially involves the maintenance of an identity; the reappearance of that which appeared before.

In fact, artistic representation has always relied upon specific materials and techniques for reproducing appearances, which inevitably introduce a difference into the appearance reproduced. The question is not whether painting ever in fact achieved the representation of appearances in any strict sense, but what it took to be its objective and goal. For the tradition of realist or representational art, the goal was the reduction and eventual elimination of observable difference between the original and the copy. For some late modern or postmodern artists, the goal is exactly the opposite:

the production of difference, the manifestation or illustration of difference, by means of perceptual similarity. Borges gave a literary formulation of this strategy in imagining the project of a little-known twentieth-century poet and novelist who undertakes to recreate Cervantes's *Don Quixote*. Borges's story tells us that he succeeded at least in composing some fragments that repeated the original word for word, yet the different possibilities for interpreting the twentieth century text mean that it is not the same novel: "The text of Cervantes and that of Menard are verbally identical, but the second is almost infinitely richer. (More ambiguous, his detractors will say; but ambiguity is a richness)" (Borges 1962, p. 52). Deleuze comments that this story shows us how "the most exact, the most strict repetition has as its correlate the maximum of difference" (Deleuze 1968, p. 5). Duchamp and then Warhol offered visual realizations of a similar strategy, the former by employing ready-made objects as sculptural artworks, thereby transforming the status and nature of the appearance represented, the latter by recreating a series of banal objects, Brillo boxes made from plywood and hand-painted to resemble the mass-produced commercial item. The rediscovery and reutilization of such gestures in the postmodernist work of Sherrie Levine and others is therefore not a return to the old ideal of art as the representation of appearances, unless we understand "return" in precisely the sense Deleuze gives to both repetition and the eternal return: repetition is the displacement, disguise, or transformation of that which is repeated; return is the mode of being of that which differs. The return of representation in this sense is the differentiation or transformation of representation itself: no longer the maintenance of identity, but the production of difference. Modern art has come to see its task not as the representation of appearances, but as their repetition; not as the production of copies, but as the production of simulacra.

In *Différence et répétition*, Deleuze announces that "the task of modern philosophy has been defined: to overturn [*renverser*] Platonism" (Deleuze 1968, p. 82). What this means depends both upon what one understands by Platonism and what this operation of "overturning" is supposed to involve. *Renverser* carries both the sense of "overcoming" as well as that of "overturning" or "reversing," an ambiguity that is reflected in the fact that various English translations of Deleuze's formulation of the task of philosophy have used both of these terms. In fact, I shall argue, both senses are involved in Deleuze's version of the escape from philosophy's Platonic past: like Nietzsche, he proposes an overcoming that proceeds by inverting certain aspects of Platonism. It was Nietzsche who in the first instance proposed this definition of the task of philosophy. In a note in the *Nachlass*, he referred to his own philosophy as an "inverted" or "reversed" Platonism (*umgedrehter*

Platonismus).[2] For Nietzsche, Platonism was both a moral and a metaphysical construct, and something to be overcome on both of these planes. From a metaphysical point of view, Platonism consisted of the distinction between the realm of Ideas or that which truly is, and the sensuous realm of relative nonbeing or mere appearance. Platonism constructs a hierarchy within reality, and a corresponding hierarchy within ourselves, which makes even the best parts of human life no more than copies or imitations of the truly real. Overturning Platonism on this plane cannot consist in simply inverting the metaphysical order and affirming the reality of the sensuous, for that merely changes the places occupied within the same persistent structure. What is required is the abolition of that structure itself, as Nietzsche suggests in "How the 'Real World' at Last Became a Myth": "We have abolished the real world: what world is left? the apparent world perhaps? . . . But no! with the true world we have also abolished the apparent world!" (Nietzsche 1968, p. 41). Commenting upon the need to change the ordering structure as a whole, Heidegger describes this overcoming of Platonism as an inversion such that "philosophical thinking twists free of it" (Heidegger 1981, p. 201).

Nietzsche's attempt to think beyond the moral structure of Platonism is, if anything, a clearer example of such an evasive maneuver. From Nietzsche's own supramoral point of view, Platonism was the primary form of the nihilism that has dominated European thought. This "dogmatist's error," as he calls it in the preface to *Beyond Good and Evil* (Nietzsche 1973, p. 14), amounted to the devaluation of temporal and corporeal human existence by opposing to it a higher realm that is the natural home of gods, "the good in itself", and of the soul once freed of "that prison house which we are now encumbered with and call a body" (Phaedrus, 250c). In its Christian form, "Platonism for the people," as Nietzsche calls it, this nihilism has defined the nature of human existence up until the modern period. For several reasons, overturning Platonism on the moral plane cannot mean simply inverting the existing hierarchy of value: firstly, because that is the path that leads to secondary nihilism or loss of faith in the highest values, and thus to the kind of despair expressed by Zarathustra's prophet, for whom "Truly, we have grown too weary even to die; now we are awake and we live on in sepulchers!" (Nietzsche 1969, p. 156); secondly, because what we have become is in part the result of centuries of Christian education of the human spirit. As a result, Nietzsche argues in *On the Genealogy of Morals*, the very possibility of overcoming nihilism depends in part on the attachment to values such as truthfulness, which are themselves the products of the Christian-Platonic tradition. Rather than simply inverting the respective values attached to soul and body, the overturning of Platonism requires the development of a new conception of what we are as embodied beings, and a new evaluation of the life of such beings: a new ontology and a new ethics of human existence.

For Deleuze, overturning Platonism is both a part and an emblem of the larger task undertaken in *Différence et répétition,* namely the critique of the representational conception of thought that has dominated the history of philosophy since Plato, and the elaboration of an alternative conception of "thought without image." Thought understood as a process of representing some external reality means that the distinctions drawn in thought are projected back onto the object itself, so that thinking properly becomes a matter of following what Socrates calls the "objective articulation" of the object (Phaedrus, 265e). Deleuze argues that the philosophy of representation relies upon a series of timid and conservative presuppositions regarding the activity of thought. According to this dogmatic image derived from common sense, thought is supposed to be a fundamentally benign activity, the exercise of a universal human faculty that has a natural affinity with the truth. Its paradigm cases are not creative acts such as the invention of new concepts, but simple acts of recognition (this is a finger, or a piece of wax; snow is white), which are supposed to involve only the application of existing concepts to sense experience. Its products are discrete and disinterested items of knowledge, rather than a violence we do to things ("thought is primarily trespass and violence" [Deleuze 1968, p. 181]). Against this image of thought, Deleuze defends a conception of thought as something to which we are provoked precisely by those phenomena we do not recognize, or by forces from outside our habitual range of experience. Only by abandoning the banal model of recognition in favor of something closer to the Kantian sublime is it possible to conceive of thought as an essentially creative activity: thought as the creation of concepts, where concepts themselves are understood as existing only in immediate relations with forces and intensities outside thought.

The dominant tradition in the history of philosophy has developed a theory of thought within the shadow of this dominant image. In general terms, the successive accounts of the instruments and means of representation given by particular philosophies have contributed to a shared philosophical understanding of the nature of conceptual thought. For Deleuze, the coherence of this tradition is defined by its suppression or exclusion of difference in favor of a logic based upon identity, resemblance and similitude. These have become the unquestioned values that govern the theorization of thought itself, with the result that it becomes impossible to think difference as such. Plato occupies a place apart in the development of this philosophy of representation, both with respect to the presuppositions of the dogmatic image of thought, which he does not always accept, and with respect to the precedence of identity over difference. While he agrees that metaphysics, understood as the theory of conceptual representation, should be defined with reference to Platonism, Deleuze argues that Plato provided a somewhat incomplete version of the philosophy of representation. The doctrinal basis of representation in Plato is confined to his theory of Ideas or Forms. As such, it lacks the systematic character of the theory of categories later developed by Aristotle. Only with the theory of categories defined as the conditions of possible experience does philosophy acquire "the elementary concepts of representation" (Deleuze 1968, p. 93). By contrast, the aim of the theory of Ideas is not the specification of objects in terms of their place within a differential tableau of genus and species, but rather selection among rival claimants, the separation of the true or the authentic from the merely apparent or the inauthentic by tracing the lineage back to a foundation. With Aristotle, difference is specified within a conceptual order that covers the entire range of possibilities, from the largest differences, which appear in the form of the analogical relation to being among its genera, to the smallest differences, which distinguish the various species of object. With Plato, difference as such, or pure difference, still appears in the intervals between founded and unfounded claimants, or between things themselves and their simulacra (Deleuze 1968, p. 84).

Deleuze's attempt to think beyond the terms of the dominant metaphysical tradition involves precisely the attempt to develop a thought capable of comprehending pure difference. In order to do so, he draws upon some of the elements of anti-Platonism scattered across the pages of Plato's dialogues. He suggests that the ambivalence toward representation found in these texts makes it both inevitable and desirable that the overturning of Platonism should conserve aspects of Plato's thought. Insofar as it is correct to see Deleuze's "overturning" of Platonism as proceeding from a reversal of sorts between conflicting aspects of Plato's thought, then this procedure mimics in advance Deleuze's larger strategy in relation to the philosophy of representation. For here too, having traced its elaboration through the philosophies of Aristotle, neo-Platonists, Descartes, Leibniz, Kant, and Hegel, Deleuze then draws upon neglected aspects of the work of these thinkers, as well as the work of others who form a "minor tradition," such as Duns Scotus, Spinoza, Nietzsche, and Bergson, to develop an alternative conception of the nature of thought. A closer examination of the treatment of Platonism by Deleuze may therefore serve to illustrate the nature of his critique of the philosophy of representation as a whole.

Plato's texts provide a conception of a world whose basic structure is that of a system of representation. Only the Forms are ultimately and absolutely real. The earthly manifestations of qualities such as beauty or justice, or material objects, such as a bed, are only imitations of the Forms themselves.

In the "*Timaeus,*" for example, the world itself is presented as a copy or "likeness of that which is apprehended by reason and mind and is unchallengeable" (*Timaeus,* 29a–b). The Forms are the key to Plato's representationalism, since they are the original or essential natures that serve as foundations for the true nature of objects and qualities in the sensuous world of human existence. Platonism thus turns on this distinction between the original and its imitations, the model and its subsequent copies. Moreover, it is this distinction that underpins the subordination of difference to identity. For the original or model is supposed to be defined by an exemplary self-identity: only the Forms are nothing other than what they are, Courage being nothing but courageous, Piety nothing but pious, and so on. These qualities are then defined in terms of their "participation" in the original. They are likenesses or copies, which truly express the nature of the Form, defined as such by virtue of a special kind of internal resemblance to the original. Thus, for example, the cabinetmaker does not make "that which really is" but rather "something that resembles real being" (*Republic,* 597a). In this way, Deleuze argues, the ontological difference between original and copy is defined with reference to a prior identity and resemblance. Difference itself is a derivative term, coming in third place, as it were, behind identity and resemblance: "Difference is only understood in terms of the comparative play of two similitudes: the exemplary similitude of an identical original and the imitative similitude of a more or less accurate copy" (Deleuze 1968, p. 166). The theory of Forms thus provides key elements on which subsequent metaphysics was able to build. In this respect, Deleuze argues, "Platonism thus founds the entire domain that philosophy will later recognize as its own: the domain of representation filled by copies-icons and defined not by an extrinsic relation to the object, but by an intrinsic relation to the model or foundation. The Platonic model is the Same, in the sense that Plato says that Justice is nothing more than just . . . The Platonic copy is the similar: the pretender who possesses in a secondary way" (Deleuze 1990, p. 259).

With Plato, Deleuze argues, we see a philosophical decision of the utmost importance being taken, that of subordinating difference to the primary relations of identity and resemblance. However, precisely because Plato was the first to theorize the world of representation, and because he does so with only the meager resources of the theory of Forms, this conceptual configuration does not go unchallenged within the dialogues. The subordination of difference to identity in Platonism, he suggests, is analogous to the situation of a recently captured wild animal, whose resistance testifies to its untamed nature—soon to be lost—better than would its behavior in a natural state (Deleuze 1968, p. 83). In particular, the ordered and hierarchical world of representation is constantly threatened by figures of another kind, or another nature, whose essence lies precisely not in resemblance to the real nature of things, but in their capacity to simulate such natures. Chief among these is the archenemy of the Platonic philosopher, the Sophist, who is described as "a sort of wizard, an imitator of real things" (*Sophist*, 235a). At the end of the dialogue, Socrates defines the Sophist by his power to simulate or "mimic" the wise, mimicry having been defined in turn as the production of semblances using one's own person as instrument. As such, he concludes that "the Sophist was not among those who have knowledge, but he has a place among mimics" (*Sophist*, 267e). Similarly, writing, which is described in the *Phaedrus* as "a kind of image" of living discourse, does not produce true wisdom, but only its semblance (*Phaedrus*, 275b, 276a). Finally, the "imitative poets" discussed in book 10 of the *Republic* do not produce imitations of the true nature of things, but only imitations of their appearances (*phantasma*). As such, they threaten to corrupt the minds of all those who do not possess the antidote of knowledge (*Republic*, 595b). Because of this, Socrates recommends their exclusion from the ideal community: "On this, then, as it seems, we are fairly agreed, that the imitator knows nothing worth mentioning of the things he imitates, but that imitation is a form of play, not to be taken seriously, and that those who attempt tragic poetry . . . are altogether imitators" (*Republic*, 602b).

It may seem that the difference between these two figures is a difference within the order of representation itself. On the one hand, the poets who recount myths are assimilated to painters and condemned as "altogether imitators." On the other hand, Socrates himself has recourse to myth in the *Phaedrus* in order to explain the true nature of love, thereby painting "after a fashion, a picture of the lover's experience in which perhaps we attained some degree of truth" (*Phaedrus*, 265b). On this basis, it is tempting to suggest that the ambivalence within Platonism with regard to representation emerges within the concept of imitation (*mimēsis*), in terms of which the order of representation is defined, threatening the very coherence of that concept. One might therefore seek to undermine the Platonic order of representation from within, by arguing that the very concept of imitation/ representation is infected with the same kind of ambivalence or indeterminacy found in other terms such as *pharmakon*.

This is the strategy adopted by Derrida in his brief discussion of the notion of imitation in "Plato's Pharmacy" (Derrida 1981, pp. 137–139). He argues that the very deficiency for which Plato condemns the painters and poets is already present in the notion of imitation. Painters only represent the bed as seen from a certain angle, thereby internalizing in their images a certain difference between the appearance and the bed itself: "Does a couch differ from itself according as you view it from the side or the front or in any other way? Or does it differ not at all in fact though it appears different, and so of other things?" (*Republic*, 598a). However, copies already internalize a difference between themselves and the object copied, necessarily so if they are to remain copies or imitations. Derrida is here relying upon the argument of the *Cratylus*, to the effect that a perfect imitation is no longer an imitation at all but another instance of the same thing.[3] In other words, imitation or copying depends upon the maintenance of a difference between the copy and the thing imitated: "If one eliminates the tiny difference that, in separating the imitator from the imitated, by that very fact refers to it, one would render the imitator absolutely different: the imitator would become another being no longer referring to the imitated" (Derrida 1981, p. 139). The concept of imitation appears to cover a continuum: at one end of the scale, imitation becomes the reproduction of the real itself, the repetition of the same; at the other end, where it copies only the appearance of the thing, it becomes mere simulation. Whereas the poets are rejected by Plato because they produce mere simulacra, Derrida suggests not without irony that writing, which Plato elsewhere describes as "a kind of image" of living speech, imitates speech perfectly because it no longer imitates at all. Imitation (*mimēsis*) is thus an inherently ambivalent concept, Derrida argues, structurally analogous to *pharmakon*:

> [I]mitation affirms and sharpens its essence in effacing itself. Its essence is its nonessence. And no dialectic can encompass this self-inadequation. A perfect imitation is no longer an imitation . . . Imitation does not correspond to its essence, is not what it is—imitation—unless it is in some way at fault or rather in default. It is bad by nature. Since (de)fault is inscribed within it, it has no nature; nothing is properly its own. Ambivalent, playing with itself by hollowing itself out, good and evil at once—undecidably, *mimēsis* is akin to the *pharmakon* (Derrida 1981, p. 139).

For Deleuze, by contrast, the difference between two kinds of imitation or copy is only apparently a distinction drawn within the realm of representation itself. In reality, it is a distinction between those figures that truly or internally resemble what they appear to resemble, and those which only superficially resemble that of which they are images. Between copies and simulacra there is no common ground, they are not like two species of the same genus but two completely different kinds of being. It is sometimes suggested that the distinction is one between more or less degenerate copies, copies more or less removed from the original, as suggested by the trilogy of Form-couch-imitation in *Republic* book 10. Deleuze insists that this obscures the real difference, which is one of kind. In the *Sophist*, Plato draws a distinction among images themselves between "likenesses" (copies) and "semblances" (simulacra) (*Sophist*, 236b–c). The former truly resemble the original, as in the example of life-size portraiture, which "consists in creating a copy that conforms to the proportions of the original in all three dimensions and giving moreover the proper color to every part" (*Sophist,*, 235e). The latter only appear to be likenesses to the unfavorably placed spectator. To a spectator with an adequate view of the illusory object it "would not even be like the original it professes to resemble" (*Sophist*, 236b). The class of such semblances would include, for example, sculptures of colossal size, which involve distortion of the true proportions so that the figure appears correct to the observer; or the image produced by a painter, which only appears to be a bed when seen from a certain angle in front of the frame.

The difference between likenesses (copies) and semblances (simulacra) is a matter of the basis of resemblance in each case: identity of dimensions, proportions, and tones in the one case; superficial or apparent resemblance on the basis of difference from the original in the other. Copies represent the Forms because they resemble them. They share an internal, spiritual resemblance with the ultimately real things themselves. In this sense, Deleuze argues, the Platonic model is defined by its self-identity, while the copy is defined by its exemplary similarity to the model. By contrast, the simulacrum "is built upon a disparity or upon a difference, it internalizes a dissimilarity" (Deleuze 1990, p. 258). Thus, in the case of the colossal sculptures, the appearance of correct proportion is only produced by the departure from parallel proportions, by the difference between the internal relations of the illusory copy and those of the figure it resembles. Or in the case of the painter, the appearance of a bed necessarily internalizes one perspective on the object, thus a difference between a bed and any such appearance of a bed. In sum, simulacra produce an effect of resemblance, but only on the basis of internal differences between themselves and the object resembled. With simulacra, the priority of identity and sameness over difference, which characterizes the world of representation, is reversed.

The exclusion of the poets is supported by the claim that they do not imitate the real nature of those things of which they speak, but only their appearances. For this claim to be sustained in turn, Plato needs some criterion for distinguishing between proper imitations or representations and simulacra. Similarly, in order to secure the crucial differences between the philosopher and the Sophist, or between speech and writing, there must be some criterion for distinguishing between the two terms in each case. On this basis, Deleuze argues, "the whole of Platonism . . . is dominated by the idea of drawing a distinction between 'the thing itself' and the simulacra" (Deleuze 1968, p. 91). This, rather than the opposition between Forms and imitations or representations, is the crucial task of Platonism. Deleuze argues that the intention of Platonism is not just to distinguish the true claimant from the false, but to exclude the latter, thereby establishing the priority of the well-founded copies, and repressing the simulacra. "Platonism as a whole is erected on the basis of this wish to hunt down the phantasms or simulacra which are identified with the Sophist himself, that devil, that insinuator or simulator, that always disguised and displaced false pretender" (Deleuze 1968, p. 166). Frequently, this result is achieved by recourse to myths, such as the account of the soul as a winged chariot in the *Phaedrus*. Deleuze argues that such myths are precisely the means by which Plato's method of division is able to provide a foundation for the distinction it seeks to draw between true claimants and mere pretenders.

But why this desire to repress or exclude simulacra? It would be easy to interpret the hostility toward the poets in the *Republic* book 10, as little more than a self-serving exercise designed to establish and protect the cultural authority of those equipped with the antidote of knowledge. The use of the theory of Forms to draw a threefold distinction between truth, opinion, and mere illusion allows Plato to disqualify the poets from the ranks of those who know. However, is this anything more than a rhetorical exercise that implies, but does not prove, that philosophers are able to represent the true nature of things? Perhaps it is not, but the argument serves a deeper, moral purpose, as the remainder of the argument against the poets shows. Whereas poets have a tendency to corrupt the minds even of the good, and to encourage and nourish the lower parts of the soul, the Platonic philosopher embodies a different kind of world: a stable and hierarchical world without excessive emotion, where neither persons nor things appear as other than they are. This is a world that prefers the calm, ordered life of the soul governed by reason to the disorderly and passionate life of the soul moved by poetry. "What appears then, in its purest state, before the logic of representation could be deployed, is a moral vision of the world. It is in the first instance for these moral reasons that simulacra must be exorcised and difference thereby subordinated to the same and the similar" (Deleuze 1968, p. 166). It is this desire to exorcise simulacra that ensures the primacy of identity and the subjection of difference. In Plato's case, Deleuze argues, "a moral motivation in all its purity is avowed: the will to eliminate simulacra or phantasms has no motivation apart from the moral. What is condemned in the figure of simulacra is the state of free, oceanic differences, of nomadic distributions and crowned anarchy, along with all that malice which challenges both the notion of the model and that of the copy" (Deleuze 1968, p. 341).

Given this understanding of Platonism, Deleuze's manner of overturning it is, at one level, a straightforward reversal: "Overturning Platonism then

COLLEGE OF THE SEQUOIAS
LIBRARY

means denying the primacy of original over copy, of model over image; glorifying the reign of simulacra and reflections" (Deleuze 1968, p. 92). However, given that simulacra are defined in terms of their power to create an illusion of sameness, to assert the primacy of simulacra is also to deny the very existence of the world of representation. For to the extent that simulacra do imitate the appearances of things, they threaten to undermine the very possibility of distinguishing between true and false, or between things themselves and mere illusions. In line with his suggestion that Plato himself provides the means to overturn Platonism, Deleuze suggests that this is what occurs at the end of the *Sophist*: the Eleatic Stranger offers a definition of the Sophist such that he can no longer be distinguished from Socrates himself. "Socrates distinguishes himself from the Sophist, but the Sophist does not distinguish himself from Socrates, placing the legitimacy of such a distinction in question." (Deleuze 1968, p. 168) Twilight of the icons .

To assert the primacy of simulacra is to affirm a world in which difference rather than sameness is the primary relation. In such a world, there are no ultimate foundations or original identities; everything assumes the status of a simulacrum. Things are constituted by virtue of the differential relations that they enter into, both internally and in relation to other things. This is a world of bodies defined only by their differential intensities or powers to affect and be affected, a world of qualitative multiplicities defined only by their powers of transmutation, a world of rhizomatic assemblages and nomadic war-machines. In such a world, the mode of individuation of things would be more akin to that of an electrical signal, understood as that which flashes between differential potentials, or to that of haecceities, understood as complex configurations of intensities. In this sense, Deleuze's "overturning" of Platonism prefigures the means by which he develops a conception of a world in which the play of difference rather than the relations of identity and resemblance expresses the nature of things. Asserting the primacy of simulacra thus "makes the Same and the Similar, the model and the copy, fall under the power of the false (phantasm). It renders the order of participation, the fixity of distribution, the determination of hierarchy impossible. It establishes a world of nomadic distributions and crowned anarchies" (Deleuze 1990, p. 263).

Because this "overturning" is also a means of overcoming the order of representation, Deleuze's critical strategy may appear to resemble the double gesture of deconstruction. It appears to involve a similar succession of phases: first, the overturning of the hierarchy established between identity and difference, and the resultant affirmation of a conception of thought based upon difference, where sameness becomes a derivative or resultant effect; second, and as a result of this initial overturning, the very structure of representation, which established the hierarchy in the first place, is dissolved: "The simulacrum is not a degraded copy. It harbors a positive power which denies the original and the copy, the model and the reproduction" (Deleuze 1990, p. 262). The excluded term thus returns to disorganize and subvert the very structure that ensured its exclusion. However, this apparent resemblance conceals a fundamental difference between Deleuze and the strategy of deconstruction. Whereas the Derridean response to the primacy of identity within Platonism is to seek to reduce its stable structures of opposition to shifting sands of ambivalence or undecidability, the Deleuzian response amounts to pursuing differences such as that between copies and simulacra to the point at which they become differences in kind. In this case, the difference in kind emerges with regard to the concept of difference itself.

Derrida does not pursue the interrogation of representation in Plato beyond showing that difference is internal to both the notion of simulacrum and that of likeness or copy itself. In particular, he does not ask whether it is in fact the same difference in each case. That it is the same is suggested by the fact that he refers to simulacra as copies of copies (Derrida 1981, p. 138).[4] In the case of the imitation of appearances, the difference between imitator and imitated, which is necessary for imitation to occur, is redoubled. It is of this difference in the second degree which makes the product a simulacrum rather than a copy. The simulacrum would then be a second-order copy, the difference between copy and original redoubled. This understanding of simulacra is explicitly rejected by Deleuze: "If we say of the simulacrum that it is a copy of a copy, an infinitely degraded icon, an infinitely loose resemblance, we then miss the essential, that is the difference in nature between simulacrum and copy" (Deleuze 1990, p. 257). In other words, Deleuze does ask whether it is the same difference in each case, and answers in the negative. His answer relies upon the claim that Plato himself introduces a qualitative distinction between two kinds of imitation: good imitations or copies and bad imitations or simulacra. The difference between them depends upon the nature of the similitude in each case; for the good copies, an exemplary similitude based upon a sameness of proportion, or "internal resemblance" to the thing itself; for the bad copies or simulacra, an apparent resemblance based upon difference in proportion, or difference in kind from the thing itself.

The difference between these two kinds of imitation, however, affects the nature of the difference between the imitation and the imitated in each case. In the case of the good copies, the difference between imitation/copy and original is a difference within resemblance, so to speak; a difference between things that are in the essential respects the same. Within the Platonic world of representation, difference is a secondary or derived relation, the similarity of the copy to original (hence their sameness or generic identity) being primary. The difference between a simulacrum and what it simulates, by contrast, is of another order altogether. The simulacrum is not in essential respects the same as what it simulates, but different. Although it reproduces the appearance of the original, it does so as an effect. Here, the apparent identity of the two is the secondary, derived relation, while it is their difference that is primary. Deleuze takes this feature of simulacra as the basis for identifying another conception of difference, a "free difference" not subject to the structure of representation that governs the Platonic universe.

Aesthetic modernity provides Deleuze with one example of a world in which difference has free reign. He suggests that modernity is defined by the power of the simulacrum (Deleuze 1990, p. 265). Since simulacra in turn are defined by their power to produce an effect of resemblance by means of difference, the power of the simulacrum is equivalent to the power of repetition, in the sense in which Deleuze opposes repetition to representation. Just as difference takes on a new sense within the context of a world in which difference is the primary relation, so repetition in this context is no longer repetition understood as the recurrence of the same. Art has always involved repetition, but repetition in the sense that simulacra "repeat": "Art does not imitate, above all because it repeats . . . (an imitation is a copy, but art is simulation)" (Deleuze 1968, p. 375). The distinctive feature of modern art is that it has come to appreciate this aspect of its own nature. One of the exemplary moments at which it does so is in pop art.

With pop, art became conscious of itself as the production of simulacra. Warhol's "serial" works, with their reproductions of newspaper and publicity photographs in different tones and sizes, self-consciously draw attention to the manner in which they reproduce images of images. However, because these works repeat images, thereby simulating a pervasive feature of modern life, they risk missing the essential point in relation to the simulacral character of art. Even before those works, Warhol had exhibited a whole room full of simulacra at his Stable Gallery show in 1964: hundreds of plywood boxes silk-screened so as to closely resemble boxes of Brillo, Campbell's soup, Kellogg's Cornflakes, and other supermarket merchandise.[5] However, Warhol was not engaged in trompe l'oeil. It is important to distinguish the material objects exhibited by Warhol, which were simulacra in the strict Platonic sense, from the artwork proper, which, as Arthur Danto has convincingly shown, cannot be identified with its material support.[6] Warhol's installation makes the point that artistic invention (the production of difference within the art world) is possible using simulacra as the material support. His choice of banal objects to simulate only serves to emphasize the fact that it is not the resemblance to real objects that makes these artworks. More generally, this work shows that art is a matter of simulation, but that simulation is a matter of displaced or disguised repetition. Simulation is the production of an effect rather than the reproduction of an appearance. The effect in question may be an effect of resemblance, or may be produced by means of an effect of resemblance, but these have no particular privilege in a world of simulacra.

To the extent that Warhol's work still plays with the idea of representation, it is not the most appropriate aesthetic correlate to Deleuze's nonrepresentational conception of thought. Abstract expressionism is perhaps a better example: the huge canvases of Pollock or Newman make no attempt to represent anything—unless perhaps in the paradoxical sense in which Kant speaks of representing the unrepresentable—but every attempt to transmit states of experience or to produce effects in the viewer. It is with this function of art that Deleuze seeks to align a nonrepresentational conception of thought. Concepts would no longer be considered images of things, but things in their own right, which might transmit intensities or provide means of interaction with other events and processes. The countertradition in the history of philosophy provides numerous instances of such a practice of thought. For example, Deleuze proposes a "double reading" of Spinoza's thought, such that it would be defined not just in terms of its extraordinary conceptual apparatus, but also in terms of the effects or vital impulses generated by the *Ethics*, and which make Spinoza "an encounter, a passion" (Deleuze 1988, p. 130). Kierkegaard and Nietzsche are also precursors in this project, insofar as they can be considered creators "of an incredible equivalent of theater within philosophy" (Deleuze 1968, p. 16). This is a theater that deploys concepts as signs capable of directly affecting the souls of readers. The practice of philosophy that is entailed by Deleuze's nonrepresentational conception of thought is therefore one that embraces precisely that power of poetry that rendered it most dangerous in Plato's eyes.

Notes

I am grateful to Moira Gatens and Paul Thom for their helpful comments on this paper.

1. On philosophy, see, for example, Jean-François Lyotard, "Presenting the Unpresentable: the Sublime," *Artforum* 20, no. 8 (1984). On painting, see Arthur Danto, "The End of Art," *The Philosophical Disenfranchisement of Art* (New York: Columbia University Press, 1986) and "Approaching the End of Art," *The State of the Art* (New York: Prentiss Hall, 1987).

2. "My philosophy reversed Platonism: the farther from true beings, all the more purer more beautiful better it is. Life in illusion as goal" (Stanley Rosen, *The Ancients and the Moderns: Rethinking Modernity* [New Haven and London: Yale University Press, 1989], p. 210).

3. "Let us suppose the existence of two objects. One of them shall be Cratylus, and the other an image of Cratylus, and we will suppose, further, that some god makes not only a representation such as a painter would make of your outward form and color, but also creates an

inward organization like yours, having the same warmth and softness, and into this infuses motion, and soul, and mind, such as you have, and in a word copies all your qualities, and places them by you in another form. Would you say that this was Cratylus and the image of Cratylus, or that there were two Cratyluses? Cratylus: I should say that there were two Cratyluses" (*Cratylus,* 432b–c).

4. Christopher Norris restates this conception of simulacra: "It is on these grounds that Plato argues his case against poetry, along with other forms of aesthetic mimesis. For what the mind is taken in by when it credits such manifest illusions is in truth the mere copy of a copy . . . This bad mimesis thus operates at a double remove from reality" (Christopher Norris, *Derrida* [London: Fontana, 1987], p. 61).

5. Charles F. Stuckey, "Warhol in Context," in G. Garrels, ed., *The Work of Andy Warhol* (Seattle: Bay Press, 1989), p. 14.

6. Arthur Danto, *The Transfiguration of the Commonplace* (Cambridge, Mass.: Harvard University Press, 1981). In arguing this point, Danto also makes use of Borges's story "Pierre Menard, Author of Don Quixote."

IV. The Question of Becoming-Woman

9

Toward a New Nomadism: Feminist Deleuzian Tracks; or, Metaphysics and Metabolism

Rosi Braidotti

Beispiele paranormaler Tonbandstimmen
Was sind paranormale Tonbandstimmen?
Es sind Stimmen unbekannte herkunft.
Es sind paranormaler Tonbandstimmen.
—Laurie Anderson, "Example #22," Big Science

Introduction

FEMINISTS' RELATIONSHIP to Deleuze's thought is ambivalent. In this paper I will try to spell out the points of intersection between the Deleuzian project to transform the images of thought and feminist theorists' figurations of changing female subjectivities, taking as my guiding light the notion of materialism. I will approach "feminist theory" not in a monolithic mode, but in Deleuze's sense of the problematic one.[1] It refers both to a political practice and a discursive field marked by a specific set of methodological and epistemological premises, which I would call the political practice of sexual difference. This practice is the claim to material and symbolic recognition on the part of politically motivated women: the "female feminist subject"[2] is a new epistemological and political entity to be defined and affirmed by women in the confrontation of their multiple differences, of class, race, sexual preference.[3]

Feminist thought is the movement that makes sexual difference operative, through the strategy of fighting for the social equality of the sexes. Feminism

159

is the question; the affirmation of sexual difference as positivity is the answer. Feminist thought aims to locate and situate the grounds for the new female feminist subjectivity. Feminism is about not restoring another memory, but rather installing a countermemory, that is to say, to paraphrase Foucault, a critical genealogy. Accordingly, I see feminist theory today as the activity aimed at articulating the questions of individual gendered identity with issues related to political subjectivity, connecting them with the problems of knowledge and epistemological legitimation.

I would like to pursue here the central notion of feminist poststructuralism, namely, the revaluation of metadiscursive language, which Jane Flax describes as the metamethodological mode[4] and Teresa de Lauretis, as critical theory.[5] At this particular moment of feminist theory,[6] it is urgent to think about the nature and the status both of thinking in general and of the specific activity known as theory. One of the central issues in feminist theories of subjectivity today is how to reconcile historicity, and therefore agency, with the political will to change, which entails the (unconscious) desire for the new, which, in turn, as Deleuze teaches us, implies the construction of new desiring subjects.

I want to emphasize that desire is what is at stake in the feminist project of elaborating alternative definitions of female subjectivity. The attempt to activate a discursive ethics based on sexual difference as a site of empowerment of women is both an epistemological and a political move. The question is how to determine what I call the points of exit from the phallogocentric mode, i.e., the angles through which women can gain access to a nonlogocentric mode of representation of the female feminist subject. The notion of desire in this configuration is not a prescriptive one: the desire to become and to speak as female feminist subjects does not entail the specific content of women's speech. What is being empowered is women's entitlement to speak, not the propositional content of their utterances. What I want to emphasize is women's desire to become, not a specific model for their becoming.

The feminism of sexual difference should be read as emphasizing the political importance of desire as opposed to the will, and as stressing the role of desire in the constitution of the subject. Not just libidinal desire, but rather ontological desire, the desire to be, the tendency of the subject to be, the predisposition of the subject toward being. Jean-François Lyotard, in his work on postmodernism,[7] supports this distinction and stresses its conceptual importance. The modernist project is understood, firstly, in terms of the complicity of reason, truth, and progress with domination and, secondly, as the marriage of the individual will with the concept of capital. In other words, argues Lyotard, modernism marks the triumph of the will to have, to own, to possess, with the correlative objectification of the subject; postmodernism undoes this connection, emphasizing the libidinal, i.e., unconscious roots of subjectivity.

In other words, feminist theory, far from being a reactive kind of thought, expresses women's ontological desire, women's structural need to posit themselves as female subjects, that is to say, not as disembodied entities, but rather as corporeal and consequently sexed beings. Following Adrienne Rich[8] I believe that the redefinition of the female feminist subject starts with the revaluation of the bodily roots of subjectivity and the rejection of the traditional vision of the knowing subject as universal, neutral, and consequently gender-free. This "positional" or situated way of seeing the subject is based on the understanding that the most important location or situation is the rooting of the subject into the spatial frame of the body. The first and foremost of locations in reality is one's own embodiment. Rethinking the body as our primary situation is the starting point for the epistemological side of the "politics of location," which aims at grounding the discourse produced by female feminists in a network of local, i.e., very specific conditions (sex, race, class).

The body, or the embodiment of the subject, is a key term in the feminist struggle for the redefinition of subjectivity; it is to be understood as neither a biological nor a sociological category, but rather as a point of overlap between the physical, the symbolic,[9] and the material social conditions.[10]

In other words, the starting ground for feminist redefinitions of female subjectivity is paradoxical: it is a new form of materialism that inherits the corporeal materiality of the poststructuralists (especially Foucault and Deleuze) and thus places emphasis on the embodied and therefore sexually differentiated structure of the speaking subject. The variable of sexuality has priority in the bodily materialism thus advocated. In feminist theory one *speaks as* a woman, although the subject "woman" is not a monolithic essence defined once and for all, but rather the site of multiple, complex, and potentially contradictory sets of experience, defined by overlapping variables.

The female feminist subject thus defined is one of the terms in a process that should not and cannot be streamlined into a linear, teleological form of subjectivity: it is rather the site of intersection of subjective desire with willful social transformation. As de Lauretis puts it, feminist theory embodies its own specific difference, which is the simultaneous "double pull" of critical negativity (the deconstruction of phallo-logocentric knowledge) and the "affirmative positivity of its politics." Feminist thought is "a developing theory of the female-sexed or female-embodied social subject, whose constitution and whose modes of social and subjective existence include most obviously sex and gender, but also race, class and any other significant sociocultural divisions and representations; a developing theory of the female-embodied social subject that is based on its specific, emergent, conflictual history."[11]

The feminist subject of knowledge as "eccentric"[12] is an intensive, multiple subject, functioning in a net of interconnections. I would add that it is rhizomatic, embodied, and, therefore, perfectly artificial; as an artifact it is machinic, complex, endowed with multiple capacities for interconnectedness in the impersonal mode. It is abstract and perfectly, operationally real.

The task for feminist theory is how to think of identity as a site of differences. Women occupy different subject-positions at different times; the task is also how to think through this multiplicity. In turn, this puts a great deal of emphasis on the question of how to rethink alterity and otherness. What is at stake here is how to restore intersubjectivity so as to allow differences to create a bond—a political contract among women—so as to affect lasting political changes. It is the affirmation of a new kind of bonding, a collectivity resting on the recognition of differences, in an inclusive, i.e., nonexclusionary manner.

This definition of the feminist subject as a multiple, complex process is also an attempt to rethink the unity of the subject, without reference to humanistic beliefs and without dualistic oppositions, linking instead body and mind in a new flux of self. The implications are far-reaching. The first level is the issue of what counts as human in a posthumanist world. What is at stake in the question is how to evolve forms of representation for the alternative female feminist subjectivity: what is the form of thought best suited to a feminist humanity, i.e., to a feminist collective subject?

The second issue concerns feminism specifically, and it involves the challenge to reassemble a vision of subjectivity after the certainties of gender dualism and sexual polarization have collapsed, privileging notions of process, complexity, and the multilayered technology of the self. In other words, feminism is about accountability; it is about grounding a new epistemology and a situated ethics; it is about foundations.

All other differences notwithstanding—and they are considerable—I want to argue that the various feminist figurations of a new female subjectivity gain by intersecting with Deleuze's project of transforming the very image we have of thinking, and with his new vision of subjectivity as an intensive, multiple, and discontinuous process of interrelations. The aim is what bell hooks rightly calls "radical postmodernism,"[13] namely, the bringing about of an antirelativistic, specific community of historically located, semiotic, material subjects, seeking connections and articulations in a manner that is neither ethnic- nor gender-centered. And the question is how to do so concretely, in the here and now of the feminist political practice.

Rhizomatic Thinking[14]

The imperative to think differently about our historical condition brings critical philosophers like Deleuze together with feminist intellectuals; they share a concern for the urgency, the necessity, to redefine, refigure, and reinvent theoretical practice, and philosophy with it, in a mode that is not molar/reactive/sedentary, but rather molecular/active/nomadic. The central concern that ties them together is the crisis of the philosophical logos and the need to invent new images of thought to put in place of the classical system of representation of theoretical thought. The challenge for feminism and philosophy alike is how to think about and adequately account for changes and changing conditions: not static formulated truths, but the living process of transformation.

In a previous study[15] on Deleuze, I ran a two-pronged argument: while stating my skepticism at the idea of a "crisis" of the philosophical subject that takes place at the same time as the historical emergence of women as a political and theoretical force, I argued for the relevance and usefulness of Deleuze's critique of the language of metaphysics to feminist theory. I stressed the point that Deleuze is relevant not only for what he has to say about women, the positivity of desire,[16] or sexuality and embodied, sexed identities. Of rather greater relevance is the redefinition of thinking, and especially of the theoretical process, as a nonreactive mode that accompanies Deleuze's new vision of subjectivity.

These two points are interrelated. The embodiment of the subject is for Deleuze a form of bodily materiality, but not of the natural, biological kind. He rather takes the body as the complex interplay of highly constructed social and symbolic forces. The body is not an essence, let alone a biological substance. It is a play of forces, a surface of intensities: pure simulacra without originals. Deleuze is therefore of great help to feminists because he deessentializes the body, sexuality, and sexed identities. The embodied subject is a term in a process of intersecting forces (affects), spatiotemporal variables that are characterized by their mobility, changeability, and transitory nature.

Accordingly, thinking is for Deleuze not the expression of in-depth interiority, or the enactment of transcendental models; it is a way of establishing connections among a multiplicity of impersonal forces.

I think that the most fruitful starting point for a feminist adaptation of Deleuze's thought is precisely his effort to image the activity of thinking differently.

In his determination to undo the Western style of theoretical thought, Deleuze moves beyond the dualistic oppositions that conjugate the monological discourse of phallo-logocentrism.

Quoting Scotus, Deleuze stresses the extent to which, in Western thought, being is univocal, it is One, the Same, and it asserts its sameness through a series of hierarchically ordained differences. In other words, the classical notion of the subject treats difference as a subset of the concept of identity as sameness, that is to say, adequation to a normative idea of a being that remains one and the same in all its varied qualifications and attributes.

This univocity has been captured by the moral discourse of Western metaphysics, which therefore rests on an inherently normative image of thought. Modernity is for Deleuze the moment when this image collapses, opening the way to other forms of representation.

In trying to define the conceptual landscape of modernity, Deleuze goes back to the classical roots of materialism. In so doing, he gives a genealogical line of thinking that, through Lucretius, the empiricists, Spinoza, and Nietzsche, emphasizes activity, joy, affirmation, and dynamic becoming. Deleuze opposes it to the "sedentary," guilt-ridden, life-denying moralizing tone of most Western philosophy: a dogmatic image of thought that Deleuze tracks all the way down to psychoanalysis.

Adopting Nietzsche's figurative style of speech, Deleuze dubs as "slave morality" Lacan's negative vision of desire, his metaphysical notion of the unconscious, and his emphasis on castration and repression.[17] Deleuze explodes the myth of interiority and in so doing undermines psychoanalysis in its very foundations—the notions of desire as negativity and the unconscious as a neometaphysical container of deep "inner" truths. He prefers to posit the unconscious in terms of displacement and production, and desire as affirmation. He stresses the importance of thinking "difference" not as the reactive pole of a binary opposition organized so as to affirm the power and primacy of the same. What Deleuze aims at is the affirmation of difference in terms of a multiplicity of possible differences; difference as the positivity of differences. In turn, this leads him to redefine the unconscious not as the deep container of yet-unknown sources, but rather as marking the structural noncoincidence of the subject with his/her consciousness. This noncoincidence is a radical disjunction that separates the thinking subject from the illusion of plenitude and self-transparence, the monolithic image of the self that rests on the phallo-logocentric system.

The rejection of the principle of adequation to and identification with a phallo-logocentric image of thought lies at the heart of the nomadic vision of subjectivity that Deleuze proposes as the new, postmetaphysical figuration of the subject. Deleuze argues and acts upon the idea that the activity of thinking cannot and must not be reduced to reactive (Deleuze says "sedentary") critique. Thinking can be critical if by critical we mean the active, assertive process of inventing new images of thought—beyond the old icon where thinking and being joined hands together under the Sphinx-like smile of the sovereign phallus. Thinking for Deleuze is instead life lived at the highest possible power—thinking is about finding new images. Thinking is about change and transformation.

It is important to stress that the new subjectivity proposed by Deleuze is eminently political: his is the kind of poststructuralist thought that aims at reconnecting theory with daily practices of resistance. Foremost among Deleuze's concerns is the idea that the philosophy and the politics of dif-ference must take into account the experiences of oppression, exclusion, and marginality. The emphasis on "becoming," against the static nature of being, is therefore also a way of reaching for the standpoint of the exploited and excluded.

The notion of rhizome is Deleuze's leading figuration: it points to a redefinition of the activity of philosophy as the quest for new images of thought, better suited to a nomadic, disjunctive self. One of these figura-tions is the notion of an idea as a line of intensity, marking a certain degree or variation in intensity. An idea is an active state of very high intensity, which opens up hitherto unsuspected possibilities of life and action. For Deleuze, ideas are events, lines that point human thought toward new horizons. An idea is that which carries the affirmative power of life to a higher degree. The force of this notion is that it finally puts a stop to the traditional search for ideas or lines that are "just" (in theory and politics alike). For if ideas are projectiles launched into time they can be neither "just" nor "false."

For Deleuze, thought is made of sense and value: it is the force, or level of intensity, that fixes the value of an idea, not its adequation to a preestab-lished normative model. Philosophy as critique of negative, reactive values is also the critique of the dogmatic image of thought; it expresses the force, the activity of the thinking process in terms of a typology of forces (Nietzsche) or an ethology of passions (Spinoza). In other words, Deleuze's rhizomatic style brings to the fore the affective foundations of the thinking process. It is as if beyond/behind the propositional content of an idea there lay another category—the affective force, level of intensity, desire, or affirmation—that conveys the idea and ultimately governs its truth-value. Thinking, in other words, is to a very large extent unconscious, in that it expresses the desire to know, and this desire is that which cannot be adequately expressed in language, simply because it is that which sustains language. Through this intensive theory of the thinking process, Deleuze points to the prephilosophical foundations of philosophy.

Deleuze's analysis of thinking (especially in *Nietzsche and Philosophy* and *Différence et répétition*) points in fact to a sort of structural aporia in philosophical discourse. Philosophy is both logophilic and logophobic, as Foucault has already astutely remarked.[18] Discourse—the production of ideas, knowledge, texts, and sciences—is something that philosophy relates to and rests upon, in order to codify it and systematize it; philosophy is therefore logophilic. Discourse being, however, a complex network of interrelated truth-effects, it far exceeds philosophy's power of codification. So philosophy has to "run after" all sorts of new discourses (women, postcolonial subjects, the audiovisual media and other new technologies, etc.) in order to incorporate them into its way of thinking; in this respect philosophy is logophobic.

The question then becomes: What can motivate today the choice of/for philosophy? How can one go on doing philosophy? Deleuze and Irigaray, in very different ways, point to what I see as the answer: They focus on the "desire for philosophy" as an epistemophilic drive, i.e., a will to know that is fundamentally affective. They build on the logophilic side of philosophy and remind us that philosophy used to signify the love of, the desire for, higher knowledge.

Thus, quoting Spinoza and Nietzsche, Deleuze banks on the affective substratum as a force capable of freeing philosophy from its hegemonic habits. Affectivity, in this scheme, is prediscursive: There is such a thing as a prephilosophical moment in the establishment of a philosophical stance, a moment in which one chooses for philosophy. This prephilosophical moment of desire not only is unthought, but remains nonthought at the very heart of philosophy, because it is that which sustains the very activity of philosophizing.

We are faced here with the problem of what is ontologically there but propositionally excluded by necessity in the philosophical utterance. There is the unspoken and the unspeakable desire for thought, the passion for thinking, the epistemophilic substratum on which philosophy later erects its discursive monuments.

Pursuing this insight in a Spinozist mode, Deleuze rejects the phantoms of negation, putting thought at the service of creation. From this perspective, we shall call philosophy all that expresses and enriches the positivity of the subject as an intensive, libidinal entity.

The Deleuzian approach calls for a new theoretical style that resists the elaboration of dogmatic ideas, untouchable sacred dogmas sanctified by a socially dominant notion of "scientificity" or of "political correctness." Deleuze's redefinition of ideas as nomadic forms of thought offers us a theoretical defense against all mental and theoretical codifications. Innovating even on Foucault's radical notion of the text as a toolbox, Deleuze sees the philosophical text as the term in an intensive process of fundamentally extra-textual practices. These practices have to do with displacing the subject through flows of intensity or forces.

Another extremely important implication of the new conceptual scheme proposed by Deleuze is the way in which it alters the terms of the conventional pact between the writer and his/her readers. If the philosophical text is the act of reading on the model of connection, the text is relinquished into the intensive elements that both sustain the connections and are generated by them. The writer/reader binary couple is split up accordingly, and a new impersonal mode is required as the appropriate way of doing philosophy.

This impersonal style is rather "postpersonal" in that it allows for a web of connections to be drawn, not only in terms of the author's "intentions" and the reader's "reception," but rather in a much wider, more complicated set of possible interconnections that blur established, that is to say hege-monic, distinctions of class, culture, race, sexual practice, and so on. The image of the rhizome pops up here as a figuration for the kind of political subjectivity Deleuze is promoting.

As interlocutors in a Deleuzian philosophical text, we are expected to be not just traditional intellectuals and academics, but also active, interested, and concerned participants in a project of research and experimentation for new ways of thinking about human subjectivity. As readers in an intensive mode, we are transformers of intellectual energy, processors of the "insights" Deleuze is giving us. These "in"-sights are not to be thought of as plunging us inward, toward a mythical "inner" reservoir of truth. On the contrary, they are better thought of as propelling us along the multiple directions of extratextual experiences. Thinking is living at a higher degree, at a faster pace, in a multidirectional manner.

This philosophical stance imposes not only the conventional academic requirements of passionless truth, but also the passionate engagement in the recognition of the theoretical and discursive implications of rethinking the subject. It is all a question of what kind of rhizomatic connections we can draw among ourselves, here and now, in the act of doing philosophy. This choice of a theoretical style that leaves ample room to the exploration of subjectivity calls for "passionate detachment" in theory-making.[19]

I want to argue that this redefinition of the image, the practice, and the textual structure of philosophy as an activity (not as an institution, on which Deleuze has many harsh things to say) rests on a change not only of propo-sitional content, but also of speaking stance. It is my belief that the change thus advocated can be of use and inspiration to the aims of feminist theory.

The Paradoxes of Materialism

Feminism shares with other philosophies of modernity (one only has to think of the controversy between Habermas and Foucault on the nature, structure and historical span of "the modern") the dubious privilege of having an unresolved relationship toward both subjectivity and materialism.

The latter has suffered from a double cramp: that of being dialectically opposed to idealism and that of having been colonized by the tradition of historical materialism. As far as the feminist theoretical tradition is concerned, the central figure in this debate is Simone de Beauvoir.

Feminist readings of de Beauvoir in the nineties are framed by the debate that, since the seventies, has opposed the neomaterialists such as Christine Delphy[20] and Monique Wittig to the strategic essentialism of the sexual difference school, such as Hélène Cixous[21] and, especially, Luce Irigaray.

More than a debate, the confrontation between the two positions turned into a polemic, and it resulted in sterile polarizations and mutual excommunications. As the history of this period has been written[22] and the analyses are forthcoming,[23] I shall not insist on this point here. I just wish to stress both the roles that Deleuze's thought, concepts, and imagery were called upon to play in the framework of this polemic, and the innovative role his philosophy could still play in the feminist debate on an alternatively gendered subjectivity.

Previously, references to Deleuze have been rather rare in feminist theory;[24] more often than not, they have been voiced on a polemical note. For instance, in her defense of sexual difference against a hasty dismissal or deconstruction of the postmetaphysical subject, Irigaray[25] refers negatively to the Deleuzian diagram of the desiring machines. The notion of the body without organs is for Irigaray reminiscent of a condition of dispossession of the bodily self, a structurally splintered position that is traditionally associated with femininity. She points out that the emphasis on the machinic, the inorganic, as well as the notions of loss of self, dispersion, and fluidity are all too familiar to women: Is not the body without organs women's own historical condition?[26] Irigaray's critique of Deleuze is radical: She points out that the dispersal of sexuality into a generalized "becoming" results in undermining the feminist claims to a redefinition of the female subject.

Stressing that the root of the term materialism is *mater* and that the material is the site of origin of the subject, is the instance that expresses the specificity of the female subject, Irigaray reattaches materialism to its maternal roots and thus starts also the long climb toward the peaks of an alternative female symbolic.[27] Central to her projects is the quest for an alternative female genealogy,[28] to be accomplished by immersion into the maternal imaginary. For Irigaray this takes the form of the exploration of images that represent the female experience of proximity to the mother's body,[29] and the sense of a female humanity and of a female divinity.[30]

Building on this insight, I have argued that one cannot deconstruct a subjectivity one has never been fully granted control over; one cannot diffuse a sexuality that has historically been defined as dark and mysterious. In order to announce the death of the subject, one must first have gained the right to speak as one. I have concluded that Deleuze gets caught in the contradiction of postulating a general "becoming-woman" that fails to take into account the historical and epistemological specificity of the female feminist stand-point. A theory of difference that fails to take into account sexual difference leaves me, as a feminist critic, in a state of skeptical perplexity.

Or, to put it differently, Deleuze's critique of dualism acts as if sexual differentiation or gender dichotomies did not have as the most immediate and pernicious consequence the positioning of the two sexes in an asymmetrical relationship to each other.

In my reading, Irigaray's version of materialism binds together both the notions of embodiment and of sexual difference, and the link between the two is made by the political will and determination to find a better, a more adequate, representation of female subjectivity. In this line of thought, great care is taken to disengage the question of the embodied subject from the hold of naturalistic assumptions and to propose instead a vision of materialism as embodied materiality. By emphasizing the embodied structure of female subjectivity, I mean to politicize the issue, and by setting the questions of political subjectivity in the framework of a critique of phallo-logocentrism, I aim at the empowerment of women. Embodiment provides a common ground on which to postulate the political project of feminism.

Clearly, for feminist corporeal materialism, the body is not a fixed essence, a natural given. In a postpsychoanalytic mode—which I choose to use with Nietzsche and, more specifically, with Deleuze—the "body" as theoretical *topos* is an attempt to overcome the classical mind-body dualism of Cartesian origins, in order to think anew about the structure of the thinking subject. The body is then an interface, a threshold, a field of intersecting material and symbolic forces. The body is a surface where multiple codes (race, sex, class, age, etc.) are inscribed; it is a linguistic construction that capitalizes on energies of a heterogeneous, discontinuous, and unconscious nature. The body, which, for de Beauvoir, was one's primary "situation" in reality, is now seen as a situated self, as an embodied positioning of the self.

If the reader finds this difficult to visualize, s/he can just think of the body art of Laurie Anderson—the contemporary performing artist who cables herself to a series of wonder-making computers and wears acoustic masks in order to subtract herself from the gaze of the audience that would fix her to a feminized, i.e., objectified, position.[31] Think also of Barbara Kruger,[32] who takes photographs all the better to show the unrepresentable aspects of female subjectivity and sexuality, and of many other women artists.[33] A great number of contemporary feminist performers offer perfect examples of counterrepresentations or affirmations of denaturalized, deessentialized bodies, which they turn into fields of alternative signification.

To sum up this theory of sexual difference, I would emphasize these features: Firstly, the belief that "woman" is that which is excluded in the masculine system of representation, because she is in excess of it and as such she is unrepresentable. "Woman" thus marks the possibility of an-other system of representation.

Secondly, this belief turned into the textual strategy of *mimesis*. This means that the quest for a point of exit from phallo-logocentric definitions of "woman" requires a strategy of working through the images and representations that the (masculine) knowing subject has created of woman as other. Irigaray's mimesis is a way of retracing backward the multilayered levels of signification, or representations, of women. In other words, "woman" is the anchoring point from which, through strategically motivated repetitions, new definitions and representations can emerge. It is an active process of becoming.[34]

Thirdly, sexual difference requiring the opening out toward issues of transcendence and universality. It is precisely on this point that sexual difference has often been criticized: for its globalizing tendency that cancels out all other differences by submitting them to its overarching importance. This is a very powerful objection, which I regret not to be able to pursue here.[35]

The assertion of sexual difference challenges the centuries-old identifications of the thinking subject with the universal and of both of them with the masculine. It posits as radically other a female, sexed, thinking subject, who stands in an asymmetrical relationship to the masculine. The apparent repetition or reassertion of feminine positions is a discursive strategy that engenders difference. For if there is no symmetry between the sexes, women must speak their own embodied version of the feminine; they must think it, write it, and represent it in their own terms.

It is precisely on the basis of the asymmetry between the sexes that Irigaray, while remaining very close conceptually to Deleuze's structures of thought, and especially his emphasis on the positive role of the unconscious in the production of theoretical discourse, is nonetheless politically opposed to his proposal of "becoming" as a way of overcoming the sexual bipolarization. Where the two differ, in other words, is in the political priority that must be granted to the elaboration of adequate systems of representation for an alternative female subject.

In my view, the paradox of Irigaray's position is that, while it is based on a notion of materiality that I find very deessentialized, it seems to move ineluctably toward issues of transcendence and incorporeal materiality. This tendency is explicit in her work on the "divine," where she argues that the female being can carry her femaleness all the way into the recognition of a common link among all women. In other words, the portion of being that a woman is, is sexed female; it is sensible matter, endowed with sex-specific forms of transcendence. By advocating a feminine form of transcendence through "radical immanence,"[36] Irigaray postulates a definition of the body not only as material, but also as the threshold to a generalist notion of female being, a new feminist humanity.

This materialism is not one, but rather involves the assertion of the importance of a multiplicity that can make sense, i.e., grant symbolic recognition to women's way of being. Like the first stone of a new civilization, Irigaray's "divine" aims at materializing for feminist practice the *a priori* conditions for achieving changes in our symbolic as well as material structures. No bodily materialism without transcendence; no female embodied subject without incorporeality. I think that the position of strategic essentialism invites the reader to dwell upon this paradox and not to seek hasty ways out of this vicious ontological circle.

Another, and quite opposite, example of feminist readings of Deleuze is the way in which Judith Butler[37] adapts Monique Wittig's[38] appeals to some of Deleuze's ideas, in her vehement critique of Irigaray's notion of "difference."[39] In her attack on the concept of difference in general and of sexual difference in particular as being biologically deterministic, Wittig calls upon Deleuze to defend her politicoepistemological hypothesis of a multiple, nonphallic sexuality. Speaking on behalf of the gay and lesbian movement, Wittig starts from the assumption that "the official discourse on sexuality is today only the discourse of psychoanalysis that builds on the *a priori* and idealist concept of sexual difference, a concept that historically participates in the general discourse of domination." She consequently argues that "for us there are, it seems, not one or two sexes but many [cf. Guattari and Deleuze], as many sexes as there are individuals. For though they have enclosed us in a sexual ghetto, we do not accord to sexuality the same importance as heterosexuals."[40]

From this perspective, Deleuze and Guattari's notion of "polysexuality" is taken as an apology not only for gay and lesbian politics, but also for the seemingly antipsychoanalytic hypothesis of "as many sexes as there are individuals."

It is important at this point to make a distinction between Butler's and Wittig's work: whereas the former is in fact firmly inscribed in the philosophical tradition, the latter is not a theoretician, but primarily a creative writer. Wittig's remarks on theory are not only scattered, but consciously polemical in their aim and style, so that one cannot speak of Wittig's system of thought at all. This does leave open for me a serious question about how Butler herself reconciles her poststructuralist outlook with her manifest sympathy for Wittig's neomaterialist approach. But I shall not pursue this point here.

It is also worth remembering that the aim of Wittig's provocative strategy is to empower women to act as authoritative speaking subjects. Here too, she opposes violently the practitioners of sexual difference—thus, contrary to Irigaray, who sees the subject-position as structurally masculine, Wittig has faith in the infinite potentials of language, in its plasticity. She therefore encourages women to use language to express their own meanings, without falling into the deconstructive complexities of Irigaray's *écriture feminine* or quests for an alternative symbolic. Contrary to Irigaray who sees the speaking position of the subject as structurally masculine (and then develops strategies for dealing with that), Wittig sees language as recyclable, malleable. She therefore encourages women to enter the subject-position, accepting therefore a position of philosophical presence: woman as the new subject of a renewed plenitude. Wittig is vehemently antipoststructuralist in rejecting the position of the split or open subject.

Wittig innovates on the classic sex/gender distinction[41] and rejects the emphasis that both Cixous and Irigaray place on what they carefully define as "female homosexual libidinal economy" and the specificity of feminine writing that goes with it. Wittig emphasizes the need to free female sexuality from its subjugation to the signifier "woman." In her view "woman" as the privileged other of the patriarchal imaginary is an idealized construction of the same order as the Phallus: it is a man-made notion, ideologically contaminated and untrustworthy. Wittig radicalizes de Beauvoir's point about the constructed nature of femininity. She proposes that we dismiss the signifier "woman" as epistemologically and politically inadequate and suggests that we replace it with the category of "lesbian." The lesbian is not a woman because a lesbian has subtracted herself from identities based on the phallus.

Butler emphasizes the fact that for Wittig "gender" is not a substantive reality, but rather an activity; she then proceeds to reinterpret Wittig's notion of "gender" as a performative utterance that constructs categories such as "sex," "women," "men," "nature" for the specifically political purpose of reproducing compulsory heterosexuality. Gender is the process by which women are marked off as "the female sex," men are conflated with the universal, and both of them are subjugated to the institution (in Foucault's sense)[42] of compulsory heterosexuality. Insofar as the lesbian refuses this process, Wittig argues that she is subversive because she problematizes the whole scheme of sexuality. The strategy supported by Wittig is, according to Butler, to allow other kinds of gendered identities to proliferate: the lesbian is the first step toward exploding the monolithic structures of gender. Again, Butler's interpretation goes much further than Wittig's own texts.

Thus, in what I see as her most Deleuzian text, though it singularly lacks all reference to Deleuze's work, Wittig reiterates her rejection of anything specifically feminine, let alone *une écriture feminine*. She argues: "[W]oman cannot be associated with writing"; because "'woman' is an imaginary formation and not a concrete reality, she is the enemy's old brand-mark, which now some relish as a long-lost and hard-won attire."[43]

Dismissing as biologically deterministic and "naturalistic" all reference to feminine specificity, Wittig confronts the problem of the masculine appropriation of the universal, and the subsequent confinement of the feminine to the particular. The question is: How then can a feminist woman express notions of a general human value?

In attempting to answer this question, Wittig proposes the category of minority subject (*sujet minoritaire*); in order to gain access to the *minoritaire* position, one has to be a member of a minority, but that alone does not suffice. "A text written by a minority writer is operational only if it manages to pass off as universal the minority viewpoint."[44]

For instance, a writer like Djuna Barnes is literally and politically subversive in that, starting from her lesbian existence, she formulates views of general value for all, nonlesbians included. This kind of consciousness is what Wittig wants to defend, against the emphasis on the feminine proposed by the sexual difference theorists.

I find this argument extremely similar to Deleuze's defense of the *devenir minoritaire,* but also paradoxically opposed to his vision of the subject as a libidinal entity. Wittig, in the passage quoted at the beginning, supports the notion of polysexuality; here she stands for a notion of becoming as the deterritorialization of the subject. In both cases she, however, does not expand on her Deleuzian leanings and pushes her conclusions to a very different direction from Deleuze's epistemological nomadism. Butler's reading of Wittig therefore achieves the double aim of passing Wittig off for the philosopher she is not and introducing Deleuze in the feminist debate in a highly polemical mode.

Butler comments very critically on Wittig, whom she sees as using the language of poststructuralist theory, especially that of Deleuze, while still believing in the humanist philosophy of plenitude. For Butler, Wittig continues to support the position that valorizes the speaking subject as autonomous and universal, whereas Deleuze is committed to displacing the speaking subject from the center of discursive power. For Butler, it is as if Wittig were quite happy to simply replace the old phallic subject and his annexed feminine with the lesbian as the next authoritative, sovereign subject.

Whether her account of Wittig is satisfactory or not, Butler's analysis has the merit of pointing out that Deleuze's post-Lacanian reading of the subject as a libidinal entity, in constant displacement in language, situates desire not only as a positive force, but also as the point of vanishing of the willful, conscious self. This differs radically from any prepsychoanalytic definition of sexuality as self-determination by the individual subject, and of desire as the ideological transcription and internalization of social codes.

In other words, Butler reminds us of the necessity not to neglect the central lesson of psychoanalysis: that subjects do *not* coincide with their consciousness—that the unconscious means the impossibility of coherence for the subject. Feminists tend to mistake volition for desire, or rather to work with radically opposed definitions of desire: on the one hand, desire as the death of the sovereign subject, on the other, desire as the willful affirmation of a politically conscious one.[45]

I think that, although she occasionally quotes Deleuze's defense of polysexuality and multiple sexualities, Wittig's line of argumentation is caught in a contradiction vis-à-vis the basic assumptions of the poststructuralist framework within which Deleuze works. What makes it contradictory in my eyes is the relationship to language and the unconscious. By being so simplistic about the *locus* of social power and so relentlessly dismissive of "women" as "female sex," Wittig ends up with a paradoxically *idealist* notion of both "women," or the female sex, and of sexed identities. The latter, for Wittig, is the direct result of social imprints that are reduced to mental constructs: Identity is an idea sustained for the purpose of social control.

I want to argue that this position highlights one of the paradoxes of feminist theory in the nineties: Namely, that it is grounded on the very concepts that it must deconstruct and deessentialize in all its aspects: gender and sexual difference.

I have outlined so far two different strategies of deconstruction of traditional femininity: On the one hand, we have the strategy of extreme sexualization through embodied female subjectivity: Irigaray's "transcendence via radical immanence." On the other hand we have the rejection of femininity in favor of a position "beyond gender." To these different positions there correspond different understandings of "materialism." For Irigaray it has to do with *mater*/matter and the sexed body, hence her emphasis on verticality and transcendence. For Wittig it is a paradoxically idealist position on language and volitional changes.

I have accordingly highlighted two paradoxes: one in the quest for a new gendered universal (strategic essentialism)[46] and one in the move beyond gender, toward a third sex position (lesbian neomaterialism). These parallel paradoxes also defend and build upon quite different representations of female sexuality and more particularly of female homosexuality.[47] This is very different from the early eighties when the great feminist divide was between homo- and heterosexual theoretical frameworks. Now the debate seems to have shifted into the homosexual sphere: as Antoinette Fouque astutely observed in her comparative readings of the strategic essentialists and the lesbian materialists, on the one hand, there is female homosexuality as the foundational theory for a new vision of subjectivity (sexual difference) and, on the other, lesbianism as a radical antifoundationalism that results in the ultimate dismissal of the feminine (lesbian neomaterialism). In her witty commentary on Wittig, Fouque sums it up as follows: "Wittig is a misogyne," she says. "[S]he's phallic about women."[48] For Fouque, Wittig fails to see the implicit relationship that exists between women and the female homosexual libidinal economy. Wittig thinks that the choice of object is all that matters, whereas what counts is the structure of desire, and when it comes to that, argue Fouque, Cixous, and Irigaray, every woman is homosexual because her first and main object of desire is another woman—her mother.

I think these paradoxes in turn illuminate the ways in which each feminist position respectively appeals to Deleuze's thought: that Irigaray should criticize Deleuze's notion of multiplicity and the dispersion of sexed identities as interfering with the affirmation of a new female subjectivity while Wittig, on the contrary, should welcome it as a way out of the sexual polarizations of the gender system seems to make perfect sense. The point for me, however, is that this "adaptation" of Deleuze's work, in what I can only describe as a polemical mode, is not the most useful way of approaching his thought.

In the next section, I would like to outline another, and, for me, more creative, line of feminist intersection with the Deleuzian conceptual universe. I will argue that this new approach can also open up new perspectives for feminist theory and its many paradoxes.

Speaking Nomadically; or, Feminist Figurations

Irigaray and other strategic essentialists propose the figuration of the "woman divine" as marking forms of representation of a specific form of transcendence, a female humanity with its own forms of discursive presence. Wittig, on the other hand, suggests that we eliminate "woman" as a category of thought altogether and instead base the feminist project upon a figuration of the "lesbian" as a third sex. In juxtaposition to both, Haraway recommends new figurations of the feminist subject in the impersonal mode, tuned in to the high-technology reality of the contemporary world.

In trying to work out a new style of thought opposed to phallo-logocentrism, most feminist theorists deliberately break with the academic convention of Aristotelian linearity. The set of interconnected relationships between women and scientific theoretical discourse is such that the discussion cannot have a beginning, a middle, and an end.

This unconventional style of thinking falls into what Haraway defines[49] as the new quest for feminist figurations, that is to say, ways of representing feminist forms of knowledge that are not caught in a mimetic relationship to dominant scientific discourse. The issue about figuration is no mere formal concern, rather it marks the shift in speaking stance that I outlined earlier, and not only in terms of its propositional content.[50] The rhizomatic construction implies a new connection between the lived experience and the activity of the critical intelligence.

The rhizomatic mode is crucial to feminism: It rests on a new interconnection between the lived experience (life) and the activity of the critical, theoretical mind, with its baggage of phallo-logocentric premises. In its post-de Beauvoir phase, feminist theory aimed at bridging the dualism that is one of the marks of the phallo-logocentric mode. Feminist theory has thus asserted the extreme proximity of the thinking process to existential reality, not in a vitalistic mode, but rather as an attempt to overcome centuries-old dichotomies.[51]

Feminism, insofar as it has drawn up the parameters for an-other speaking stance, has also redefined the relation between thought and life, splitting open the conventions of rational discourse. These have been formalized in the Pythagorean table of oppositions which Lloyd analyzes in her work in philosophy:[52] body/mind, passive/active, night/day, feminine/masculine, theory/practice, nature/culture, inside/outside, etc. What is at stake in the feminist project is the redefinition of what thinking, thought, and especially theory actually mean.

The centrality of the relationship thought/life in feminism brings it close to Deleuze's attack on the binary logic of the logocentric system. Deleuze proposes to overcome the structure of thought on which the dichotomous oppositions are based, rather than simply reverse the terms of the opposition. Applied to feminism, this gives a critique of the emancipatory model of women's liberation, whose aim is—perhaps too hastily—summed up as wanting to integrate women as first-class citizens in the system of power that traditionally confined them to a secondary position. This model came under criticism by Irigaray[53] for its implicit conservatism: a mere reversal of the subordinate position leaving the general structure unchanged might have benefited some women in the short range, but in the long run it would not only have excluded large proportions of women, especially "minority women," but it would also have confirmed the basic structure of the present system. The quest for an active affirmation of differences has since emerged as the new political and theoretical focus of feminist theory and practice.

The task of giving a name, a shape, and a structure to the new feminist consciousness and, through that, to female subjectivity is precisely what the project of feminist figurations is all about. What is at stake is the quest for adequate representations of that which, by definition, cannot be expressed within the parameters of the phallo-logocentric discourse of which even the most radical of feminists is a part-time member. The idea of figurations therefore provides an answer not only to political, but also to both epistemological and aesthetic questions: How does one invent new structures of thought? Where does conceptual change start from? What are the conditions that can bring it about? Is the model of scientific rationality a suitable frame of reference in which to express the feminist subjectivity? Is the model of artistic creativity any better? Will mythos or logos prove to be a better ally in the big leap across the postmodern void?

I think that the term "transdisciplinary" is a rather adequate one in describing the new rhizomatic mode in feminism. It means going in between different discursive fields, passing through diverse spheres of intellectual discourse. The feminist theoretician today can only be "in transit," moving on, passing through, creating connections where things were previously disconnected or seemed unrelated, where there seemed to be "nothing to see." In transit, moving, displacing—this is the grain of hysteria without which there is no theorization at all.[54] In a feminist context, "transdisciplinary" also implies the effort to move on to the invention of new ways of relating, of building footbridges between notions. The epistemic nomadism I am advocating can only work, in fact, if it is properly situated, securely anchored in the "in-between" zones.

The significance of Haraway in this debate on female subjectivity is her radical redefinition of materialism.

Firmly implanted in the tradition of materialist praxis, but determined to adapt it to the postmodern condition, Haraway reminds us that rethinking the subject amounts to rethinking his/her bodily roots. The body stands for the radical materiality of the subject. I see Haraway as pursuing in a feminist way the Foucauldian and Deleuzian line about bodily materiality, though she would rather speak the language of science and technology than that of postmetaphysical philosophy. She is an utterly nonnostalgic posthuman thinker: Her conceptual universe is the high-technology world of "informatics" and telecommunications.

In this respect, she is conceptually part of the same epistemological tradition as Bachelard and Canguilhem, and consequently Foucault and Deleuze, for whom the scientific ratio is not necessarily hostile to humanistic approaches and values. Moreover, in this line of thinking, the practice of science is not seen as narrowly rationalistic, but rather allows for a broadened definition of the term, to include the play of the unconscious, dreams, and the imagination in the production of scientific discourse.

Following Foucault,[55] Haraway draws our attention to the construction and manipulation of docile, knowable bodies in our present social system. She invites us to think of what new kinds of bodies are being constructed right now, i.e., what kind of gender system is being constructed under our very noses.

Haraway also challenges the androcentrism of the poststructuralists' corporeal materialism. Thus, while sharing many of Foucault's premises about the modern regime of truth as "bio-power," Haraway also challenges his redefinition of power. Supporting Jameson's idea that a postmodernist politics is made necessary by the historical collapse of the traditional Left, and that it represents the Left's chance to reinvent itself from within, Haraway notes that contemporary power no longer works by normalized heterogeneity, but rather by networking, communication redesigns, and multiple interconnections. She concludes that Foucault "names a form of power at its moment of implosion, (and that) the discourse of bio-politics gives way to technobabble."[56]

Two points are noteworthy here: Firstly, Haraway analyzes the contemporary scientific revolution in more radical terms than Foucault does, mostly because she bases it on first-hand knowledge about today's technology. Haraway's training in biology and sociology of science are very useful here. By comparison with her approach, Foucault's analysis of the disciplining of bodies appears already out-of-date, apart from being, of course, intrinsically androcentric.

Secondly, Haraway raises a point that Deleuze also noted in his analysis of Foucault, namely, that the Foucauldian diagrams of power describe what we have already ceased to be; like all cartography, they act *a posteriori*, and therefore fail to account for the situation here and now. In this respect, Haraway opposes to Foucault's bio-power a deconstructive genealogy of the embodied subjectivities of women. Whereas Foucault's analysis rests on a nineteenth-century view of the production system, Haraway inscribes her analysis of the condition of women into an up-to-date analysis of the post-industrial system of production. Arguing that white capitalist patriarchy has turned into the "informatics of domination" (p. 162), Haraway argues that women have been cannibalized by the new technologies; they have disappeared from the field of visible social agents. The postindustrial system makes oppositional mass politics utterly redundant; a new politics must be invented, on the basis of a more adequate understanding of how the contemporary subject functions.

More than ever, therefore, the question then becomes: What counts as human in this posthuman world? How do we rethink the unity of the human subject, without reference to humanistic beliefs, without dualistic oppositions, linking instead body and mind in a new flux of self? What is the view of the self that is operational in the world of the "informatics of domination"?

Drawing her conclusions from the notion of identity as a site of differences, Haraway reminds us that feminists in the nineties must replace naive belief in global sisterhood or more strategic alliances based on common interests, with a new kind of politics, based on temporary and mobile coalitions and therefore on affinity. Arguing that "innocence and the corollary insistence on victimhood as the only ground for insight has done enough damage," Haraway calls for a kind of feminist politics that could embrace "partial, contradictory, permanently unclosed constructions of personal and collective selves" (p. 157).

Hence the importance of figurations in providing new images of thought, new forms of representation of our experience. The challenge is how to speak cogently of the technoscientific world, while maintaining a certain level of mythical wonder and admiration about it. Instead of giving in to negative assessment about the technological universe, Haraway argues that we simply need new forms of literacy in order to decode today's world. For Haraway it means the world is a semiotic and symbolic agent; not passive, not dualistically opposed to the mind, but a partner in a dialogic approach to understanding.

Figurations also entail a discursive ethics, that one cannot know properly, or even begin to understand, that toward which one has no affinity. Critical intelligence for Haraway is a form of sympathy. One should never criticize that which one is not complicitous with: Criticism must be conjugated in a nonreactive mode, a creative gesture, so as to avoid the Oedipal plot of phallo-logocentric theory.

It is in this framework that Haraway proposes a new figuration for feminist subjectivity: the cyborg. As a hybrid, or body-machine, the cyborg is a connection-making entity; it is a figure of interrelationality, receptivity, and global communication that deliberately blurs categorical distinctions (human/machine, nature/culture, male/female, Oedipal/non-Oedipal). It is a way of thinking specificity without falling into relativism. The cyborg is Haraway's representation of a generic feminist humanity; it is her answer to the question of how feminists reconcile the radical historical specificity of women with the insistence on constructing new values that can benefit humanity as a whole by redefining it radically.

Moreover, the body in the cyborg model is neither physical nor mechanical—nor is it only textual. It is rather a counterparadigm for the interaction between the inner and the external reality. It is a modern reading not only of the body, not only of machines, but rather of what goes on between them. As a new powerful replacement of the mind/body debate, the cyborg is a postmetaphysical construct.

In my reading, the figuration of the cyborg reminds us that metaphysics is not an abstract construction—it is a political ontology. The classical dualism body/soul is not simply a gesture of separation and of hierarchical coding; it is also a theory about their interaction, about how they hang together. It is a proposition, however unsatisfactory, about how we should go about rethinking the unity of the human being. In this respect, Haraway is right in stating that "the cyborg is our ontology; it gives us our politics" (p. 150). What is at stake here is the definition and the political viability of a technological form of materialism as a paradigm for a rhizomatic subjectivity.

An important moment in Haraway's cybernetic imaginary is the notion of "situated knowledges." Answering implicitly the standard humanistic accusation that emphasis on multiplicity necessarily leads to relativism, Haraway argues for a multifaceted foundational theory and an antirelativistic acceptance of differences in a historically located semiotic and material subjectivity which seeks connections and articulations in a non-gender-centered and nonethnocentric perspective.

In her rejection of classical dualism, Haraway emphasizes a network of differences, especially the differences organic/inorganic and human/machine, in opposition to the primacy granted to the binary opposition of masculine to feminine in sexual difference theories. She proposes a sort of deessentialized, embodied genealogy as the strategy to undo the dualism. She calls for political accounts of constructed embodiments, like theories of gendered racial subjectivities, which have to be situated in certain social realities so as to support claims on action, knowledge, and belief.

I see the cyborg, as a feminist figuration, to be an illuminating example of the intersection between feminist theory and Deleuzian lines of thought, in their common attempt to come to terms with the posthumanist world. Feminist figurations refer to the many, heterogeneous images feminists use to define the project of becoming-subject of women, a view of feminist subjectivity as multiplicity and process, as well as the kind of texts feminists produce. For Wittig who chooses the figuration of the "lesbian," echoed by Butler with her "parodic politics of the masquerade," many others, quoting Nancy Miller[57] prefer to become "women," i.e., the female feminist subjects of another story. If, according to Haraway, feminists can be seen as "cyborgs"[58] they can also be imaged as de Lauretis's "eccentric" subjects, or as "fellow-commuters" in an in-transit state,[59] or as "inappropriated others,"[60] or as "postcolonial"[61] subjects .

Figurations are not pretty metaphors: They are politically informed maps, which play a crucial role at this point in the cartography of feminist corporeal materialism in that they aim at redesigning female subjectivity. They are relational images; they are rhizomes. In this respect, the more figurations are disclosed in this phase of feminist practice, the better.

I think that these new figurations can be taken as an attempt to come to terms with what I have chosen to call the new nomadism of our historical condition. I have argued that the task of redefining female subjectivity requires as its preliminary method the working through of the stock of cumulated images, concepts, and representations of women and of female identity, such as they have been codified by the culture we are in. If "essence" means this stock of culturally coded definitions, requirements, and expectations about women and female identity—this repertoire of regulatory fictions that are tattooed on our skins, then it would be false to deny that such an essence not only exists, but also is powerfully operational. History is women's destiny. In other words, because of this history and because of the way in which phallo-logocentric language structures our speaking positions as subjects, before feminists relinquish the signifier "woman," we need to repossess it, to revisit its multifaceted complexities, because these complexities define the one identity we share—female feminists. This is the starting point, however limited, for the political project of the feminism of difference.

In other words, I am very resistant to a position of willful denial of something feminists know perfectly well: that identity is not just volition, that the unconscious structures one's sense of identity through a series of vital (even when they are lethal, they are vital) identifications, which affect one's situation in reality. Feminists must know better than to confuse, to merrily mix up, willful choice—political volition—with unconscious desire. Identity is not the same thing as subjectivity: One is also and primarily the subject of one's own unconscious.

To put it more plainly: Following Nietzsche, Deleuze, and Irigaray, I do not believe that changes and transformations—such as the new symbolic system of women—can be created by sheer volition. The way to transform psychic reality is not by willful self-naming: at best that is an extreme form of narcissism; at worst it is the melancholic face of solipsism. Rather, transformation can only be achieved through deessentialized embodiment or strategically reessentialized embodiment—by *working through* the multi-layered structures of one's embodied self.

Like the gradual peeling off of old skins, earned by carefully working Freud's totemic meal, it is the metabolic consumption of the old that can engender the new. Difference is not the effect of willpower, but the result of many, of endless, repetitions. Until we have worked through the multiple layers of signification of "woman"—phallic as it may be—I am not willing to relinquish the signifier.

That is why I want to continue working through the very term—women as the female feminist subjects of sexual difference—that it needs to be deconstructed follows from an emphasis on the politics of desire. I think, with Deleuze, that there cannot be social change without the construction of new kinds of desiring subjects as molecular, nomadic, and multiple. I take it as the task of the feminist as critical intellectual here and now to resist the recoding of the subject in/as yet another sovereign, self-representational language. One must start by leaving open spaces of experimentation, of search, of transition. I think that politics begins with our desires, and our desires are that which evade us, in the very act of propelling us forth, leaving as the only indicator the traces of where we have already been, that is to say, of what we have already ceased to be. The cartography of the female embodied subject, just like Foucault's diagrams of power, is always already the trace of what no longer is the case. As such it needs to be started all over again, constantly. In this repetition of the cartographic gesture there lies the potential for opening up new angles of vision, new itineraries. Nomadism is therefore neither a rhetorical gesture nor a mere figure of speech, but a political and epistemological necessity for critical theory at the end of this century.

Notes

I wish to thank the participants of the graduate research seminar in women's studies in my department for their comments. Special thanks also to Teresa de Lauretis and Anneke Smelik.

1. See Rosi Braidotti, "The Politics of Ontological Difference," in Teresa Brennan, ed. *Between Feminism and Psychoanalysis* (London, Routledge, 1989).

2. This expression is used extensively by Teresa de Lauretis, for instance in her *Technologies of Gender* (Bloomington: Indiana University Press, 1986).

3. For a fuller elaboration of my understanding of sexual difference, see "The Politics of Ontological Difference."

4. Jane Flax, "Postmodernism and Gender Relations in Feminist Theory," *Signs* 12:4 (1987). Of the same author, see also *Thinking Fragments* (Berkeley: University of California Press, 1990).

5. Teresa de Lauretis, ed., *Feminist Studies/Critical Studies* (Bloomington: Indiana University Press, 1986); *Technologies of Gender* (Bloomington: Indiana University Press, 1987).

6. See Julia Kristeva, "Women's Time," *Signs* 7:1 (1981), reprinted in Nannerl O. Keohane, Michelle Z. Rosaldo and Barbara C. Gelpi eds., *Feminist Theory: A Critique of Ideology* (Chicago: Chicago University Press, 1982).

7. Jean-François Lyotard, *Le postmodernisme expliqué aux enfants* (Paris: Galilée, 1985).

8. See Adrienne Rich, *Of Woman Born* (New York: W. W. Norton, 1976); *On Lies, Secrets and Silence* (New York: W. W. Norton, 1979); and *Blood, Bread and Poetry* (New York: W. W. Norton, 1985).

9. The term "symbolic" is complex; I am using it here in a post-Lacanian sense, as referring to the cumulated and multilayered structure of signification of language, where language encapsulates the fundamental structures of a given culture. The literature on Lacanian feminism is so vast that I shall not even attempt to discuss it here; for an excellent summary see Teresa Brennan's introduction to Teresa Brennan, ed., *Between Feminism and Psychoanalysis* (London: Routledge, 1989).

10. For a fuller analysis of this vision of the body, allow me to refer you to my article "Organs without Bodies," *Differences* 1:1 (1989). See also Elizabeth Grosz, "Notes Towards a Corporeal Feminism," *Australian Feminist Studies* 5 (1987).

11. Teresa de Lauretis, "Upping the Anti (sic) in Feminist Theory," in *Conflicts in Feminism*, Marianne Hirsch and Evelyn Fox Keller, eds. (New York: Routledge, 1990), p. 266.

12. Teresa de Lauretis, "Eccentric Subjects: Feminist Theory and Historical Consciousness," *Feminist Studies*, vol. 16, no. 1 (1990).

13. bell hooks, "Postmodern Blackness," in *Yearning* (Toronto: Between the Lines, 1990).

14. I refer here to the concept elaborated by Gilles Deleuze in collaboration with Félix Guattari; see *Rhizome* (Paris: Minuit, 1976).

15. Rosi Braidotti, *Patterns of Dissonance* (Cambridge: Polity Press/New York: Routledge, 1991), chapters 3, 4, and 5.

16. On this point, see Judith Butler, *Subjects of Desire* (New York: Columbia University Press, 1987), especially chapter 4.

17. See Gilles Deleuze and Félix Guattari, *L'Anti Oedipe* (Paris: Minuit, 1980).

18. Michel Foucault, *L'Ordre du discours* (Paris: Gallimard, 1977).

19. This expression, originally coined by Laura Mulvey in film criticism, has been taken up and developed by Donna Haraway in "Situated Knowledges: The Science Question in Feminism and the Privilege of Partical Perspective," and in "A Cyborg Manifesto: Science, Technology and Socialist-Feminism in the Late Twentieth Century," both in *Simians, Cyborgs and Women* (London: Free Association Press, 1991).

20. See Christine Delphy, "Pour un matérialisme féministe," *L'Arc* 61 (1975) and see *Close to Home* (London: Hutchinson, 1984).

21. See Hélène Cixous, "Le rire de la Meduse," *L'Arc* 61 (1975); "Le sexe ou la tête," *Les Cahiers du grif* 5 (1977); *Entre l'écriture*, (Paris: des femmes, 1986); and *Le livre de Promethea* (Paris: Gallimard, 1987).

22. See Claire Duchen, *Feminism in France* (London: Routledge, and Kegan Paul, 1986).

23. See Rosi Braidotti, "Essentialism," forthcoming in Elizabeth Wright, ed., *Dictionary of Feminism and Psychoanalysis* (London: Routledge).

24. See Rosi Braidotti, "Féminisme et philosophie: la critique du pouvoir et la pensée féministe contemporaine," doctoral dissertation, May 1981, Pantheon-Sorbonne University, Paris; "Femmes et philosophie: questions à suivre," in *La revue d'en Face* 13 (1984); "Modelli di dissonanza: donne e/in filosofia," in Patrizia Magli, ed., *Le Donne e i segni* (Urbino: Il Lavoro editoriale, 1985); and *Patterns of Dissonance* (Cambridge: Polity, 1991); Alice Jardine, *Gynesis* (Ithaca: Cornell University Press, 1985); Judith Butler, *Gender Trouble* (New York: Routledge, 1990); Karin Emerton, "Les femmes et la philosophie: la mise en discours de la différence sexuelle dans la philosophie contemporaine," unpublished doctoral dissertation, November 1986, Pantheon-Sorbonne University, Paris, and "From Conducting Bodies to Natural Science," catalogue of Marilyn Fairskye, *Natural Science* (Sydney: Bench Press, 1989).

25. Luce Irigaray, *Speculum: de l'autre femme* (Paris: Minuit, 1974); *Ce sexe qui n'en est pas un* (Paris: Minuit, 1977); *Amante Marine* (Paris: Minuit, 1980); *L'ethique de la différence sexuelle* (Paris: Minuit, 1984); *Sexe et parenté* (Paris: Minuit, 1988); *Le temps de la différence* (Paris: Minuit, 1989); and *Je, tu, nous* (Paris: Minuit, 1990).

26. *Ce sexe qui n'en est pas un*, p. 140.

27. See on this point the magisterial study by Margaret Whitford, *Luce Irigaray: Philosophy in the Feminine* (London: Routledge, 1991).

28. See *Le temps de la différence*.

29. See *Luce Irigaray*.

30. For a study of the aesthetics of sexual difference, see Laura Guadagnin and Valentina Pasquon, eds., *Parola, Mater-Materia* (Venezia: Arsenale Editrice, 1989).

31. Laurie Anderson's contribution to performance art has been widely recognized; see, as an example, Andreas Huyssen, *After the Great Divide* (Bloomington: Indiana University Press, 1986). For a more feminist analysis of her work, see Susan McClary, *Feminine Endinas: Music, Gender and Sexuality* (Minneapolis: Minnesota University Press, 1991).

32. Barbara Kruger, *We Won't Play Nature to Your Culture* (London: ICA, 1983).

33. For instance, Mary Kelly, *Post-Partum Document* (New York: Routledge, 1984) and Jana Sterbak, *States of Being/Corps à Corps*, National Gallery of Canada, Ottawa, 1991.

34. In the article "The Politics of Ontological Difference," I have summed up the process of mimesis as strategic essentialism as the temporary strategy that defines as "woman" the stock of cumulated knowledge about the female, sexed subject—whose traits, qualities, and representations affect each and every empirical woman. For each woman is the direct empirical referent of all that has been symbolized as and theorized about femininity, the female subject, and the feminine.

35. This criticism has been particularly vehement on the part of black feminists and the so-called postcolonial critics.

36. I am grateful to Anne Claire Mulder for this formulation, which is central to her theological research on the notion of incarnation in the work of Irigaray.

37. *Gender Trouble*, p. 167.

38. See Monique Wittig, *Le Corps lesbien* (Paris: Minuit, 1973); "La Pensée straight," *Questions Féministes* 7 (1980); and "Paradigm," in George Starobian and Elaine Marks, eds., *Homosexualities and French Literature* (Ithaca: Cornell University Press, 1979).

39. In her work as a creative writer, however, and especially with her novel *Le Corps lesbiens*, Wittig has contributed tremendously to the radical redefinition of female sexuality and women's desire, but she has done so in a manner quite opposed to sexual difference theorists.

40. Both quotations are from "Paradigm," in G. Stambolian and E. Marks (eds.), *Homosexualities and French Literature*, p. 119.

41. See on this point my brief account *Theories of Gender* (Utrecht: University of Utrecht, September 1991).

42. See Michel Foucault, *Surveiller et punir* (Paris: Gallimard, 1977).

43. Monique Wittig, "Postface" in Djuna Barnes, *La passion* (Paris: Flammarion, 1982), p. 111. My translation follows; the exact quotation is:

   "La femme" ne peut pas être associée avec écriture, parce que "la femme" est une formation imaginaire et pas une realité concrète, elle est cette vieille marque au fer rouge de l'ennemi maintenant brandie comme un oripeau retrouvé et conquis de haute lutte.

44. "Postface" in *La passion*, p.116. My translation; the exact quotation is:

   Un texte écrit par un écrivain minoritaire n'est efficace que s'il réussit à rendre universel le point de vue minoritaire.

45. The debate about lesbian desire in feminist theory was introduced also by Adrienne Rich, whose idea of the "lesbian continuum" differs radically from Wittig's definition of the lesbian as nonwoman.

46. In a previous study, I have outlined the theoretical structure of this new gendered universalism. "From She-Self to She Other," forthcoming in Gisela Bock and Susan James, eds., *Beyond Equality and Difference* (London: Routledge, 1992).

47. This point will be developed in my forthcoming study, *Organs Without Bodies* (London: Routledge).

48. Antoinette Fouque, "Notre pays, notre terre de naissance, c'est le corps maternel," *Des femmes en mouvement/Midi Pyrennées* no. 1 (1982).

49. In "'Gender' for a Marxist Dictionary: the Sexual Politics of a Word," in *Simians, Cyborgs and Women*.

50. See Donna Haraway, "The Promises of Monsters," paper delivered at the Women's Studies department of the University of Utrecht, October 1990.

51. The notion of "experience" has been the object of intense debates in feminist theory; see, as examples, Teresa de Lauretis, *Alice Doesn't* (Bloomington: Indiana University Press, 1984); and Sandra Harding, *The Science Question in Feminism* (London: Open University Press, 1986) and *Feminism and Methodology* (London: Open University Press, 1987).

52. Genevieve. Lloyd, *The Man of Reason* (London: Methuen, 1985).

53. Luce Irigaray, "Egales à qui?" *Critique*, no. 489 (1987); English translation in "Equal to whom?" *Differences* 1:2 (1989).

54. As Monique David-Menard argues in *L'Hysterique entre Freud et Lacan: Corps et Langage en Psychanalyse* (Paris: Édition Universitaires, 1983).

55. *Surveiller et punir.*

56. "A Cyborg Manifesto," p. 245, footnote.

57. See Nancy K. Miller, "Subject to Change," in Teresa de Lauretis, ed., *Feminist Studies/Critical Studies* (Bloomington: Indiana University Press, 1986).

58. My reading of cyborgs as rhizomatic figurations of thought does not mean to suggest any structural comparison between Haraway and Deleuze. In some respects, nothing could be further removed from Haraway's scheme of thought than references, let alone close attention to the unconscious or the politics of subjective desire.

59. Maurizia Boscaglia, "Unaccompanied Ladies: Feminist, Italian and in the Academy," *Differences* 2:3 (1991).

60. Trinh T. Minh-ha, *Woman, Native, Other* (Bloomington: Indiana University Press, 1989).

61. See Chandra Mohanty, "Under Western Eye: Feminist Scholarship and Colonial Discourse," *Boundary* 2,3 (1984) and Gayatri Spivak, *In Other Worlds* (New York: Routledge, 1989).

10

A Thousand Tiny Sexes: Feminism and Rhizomatics

Elizabeth Grosz

DELEUZE AND GUATTARI'S work is rarely discussed in the texts of feminist theory, even in those explicitly addressed to what is commonly called "French theory" or French postmodernism.[1] This omission is even more striking, given the ready availability of English translations of most of their major (solo and collaborative) works. Could it be that their work has little to offer feminist theory? Or that feminists, even those working on "French theory," have, for whatever reasons, simply not read them? Or is it that their work is difficult—difficult to read, to enter and to feel at ease in, to use? This paper undertakes a preliminary exploration of the theoretical terrain, and some of the basic concepts, in Deleuze and Guattari's *A Thousand Plateaus*[2] with the aim of seeing their possible value for feminist concerns; their potential for contesting and reorienting feminist commitments; and their utility, or otherwise, for feminist methodologies.

1. Feminist Suspicions

Those feminists who have explicitly addressed Deleuze and Guattari's work, in the main, have tended to be rather critical, or, at the very least, suspicious of the apparently masculine interests, orientations, and metaphors in their writings; worried about the models and images of machines, assemblages, planes, forces, energies, and connections advocated; suspicious regarding their use of manifestly misogynist writers like Henry Miller and D. H. Lawrence; critical of an *apparently* phallic drive to plug things, make connections, link with things. If I may be permitted to quote myself from an earlier paper, this may help to capture some of the common feminist responses I have heard with regard to their work:

> They exhibit a certain blindness to their own positions as masculine (not because they are men, but because they are blind to their own processes of production, their own positions as representatives of particular values and interests that are incapable of being universalized or erected into a neutral theoretical method). They have paid lip service to feminist interests in their advocacy of the processes of becoming-marginal or becoming-woman as part of their challenge to totalizing procedure. But they exhibit a certain blindness to feminine subjectivity, a feminist point of view and the role of women in their characterizations of the world . . . They fail to notice that the process of becoming-marginal or becoming-woman means nothing as a strategy if one is already marginal or a woman . . . What they ignore is the question of sexual difference, sexual specificity and autonomy.[3]

Expressed here are a series of reservations about the relevance of their work to questions of sexual difference: There is the claim that their work does not acknowledge its investments in masculine perspectives; the claim that they describe as "neutral" a position that is manifestly not neutral with respect to the specificity of female experience; and a refusal to accept that their use of the metaphor of woman, or becoming-woman, has very real effects, not in the valorization of femininity, but, on the contrary, in its neutralization or neuterization. One of the few feminist theorists who has published material on Deleuze and Guattari, Alice Jardine, makes a similar series of charges against them in her text *Gynesis*, where she claims:

> [T]o the extent that women must "become woman" *first* . . . might that not mean that she must also be the first to disappear? Is it not possible that the process of "becoming woman" is but a new variation of an old allegory for the process of women becoming obsolete? There would remain only her simulacrum: a female figure caught in a whirling sea of male configurations. A silent, mutable, head-less, desireless spatial surface necessary only for *his* metamorphosis? (Jardine 1985, p. 217).

The suspicion that "becoming-woman," "desiring machines," and other similar concepts are merely excuses for male forms of appropriation of whatever is radical and threatening about women's movements is also hinted at, though less directly and without specifically referring to Deleuze and Guattari by name, in Irigaray's writing. She claims that for women to accept Deleuzian perspectives regarding notions like desire, machinic functions, assemblages, and so on is to once again subsume women under the neutralized masculinity of the phallocratic:

> [D]oesn't the "desiring machine" still partly take the place of woman or the feminine? Isn't it a sort of metaphor for her that men can use? Especially in terms of their relation to the techno-cratic?

Or again: [C]an this "psychosis" be "women's"? If so, isn't it a psychosis that prevents them from acceding to sexual pleasure? At least to their pleasure? That is, to a pleasure different from an abstract—neutral?—pleasure of sexualized matter. That pleasure which perhaps constitutes a discovery for men, a supplement to enjoyment, in a fantasmatic "becoming-woman," but which has long been familiar to women. For them isn't the [Body without Organs] a historical condition? And don't we run the risk once more of taking back from woman those as yet unterritorialized spaces where her desire might come into being? Since women have long been assigned to the task of preserving "body-matter" and the "organless," doesn't the [Body without Organs] come to occupy the place of their own schism? Of the evacuation of women's desire in women's body? . . . To turn the [Body without Organs] into a "cause" of sexual pleasure, isn't it necessary to have had a relation to language and to sex—to the organs—that women have never had?[4]

Here, Irigaray voices a number of reservations about the Deleuzian project, which could be briefly listed in the following points:

1. The metaphor of becoming-woman is a male appropriation and recuperation of the positions and struggles of women. As such, it risks depoliticizing, possibly even aestheticizing, struggles and political challenges crucial to the survival and self-definition of women;

2. Such metaphors serve to neutralize men's search for their own dissolution and reorganization, making the struggles around the question of "becoming" a broadly human, or even more broadly, a universal, rather than a specifically masculine, enterprise, and thus participate in the kind of desexualization or despecification characteristic of phallocentric thought;

3. While they may be understood as masculine appropriations of femininity, metaphors of becoming-woman also, paradoxically, prevent women from exploring and interrogating their own specific, and nongeneralizable, forms of becoming, desiring-production, and being;

4. Like all phallocentric systems of thought, the Deleuzian project may, once again, be accused of simply using women as the ground, object, or excuse for his own involvements; of using woman to obscure an examination of his own investments in women's subjugation. Woman, once again, becomes the object or the prop of man's speculations, self-reflections, and intellectual commitments;

5. To invoke the notion of "becoming-woman" in place of a concept of "being woman," Deleuze and Guattari participate in the subordination, or possibly even the obliteration, of women's struggles for autonomy, identity, and self-determination, an erasure of a certain, very concrete and real set of political struggles, which, if it were directed to, say, the struggles of other "minority" groups (women of course are not a minority, statistically

speaking), would provoke horror and outrage. For example, for white, middle-class men to invoke the metaphor of becoming-black, or becoming-Hispanic, would provoke scathing condemnation and great suspicion;

6. Deleuze and Guattari are invested in a romantic elevation of models of psychosis, schizophrenia, and madness that, on the one hand, ignore the very real pain and torment of individuals, and, on the other hand, raise pathology to an unlivable, unviable ideal for others. Moreover, in making becoming-woman the privileged site of all becomings, Deleuze and Guattari confirm a long historical association between femininity, women, and madness that ignores the sexually specific forms that madness takes (as Irigaray's own earliest researches have demonstrated); and

7. In evoking metaphors of machinic functioning, Deleuze and Guattari, like other masculinist philosophers, utilize models and metaphors that have been made possible only at the expense of women's exclusion and denigration: technocracies, while not inherently masculinist, are so de facto insofar as they are historically predicated on women's exclusion.

Admittedly Irigaray, Jardine, and I, in my earlier text, were referring, not to *A Thousand Plateaus,* but to Deleuze and Guattari's earlier works, most notably, *Anti-Oedipus*[5]—in itself a very complex and highly specifically directed text, with a different orientation and different perspectives from those developed in their later texts. But many of the concerns expressed in the preceding quotations may, with equal relevance, be directed toward *A Thousand Plateaus.* It will be the task of this paper to explore whether in fact such reservations and suspicions are warranted regarding what Deleuze and Guattari call their "rhizomatics," and whether indeed rhizomatics may provide a powerful ally and theoretical resource for feminist challenges to the domination of philosophical paradigms, methods, and presumptions that have governed the history of Western thought and have perpetuated, rationalized, and legitimated the erasure of women and women's contributions from cultural, sexual, and theoretical life. In other words, even if their work is deemed patriarchal or phallocentric (no text—not even "feminist" texts—can in a sense be immune to this charge, insofar as the very categories, concepts, and methodologies available today are those spawned by this history), it may still serve as a powerful tool or weapon in feminist challenges to phallocentric thought. Insofar as feminist theory and Deleuzian rhizomatics share a common target—the reversal of Platonism[6]—a reversal that problematizes the opposition, so integral to Western thought, between the ideal and the real, the original and the copy, the conceptual and the material, and, ultimately, between man and woman, it may in fact turn out that a (provisional, guarded) alliance may be of great strategic value.

In this paper, I would like to temporarily suspend critical feminist judgment in order to "enter into" the project(s) articulated in Deleuze and Guattari's *A Thousand Plateaus*. I would like to explore how this text might possibly be used by and for feminist theoretical projects, which involves some commitment to their overarching framework, basic presuppositions, and central concepts. It will be necessary to outline a number of their central concepts and images that may be of relevance to feminists, especially those concerned with bodies, sexualities, pleasures, and desire—the Body without Organs, the desiring machine, becoming-woman; and those of more general methodological relevance, such as the notions of rhizomatics, cartography, intensities, speed, planes.

2. Feminist Conjunctions

There are a number of prima facie reasons why, in spite of their apparently peripheral or oblique relations to feminist theory, nevertheless Deleuze and Guattari's writings may prove fruitful for various forms of feminist research. I would like to briefly indicate what these congruities, points of overlap, and common interests may be, even if only schematically. This provisional and schematic overview, a first attempt to explore and navigate paths through the nomadic grounds they explore, is preliminary to a deeper investigation into their work.

In the first place, like a number of their contemporaries, Deleuze and Guattari challenge and displace the centrality and pervasiveness of the structure of binary logic that has exerted a domination in Western philosophy since the time of Plato. Not only do they seek out alternatives with which to contest or bypass the metaphysical bases of Western philosophy (which Derrida terms "logocentrism": the necessary presumption of givenness or presence); they seek to position traditional metaphysical identities and theoretical models in a context that renders them merely effects or surface phenomena within a broader or differently conceived ontology or metaphysics. Systems of thought based on the centrality of the subject and the coherence of signification can be put to work in such a way that they are no longer privileged or causal terms, but effects or consequences of processes of sedimentation, the congealing or coagulation of processes, interrelations, or "machines" of disparate components, functioning in provisional alignment with each other to form a working ensemble. Given that it is impossible to ignore binarized or dichotomous thought, and yet, given that such theoretical paradigms and methodologies are deeply implicated in regimes of oppression and social subordination—of which the oppression of women is the most stark—any set of procedures, including rhizomatics, which seeks to problematize and render them anachronistic may well be worth closer feminist inspection. As they claim: "We employ a dualism of models only in order to arrive at a process that challenges all models. Each time, mental correctives are necessary to undo the dualisms we had no wish to construct but through which we pass" (Deleuze and Guattari 1987, p. 20).

For this reason, if for no other, their use of rhizomatics, cartography, schizoanalysis, etc., like deconstruction or grammatology, are at least of indirect relevance to feminists. Even if their procedures and methods do not actively affirm or support feminist struggles around women's autonomy and self-determination, they may nevertheless help clear the ground of metaphysical concepts so that women may be able to devise their own knowledges and accounts of themselves and the world.

In addition, and also aligned with feminist challenges to prevailing forms of masculinism in philosophy, is their interest in the question of difference, a difference capable of being understood outside the dominance or regime of the One, the self-same, the imaginary play of mirrors and doubles, the structure of binary pairs in which what is different can be understood only as a variation or negation of identity. Deleuze claims to conceptualize difference in terms beyond the four "illusions" of representation: identity, opposition, analogy, and resemblance. In conceptualizing a difference in and of itself, a difference that is not subordinated to identity or the same, Deleuze and Guattari invoke two forms of energy and alignment: the processes of becoming and the notion of multiplicity, a becoming beyond the logic, constraints, and confines of being, and a multiplicity beyond the merely doubling or multicentering of proliferating subjects:

> It is only when the multiple is effectively treated as a substantive, "multiplicity," that it ceases to have any relation to the One as subject or object, natural or spiritual reality, image and world . . . A Multiplicity has neither subject nor object, only determinations, magnitudes and dimensions that cannot increase in number without the multiplicity changing in nature (Deleuze and Guattari 1987, p. 8).

A multiplicity is not a pluralized notion of identity (identity multiplied by *n* locations), but is rather an ever-changing, nontotalizable collectivity, an assemblage defined, not by its abiding identity or principle of sameness over time, but through its capacity to undergo permutations and transformations, that is, its dimensionality: "Multiplicities are defined by the outside: by the abstract line, the line of flight or deterritorialization according to which they change in nature and connections with other multiplicities" (Deleuze and Guattari 1987, p. 9).

While the notion of becoming has proved an enormously fertile ground for a surprisingly large number of post-Nietzschean thinkers—Derrida, Irigaray, and Levinas, to name but a few—it has functioned to provide nonteleological notions of direction, movement, and process. Part of a Heraclitean tradition, and strongly associated with the model of the Hegelian dialectic, becoming in Deleuze's writings has stronger affinities with the pre-Socratics, with Spinoza, and with the post-Nietzscheans than it may have in the texts of other contemporary French philosophers. However, exactly how such notions of multiplicity and becoming function in Deleuze's work and how they may (or may not) be of use in feminist challenges to the structure of binary oppositions, to the formalized notions of identity or equivalence that have been used to define and exclude women, remains an open question, one to be explored in further detail beyond the limited confines of this paper.

Furthermore, there seems to be an evident allegiance between Deleuze and Guattari's notions of political struggle, decentered, molecular, multiple struggles, diversified, nonaligned, or aligned in only provisional or temporary networks, in nonhierarchical, rhizomatic connections, taking place at those sites where repression or antiproduction is most intense—and feminist conceptions of, and practices surrounding political struggle. In a sense, it could be argued that the Deleuzian-Foucauldian understanding of politics[7] theorizes, in a clearer and more direct form than rival or alternative political philosophies (including Marxism, socialism, liberalism, and anarchism), the kinds of theoretical and political struggles in which feminists are involved. Such struggles cannot be conceived simply as collectivized or group actions (they imply notions of the collectivity or multiplicity and the group that have not, before Deleuze and Guattari, been adequately theorized); struggles occur not only in group-sized multiplicities, but also in those multiplicities internal to or functional through and across subjects, within subjects, against the control of the ego and the superego, against processes of oedipalization, which will enable a proliferation of becomings and the production of marginalities of all kinds. In short, Deleuze and Guattari's understanding of micropolitics, their affirmation of localized, concrete, nonrepresentative struggles, struggles without leaders, without hierarchical organizations, without a clear-cut program or blue-print for social change, without definitive goals and ends, confirms, and indeed, borrows from already existing forms of feminist political struggle, even if it rarely acknowledges this connection.

Finally, Deleuze and Guattari's notion of the body as a discontinuous, nontotalized series of processes, organs, flows, energies, corporeal substances and incorporeal events, intensities, and durations may be of great relevance to those feminists attempting to reconceive bodies, especially women's bodies, outside of the binary polarizations imposed on the body by the mind/body, nature/culture, subject/object, and interior/ exterior oppositions. They provide an altogether different understanding of the body than those that have dominated the history of Western thought in terms of the linkage of the human body to other bodies, human and nonhuman, animate and inanimate; they link organs and biological processes to material objects and social practices while refusing to subordinate the body to a unity and homogeneity provided either by the body's subordination to consciousness or to organic organization. Following Spinoza, the body is regarded neither as a locus for a conscious subject nor as an organically determined object; instead, like the book itself, the body is analyzed and assessed more in terms of what it can do, the things it can perform, the linkages it establishes, the transformations it undergoes, the machinic connections it forms with other bodies, what it can link with, and how it can proliferate its capacities—a rare, affirmative understanding of the body:

> Spinoza's question: *what is a body capable of*? What affects is it capable of? Affects are becomings: sometimes they weaken us to the extent they diminish our strength of action and decompose our relations (sadness), sometimes they make us stronger through augmenting our force, and making us enter into a vaster and higher individual (joy). Spinoza never ceases to be astonished at the body: not having a body, but at what the body is capable of. Bodies are not defined by their genus and species, nor by their organs and functions, but by what they can do, the affects they are capable of, in passion as in action.[8]

The notion of the Body without Organs (BwO) will be explored in more detail later in this paper, but at least at first glance, feminist theorists need to devise alternative accounts of corporeality that go beyond the confines of the mind/body polarization if women's specificity is to be rethought, and the domination of phallocentric representations is to be overcome. If this means turning to philosophers whose work has in the past been vilified or treated as suspect by feminists—as has Nietzsche's work, not to mention Deleuze's—this seems to me to be a risk worth taking, given the enormous theoretical stakes invested in reconceptualizing the body, and with it, subjectivity, in rethinking the relations between men and women, and between women, in social relations.

In the fifth place, just as Deleuze and Guattari provide notions of the body alternative to those usually dominant in Western thought, so too, they have reconsidered the notion of desire in active and affirmative terms. It has been plausibly argued[9] that in the tradition reaching from Plato to Lacan and beyond, desire has been understood as negative, abyssal, a lack at the level of ontology itself (this was most ably articulated in Hegel's understanding of the lack [of object] of desire being the necessary condition for the maintenance of desire), a lack in being that strives to be filled through the (impossible) attainment of an object—the object, for man, being, presumably, the attainment or possession of woman, woman being the perennial object of man's desire, though without a congruous desire herself (for woman to have desire is to put her on the same ontological level as man—a theoretical impossibility in phallocentric texts, hence the enigmatic and perpetual question of woman's desire: what does woman want?). Instead of understanding desire as a lack or a hole in being, desire is understood by Deleuze—again following Spinoza and Nietzsche—as immanent, as positive and productive, a fundamental, full, and creative relation. Desire is what produces, what makes things, forges connections, creates relations, produces machinic alignments. Instead of aligning desire with fantasy and opposing it to the real, as psychoanalysis does, for Deleuze, desire is what produces the real; instead of a yearning, desire is an actualization, a series of practices, action, production, bringing together, making machines, making reality. "Desire is a relation of effectuation, not of satisfaction."[10]

Since Plato, desire has been conceived under the dominance of the subject and the sign. Whether the subject has been conceived in terms of consciousness and ideas (as in Plato or Hegel) or the unconscious (as in Freud and Lacan) desire has been that yearning to fill in, to reproduce a lost plenitude, whether the plenitude of the Idea or that of the pre-Oedipal. So too, desire must transform itself into signification: for Lacan, it is the lack constitutive of desire that propels the subject into the order of signification, which, in its turn, marks the subject with a lack impossible to fill (this is the advent of demand from the order of the Real). It seeks its various satisfactions—satisfactions of the same order, governed by a master signifier, the phallus—always and only at the level of representations, whether in hallucinatory form (the dream as the fulfillment of desire) or in the form of verbalized free associations. Desire is then a property of the subject; it is enacted through representations and is thwarted or frustrated by the Real.

By contrast, for Deleuze and Guattari, following Spinoza, Platonism is inverted, if not reversed: desire is primary and given rather than lack; it is not produced, an effect of frustration or ontological lack, but is primitive and primary, not opposed to or postdating reality, but productive of reality. Desire does not take for itself a particular object whose attainment it requires; rather, it aims at nothing in particular above and beyond its own proliferation or self-expansion. It assembles things out of singularities, and it breaks down things, assemblages, into their singularities: "If desire produces, its product is real. If desire is productive, it can be so in reality, and of reality" (Deleuze and Guattari 1977, p. 26). As production, desire does not provide blueprints, models, ideals, or goals. Rather, it experiments; it makes; it is fundamentally aleatory; it is bricolage. Such a notion of desire cannot but be of interest to feminist theory insofar as women have been the traditional depositories and guardians of the lack constitutive of (Platonic) desire, and insofar as the opposition between presence and lack, between reality and fantasy, has traditionally defined women and constrained them to inhabit the place of man's other. Lack only makes sense to the (male) subject insofar as some other (woman) personifies and quite literally embodies it for him. Any model of desire that dispenses with its reliance on the primacy of lack seems to be a positive step forward, and for that reason alone worthy of careful consideration.

And, in the sixth place, Deleuze and Guattari resurrect the question of the centrality of ethics, of the encounter with otherness in a way that may prove highly pertinent to feminist attempts to rethink relations between the mainstream and the margins, between dominant and subordinated groups, oppressor and oppressed, self and other, as well as between and within subjects. Here ethics is no longer conceived on the basis of an abstract system of moral rules and obligations, such as proposed by Kantian or Christian morality (that is, in terms of moral prescriptions and imperatives), nor in opposition to conceptions of politics (as it commonly has in, for example, Marxist theory). Rather, Deleuze and Guattari are participants in what might be described as the advent of a "postmodern ethics," an ethics posed in the light of the dissolution of both the rational, judging subject and the contract-based, liberal accounts of the individual's allegiance to the social community. In the wake of Spinoza's understanding of ethics, ethics is conceived of as the capacity for action and passion, activity and passivity; good and bad refer to the ability to increase or decrease one's capacities and strengths and abilities. Given the vast and necessary interrelation and mutual affectivity and effectivity of all beings on all others (a notion, incidentally, still very far opposed to the rampant moralism underlying ecological and environmental politics, which also stress interrelations, but do so in a necessarily prescriptive and judgmental fashion, presuming notions of unity, wholeness, integration and cooperation rather than, as do Deleuze and Guattari, simply describing interrelations and connections without subordinating them to an overarching order, system, or totality), the question of ethics is raised whenever the question of a being's, or an assemblage's, capacities and abilities are raised. Unlike Levinasian ethics, which is still modeled on a subject-to-subject, self-to-other, relation, the relation of a being respected in its autonomy from the other, as a necessarily independent autonomous being—the culmination and final flowering of a phenomenological notion of the subject—Deleuze and Guattari in no way privilege the human, autonomous, sovereign subject; the independent other; or the bonds of communication and representation between them. They are concerned more with what psychoanalysis calls "partial objects," organs, processes, and flows, which show no respect for the autonomy of the subject. Ethics is the sphere of judgments regarding the possibilities and actuality of connections, arrangements, lineages, machines:

> All individuals exist in Nature as on a plane of consistence whose entire figure, variable at each moment, they go to compose. They affect one another insofar as the relation that constitutes each individual forms a degree of power [*puissance*], a power of being affected. Everything in the universe is encounters, happy or unhappy encounters (Deleuze and Parnet 1987, p. 74).

There are, then, at least these points of shared interest, of potential interaction and linkage between the Deleuzian project and those designated as feminist. This is not to say that an "alliance" between feminism and Deleuzianism is possible or even fruitful, nor even that they may be able to offer each other new insights or methods; rather, not only are there possible conjunctions and interactions, but also possible points of disjunction, of disruption, and of mutual questioning that may prove as fruitful as any set of alignments or coalition of interests.

3. Rhizomatics, Multiplicity, and Becoming

In this and the following section, I will concentrate on a relatively small cluster of concepts that I believe may overlap with feminist interests: the notions of rhizome, assemblage, machine, desire, multiplicity, becoming, and the Body without Organs. As I understand them, these concepts are linked together as part of the schizoanalytic project of rejecting or displacing prevailing centrisms, unities, and rigid strata. In order to adequately understand their apparently idiosyncratic contributions, contributions that very commonly have appeared hermetically sealed to the outsider or the uninitiated, ridden with jargon and with a mysteriously ineffable systematicity, it is necessary to let go of a number of preconceptions and inherited conceptual schemas of notions of subjectivity and conventional modes of explanation. In Deleuze and Guattari's work, the subject is not an "entity" or thing, or a relation between mind (interior) and body (exterior). Instead, it must be understood as a series of flows, energies, movements, and capacities, a series of fragments or segments capable of being linked together in ways other than those that congeal it into an identity. "Production" consists in those processes that create linkages between fragments—fragments of bodies and fragments of objects—and "machines" are heterogeneous, disparate, discontinuous assemblages of fragments brought together in conjunctions (x plus y plus z) or severed through disjunctions and breaks, a concept not unlike a complex form of bricolage or tinkering described by Lévi-Strauss. A "desiring machine" opposes the notion of unity or One: the elements or discontinuities that compose it do not belong either to an original totality that has been lost (Plato or Freud), or to one that finalizes or completes it— a telos (Hegel). They are multiplicities of (more or less) temporary alignments of segments. They do not *represent* the real; they *are* the real. They constitute, without distinction, individual, collective, and social reality. Desire does not create permanent multiplicities, which would produce what is stable, self-identical, the same. It experiments rather than standardizes, producing ever-new alignments, linkages, and connections. Rhizomatics, or schizoanalysis, does not study the coagulations of entities, the massifications of diverse flows and intensities, but lines of flow and flight, trajectories of territorialization, deterritorialization, and reterritorialization.

Probably the clearest characterization of this project comes from the introductory "plateau" of *A Thousand Plateaus*, called "Rhizome." Here Deleuze and Guattari make explicit that their project has nothing to do with conventional modes of explanation, interpretation, and analysis: they refuse the domination of linguistic/literary/semiological models, which all seek some kind of hidden depth underneath a manifest surface. Rather, they are interested precisely in connections and in interrelations that are never hidden, connections, between not a text and its meaning, but, say, a text and other objects, a text and its outside:

> We shall never ask what a book, a signifier and signified means, we shall not look for anything to understand in a book; instead, we shall wonder with what it functions, in connection with what it transmits intensities or doesn't, into what multiplicities it introduces and metamorphoses its own, with what body without organs it makes its own converge. A book only exists by means of an outside, a beyond. Thus, a book being itself a little machine, what measurable relationship does this literary machine have in turn with a war machine, a love machine, a revolutionary machine etc. (Deleuze and Guattari 1987, p. 4).

Writing, they suggest, has "nothing to do with signifying. It has to do with surveying, mapping, even realms that are yet to come" (Deleuze and Guattari

1987, p. 4). It is thus no longer appropriate to ask what a text means, what it says, what is the structure of its interiority, how to interpret or decipher it. Instead, one must ask what it does, how it connects with other things (including its reader, its author, its literary and nonliterary context). Rhizomatics opposes itself to both what Deleuze and Guattari call the tree image and what they call the root image. The tree metaphor is an emblem of linear, progressive, ordered systems (presumably it dates from the ideal model of argument derived from Greek philosophy now known as Porphyry's tree, which functions through the operation of disjunctive syllogism); the root metaphor also presumes a unity, but like the root itself, this unity is hidden or latent, and thus may present itself as if it were decentered or nonunified. Unlike the manifest unity of the tree, the unity of the root is more hidden; it evokes a kind of nostalgia for the lost past or an anticipated future. In opposition to both of these models of a text, Deleuze and Guattari use the metaphor of the rhizome, an underground—but perfectly manifest—network of multiple branching roots and shoots, with no central axis, no unified point of origin, and no given direction of growth—a proliferating, somewhat chaotic, and diversified system of growths:

> The rhizome is reducible neither to the One nor the multiple . . . It is not a multiple derived from the One, or to which the One is added (n+1). It is composed not of units but of dimensions, or rather, directions in motion. It has neither beginning nor end, but always a middle . . . from which it grows and which it overspills. It constitutes linear multiplicities with *n* dimensions having neither subject nor object . . . and from which the One is always subtracted (n-1) . . . Unlike a structure, which is defined by a set of points and positions, with binary relations between points and biunivocal relationships between the positions, the rhizome is made only of lines: lines of segmentarity and stratification as its dimensions . . . The rhizome operates by variation, expansion, conquest, capture, offshoots . . . The rhizome is acentered, non-hierarchical, non-signifying system (Deleuze and Guattari 1987, p. 21).

The rhizome may be summarily described in the following terms:
1. It is based on connections, bringing together diverse fragments—not only different theories, but also theories with objects and practices;
2. It is based on heterogeneity: these multiple connections are not only massified linkages, but also microlinkages, which bring together very diverse domains, levels, dimensions, functions, effects, aims, and objects;
3. It is based on multiplicity: multiplicity here does not mean a multiplicity of singularities, of ones, a repetition of the self-same, but a genuine proliferation of processes that are neither ones nor twos;

4. It is based on ruptures, breaks, and discontinuities: any one of the rhizome's connections is capable of being severed or disconnected, creating the possibility of other, different connections; and
5. It is based on cartography—not a reproduction or tracing, model-making or paradigm-construction, but map-making or experimentation:

> The rhizome is altogether different, *a map and not a tracing*. The orchid does not reproduce the tracings of the wasp; it forms a map with the wasp, in a rhizome. What distinguishes the map from the tracing is that it is entirely oriented toward an experimentation in contact with the real. The map does not reproduce an unconscious closed in upon itself; it constructs the unconscious . . . The map is open and connectable in all of its dimensions; it is detachable, reversible, susceptible to constant modification. It can be torn, reversed, adapted to any kind of mounting, reworked by an individual, group or social formation . . . A map has multiple entryways, as opposed to the tracing, which always comes back "to the same." The map has to do with performance, whereas the tracing always involves an alleged "competence" . . . *The tracing should always be put back on the map* (Deleuze and Guattari 1987, p. 12).

Rhizomatics, then, is a name for a method and an objective: it names a decentered set of linkages between things, relations, processes, intensities, speeds or slownesses, flows—proliferations of surface connections. In this sense, rhizomatics is opposed to hermeneutics, psychoanalysis, and semiotics, each of which seeks, in its different way, to link an object (a text, a subject, a sign) with a hidden depth or latency—sense, the unconscious, the signified. Rhizomatics is a form of pragmatics: it is concerned with what can be done; how texts, concepts and subjects can be put to work, made to do things, make new linkages. Pivotal concepts within a rhizomatic cartography are the notions of the body without organs and becoming-woman, to which I will now turn.

4. Bodies Without Organs and Becomings . . .

Deleuze and Guattari's notion of the Body without Organs (BwO) constitutes their attempt both to denaturalize the human body and to place it in direct relations with the flows or particles of other bodies or entities. In relying on a Spinozist conception of the univocity of being, in which all things, regardless of their type, have the same ontological status, the BwO refers indistinguishably to human, animal, textual, sociocultural, and physical bodies. Rather than, as psychoanalysis does, regard the body as the developmental union or aggregate of partial objects, organs, drives, and bits, each with their own significance and their own pleasures, which are, through oedipalization, brought into line with the body's organic unity, Deleuze and Guattari instead invoke Antonin Artaud's conception of the Body without Organs. This is the body disinvested of all fantasies, images, and projections, a body without a psychical interior, without internal cohesion or latent significance.

The Body without Organs is not a body evacuated of a psychic interiority; rather, it is a limit or a tendency to which all bodies aspire. Deleuze and Guattari speak of it as an egg, a surface of intensities before it is stratified, organized, and hierarchized. It lacks depth or internal organization, and can instead be regarded as a flow, or the arresting of a flow, of intensities:

> The BwO causes intensities to pass: it produces and distributes them in a spatium that is itself intensive, lacking extension . . . It is non-stratified, unformed, intense matter . . . that is why we treat the BwO as the full egg before the extension of the organism and the organization of the organs, before the formation of strata . . . (Deleuze and Guattari 1987, p. 153).

The Body without Organs does not oppose or reject organs, but rather is opposed to the structure or organization of the body, insofar as it is stratified, regulated, ordered, and functional; insofar as it is subordinated to the exigencies of property and propriety. It is the body before and in excess of the coalescence of its intensities and their sedimentation into meaningful, functional, organized, transcendent totalities, which constitute the unification of the subject and of signification. Deleuze and Guattari regard the Body without Organs as a limit; a tendency; a becoming that resists centralized organization or meaningful investment; a point or process to which all bodies, through their stratifications, tend; a becoming that resists the processes of overcoding and organization according to the three great strata or identities it opposes: the union of the *organism*, the unification of the *subject*, and the structure of *significance*. The BwO resists any equation with a notion of identity or property: "The BwO is never yours or mine. It is always *a* body" (Deleuze and Guattari 1987, p. 164).

Deleuze and Guattari distinguish between two kinds of Body without Organs: the emptied Body without Organs, exemplified by the drug addict, the masochist, and the hypochondriac, and the full Body without Organs, in and through which intensities circulate and flow, where powers, energies and productions are engendered. In the case of the emptied Body without Organs, the body is not only evacuated of organs and forms of organization, but also of its intensities and forces. The hypochondriac, for example, destroys both organs and the flow of matter and intensities; the masochist's BwO is a body sewn up, smothered, filled only with what he or she calls "pain waves." The junkie's Body without Organs is filled, by contrast, with "refrigerator waves," the Cold:

> [A junky] wants The Cold like he wants his junk—NOT OUTSIDE where it does him no good but INSIDE so he can sit around with a spine like a frozen hydraulic jack . . . his metabolism approaching Absolute Zero.[11]

The empty Body without Organs does not deny a becoming; rather, it establishes a line of flight that is unable to free the circulation of intensities, making other, further connections with other BwOs possible. It is a line of flight that ends in its own annihilation:

> Instead of making a body without organs sufficiently rich or full for the passage of intensities, drug addicts erect a vitrified or emptied body, or a cancerous one: the causal line, creative line or line of flight immediately turns into a line of death and abolition (Deleuze and Guattari 1987, p. 285).

While being neither a place nor a plane, a scene, or a fantasy, the BwO is a field for the production, circulation, and intensification of desire, the locus of the immanence of desire. Although it is the field for the circulation of intensities, and although it induces deterritorializations, lines of flight, and movements of becoming, the ability to sustain itself is the condition that seems to be missing in the empty BwO. There must, it seems, be a minimal level of cohesion and integration in the BwO in order to prevent its obliteration: there must be small pockets of subjectivity and signification left in order for the BwO's survival in the face of the onslaughts of power and reality. A complete destratification renders even the BwO unfunctional:

> You have to keep enough of the organism for it to reform each dawn; and you have to keep small supplies of significance and subjectification, if only to turn them against their own systems when the circumstances demand it, when things, persons, even situations, force you to; and you have to keep small rations of subjectivity in sufficient quantity to enable you to respond to the dominant reality. Mimic the strata. You don't reach the BwO, and its plane of consistency, by wildly destratifying. That is why we encountered the paradox of those emptied and dreary bodies at the very beginning: they had emptied themselves of their organs instead of looking for the point at which they could patiently and momentarily dismantle the organization of the organs we call the organism (Deleuze and Guattari 1987, pp. 160-61).

Destratification, freeing lines of flight, the production of connections, and the movements of intensities and flows through and beyond the Body without Organs are thus trajectories or tendencies rather than fixed states or final positions. Deleuze and Guattari advocate not a dissolution of identity, a complete destabilization and defamiliarization of identity, but rather microdestratifications, intensifications of *some* interactions but not necessarily all:

> Staying stratified—organized, signified, subjected—is not the worst that can happen; the worst that can happen is that you throw the strata into demented or suicidal collapse, which brings them back down on us heavier than ever (Deleuze and Guattari 1987, p. 161).

The Body without Organs is the field of becomings. Becoming (-woman, -animal, -imperceptible) is, in feminist terms, perhaps the most controversial element of Deleuze and Guattari's work. In order to know what a body is, it is vital to know what it is capable of, what its energies are, what relations it establishes, and what interactions and effects it has on other bodies. The body cannot be conceived as a block, an entity, an object or a subject, an organized and integrated being. In order to make the body more amenable to transformations, realignments, reconnections with other Bodies without Organs, there are struggles within the body that require recognition.

As Deleuze and Guattari distinguish the Body without Organs from the body's organization as a singular, unified, organic and psychic totality, so too they distinguish between molar and molecular forms of subjectivity, minoritarian and majoritarian collective groupings. Becomings are always molecular, traversing and realigning molar "unities":

> If we consider the great binary aggregates, such as the sexes or classes, it is evident that they also cross over into molecular assemblages of a different nature, and that there is a double reciprocal dependency between them. For the two sexes imply a multiplicity of molecular combinations bringing into play not only the man in the woman and the woman in the man, but the relation of each to the animal, the plant, etc.: a thousand tiny sexes (Deleuze and Guattari 1987, p. 213).

If molar unities, like the divisions of classes, races, and sexes, attempt to form and stabilize identities, fixities, systems that function homeostatically, sealing in their energies and intensities, molecular becomings traverse, create a path, destabilize, enable energy seepage within and through these molar unities. In his paper "Politics,"[12] Deleuze makes a distinction between three types of "lines" relevant to understanding the nexus between the individual and the social: First, there is the rigidly segmented line, the line that divides, orders, hierarchizes, and regulates social relations through binary codes, creating the oppositions between sexes, classes, and races, and dividing the real into subjects and objects. This is a stratifying or *molar* line. Second, there is a more fluid, *molecular* line, which forms connections and relations beyond the rigidity of the molar line. It is composed of fluid lines, which map processes of becoming, change, movement, and reorganization. While it is not in itself "revolutionary" (if it is still meaningful today to say this), it accounts for both sociopolitical and micro becomings, demassifies molar segmentations, and creates overcoded territories, passages, or cracks between segments so that they may drift and yet something may pass between them. And, third, there is a more *nomadic* line, not always clearly distinguishable from the molecular line, which moves beyond given segments to destinations unknown in advance, lines of flight, mutations, even quantum leaps. Thus if the division, the binary opposition, between the sexes—or, for that matter, the global systems constituting patriarchy—can be considered molar lines of segmentation, then the process of becoming-woman—for both men and women—consists in the releasing of minoritarian fragments or particles of "sexuality" (sexuality no longer functioning on the level of the unified, genitalized organization of the sexed body), lines of flight, which break down and seep into binary aggregations. But this process of the multiplication of sexualities is only a step in the creation of a nomadic line, a line of becoming-imperceptible, which disaggregates the molar structures.

If the Body without Organs never "belongs" to a subject, nor functions simply as an object, if it is never "yours" or "mine," but simply *a* Body without Organs, then becomings, by contrast, are never generic, never intermediate: they are always becoming-something. Becomings are always specific movements, specific forms of motion and rest, speed and slowness, points and flows of intensity: they are always a multiplicity, the movement of transformation from one "thing" to another that in no way resembles it. Captain Ahab becomes-whale, Willard becomes-rat, Hans becomes-horse, the Wolf Man becomes-wolf.[13] These are not based on the human's imitation of the animal, a resemblance with the animal, or a mimicry of the animal's behavior or, by contrast, of the animal's ability to represent the subject's fantasies or psychic significances, its metaphoric or symbolic relation to the subject. Deleuze and Guattari suggest that becomings, and especially becoming-animal, involve a mediating third term, a relation to something else, neither human nor animal, to which the subject relates, and through which relation it enters into connections with the animal:

> An example: Do not imitate a dog, but make your organism enter into composition with something else in such a way that the particles emitted from the aggregate thus composed will be canine as a function of the rela-

tions of movement and rest, or of molecular proximity, into which they enter. Clearly, this something else can be quite varied, and be more or less directly related to the animal in question: it can be the animal's natural food (dirt and worm), or its exterior relations with other animals (you can become-dog with cats, or become-monkey with a horse), or an apparatus or prosthesis to which a person subjects the animal (muzzle for reindeer, etc.), or something that does not have a localizable relation to the animal in question . . . we have seen how Slepian bases his attempt to become-dog on the idea of tying shoes to his hands using his mouth-muzzle (Deleuze and Guattari 1987, p. 274).

While becoming-animal is a major line of flight from identity, the mode of becoming most privileged in Deleuze and Guattari's writings is becoming-woman, through which, they claim, all other becomings are made possible: "Although all becomings are already molecular, including becoming-woman, it must be said that all becomings begin with and pass through becoming-woman. It is the key to all other becomings" (Deleuze and Guattari 1987, p. 277). The process of becoming-woman, while never specified, cannot be based on any recognition of, identification with or imitation of woman as molar entities. It is for this reason they claim that not only must men become-woman, but so too must women. Presumably this means that for women, as much as for men, the process of becoming-woman is the destabilization of molar (feminine) identity:

> What we term a molar entity is, for example, the woman as defined by her form, endowed with organs and functions, and assigned as a subject. Becoming-woman is not imitating this entity or even transforming oneself into it . . . not imitating or assuming the female form, but emitting particles that enter the relation of movement and rest, or the zone of proximity, of a microfemininity, in other words, that produce in us a molecular woman (Deleuze and Guattari 1987, p. 275).

Deleuze and Guattari explain that they are not here advocating the development of any form of "bi-sexuality." For them, bisexuality is simply an internalization of binarized sexuality, the miniaturization of the great molar polarities of the sexes without in any way contesting them. Becoming-woman disengages the segments and constraints of the molar identity in order to reinvest and be able to use other particles, flows, speeds, and intensities of the Body without Organs. This enables them, paradoxically, to suggest that even the most phallocentric and notorious male writers—they mention Lawrence and Miller—have, in their writings, become-woman, or relied on processes of becoming-woman, a statement whose validity remains problematic from a feminist point of view. While it may be argued (as they do) that writers like Virginia Woolf produce such texts, and while it is plausible to claim, as Kristeva does, that men too, with certain risks to their masculine, phallic position, can write as women—Joyce, Mallarmé, Artaud, etc.—it remains considerably less convincing to hold up the most notoriously phallic and misogynist writers to exemplify this mode of becoming:

> When Virginia Woolf was questioned about a specifically women's writing, she was appalled at the idea of writing "as a woman." Rather, writing should produce a becoming-woman as atoms of womanhood capable of crossing and impregnating an entire social field, and of contaminating men, of sweeping them up in that becoming . . . The rise of women in English novel writing has spared no man: even those who pass for the most virile, the most phallocratic, such as Lawrence and Miller, in their turn continually tap into and emit particles that enter into the proximity or zones of indiscernibility of women. In writing, they become-women. The question is not, or not only, that of the organism, history, and subject of enunciation that oppose masculine to feminine in the great dualism machines. The question is fundamentally that of the body—the body they steal from us in order to fabricate opposable organs (Deleuze and Guattari 1987, p. 276).

It is never clear who is the "they" and who is the "us" referred to here. If this description is appropriate (and it is not entirely clear to me how appropriate it is), then to become-woman, writers like Miller and Lawrence must "steal" the body—or something of the body—of women: but, then, in what ways is this in any sense critical of, rather than simply affirmative of, men's patriarchal exploitations of women? In what way does this contest, ameliorate, or act as restitution for the robbery of women's bodies by men, in the service of their goals, interests, machines, and habitual power positions?

This question is clearly linked to a series of others: Why is woman (or child or animal) privileged, at least in name, in the advocacy of becoming? If women, too, need to become-woman, and children to become-child, then why refer at all to women and children? Why not simply explain it in terms of the more general trajectory of becoming, the nonorganic, asubjective, and asignifying becoming-imperceptible? Is this another form of the phallic appropriation and exploitation of women and femininity as the object of male speculation and systems-building? Where does it leave women in relation to men, and children in relation to adults? What effects do such characterizations have on the great molar divisions between ages and sexes? In other words, what are its short- and long-term political effects?

To be fair to Deleuze and Guattari, they do attempt to clear up some of these confusions, although it remains uncertain how successful they are.

They describe all processes of becoming as "minoritarian" and molecular, rather than as majoritarian and molar. The minority is not a quantitative concept: It refers only to molecular processes, while the majority refers to the great divisions of groups in terms of prevailing power relations:

> Majority implies a state of domination, not the reverse . . . it is perhaps the special situation of women in relation to the man-standard that accounts for the fact that becomings, being minoritarian, always pass though a becoming-woman. It is important not to confuse "minoritarian," as becoming or process, with a "minority" as an aggregate or a state . . . There is no becoming-man because man is the molar entity par excellence, whereas becomings are molecular (Deleuze and Guattari 1987, pp. 291–2).

Becoming-woman involves a series of processes and movements outside of or beyond the fixity of subjectivity and the structure of stable unities. It is an escape from the systems of binary polarization that privilege men at the expense of women. In this sense, even if in no other, Deleuze and Guattari's work is clearly of some value to feminist theory. However, it then becomes clear that exactly what becoming-woman means or entails is different for the two sexes: for men, it implies a de- and restructuring of male sexuality, the bringing into play of microfemininities, of behaviors, impulses, and actions that may have been repressed or blocked in their development, but exactly what it means for women remains unspecified. Deleuze and Guattari state that for women to become-woman does not mean renouncing feminist struggles for the attainment of a self-determined (molar) identity and taking up a different path; the paths of becoming can only function, as they claim, through the relative stability afforded by subjective identity and signification:

> It is, of course, indispensable for women to conduct a molar politics, with a view to winning back their own organism, their own history, their own subjectivity . . . But it is dangerous to confine oneself to such a subject, which does not function without drying up a spring or stopping a flow (Deleuze and Guattari 1987, p. 276).

Becoming-woman means going beyond identity and subjectivity, fragmenting and freeing up lines of flight, "liberating" a thousand tiny sexes that identity subsumes under the One. Deleuze and Guattari imply that man's becoming-woman relies on or presupposes woman's, that her becoming-woman is the condition of his:

> A woman has to become-woman, but in a becoming-woman of all man . . . A becoming-minoritarian exists only by virtue of a deterritorialized medium and subject that are like its elements. There is no subject of

becoming except as a deterritorialized variable of a majority: there is no medium of becoming except as a deterritorialized variable of a minority (p. 292).

If becoming-woman is the medium through which all becomings must pass, it is, however, only a provisional becoming, or a stage in a trajectory or movement, which takes as its end the most microscopic and fragmenting of processes, which Deleuze and Guattari describe as "becoming-imperceptible." This becoming is the breakdown of all identities, molar and molecular, majoritarian and minoritarian; the freeing of infinitely microscopic lines; a process whose end is achieved only with complete dissolution and the production of the incredible shrinking "man":

> If becoming-woman is the first quantum, or molecular segment with the becomings-animal that link up with it coming next, what are they all rushing toward? Without a doubt, toward becoming-imperceptible. The imperceptible is the immanent end of becoming, its cosmic formula. For example, Matheson's Shrinking Man passes through the kingdoms of nature, slips between molecules, to become an unfindable particle in infinite meditation on the infinite (Deleuze and Guattari 1987, p. 279).

There is, then, a kind of "progression" in becomings, an order or "system" in which becoming-woman is, for all subjects, a first step, proceeded by becoming-animal, and then toward becoming-imperceptible. Indiscernibility, imperceptibility, and impersonality remain the end points of becoming, their immanent direction or internal impetus, the freeing of absolutely minuscule microintensities to the nth degree. Establishing an identity as a woman is thus only setting the stage for the process of becoming-woman; becoming-woman is the condition of human-becomings; and human-becomings, in turn, must deterritorialize and become-animal. The chain of becomings follows the traditional scientific "order of being" from the most complicated organic forms through the animal world to inorganic matter, down to the smallest point or quantum of energy, the sub-subatomic particle.

Such formulas in which the "liberation of women" is merely a stage or stepping stone in a broader struggle, must be viewed with great suspicion: these are common claims, claims that have been used to tie women to struggles that in fact have very little to do with them, or rather, to which women have been tied through a generalized "humanity," which is in fact a projection or representation of men's specific fantasies about what it is to be human. The Marxist subordination of women's struggles to the class struggle, the subsumption of women's call for identities as women under the general call for the dissolution of all identities (Kristeva and Derrida), and the positioning of women's pleasures and desires as the means of access to the Other (Lacan and Levinas) all serve as relatively current examples of such phallocentrism. It is not something to which women are immune either: the fact that women perpetrate this maneuver is a function of the uncritical internalization of perspectives and interests devised and developed by men. This means, at the least, that feminists need to be wary of Deleuze and Guattari's work—as wary as of *any* theoretical framework or methodology. But it clearly does not mean that their work needs to be shunned, avoided, or ignored because of some risk of patriarchal contagion. After all, in spite of more and more subtle forms of political appropriation of women and femininity enacted by Marxism, psychoanalytic theory, deconstruction—and many other forms of theory—nevertheless, feminist theory is considerably richer because of its encounters and alliances with these theories than it would have been without them.

There is no doubt that rhizomatics has something of importance to offer feminists. If it does not actually augment feminist theory (which in any case would imply some kind of theoretical commensurability), then at least it may imply a complementarity, and it may also force critical reevaluations of the forms of struggles that women have undertaken and will continue to undertake against their containment within phallocentric discourses, knowledges, and representations. Deleuze and Guattari's work raises a number of crucial questions about the political investments of specific positions within feminism—liberal, Marxist, and socialist forms—which can be seen to participate in a molarization, a process of reterritorialization, a sedimentation of women's possibilities of becoming. It provides a mode of analysis and contestation of the ontological commitments and intellectual frameworks of models of knowledge that must surely be of some interest and value to feminists, insofar as it is experimental, innovative, and self-consciously political. Its concrete and specific value must remain an open question: This depends entirely on what feminists are able to do utilizing their work in the future, what systems of desire it can function to produce, and what networks or machines of power it can serve to support or destabilize. The more varied, the bolder such feminists thought-experiments may be, the easier it will become to assess Deleuze and Guattari's value for feminist theory. But feminists must remain wary, insofar as Deleuze and Guattari too sever becoming-woman from being-woman, and in making the specificities of becoming-woman crucial to man's quest for self-expansion, they render women's becoming, their subversions, and their minoritarian and marginal struggles subordinate to a movement toward imperceptibility, which could, in effect, amount to a political obliteration or marginalization of women's struggles.

Notes

1. There are some exceptions to this general claim. See, for example, Alice Jardine's *Gynesis: Configurations of Woman and Modernity* (Ithaca: Cornell University Press, 1985); Gaylyn Studlar, *In the Realm of Pleasure: Von Sternberg, Dietrich and the Masochistic Aesthetic* (Urbana: University of Illinois Press, 1988); and Rosi Braidotti, *Patterns of Dissonance* (Cambridge: Polity Press, 1991). As well, there are a number of unpublished feminist pieces of which I am aware, for example, Karin Emerton, "Figures of the Feminine" (1987); Petra Kelly, "Deleuze and Nietzsche: The Secret Link" (paper delivered to the MLA, 1988); and Marie Curnick, "Tales of Love" (1990).

2. Gilles Deleuze and Félix Guattari, *Capitalism and Schizophrenia*, vol. 2, *A Thousand Plateaus*, trans. Brian Massumi (Minneapolis: University of Minnesota Press, 1987).

3. Elizabeth Grosz, "Male Theories of Power" (unpublished paper, 1985).

4. Luce Irigaray, *This Sex which is not One*, trans. Catherine Porter with Carolyn Burke (Ithaca: Cornell University Press, 1985), pp. 140–41.

5. Gilles Deleuze and Félix Guattari, *Capitalism and Schizophrenia*, vol. 1, *Anti-Oedipus*, trans. Robert Hurley, Mark Seem, and Helen Lane (New York: Viking Press, 1977).

6. See Gilles Deleuze's *The Logic of Sense*, trans. Mark Lester with Charles Stivale (New York: Columbia University Press, 1990) and Luce Irigaray's "Plato's Cave," in *Speculum of the Other Woman*, trans. Gillian Gill (Ithaca: Cornell University Press, 1984).

7. See Michel Foucault and Gilles Deleuze, "Intellectuals and Power," in Donald F. Bouchard, ed., *Language, Counter-Memory-Practice* (Ithaca: Cornell University Press, 1977).

8. Gilles Deleuze and Claire Parnet, *Dialogues*, trans. Hugh Tomlinson and Barbara Habberjam (New York: Columbia University Press, 1987), p. 74.

9. In Dominique Grisoni, "The Onomatopoeia of Desire," in Peter Botsman, ed., *Theoretical Strategies*, trans. Paul Foss (Sydney: Local Consumption Publications, 1982).

10. Colin Gordon, "The Subtracting Machine," in *I and C*, no. 8: p. 32.

11. William Burroughs, *The Naked Lunch* (New York: Grove Press, 196), pp. xcv–xcvi.

12. Gilles Deleuze, "Politics," *On the Line*, trans. John Johnston (New York: Semiotexte Foreign Agents Series, 1983).

13. See also *Dialogues*, p. 73.

V. Minor Languages and Nomad Arts

11

On the Concept of Minor Literature From Kafka to Kateb Yacine

Réda Bensmaia

We would call this a blur, a mixed-up history, a political situation, but linguists don't know about this, don't want to know about this, since, as linguists, they are "apolitical," pure scientists.
—Gilles Deleuze and Félix Guattari,
Kafka: Toward a Minor Literature

In 1975, WHEN Gilles Deleuze and Félix Guattari presented their modest book on Kafka, many critics thought that the thesis defended in it could be chalked up to the militant "schizoanalysis" of *Anti-Oedipus*. For such critics, as for other skeptical readers of Deleuze and Guattari, this book was merely a more popular way of defending the ideas that they had previously put forward: linguistic pragmatism, desiring-machines, lines of escape, and other deterritorializing Bodies without Organs.[1] With the benefits of hindsight, it is much clearer now that this seemingly marginal book was not based on a need for publicity or propaganda; rather it was a book that ushered in a sound, new way of thinking and writing, and—more importantly—it was a text that discovered a new theoretical "continent": that of "minor literature." Indeed, before Deleuze and Guattari took on the task of bringing to light what is at stake (politically and ideologically, but also pragmatically and experimentally) in Kafka's work, Kafka still enjoyed a secure place in the hierarchy of "great authors," and one could hardly have thought it possible to discover such a theoretical time bomb within his "canonized" texts. If there were critics who dared broach the question of whether or not it was necessary to "burn Kafka" for the heresy of not conforming to genre codes or to the laws of narratology, no one was truly prepared to disclose the fact that

Kafka's work had sufficient resources to allow it to be no longer liable to the sort of questioning to which it had been subjected until that point. Kafka's name was still inextricably connected to a conception of literature according to which Flaubert, Goethe, Hegel, Marx, and Freud called the shots; only by invoking all these names in relation to Kafka could one claim access to his work and become one of the "initiated." Later, undoubtedly because Kafka's polymorphous work—somewhat in the sense in which Freud speaks of "polymorphous" sexuality—continued to resist the psychological analyses to which it was subjected, it was even to be pushed in the direction of theology and the cabala.

All this commotion would undoubtedly have continued or even escalated—has Kafka not been imagined as visiting professor at an American university in a short story by Philip Roth?!—had not Deleuze and Guattari intervened with their gentle jolt. This jolt was the result not of a new attempt to enrich Kafka's work artificially by trying to "swell it up through all the resources of symbolism, of oneirism, of esoteric sense, of a hidden signifier";[2] nor from a new attempt at a totalizing interpretation of Kafka's work; on the contrary, the break that Deleuze and Guattari brought about came from the radical reversal of this "perspective." For Deleuze and Guattari, the revolution that Kafka introduced is not the outcome of any particular philosophical proposition; neither does it stem from this or that thematic invention or rhetorical *dispositio*, but rather from the enactment of new operational principles for literature: in Kafka's hands, literature refuses to play the game of what people call "literature (with a capital L)"; for him literature becomes experimental, but in a new sense. Indeed, for Kafka, literature is no longer related to the desire to tell extraordinary and edifying stories; nor is it a question of inventing a new style or improving upon what the "masters" did, in the hope of relieving what Bloom calls the "anxiety of influence." It is the creation of a new regime of writing that enables us to account for what the writer currently apprehends as a situation of underdevelopment with which he or she experiments as if it were an extreme solitude or desert. The Kafka that Deleuze and Guattari give us anew is no longer seen as a writer preoccupied with the question of deciding in which language he should write, but rather as the writer who for the first time radically throws open the question of "literature" to the forces and the differences (of class, race, language, or gender) that run through it.

Creating the concept of "minor literature" with respect to Kafka's work, Deleuze and Guattari have brought about not merely a simple reterritorializing revaluation of literature, but a drastic change of the entire economy of "literature" itself as a compendium of hierarchically ordered literary genres or as a center of subjectification. Literature no longer begins with man in general—"*Der Mensch überhaupt*"—but rather with this particular man or that particular woman: here a Jew, a Czech, one who speaks Yiddish and Czech but writes in German in a Prague ghetto; later on a Berber, but of Algerian nationality, who speaks French and Arabic but who must write in French for an illiterate public!; or again, a Mexican American who speaks Spanish at home but writes in English. "How many people," Deleuze and Guattari ask forcefully,

> today live in a language that is not their own? Or no longer, or not yet, even know their own and know poorly the major language that they are forced to use? This is the problem of immigrants, and especially of their children, the problem of minorities, the problem of a minor literature, *but also a problem for all of us*: how to tear a minor literature away from its own language, allowing it to challenge the language and making it follow a sober revolutionary path? How to become a nomad and an immigrant and a gypsy in relation to one's own language? Kafka answers: *steal the baby from its crib, walk the tightrope* (Deleuze and Guattari 1986, p. 19; emphasis mine).

In this short passage, we already have enough to go on to submit without fear of going astray that in the effort to reread Kafka, to tear him away from high literature and make him the precursor of a radically new political literature, there is not the least desire—not even a repressed one—to rediscover a canon or to canonize literature all over again.[3]

From such a perspective, writing quickly acquires a network of overcoding determinations that will prohibit the writer from ever assuming a preexisting identity, language, or even subjectivity. Being a "minor" writer, in the sense that Deleuze and Guattari give the expression on the basis of Kafka's work, is no longer a matter of a simple aesthetic choice, but the result of an exigency —no longer seen as dependent on the mere will of a subject felt as transparent to itself, but on an existential situation, as it were. However, having no standard or canonical means of expression at its disposal—no abstract universal in the form of *a single* national language, *a single* ethnic affiliation, *a single* prefabricated cultural identity—this existential situation calls into being a new economy of writing and of reading. The utter uniqueness of this situation is what shapes the three principal characteristics that Deleuze and Guattari identify in what they will henceforth include in the category of "minor literature."[4]

The first fundamental characteristic has to do with the forces that determine the relationship that the writers concerned have with the languages involved. "A minor literature doesn't come from a minor language; it is rather that which a minority constructs in a major language," write Deleuze and

Guattari, who proceed to elaborate as follows: "The first characteristic of minor literature in any case is that in it language is affected with a high coefficient of deterritorialization" (Deleuze and Guattari 1986, p. 16). This characterization clearly describes the situation of a writer such as Kafka "himself" as a Jew living in Prague who, with no other language than German really available as a cultural medium, will have to leave behind his mother tongue and begin to write in a foreign language. Whence the "impasses," the series of "impossibilities" that will confront him: the "impossibility of not writing . . . the impossibility of writing other than in German . . . the impossibility of writing in German" (Deleuze and Guattari 1986, p. 16). I have said that this is clearly Kafka's "himself," but it is easy to see that such also is the situation of the Algerian, Moroccan, or Tunisian writer—or, more generally, that of the *non-French* Francophone writer: one from Canada, for example, from the Antilles or Senegal, or from Mauritania. These writers will experience the same "impossibility" of not writing, because "national consciousness, uncertain or oppressed, necessarily exists by means of literature" (Deleuze and Guattari 1986, p. 16).[5]

The second characteristic of "minor literatures," according to Deleuze and Guattari, is that "everything in them is political" (Deleuze and Guattari 1986, p. 17). Referring to Kafka's work, they have no difficulty in showing that, contrary to the many *psychological* interpretations that had accustomed us to the idea of an "individualist" and/or "intimist" Kafka, or again, of Kafka as a fitting psychoanalytic subject (Marthe Robert), everything in Kafka is political—but not at all in the sense that he speaks of *nothing but* politics (in the politician's usage of the term); rather in the sense in which what takes precedence and governs the economy of daily life is no longer a "private affair," as Kafka says, but rather the concern of the political instance (*le politique*). Here, the individual no longer appears as the product of a particular isolated consciousness (even an "unhappy" or "split" one), but rather as an arrangement of *n* elements—in other words, as a desiring-machine that functions only because it is always already connected to other "machines." Most of the time these are stronger and more efficacious machines—both more efficient and productive, to be sure—but also more "determinant": commercial machines, economic machines, but also the horde of bureaucratic and judicial machines.[6]

The third characteristic of minor literature that Deleuze and Guattari discuss and which, from a certain perspective, is derived directly from the first two, "is that in it everything takes on a collective value" (Deleuze and Guattari 1986, p. 17). Indeed, because it is not the product of agents participating in a dominant culture or language and feeling themselves to be part of an always already constituted and transparent whole—because it results from a situation "where there are no possibilities for an individuated enun-ciation" (Deleuze and Guattari 1986, p. 17)—minor literature will appear as the literature in which every statement, however slight, refers to a collectivity, or even to a community that is no longer *actual,* but essentially *virtual.* It is this state of affairs that gives minor literature its specific status and worth.[7] To speak in Althusserian terms, it is as if the system of "interpellations" that works fully in the regime of "great literature" no longer works. We must not forget that the regime of high literature is an essential system because it constitutes the transparency of the subject and its adhesion to the great symbolic subject of French or German language and nationality. As Kafka says, and as Deleuze and Guattari aptly repeat, "What in great literature goes on down below, constituting a not indispensable cellar of the structure, here takes place in the full light of day, what is there a matter of passing interest for a few, here absorbs everyone no less than as a matter of life and death" (Deleuze and Guattari 1986, p. 17).

Although recognizing here a founding and revolutionary theory—not only for "popular" literature and for literatures referred to as "marginal," but also for "literature" in general—a number of modern theorists have not failed to notice the limits or blind spots that, according to them, must be analyzed if the ruts of classical bourgeois literature are to be avoided.

In Louis A. Renza's view, Deleuze and Guattari, in writing their book on Kafka and the concept of minor literature, had attempted to introduce an antiauthoritarian and anti-"great-author" conception that would also be "third-worldly." Such a conception would finally open up a space and give voice to the literatures that escape "totalizing formulations of formalist, oedipal, bourgeois or Marxist modes of organization" (Renza 1984, p. 29). In fact, according to Renza, for Deleuze and Guattari, minor literature exem-plifies the type of *relation to* and *practice of* literature that they had already problematized in their *Anti-Oedipus;* as such, minor literature would be seen as inscribed squarely within the rather anarchist problematic that involved replacing the preformed formal entities of yesteryear—subject, author, repre-sentation, history, science—with a theory of "desiring-machines," of "deter-ritorialized flows," and/or of "bodies without organs." This change in perspective, moreover, is in Renza's eyes the best index of the distance sepa-rating Deleuze and Guattari's conception of literature—a conception that the notion of "minor" literature enables them to radicalize—and a Marxist conception, for example. In fact, Renza believes, because it has tended to deny the impact of desire on the economy of social exchanges—a denial effected by "fetishizing the discourse of labor" (Renza 1984, p. 30)—Marxism itself, despite its sensitivity to the question of oppressed minorities, has missed the revolutionary dimensions of desire and become liable to a schizoanalysis according to the rules. Moreover, it is the same logic that, according to Renza, allows Deleuze and Guattari to erect a guardrail around the oedipalizing intervention of Freudian psychoanalysis, and which leads them to criticize the Marxist regimentation (through labor) and domestication (through the "Oedipal nursery" [*la mise en pouponnière*]: "daddy-mommy-me"!) of the deterritorializing forces of desire. This critique of Freudo-Marxism is, in Renza's view, what causes Deleuze and Guattari to define an antibourgeois counterculture and to isolate a certain number of artistic works as characteristic examples of the new literature, i.e., of minor literature as a set of desiring-machines whose task it is to "short-circuit social production . . . by introducing an element of dysfunction."[8]

From such a perspective, minor literature—or, more precisely, the work called minor—would be *the ideal anti-Oedipal* text, which would conform to the theoretical exigencies of schizoanalysis, and which would come to illustrate somehow the parameters that schizoanalysis has formally assigned to it. In other words, for Renza, it is not the case that the "minor" text with its own formal and ideological characteristics made it necessary to remodel the genres and to reshuffle the cards; on the contrary, it is that a prior theoretical demand assigned a revolutionary role and function to a text *singled out arbitrarily*. From this perspective, Deleuze and Guattari are not seen as truly innovative, nor as having helped free us from the hermeneutic circle in which we were caught; rather, by setting out to challenge the validity of the criteria assigning to literary texts their place within the hierarchy of genres and (bourgeois) values, but ignoring those elements that do not fit *their* theory, Deleuze and Guattari end up establishing a system of values as rigid and dogmatic as the previous one and bringing about a return to the ideal of a literary canon. The minor literature that is then mobilized will appear simply as one kind (of literature) among others and will therefore lose its specificity.[9]

If Renza's criticism gives food for thought and calls us to vigilance, it seems nevertheless not to take into account the *politicohistorical mooring* from the vantage point of which Deleuze and Guattari have attempted to develop their analysis. For, if it is indeed true that the works of Kafka or of Edgar Allan Poe have been effectively coopted by the dominant bourgeois culture and strongly integrated into the literary canon, it is not automatically the case that they were predestined to suffer this fate. Quite the contrary, this recuperation could be one more indication of the potency of the majoritarian literary model, whose force derives precisely from the fact that it makes possible both the deflection of the destabilizing power (*dunamis*) of what can now be identified as minoritarian flows of texts, and their inscription after all as texts in the mainstream, the canon. In this sense, pulling

Kafka onto the side of minor literature, or using his work as an occasion for a reshuffling and a new theoretical deal, may be conceived as a strategy enabling a new literary theorist to kill two birds with one stone: first, to reevaluate the criteria for the definition of what "literature" is and, second, to wrest from the grip of "literature" works that would not have been integrated into the canon without having their critical (political and ideological) force *neutralized*. From such a standpoint, to appropriate Kafka or to claim his authority for the sake of minor literature would not so much reinforce the established system, as show its boundaries—suggesting a map of these at the same time as pointing to a way out of them.

It seems to me that David Lloyd understood these dynamics very well when, instead of focusing on the adequacy (or inadequacy) of any formal criterion of definition *in abstracto*, he set himself the task of providing us with new vital leads. In fact, as Lloyd sees it, while Renza may have succeeded in bringing out dramatically the contradictions inherent in all attempts to define the concept of minor literature—from Northrop Frye, through Harold Bloom and Fredrick Jameson, to Deleuze and Guattari—he nonetheless failed to assess correctly two fundamental elements: (1) the political function of the evaluations that he criticized and (2) the ideological function of the canon to which he referred without really managing to keep the necessary distance from it (Lloyd 1987, pp. 4–5). According to Lloyd, one of the touchstones for the questions posed in this debate is less the different conceptions of the subject or of subjectivity in general, less the redefinition and redistribution of literary genres for the sake of promoting a new canon, than it is the historicopolitical causes of the emergence of what we call, for the moment and for lack of a better term, "minor literature":

> Rather than shore up the notions of subjectivity that underpin canonical aesthetics, and rather than claiming still to prefigure a reconciled domain of human freedom in creativity as even surrealism does, *a minor literature pushes further the recognition of the disintegration of the individual subject of the bourgeois state, questioning the principles of originality and autonomy that underwrite that conception of the subject* (Lloyd 1987, pp. 24–25; my emphasis).

And in fact, as soon as we begin to analyze the intrinsic value of what is played out in texts that integrate the criteria proposed by Deleuze and Guattari—namely, deterritorialization of language, connection of the individual to political immediacy, collective arrangement of utterance—it becomes much easier to measure the scope of the changes that have occurred and to evaluate their nature. But the fact is that at this point the literary canon is no longer conceived in terms of an apolitical and ahistorical institutional norm concerning only the university and the school, or the (individual) affair of the critics, but rather as a *normative institution* whose fate is linked to the nature of the *states* that are its counterparts. In such a context, minor literature can no longer be considered as just another category, but must be seen as a concept that makes it possible to orient thought in a completely different direction. If, for the time being, the literary canon fails to impose itself as a necessary and sufficient system of values, it is not only because literature has changed, but also because the institutions that used to present literature as eternal are in the process of disintegrating. There are minor literatures because peoples, races, and entire cultures were in the past reduced to silence. Minor literature appears, therefore, as the practical manifestation of that very voice: the voice of Algerians, for example, men and women, who can begin to speak not only of the violence of colonization, but also of their own differences—the difference between what the state wants them to be and what they themselves want to experiment with; differences between, on the one hand, imperial conceptions of a New World Order that takes into account only the well-understood interests of affluent countries and, on the other, the "minor" conceptions that naturally belong to peoples continuing to struggle against the underdevelopment that is the legacy of years and sometimes decades of slavery; differences, finally, between East and West and, more recently, between North and South. These are some of the differences beginning to be heard *in literature* but also elsewhere, on the political scene, for example—at the price, most often, of the most costly sacrifices.[10]

In order to substantiate my claims, I would like to devote the rest of this essay to the analysis, illustrated by the theatrical experience of the writer Kateb Yacine, of certain theoretical and practical difficulties that Francophone Algerian literature has encountered in its effort, despite the obstacles it faces, to create a language of its own, to elaborate a terrain, and to find an audience.

What is the situation of a country like Algeria at the time of independence? What terrain is available for getting a cultural life off the ground? What conditions confront Algerian writers? On the one hand, Algeria inherits a state of rampant mass deculturation, in view of which the very notion of an audience seems to be a luxury or, in the best of cases, a difficult objective to reach; on the other, the number of writers, artists (including filmmakers) and intellectuals is woefully insufficient in relation to its needs, and, for the most part, these writers and artists are wholly acculturated (almost all of them have, in the best of cases, been formed in the French school system). Not only, therefore, are (cultural) products and producers lacking, but the terrain itself is missing on which these products may take root and acquire a certain significance. That is to say that at the time of

Algeria's independence, cultural problems in general, and those of literature in particular, were being posed not *in universal and abstract terms of expression,* but, first and foremost, in terms of regional and concrete territorialization. In other words, we were faced with an attempt to create from scratch —but not casually—on the ruins of a social community that escaped disaster and dislocation only in *extremis* a new collective subject, or even a national subject. It is evident here that every decision and every engagement was, to borrow one of Kafka's expressions, a question "of life or death." To create or recreate a terrain or to define something as a national characteristic sounds natural enough—but out of what? Out of the forgotten, obliterated past? Out of the ruins of popular memory? Out of folklore? Tradition? Which folklore, which tradition? In fact, not one of these instances was strong enough and cohesive enough to anchor a national culture. And in any case, even when raised in this way, the questions are not very clear and the problems remain abstract because, whether by means of folklore, the past, tradition, or anything else of that ilk, the creation of a specific, authentic culture requires first of all a solution to the problem of the medium through which it must—or can—be accomplished: specifically, the problem of language. In which language should one write? In which language should one communicate? Which language should be used on the radio, on television, in films? French—this "paper language" that only intellectuals and lettered people speak and read? Arabic? But which Arabic? The language of the educated or that of the street? Or again: What does one do with the Berber language? Prohibit it? Ostracize it?

These are the concrete and vital problems that explain the crucial tensions, contradictions, and difficulties encountered by every artist in Algeria and in any other former French colony: to write for the writers, or to make films for the filmmakers, becomes an urgent question because, as we understand very well by now, every one of the choices they make is a *founding* choice; each one of their words carves out the very flesh of the nation to come. In all cases, it is a matter of creating the missing terrain— for the terrain is indeed missing—though from a certain point of view, what is missing is also the people itself.[11] It is a matter of finding a way out from the labyrinth of languages: a matter of staking one's territory like an animal, of never leaving one's *Umwelt*—with the understanding that this declaration of a missing people is not a renunciation, but rather "the new basis on which it is founded."[12]

We know today that this lack, as well as the movements of deterritorialization that accompany it, is inseparable from the problem of language: the situation of Francophones in a country that opts very rapidly for Arabization in schools and administrative bodies; the situation of Arab-speaking writers in a country with an illiteracy rate of over 8.5 percent, and with French still the dominant language everywhere; the situation of the Berbers in the mountains and the Tuaregs in the Sahara, forced to abandon their own languages as they leave the desert or the rural areas. What is to be done with this blur of languages? Or, as Deleuze and Guattari put it, "How to become a nomad and an immigrant and a gypsy in relation to one's own language? Kafka answers: steal the baby from its crib, walk the tightrope" (Deleuze and Guattari 1986, p. 19). For Algerian writers, there have been only two possible paths to take. One has been to enrich the French language artificially, to "swell it up through all the resources of symbolism, of oneirism, of esoteric sense, of a hidden signifier" (p. 19), an approach resulting in some of the texts of writers such as Mohammed Dib, Rachid Boujedra, and, to a certain extent, Nabile Farès. But such efforts have implied once more "a desperate attempt at symbolic reterritorialization based in archetypes" (p. 19)— sexuality, blood, or death—that have only accentuated the break from the people. The alternative has been to move toward a greater sobriety, a poverty of means, a "white writing," out of which has come texts such as Boujedra's *L'escargot entêté* or the poems and later novels of Dib.

Faced with these limitations, Yacine very soon leaves off writing novels and poetry in order to give himself entirely over to theatrical production. This was a "minor" genre in Algeria when Yacine laid hold of it at the beginning of the 1970s, but he made it into an extraordinary instrument of metamorphosis, transforming a situation of extreme cultural poverty and stagnation into a revolutionary process. Having understood very early on the importance of the linguistic element in the situation/circumstances Algeria was going through during that period, Yacine quickly seized on the advantages to be gained by exploiting the resources of the popular theater. He understood at any rate that it made no sense to promote a theater limited to spoken Arabic in order to produce plays in a country with not one spoken language, but rather several vernacular languages (Arabic, French, and Berber), each with its own temporality and its own terrain. Yacine understood as well that if independence had emancipated Algeria from its politicoadministrative tutelage, it had not solved the problem of its relation to French as a vehicular language (of commercial exchange and bureaucratic transmission) and as a referential language (the instrument of politics and of *Gesellschaft*)! His understanding of this complex interplay, it seems to me, is what explains the affinities between his theater and the minor literature that Deleuze and Guattari present as emerging with Kafka. Yacine's theater, with the capacity to take all these elements into account, is able to function as a practical sociolinguistics and to fill the prevailing void. Because his work takes off from the same politicohistorical premises as Kafka's, it is no surprise that it shares in the principal traits that characterize minor literature: Yacine has spontaneously transposed these features into his work.

The first thing that strikes the reader or the viewer of his plays is the treatment to which he subjects the languages he mobilizes. Yacine found a way to transform French in order to bend it to the needs of the cause he was defending; in order to speak to the people, to address the people, to lend it a voice when it was foreign to itself. He accomplishes this by means of *underdeveloping*—developing from below—French, in order to bend it to the political and ideological demands of his people, through the elimination of syntactic and lexical forms. We should not forget the taste for "innate genitality," as Antonin Artaud would have called it, in the semantic overload of words—an overload that often reaches the pitch of a cry, or of the popular song of Cheikh Mohammed el Anka and of Rai music.[13] Having said this, we must also acknowledge that Yacine was never oriented toward a cultural reterritorialization through spoken Arabic or Berber, and even less through a hypercultural usage of French or classical Arabic. On the contrary, since *both* French *and* Arabic were themselves deterritorialized in Algeria as in the entire Maghreb, Yacine chose to push ever further in the direction of an increasingly *intensive* use of French. Indeed, although in his novels French syntax was still more or less respected, in his theater Yacine definitely dismisses "standard" French in order to draw the language nearer to the most disarticulated usages, which are also the closest to popular practice. Thus, besides the common vernacular languages used (Arabic, Berber), the knowledgeable public could also recognize the French of the immigrant worker, the French of the Berber speaker, or the French of a particular town (Algiers, Oran, or Constantine) mixed with the different accents that correspond to these. This mishmash helps explain the "becoming" that Yacine has his characters undergo: not only Tunisian president Bourguiba's becoming "short neck,"[14] but also the general's becoming "killer consonants."[15]

The other characteristic feature of this theater is obviously its political dimension. Here, as well, we are faced with a theater that is political not because of the political themes it mobilizes, but essentially because it is a theater where every "individual concern" is always and immediately connected with politics. In Yacine's theater, if an individual concern is necessary, it is, above all, insofar as it is always another story, a much larger and more complex one—the story of colonization, most definitely, but also the story of racism, of the prison and the psychiatric asylum, of the French school system, etc.—all of these stories are vibrating within the private affair, which stems from them and is played out in them. It is thus that the familial triangle will always find itself broken and exploded: in Yacine, one always abandons his mother (the motherland) and the father is always father at one remove, a phony father or a stepfather. The fact is that family ties were historically subordinated to many other laws besides those of an "integrated" society: when it is not the father who emigrates, leaving his offspring to a brother or a cousin, it is the sons who leave never to return, and who end up inventing their own genealogy.[16] Familial relations will then be replaced by *blocks of alliance,* and the Algerian will find more affinity with a Portuguese immigrant in France or a black American than with a compatriot who has accepted the "new deal" with one race, one language, and a single religion, Islam. In Yacine's universe, neither race nor religion, nor even language, sufficiently accounts for the mental world of a North African.

And it is in this context that one could say that Yacine's theater is a *political theater,* even a theater of grand politics, and not only a politicized theater. Whereas in dominant nations the family, the couple, and even the individual carry out their affairs as *private affairs,* in the theater of Yacine "the private affair merges with the social—or political—immediate."[17] Thus, as is also the case in the films of Glauber Rocha or Güney or in the novels of Gabriel García Márquez, "the myths of the people, prophetism and banditism [and, I would add, emigration and the impossibility of return] are the archaic obverse of capitalist violence, as if the people were turning and increasing against themselves the violence that they suffer from somewhere else out of a need for idolization" (Deleuze 1988, p. 218). It is this violence that Yacine, without knowing or even caring about what Kafka may have done, mobilizes in his theatrical work, which he transforms into the largest imaginable arena of agitprop, which "is no longer a result of a becoming conscious, but consists of *putting everything into a trance,* the people and its masters, and the camera [in Yacine's case, the mise-en-scène] itself, pushing everything into a state of aberration, in order to communicate violences as well as to make private business pass into the political, and political affairs into the private" (Deleuze 1988, p. 219). For Yacine and for many writers and filmmakers from former colonies, as for Kafka, it is no longer a question of invoking myths in order to discover their archaic sense and structure, "but of connecting archaic myth to the state of the drives in an absolutely contemporary society, hunger, thirst, sexuality, power, death, worship" (Deleuze and Guattari 1988, p. 219). As Yacine puts it, "plans are constantly being turned upside down!" Once again, it is not a matter of opposing "reality" (which one?) to myth, but, on the contrary, given the existing circumstances, of extracting from the myth a "lived actual" that would make it possible to account for the impossibility of living in the conditions that people have inherited. Such an impossibility could certainly drive people to madness, but it can also be transformed into a revolutionary instrument for attending to first things first—for example, to the need to give life and voice to the people. But, for Yacine, defending the people no longer means hunkering down and retreating into oneself, but, on the contrary, showing that the people are never one but always plural: a multiplicity of peoples with intersecting destinies.[18]

In this way, popular theater takes over a potential revolutionary machine, not only for short-term ideological reasons, but rather because only this machine is able to fulfill the conditions of a collective utterance that is nowhere else to be found. One must be blind therefore, or irresponsible, to accuse Deleuze and Guattari of not being political enough, or of being shortsighted from a historical point of view. One must be deaf not to hear the shout of joy let out by all writers living and writing in the conditions that they describe the day that they were able to count Kafka as one of their own and to add the multiple resources of his "minor" art to the instruments that they had created against the silence and the indifference of the literary *establishment*. Minor literature had long since made its *practical entry* into the history of literature; but its *theoretical entry* had yet to be made. Thanks to the work of Deleuze and Guattari, and judging by the renewed interest it is currently receiving and, above all, by the rich debates it has provoked, one can say that this theoretical entrance has taken place— and all to the good of literature.

—*Translated by Jennifer Curtiss Gage*

Notes

1. Cf. Deleuze and Guattari on the *CsO* (*Corps sans organes*): "It is in no way a question of a fragmented, shattered body, or of organs without a body (OwB). The CsO is precisely the opposite. It is not a matter of fragmented/piecemeal . . . organs with respect to a lost unity, nor of a return to the undifferentiated with respect to a differentiable whole . . . The BwO is desire; it is that which and through which we desire" (*Mille plateaux: Capitalisme et schizo-phrénie* [Paris: Minuit, 1980], p. 203).

2. Gilles Deleuze and Félix Guattari, *Kafka: Toward a Minor Literature,* trans. Dana Polan (Minneapolis: University of Minnesota Press, 1986), p. 19.

3. Here I have in mind, among other possible references, the beautiful, quite original text of Louis A. Renza, *"A White Heron" and the Question of Minor Literature* (Madison: University of Wisconsin Press, 1984), in which one finds the following remarks: "For Deleuze and Guattari, *then,* 'minor literature is 'schizo' literature in its subatomic-like anti-oedipal and self-deconstructing release of literary 'intensities'" (p. 33; my emphasis); or the following, which is even more clearly stated and, in its context, appears as a symptom: "Unlike the formalist or Bloomian aesthetic conceptions of minor literature, *then,* Deleuze and Guattari's includes an ideological element. And unlike the Marxist ideological conception of minor literature, theirs attempts to account for its particular aesthetic operations. Yet *no less than these other conceptions,* Deleuze and Guattari's anti-oedipal or fissionary (but not

visionary) delineation of minor literature *ends up* inviting the return of a repressed desire for canonicity" (p. 34; emphasis mine).

4. In the general context of Renza's analysis, the quotation marks produce the intended effect of once again canonizing a text whose primary task was to remove itself from the canon, whether literary or critical! In the previous note, the "then" and "ends up" seem to me, at the very least, to clash both with the overall project and with the details of the Deleuze and Guattari project. As I try to suggest here, their project is not to canonize Kafka—how could they do so, since they make Kafka the "somber precursor" (Deleuze) of a kind of minor literature that owes him its *theoretical* existence!—but rather to tear his work away from the many attempts to reduce it to the literature of the major (signifying) regimes.

5. I am thinking here of the work of writers such as Abdelkébir Khatibi in Morocco, Abdel Wahhab Meddeb in Tunisia, and, of course, writers like Nabile Farès or Kateb Yacine in Algeria, or Edouard Glissant in the Caribbean. They also found themselves, in the days following their countries' independence, in the situation that Deleuze and Guattari describe: They must write, but—whether for technical or for ideological reasons, which I will address later on with regard to Yacine—they cannot use the French language simply as a matter of course. Whatever they do, this language will remain an "official language" and the instrument par excellence of the most tragic "inner exiles." "Never," writes Yacine, "even in my days of success with the teacher, did I stop feeling deep inside myself that second rending of the umbilical cord, that internal exile that brought the schoolchild closer to his mother only to yank him away, each time a little farther, from the murmuring blood, from the reproving tremors of a banished language, secretly, of one accord, no sooner struck than broken . . . *Thus it was that together I lost both my mother and her language, the only inalienable—and yet alienated—treasures*" (*Le polygône étoilé* [Paris: Seuil, 1956], pp. 181–182; my emphasis).

6. In setting forth the elements of this problematic, I recognize the debt that Deleuze and Guattari owe to Althusser's work, particularly his work on "ideological state apparatuses." "It will be recalled that after revealing the effects of the mirror-structure of Ideology— whether 'the interpellation of "individuals" as subjects,' or 'their subjection to the (Grand) Subject,' or the 'mutual recognition of subjects by themselves and by one another,' or, lastly 'the absolute guarantee that all is well'" Althusser remarks,

> Result: caught in this quadruple system of interpellation as subjects, of subjection to the Subject, of universal recognition and of absolute guarantee, the Subjects "work," they "work by themselves" in the vast majority of cases, with the exception of the "bad subjects" who on occasion provoke the intervention of one of the detachments of the repressive state apparatus. But the vast majority of (good) subjects work all right "all by themselves," i.e. by ideology (whose concrete forms are realized in the Ideological State Apparatuses). They are inserted into practices governed by the rituals of the ISAS, etc. [Louis Althusser, "Ideology and the State," in *On Ideology* (London: Verso, 1984), p. 181.

See also "Idéologie et appareils idéologiques d'état," *La Pensée* 151 (1970): p. 35.

7. For reasons that are quite understandable in the context in which Deleuze and Guattari inscribe their analysis of the emergence of minor literature—their task is to analyze the work of an author whose work cannot yet be defined except through a demarcation from the canon and from the genres that dominate the cultural and literary scene of the moment— the collective dimension is attributed to the rarity of talents in the face of what we could term the plethora of "masters." I will attempt, later on, to show that determination by means of rarity is problematic in that it tends (unconsciously?) to confirm the validity of a model—

that of *great literature*—according to the definition of which everything that is not included in the literary canon will be considered as insufficient, secondary, or even marginal.

Deleuze and Guattari seem completely aware of this problem, since a little further on in their book, after defining the three characteristics of minor literature—deterritorialization of language, connection of the individual with the political immediacy, collective arrangement of utterance—they spontaneously invoke the relation of the notion of minor literature to that of "marginal" literature. Now, as they do so, they show that the latter can be "well understood" only in comparison with the singular economy of minor literature: "There has been much discussion of the questions 'What is a marginal literature' and 'What is a popular literature, a proletarian literature?' The criteria are obviously difficult to establish if one doesn't start with a more objective concept—that of minor literature. Only the possibility of setting up a minor practice of a major language from within allows one to define popular literature, marginal literature, and so on" (Deleuze and Guattari 1986, p. 18; my emphasis).

One final remark on this subject. In his fine book on the Irish author James Clarence Mangan, David Lloyd exhibits an acute awareness of these difficulties and makes a number of important points that I would like to begin to relate to the present study. Having acknowledged the work of the pioneer Louis A. Renza (see note 1 above), Lloyd criticizes him for deferring discussion of the *political* functions of the different evaluations of minor literature that were made by the predecessors of Deleuze and Guattari, but straightaway Lloyd extends his criticism to a certain lack of vigilance on the part of Deleuze and Guattari themselves. Lloyd writes

> To produce an adequate theory of minor literature in any sense of the term, it is necessary to analyze historically the politics of culture. Deleuze and Guattari's work goes some way toward engaging this issue, though impressionistically and largely only synchronically. What they valuably indicate, however, is the extent to which recent interest in the question of "minor" literature recognizes the prior emergence of a combative field of literature that is expressly political insofar as the literature of the Third World, of "minorities" or formerly marginalized communities, *calls into question the hegemony of central cultural values. A retrospective, even belated, analysis discovers in articulating the political structure of the canon the terms of an aesthetic culture that have already been negated by a new literature* (David Lloyd, *Nationalism and Minor Literature: James Clarence Mangan and the Emergence of Irish Cultural Nationalism* [Berkeley: University of California Press, 1987], p. 5; my emphasis).

8. Gilles Deleuze and Fèlix Guattari, *Capitalism and Schizophrenia*, vol. 1, *Anti-Oedipus*, trans. Robert Hurley, Mark Seem, and Helen R. Lane (New York: Viking Press, 1977), p. 31. Quoted in, *"A White Heron" and the Question of Minor Literature*, p. 31.

9. Cf. *"A White Heron" and the Question of Minor Literature*, pp. 32–36, particularly the following:

> Their brand of minor literature clearly becomes a *privileged double* of their antioedipal revolutionary desire to overthrow all versions of a here debased reactionary or reterritorializing major literature . . . Deleuze and Guattari thus *privilege* only a *certain kind* of minor literature, that which like Kafka's is in the process of interrogating the oedipean tropes of major literary praxis but which the major language or canonical critical codes can misrecognize as major according to their own standards (p. 34; my emphasis).

10. Who would have ever heard of Kateb Yacine, Nabile Farès, and Rachib Boujedra without the Algerian war and the independence that followed? Yacine had written and published very

beautiful texts before these events! But it is true that he still could be read only as a "minor" writer, in other words, as a *secondary* writer. As an Algerian writer, was he not still considered as a second-class French citizen from the outlying territories?

11. I am thinking here of what Gilles Deleuze writes in *Cinema 2: The Time-Image*, trans. Hugh Tomlinson and Robert Galeta (Minneapolis: University of Minnesota Press, 1988), pp. 216–18:

> [T]he people no longer exist, or not yet . . . *the people are missing* . . . No doubt this truth also applied to the West, but very few authors discovered it, *because it was hidden by the mechanisms of power and the systems of majority*. On the other hand, it was absolutely clear in the third world, where oppressed and exploited nations remained in a state of perpetual minorities, in a collective identity crisis. Third world and minorities gave rise to authors who would be in a position, in relation to their nation and their personal situation in that nation, to say: *the people are what is missing* (my emphasis, except for first).

12. *Cinema 2*, p. 217. These are the "conditions" that explain why, historically, it is the cinema or theater, and not literature, for example, that has achieved the objectives expected from the renaissance of Algerian culture, providing the vital medium that enables a people to recognize in themselves a national "character": as an identity in the diversity of local languages and cultures, as a unity in the multiplicity of *technes* and manners, and, finally, as active solidarity amid the disparity of cities and countrysides.

13. Cheikh Mohammed el Anka was a singer of the *chaabi*, or popular, style—one of the most broadly appreciated genres of music, through which the most important political, erotic, and social messages were conveyed. Rai is a form of popular dance music with strong rhythms and lyrics that often deal with the burning issues of the day, whether political, social, sexual, or affective. It is no coincidence that Rai music has been condemned by representatives of the FIS (Islamic Salvation Front) in Algeria.

14. Bourguiba is transcribed as "*bourequibat*," which in colloquial Arabic is a diminutive of "neck" and can be translated as "small neck" or "spindly neck."

15. The reference here is to the General "*Q qui tue*" ("Killer Q") in Yacine's *La Gandourie sans uniforme*.

16. Cf. Mouloud Feraoun, *Le fils du pauvre* (Paris: Seuil, 1954) and Rachid Boujedra, *Topographie idéale pour une agression caractérisée* (Paris: Denoël, 1975).

17. Cf. *Cinema 2*, p. 218.

18. I have in mind here the play *L'homme aux sandales de caoutchouc* (Paris: Seuil, 1972), written in honor of Ho Chi Minh while he was still alive; this play ultimately became a hymn to the struggle of all oppressed peoples.

12

Francis Bacon:
The Logic of Sensation

Dana Polan

OUT OF GILLES DELEUZE'S books, *Logique de la sensation* has been virtually passed over in silence. But for a review essay by Patrick Vauday at the time of its appearance and a very short appreciation by Christine Buci-Glucksmann,[1] *Logique* is a book that few writers seem to have felt is important—either for what it says about Bacon (my university's fine arts library has a number of books on Francis Bacon, but not Deleuze's), for what it teaches about aesthetic practice in the contemporary world, or, most important perhaps to our purposes here, for what it offers as confirmations or mutations in Deleuze's work when it comes to engage with the work of art.

This neglect seems to me unfortunate, and what I want to do in the following discussion is suggest some of the interest *Logique de la sensation* might hold for us. We can note, first of all, how interesting the book is simply as a reading of Bacon. In keeping with his attempt (as in *Kafka)* to rethink authorship away from psychologism, Deleuze figures here a Bacon who is almost a *scientist* of the visual arts, using the space of the tableau for operative experiments (*operatoire* is one of the recurrent words in the book). Deleuze's Bacon is, for example, quite different from the pop-psych version of the suffering artist represented in a short piece on Bacon that appeared in my local paper, the *Pittsburgh Post-Gazette*, as I was preparing this essay.[2] Here, the meaning of art is to be found *in* the artist, in the very corporeality of his being. Donald Miller, the *Post-Gazette* art critic, receives a photo of Bacon and notes that he has "differently focused eyes." For Miller, this explains the style of the art with its "interlocking planes floating indistinctly into each other, as crossing focal points would." Miller even makes an appeal to the old mythology that art is born out of suffering: "I don't admire Bacon any less . . . If anything, I marvel how Bacon, like [Henry] Koerner, has enriched his creativity through his eye problem, creating a distinctive style."

To be sure, even as he avoids such myths of a creativity tied intensely to the suffering body, Deleuze is not wanting to get rid of notions of individual authorship altogether, and there are moments when *Logique de la sensation* slips back into that romanticist appreciation of individual expressivity that often pops out in Deleuze's texts on artists. On the one hand, as in *Kafka,* with its constant reference back to the *Letters* or *Diaries* (and to a lesser extent the testimony of friends), Deleuze reverts to a faith in the ability of the artist to reveal his/her intention in moments of intimate communication. *Logique de la sensation* relies heavily on Bacon's interview with David Sylvester, and the book often treats Bacon's words as a truth that can be applied to the understanding of the work's experimentation: to take just one example from a possible many, on the second page of *Logique,* Deleuze cites from the Sylvester interview the claim that "*with modesty,* Bacon recognizes that classic painting has often succeeded in tracing this other type of relation between Figures [that is, of nonnarrative relation] and that this is still the task of the painting of the future" (p. 10; my emphasis).

On the other hand, as in Deleuze's two volumes on cinema[3], the very comparison of the artist to other sorts of workers in the realm of concepts—whether they be philosophers or scientists—bolsters a romanticism of the artist by treating him/her as a veritable thinker, a true inhabitant of a world of ideas (even if these ideas are indistinguishable from the force and sensation that go along with them). Deleuze eschews the myth of the artist as an intuitive figure for whom creativity comes welling up as a sort of ineffable inspiration or intuition; for Deleuze, instead, it seems often that it is the very fact that the artist can *reflect* on his/her practice that gives the artist a worth, a value.

Nonetheless, for all its emphasis on a specialness of the artist, Deleuze's meditation on creators avoids a full romantic mythology of expressiveness in a number of ways. First of all, the very emphasis on the artist as someone who works experimentally breaks down typical boundaries of the aesthetic and the practical: the artist rejoins the general camp of cultural workers. Second, and connected to the first point, Deleuze's mode of discourse, here as in other books on single figures, works by a deliberate process of digression in which the writing veers away from the nominal subject of the book endlessly to make comparisons with other figures. Just as the Kafka book will be about Welles or Proust as well as Franz K., just as the Leibniz book will be as much about baroque artists up to the present, so too the Bacon book offers short disquisitions on figures ranging from Rembrandt to Joseph Conrad to (again) Proust to Jacques Tati to William Burroughs to Artaud. Some of this derives from Deleuze's overall interest in writing as a form of pick-up (as he terms it in *Dialogues*), but it seems to me it also works to remind us that no artist is alone. Each artist takes his/her place in a tradition of experiments, and each artist can be read as simply one more side (or facet) of an overall project: here, with a concise explicitness, Deleuze names that project the search for *a logic of sensation.*

It is here that the quasi-romantic study of Bacon individually joins up with the larger romantic project of Deleuze: to go beyond the surface fixities of a culture and find those forces, those energies, those fluxes, those sensations that specific sociohistorical inscriptions have blocked and reified into social etiquettes and stultifying patterns of representation. Bacon, of course, seems ready-made for such a project, and one can almost have the sense that if Bacon didn't exist, Deleuze would have had to invent him for his argument. Of course, though, he does exist, and the proof of this is brought out doubly by material aspects of *Logique de la sensation.*

First, the back of the two volumes of *Logique* sport photomaton pictures of Bacon, making him seem present in directly vibrant ways. That one major argument of *Logique* deals very critically with the role of the photographic image in increasing the spread of clichés through our society only intensifies the irony of the cover of *Logique*'s appeal to a givenness of the artist through his photographic image. If, as I have already suggested, *Logique* is in a tension between a romanticism of the artist as a ground of knowledge about artistic practice, and a demythification of individuality by the reinsertion of each individual artistic praxis back into a field of general cultural experimentation, the back-cover photos of Bacon aid in the staging of this tension by offering us the image of the artist on the back of a book that critiques to a large degree the potential truth-value of images. And, in this respect, even the cover itself incorporates the tensions of the book's arguments about the need for a modern art of *defiguration* by, on the one hand, offering up the photographs with scratches, rips, technical flaws, and so on as if to figure the very breakdown of the figurative that *Logique* will discuss in its pages and, on the other hand, balancing the back-cover photography against the front-cover painting of a mutating face, as if to highlight the distinction between the powers of painterly defiguration and the limitations of photographic cliché.

Second, the very division of *Logique de la sensation* into two volumes—one just of Deleuze's commentary, one just of Bacon's paintings—sets up the tension of image and concept and yet suggests ways to overcome the developing of that tension into an irreconcilable split. How can one, on the one hand, argue that all aesthetic practices participate in a common activity of force and sensation and, on the other hand, still respect the material and formal specificity of each art? This is a question that has vexed theorists. To take just one example, film theorist Raymond Bellour argues that film is an "unattainable text," posing quite particular problems to close textual analysis.[4] Such analysis necessitates a quotability of the analyzed work (as in the "lexie" of Roland Barthes's *S/Z*), but, as Bellour argues, film is not quotable, or rather it is not quotable in any way that does not freeze the image (see, for example, Alfred Guzzetti's book on Jean-Luc Godard's *Two or Three Things I Know about Her,* which puts frame enlargements on one page and commentary on the facing page) or translate the visual into the verbal. Short of doing one's textual analysis in the same medium as the analyzed work—so that Bellour himself, to analyze the sexual ideology of the Hollywood film, has made a critical videotape that includes, or quotes, extracts from the films—analysis can only seem to betray the image.

As I have suggested in a review-essay of Deleuze's book on Foucault, there seems to be, in Deleuze, an active engagement with the theoretical question of what it means to talk in one medium about the practices of another medium.[5] Aware that all acts of translation are betrayals, Deleuze seeks experimentally, nonetheless, for those ways, those moments, in which the verbal can *invoke* the visual. First, as I argue, there is in Deleuze's writing a constant recourse to the setting up of *tableaus*—verbal descriptions of scenes that in their stylistic richness gain all the intensity of a visual presence. Second, the very language that Deleuze uses to describe the operations of force and intensity is a vivid and materialized one that makes even the most ethereal concepts seem sensuously concrete. For all his discussion of the arts as conceptual, Deleuze understands the concepts as quite physical operations, rather than as ideal abstractions. His philosophical language is one of mappings and cartographies, lines of escape and vanishing points, rhizomatic and crystalline branchings, and so on.

With apparent paradox, this evocative verbal language seems to work its spell all the more when the visual is not present. It is as if once the language of evocation gets going and starts constructing the imagination of a visuality for the reader, any actual image could only be a reductive fixity, an impoverishment, a blocking of the imagination's powers. Hence, Deleuze eschews all photos in his two cinema books, letting his own language do the work of rendering the films in their forceful intensity.

In the case of *Logique de la sensation*, what might have been initially a practical decision to present the analysis in two easily manageable parts also seems to stage the tension between verbal and visual. Most important, it seems to me that there is no apparent, easy, logical, necessary relation between the two volumes. Although the volume of pure text sports little figures in the margin keyed to particular plates in the volume of images, the very turning back and forth between the two tomes leads to a constant fragmenting of Deleuze's own argument's flow (so that I decided to read the text twice, once flipping to the images, once just concentrating on the text;

another option would be to study the images very closely and then go to the text alone). Not merely an illustration of Deleuze's argument, the volume of images is a full and beautifully produced catalogue in its own right; not merely a catalogue essay, Deleuze's volume is a general theory of modern art in its own right. As I have argued for *Foucault*, Deleuze figures his theory of art with a writing style that itself overcomes the verbal/visual dichotomy by being intensely vivid, imagistic, tableauesque. Note, for example, how evocative, how unabstracted are the opening words of *Logique de la sensation*: "A roundness often delimits the place where the character—that is, the Figure— is seated. This roundness, or this oval, more or less, takes its place: it can overflow the edges of the tableau, be in the center of a triptych, etc." (p. 9).

What theory of art emerges then in Deleuze's evaluation of the visual? It is his concept of modern art that I want to stake out in the rest of this essay by simply going through the book and rehearsing its argument. Given the relative unfamiliarity of most scholars with *Logique de la sensation*, this explanatory operation is perhaps not without interest.

Deleuze begins with a note telling us that his book will be organized by rubrics, each dealing with an aspect of Bacon's paintings. Taken together, these rubrics are intended to build a "general" logic of sensation, "whose summit is founded in the sensations of colors." At the same time, in a gesture that is familiar in the work of Deleuze, he suggests that this logic of sensation also has a historical dimension—is directly historical. Indeed, if much of Deleuze's work is geared to finding a general force or sensation behind the superficial flux of historical movement, there is also a sense in which history takes its revenge on Deleuzian antihistory and shows how the search for a logic of sensation is governed by a framework that is finally temporal throughout. One thinks here of the claim in *L'image-movement* (and repeated in the special note added to the American edition) that Deleuze intends no historical argument about the development of cinemas. Yet the two volumes on cinema quickly become historical through, and at several levels, whether that of the progress from a simple movement within the single shot of "primitive cinema" to the complex movement constructed by montage, or the movement within and between the two volumes from a goal-oriented action cinema symptomatized by Hollywood story-telling to a postwar art cinema symptomatized by errancy, passive observation, and the pure perception of time.

In *Logique de la sensation*, too, an art history argument emerges. Here, however, in contrast to the cinema books, this history never seems even vaguely totalized (except insofar as Bacon is seen as a high point of the age-old quest for defiguration) and emerges only in flashes, deliberate digressions that offer glimpses of a narrative never fully rendered. I think, for example, of the fascinating excursus in rubric 2 (pp. 13–14) on the effect of photography and modernity on art's history. Here Deleuze dispenses with the famous argument—from Malraux and now picked up by Bacon—that two conditions of modernity free modern art from the representational project: first, the rise of photography creates a new ease of documentation that will permit modern art to explore other, nondocumentary regions; second, secularization increasingly frees art from the need to *represent* religious themes and values.

Deleuze dispenses with the latter of these two arguments in a way that once and for all puts to rest the myth that it is only in our modern age that defiguration is achieved in art (to take just one example, remnants of this myth surface in Barthes's *Writing Degree Zero,* where Flaubert and 1850 stand as markers of a needed break from bourgeois representability). Deleuze argues intriguingly that traditional Christian religious art needs an element of defiguration, of abstraction, to fulfill its very aims. It needs this in order specifically to achieve a different and higher sort of representation that goes beyond realism's rendering of an earthly hereness to picture at one and the same time this figurative hereness *and* the more abstracted, unmaterial, spiritual realm of the beyond. As Deleuze puts it,

> Take an extreme example: the "Burial of Count d'Ogaz," by El Greco. A horizontal divides the tableau into two parts, inferior and superior, terrestrial and celestial. And in the bottom part, there is certainly a figuration or a narration that represents the burial of the count, even though all the coefficients of deformation of bodies, and notably of elongation, are already at work. But above, where the Count is received by Christ, there is a wild liberation, a total freedom: the figures stand up or stretch out, refine themselves without measure, outside all constraint. In spite of appearances, there is no longer any story to be told; Figures are delivered from the representative role and they enter directly into rapport with an order of celestial sensations (p. 13).

Deleuze's Francis Bacon, then, will be a modern artist, but not according to our usual sense of modernity as a radical break from the regressions of history and as a first and unique achieving of defiguration. For Deleuze, defiguration has a venerable history (just as *Logique du sens* finds antecedents for Lewis Carroll in the Stoics), and if there is a uniqueness or specificity to Bacon's defigurative project, it is that Bacon's historical moment is the moment of such phenomena of mass reproduction as the cinema and the photograph. Bacon is in a lineage with El Greco and others, but his place in that lineage is, of necessity, historically particular.

Deleuze's discussion begins fairly internally—with an analysis of Bacon's specific painterly practices—and then moves from formal analysis of the tableaus to the larger art-historical implications of what Bacon is up to. Thus, the very first rubric, "*Le rond, La piste*," examines the procedures by which Bacon frequently delimits a central figure through the effect of surrounding that figure with some oval shape. And yet, very quickly, Deleuze directs his analysis in such a way that the division of formal investigation and historical or sociological inquiry reveals itself to be little more than an expedient heuristic. The formal and the historical blur inextricably. For instance, the very simple act of delimitation by means of an oval is rewritten by Deleuze as only a single and initial step in a higher logic or series of logics.

The first rubric gives us several examples of this rewriting. First, Deleuze reminds us that the delimitation by means of the oval is itself an open-ended process of experimentation: it renders "sensible a sort of trailblazing of the Figure in its place, or on itself. It is an operative field" (p. 9). Second, as Deleuze notes, the delimitation of the single figure will have to be situated in subsequent discussions in relation to Bacon's larger procedure of linking several figures together (as in the triptychs). Third, delimitation of a figure away from all narrative context is not the only means of defiguration, even if it is the one that Bacon in particular prefers: as Deleuze says, "painting has two possible paths for escaping the figurative: toward pure form, through abstraction, or toward the pure figural, through extraction or isolation" (p. 9). If Bacon opts for the latter, another branch of art opts for the former, and much of *Logique de la sensation* will discuss the option of abstraction as much as that of a denarrativizing isolation. And this constant attention by Deleuze to the multiple paths of art history connects to yet another way the first rubric takes its place within a higher logic: already, from the beginning, Deleuze digresses from Bacon to the whole field of art experimentation. For example, he announces (p. 11) that the links of the Baconian system with Egyptian and Byzantine and other artistic systems will have to be explored at some later point.

Just as the simple strategy of the oval will be generative, then, of other Baconian strategies, so too the first rubric of *Logique de la sensation* contains the basic crystals for the remainder of Deleuze's argument. Hence, the second rubric moves, as we have already noted, into general comments geared to overcoming standard arguments (the Malrauxian ones) as to a supposed privilege of modern art in the quest for defiguration. As indicated before, Deleuze quickly disposes of the argument that the religiosity of premodernist art destined it for a project of figuration. That argument relegated to the dust bins of history, Deleuze invokes the second argument, namely, that photography's chemical reproduction of images gives it a realism that frees up other arts from the desire for realism; but he ends the second rubric with the resolution of this issue hinted at, but not fleshed out. Again, in the two short pages of rubric 2, we can see the argumentative-discursive strategy of Deleuze at work: he moves beyond the concerns immediately at hand (that is, Bacon's defigurative tactics) to general (historical) concerns, but he makes this move in a way that allows, indeed even necessitates, further discussion in later rubrics.

In regard to Malraux's second argument—photography frees up the arts so that they may go thirsting after defiguration—Deleuze accepts it *in part*. He admits that photography impacts on painting; there is a sort of anxiety of influence in which each painter begins his/her work knowing (or sensing) that that work is being done in a world already of the photograph: "[m]odern painting is invaded, besieged, by photos and clichés that install themselves on the canvas even before the painter has begun to work. In fact, it would be an error to believe that the painter works on a white and virgin surface. The surface is virtually already invested entirely by all sorts of clichés from which one must break away" (p. 14). But, where Malraux tended to see the freeing up of painting as a natural process wherein a nonvisual art easily discovered its true vocation, Deleuze argues that this process has nothing natural about it, nothing spontaneous, nothing inevitable. The world of the cliché comes to the artist as a threat, a pressure, and only a concerted effort, an intense job of work, can enable painting to eschew the cliché (this notion of art as hard work is another way Deleuze makes the practice of the painter complementary with that of the scientist or experimenter or engineer): "[H]aving renounced religious sentiment, but besieged by the photo, modern painting is in a much more difficult situation, no matter what one says, in trying to break with the figuration that would seem to be its miserable assigned lot" (p. 14).

One form of painterly hard work would be that of abstract art: "It needed the extraordinary work of abstract painting to tear modern art from figuration" (p. 14). But (and this "but" is immediately Deleuze's as much as mine) the break from figuration can also appear as a direct confrontation with figuration, a working through it, a defiguring of it. "But," asks Deleuze in the last line of rubric 2, "Isn't there another path for the tearing of modern art from figuration, one that is more direct and more sensible?"

This question allows the argument to move back to formal analysis, to an engagement with the internal systematicities of the Baconian job of work. Indeed, rubric 3 begins with the announcement of such a return: its first word is "*Revenons.*" But already the rhizomatic process of Deleuze, where any one activity reveals that it touches upon so many others, is at work here. If the first rubric had dealt especially with two elements, the figure and the surrounding oval, rubric 3's return clarifies that there are really three different elements at work here. "Let us return to Bacon's three pictorial elements: large flat areas which are spatializing material structure; the Figures, Figures and their factness; place, that is, the round shape, the arena, or the contour which is the common limit of Figure and flat area" (p. 15). In a quasi-structuralist manner, Deleuze treats the three elements of the flat tableau—space, figure, and oval—virtually as pieces in a *combinatoire* out of which various painterly combinations are possible.

Thus, on the one hand, Deleuze echoes the argument of the first rubric to note how one relation of oval to figure can construct the Baconian painting as an activity of witnessing in which the figure is delimited from an action by virtue of its seeming to be "in attendance for that which is going to happen" (p. 15). Deleuze emphasizes that the witness is not a spectator: "These [are] witnesses, not in the sense of spectator, but as marker or constant in relation to which a variation is gauged" (p. 15). In such cases, the figure is pretty much a stability around which the open space of the tableau is caught in an athletic motion: "[T]he flat space is caught up precisely in a movement by which it forms a cylinder: it rolls around the contour, the site; and it envelops, it imprisons the Figure" (p. 16).

On the other hand, in many of Bacon's paintings, it is the figure that is involved in energetic motion. Here, we see a way in which Bacon's practice— the transformative and transforming shapes—seem ready-made for a Deleuzian analysis. As Deleuze notes, the Baconian figure is that of a body, specifically a body in the process of a full and violent becoming, racked by spasms, wrenching cries, vibrant thrusts of transmuting flesh. Here, the flat space ceases to be mere background and becomes instead a virtual destiny of the fleshy figure it holds within: "Hysteric scene. The whole series of spasms in Bacon is of this type: love, vomiting, excrement, always the body which tries to escape by one of its organs, to rejoin the flat surface, the material structure . . . And the cry, Bacon's cry, is the operation by which the entire body escapes through the mouth" (p. 17). Here the oval is not so much a delimiter that turns the figure in on itself so that it can achieve self-sufficient systematicity. Quite the contrary, the oval becomes a hole, an openness toward which the figure directs itself as if it has found one of Deleuze's famous "vanishing points" (*points de fuite*). Comparing Bacon to William Burroughs with his contractions of the body that are actually prosthetic mergings of the body with its surround, and to Lewis Carroll, with his mirrors that are not reflections of the body but seductions bringing the body beyond itself, Deleuze sets up the Baconian practice as a nonstop mutation.

Not surprisingly, just as he did with Kafka, Deleuze sums up the evolutionary mechanism in Bacon as a *becoming-animal*, the concern of rubric 4. Here, Deleuze modifies the initial step of his argument, where the figure was taken to be a whole element capable of connecting up to larger processes, but not seeming divisible in itself; now, in contrast, in the fourth rubric, Deleuze examines how the figure itself is caught in an act of becoming in which it is not only the relation to the outside that is in mutation, but also the figure itself in its internal (dis)organization. In particular, the human figure reveals itself to be internally (and dynamically) divided in two productive ways. First, Deleuze notes that the figure in Bacon is that of the human body, specifically, of a body governed by a tension between *heads* and *faces*. Acknowledging in a footnote his debt to Félix Guattari, Deleuze explains how such a tension is worked out by Bacon:

> A portraitist, Bacon is a painter of heads and not of faces . . . [T]he face is a structured spatial organization that covers the head, while the head is a dependency of the body, even if it is not the endpoint of it. It is not that it lacks spirit [*esprit*] but rather that it is a spirit that is body, a corporeal and vital gust, an animal spirit, it is the animal spirit of man . . . It is thus a very special project that Bacon pursues as portraitist: to undo the face, to rediscover or cause to surge forth the head beneath the face" (p. 19).

As Deleuze argues, in Bacon there is a "*zone of indiscernability, of undecidability*, between man and animal" (p. 20; his emphasis).

Such indiscernibility is linked to the second tension Deleuze finds in Bacon's rendition of the figure of the body: namely, a tension between, on the one hand, flesh (*chair*) or meat (*viande*), and bone, on the other. Bones serve as a supportive or structuring matter that flesh mutates or moves away from: "Meat is that state of the body where flesh and bones confront locally, instead of being composed together structurally" (p. 20). Deleuze notes the importance, for Bacon, of the vertebral column—but not so much for any offer it gives to the body of solid, stable support as, quite the contrary, for the ways it serves virtually as a measure, a marker, against which the deviations of the flesh can be measured. Deleuze suggests that here we can uncover one reason for Bacon's fascination with scenes of crucifixion: on the one hand, the sublime religiosity of the crucifixion shows an attempt to redress the body upright toward the radiance of the heavens, but, on the other hand, all transcendent uplift is countered by the weighty pulling of the flesh downward toward its own animality. As Deleuze puts it, "[M]eat has a head by which it flees and descends from the cross" (p. 22).

Deleuze is moving toward an understanding of Bacon as a painter who defigures representation and breaks the figure from representation in hopes of rendering sensation in and of itself. The sixth rubric will deal explicitly, as its title announces, with "Painting and Sensation." But to get to this point, that is, for the development of Deleuze's own argument to echo fully the progress of Bacon's painterly work, Deleuze has to pass through a "Recapitulative Note: Periods and Aspects of Bacon," the concern of the fifth rubric. Predictably though, Deleuze endorses the possibility of a recapitulation (the terms of which he borrows from David Sylvester's analysis of Bacon), while at the same time he seems to call into question any totalizing summation of the career.

Sylvester discerns three periods in Bacon, and Deleuze sums these up as "the first which brings into confrontation the precise Figure and the lively and hard open space; the second which treats a *'malerisch'* form against a tonal background rendered in strips [*à rideaux*]; the third, finally, which reunites 'the two opposed conventions,' and which returns to the lovely flat background while locally inventing effects of blurriness through scratching and rubbing" (p. 24). Deleuze, however, modifies this chronology in two ways that make any attempt at positive recapitulation less easy. First, he suggests that the three practices are simultaneous, not successive:

> And that's what's essential: there is certainly a succession of periods, but there are also coexistent aspects by virtue of the three simultaneous elements of the painting that are perpetually present. The armature or the material structure, the Figure in position, contour as a limit of the two, never cease constituting a system of the utmost precision (p. 24).

Second, any recapitulation is exceeded, has the lie put to it, by the fact that Bacon's own career is open-ended and moving toward a fourth phase, one in which the full breakdown of representation might be achieved: "the zone of blurring or sweeping away, which makes the Figure surge up, will now matter in and of itself, independently of all defined form: it will appear as a pure objectless Force . . . The Figure is dissipated" (p. 25).

It is the work of defiguration to achieve pure force that Deleuze sums up as a logic of sensation, whose overall power is hinted at in the sixth rubric. Going back to phenomenological readings of Cézanne, such as the famous one by Merleau-Ponty, Deleuze suggests that sensation emerges in the encounter of a perceiving subject with the disintegrating figure of the painting: "What is painted in the tableau is the body, not insofar as it is represented as object, but insofar as it is lived as experiencing sensation . . . Following Valéry, we can say that sensation is that which is transmitted directly by avoiding the detour or the boredom of a story [*histoire*] to be told" (pp. 27–28).

Histoire has a double sense of *story* and *history*, and Deleuze plays on this ambiguity to argue that the sensation of Bacon's defiguration is also, simultaneously, an attempt to get away from narrative and from historical reference. In particular, whatever sensation a Baconian painting engenders should not come from any anecdotal value in an object represented therein:

Bacon has not stopped wanting to eliminate the "sensation," that is, the primary figuration of that which provokes a violent sensation . . . Bacon brings with himself all the violence of Ireland, the violence of Nazism, the violence of war . . . But whenever there is horror, a history is reintroduced, one has failed at rendering the cry . . . This is because violence has two very different meanings: "when one speaks of the violence of painting, this has nothing to do with the violence of war" (p. 29; the internal quotation is from Bacon).

Beyond figuration and representation, then, sensation comes from a pure power that "overflows all domains and traverses them. This power is that of Rhythm, which is deeper than vision, audition, etc. . . . 'A logic of the senses,' Cézanne said, 'that is non-rational, non-cerebral'" (p. 31). It is for this reason that Patrick Vauday in his review-essay of *Logique* argues that the book is a major revision of phenomenology's emphasis on subjectivity, but a subjectivity imagined as that of a fully centered, fully composed, fully integrated being. Deleuze's approach still strongly speaks of subjectivity, but it is now a subjectivity that is broken up, traversed by intensities, run through with energies—in short, as Deleuze puts it, *hystericized*.

"*L'hystérie*" is the title of the seventh rubric. Explaining Bacon in light of Artaud, Deleuze familiarly refers to the ways the postphenomenological workings of modern aesthetic practice produce a subjectivity, not of the *organism*, but of the *body without organs*. At the same time, though, Deleuze seeks to distinguish Bacon's practice—and the painterly tradition to which it belongs—from other modern logics of sensation that aim to break down the integrity of the human organism.

First, Deleuze makes use of Worringer (as he has in other writings on art) to set up a possible typology of modern artistic options. In particular, by using Worringer's understanding of a specificity of the Gothic tradition of art, Deleuze argues that Bacon's practice comes from a heritage that is doubly antagonistic: directed, on the one hand, against the "organic representation of classical art" and, on the other hand, against an abstraction that transforms representations into "geometric form." Bacon's Gothicism offers instead "a geometry that is no longer in the service of the essential and the eternal; it is a geometry put in the service of 'problems' or 'accidents,' ablation, adjunction, projection, intersection" (p. 34). And just as some art historians have argued in favor of the ties of Gothic art to an intense religiosity (see, most famously, Panofsky's *Gothic Architecture and Scholasticism*[6]), Deleuze himself acknowledges a spiritual dimension to this search for an intensity that would be neither abstract nor representational: "Bacon's geometry gives witness to a high level of *spirituality* since it is a spiritual will that leads this geometry away from the organic and in search of elementary forces" (p. 34).

Beyond distinguishing different goals within the overall work of aesthetic practice, Deleuze also differentiates among the various arts and suggests there is a particular force to *painting* that is different from that of, say, literature (for example, Artaud) or music. As Deleuze puts it bluntly, "We want to say in fact that there is a special connection of painting to hysteria" (p. 37). As Deleuze clarifies, this is not a hysteria of the artist (Deleuze is not offering a psychobiography) so much as a hysteria of the medium of painting itself, based as it is on the direct effect of lines, colors, and so forth on the eye of the beholder. Indeed, Deleuze will suggest that there is an optical specificity of painting that means that no matter the particular psychology of the painter, that psychology gets translated or transmuted into something quite different when used for painting:

> Abjection becomes splendor, the horror of life becomes a very pure and very intense life . . . It is cerebral pessimism that painting transmutes into nervous optimism . . . This is the double definition of painting: subjectively, it invests our eye which ceases to be organic to become a polyvalent and transitory organ; objectively, it holds before us the reality of a body, of lines, and of colors liberated from organic representations (p. 37).

However, even as he grants special privilege to painting, Deleuze acknowledges that all the modern arts can share in the quest for a logic of sensation. In particular, each art resembles the others in the way it seeks to use the materials specific to it to render something beyond it: for example, as Deleuze notes, modern music often employs the aural as a way to capture the chromatic, and painting often uses the visual to grab at the invisible.

The dialectic of visible and invisible is a central concern of the eighth rubric, "*Peindre les forces.*" From an opening statement on the unity of the project of the modern arts, Deleuze focuses in progressively on the specific work of painting, on the particular contribution of Bacon to that work ("It seems that, in the history of painting, Bacon's Figures are one of the most marvelous responses to the question: how to render visible invisible forces?" [p. 40]), and on the particular role of the cry as a special strategy in Bacon. Deleuze asks of this privilege given to the cry, "Why does Bacon see in the cry one of the highest objects of painting?" (p. 41). Deleuze suggests that the cry has a spiritual function, but one altogether other than the interpretation usually given it by writers on Bacon who would see the cry as an agonized declaration of existential pain—an expression, we might say, of "the horror, the horror." For Deleuze, such a reading is superficial in the extreme: "The forces that make the cry, and that convulse the body and arrive at the mouth . . . are not at all confused with the visible spectacle before which one cries, nor with the assignable sensible objects whose action decomposes and recomposes our pain" (p. 41).

To read the Baconian cry as an expression of horror is, for Deleuze, to remain in a representational frame of mind. Against those who would take Bacon to be a depressing painter of the ravages of existence, Deleuze adopts the affirmative approach of "*savoir gai*": "When Bacon distinguishes two violences, that of spectacle and that of sensation, and says that one has to renounce the former to attain the latter, this is a sort of declaration of faith in life" (p. 41).

Why, then, bother to paint horror at all, why not accede directly to the sensations of joyful affirmation? Deleuze's answer is that starting with the superficial appearance of horror allows Bacon's painting to become a sort of triumphant battle with the forces of pessimistic representation. Instead of easily achieving painterly optimism right from the start, Bacon figures the heroic struggle of such optimism against all the pressures that would bring it crashing down into banality:

> We must render to Bacon as much as to Beckett or Kafka the following homage: they erected unbeatable Figures—unbeatable in their insistence, in their presence, at the very moment where they "represented" horror, mutilation, prosthesis; the fall or failure. They gave life a new power of a laughter that is extremely direct (p. 42).

Having now defined a specificity both of painting in relation to the other arts and of Bacon within the history of painting, Deleuze returns more directly to Bacon's particular practice, and in the ninth rubric initiates a discussion of "Couples and Triptychs" in Bacon. Where the earliest pages of *Logique* examined the simple dynamics of, for example, figure-ground relations, now the analysis itself and the combinatory it is examining are complicated by a multiplication of the basic painterly elements. As Deleuze puts it at the beginning of the rubric: "It thus happens that sensation passes through different levels, under the action of forces. But it also happens that two sensations confront each other, each with its own level or zone and cause their respective levels to communicate with each other. We are no longer in the realm of simple vibration, but in that of resonance" (p. 45).

Although he began *Logique* with a fairly formal analysis of fundamental elements within the Baconian tableau, Deleuze has progressively complicated his initial givens. He has situated Bacon within a larger art history and he now moves back to the particularities of Baconian form to show each and every strategy is no more than one option in a larger array of endeavors of the artist. On the one hand, for example, Bacon goes beyond the initial given of the figure by means of couples of figures. Deleuze even suggests that his initial emphasis on the solitary figure may have been little more than heuristic and that, in fact, even the solitary figure is already coupled with other figures with which it is in an integral and necessary resonance: "At the limit, there are only coupled Figures in Bacon . . . Even the simple Figure is often coupled with its animal" (pp. 45–46).

On the other hand, taking a "privileged place in Bacon's oeuvre" (p. 48) are the triptychs, which Deleuze treats as a sort of dialectical surpassing of the vibratory power of the figure and the coupled figures. In a sense, Deleuze argues, the logic of sensation of the figure can only go so far, can achieve only a limited defiguration: insofar as the figure constitutes a given against which permutations are measured, there is always the danger that representation makes a reappearance and turns the figure into a stable meaning.

In the triptychs, however, no one figure stands alone; no one figure gains priority (not even the figure in the center). Even as the triptych increases the stakes of the quest for defiguration—insofar as the multiplication of figures might seem to encourage the return to the painting of narrativity, of logical and causal connections among figures—the triptych also renders all relations more vibratory, more mobile. We now have three panels, each filled with information, and this leads to increased possibilities of permutations and resonances among panels. Deleuze refers to John Russell's account of a reading or, rather, readings, of a Bacon triptych: With regard to the various figures, a number of hypotheses can be expressed, but there is never anything to ground any one interpretation at the expense of any other. What the viewer is left with finally is the sheer vibratory facticity, the thereness, or what Deleuze, borrowing from Bacon and quoting in English, terms the "matter of fact" nature of the painting, where things are simply painted and no final meaning is easily imparted to them. At the most, one might assign general roles to each of the three panels' dominant figures: activity, passivity, witnessing. But these roles are to be thought of less as deep significations of the work of art than as combinatory elements that give the painting new rhythmic powers.

Again, Deleuze's language implies that the arts are unified in their quest for an overall logic of sensation. Although he has given a special privilege to painting, Deleuze uses a musical vocabulary to invoke the powers of painting in relation to the depiction of sensation:

> [T]o paint sensation, which is essentially rhythm . . . But in simple sensation, rhythm still depends on the Figure, it presents itself as a *vibration* that traverses the body without organs, it is the vector of sensation, it is that which makes sensation pass from one level to another. [In contrast,] in the coupling of sensation, rhythm liberates itself already, since it confronts and reunites diverse levels of different sensations: it is now *resonance*, but it is

still confused with the melodic lines, the points and counterpoints of a coupled Figure; it is the diagram of the coupled Figure. With the triptych finally, rhythm takes on an extraordinary amplitude, in a *forced movement* that gives it autonomy and gives us the impression of Time: the limits of sensation are overflown, exceeded in all directions (pp. 48–49; ellipses are in the original).

In Deleuze, digressive name-dropping is often quite revealing of the larger stakes for any single point he is presently making. In this instance, as if to insist on the unity of the arts at this level of overrun rhythmic sensation, Deleuze ends the rubric with a panoply of artistic references: Stravinsky, Beethoven, Messiaen, Rembrandt, Soutine, Claudel.

Similarly, Deleuze begins the tenth rubric—"Note: What Is a Triptych?"—with references to several artists: Messiaen, but also Paul Klee, who is said to have dealt in a painterly way with the same procedures of rhythm as the musicians. Indeed, if he has earlier argued that the rhythmic power of the triptych comes from its presenting of multiple elements that can then combine in unstable ways, Deleuze now argues that this activity occurs at levels of increasing abstraction (or defiguration) in which the painterly specificity of the work is progressively left behind and purer, non-medium-specific rhythms emerge. On the one hand, the triptychs often work figuratively by playing a witnessing figure against an acting one; on the other hand, and at an entirely different level, the function of these figures can reverse in cases where the dynamic is no longer the representative one of horizontal-vertical.

In other words, Deleuze argues that the function of the elements, of the figures, in the triptychs ultimately has little to do with any identity, any anthropomorphism, that one might have assumed to accrue to such figures. To act and to witness an act might seem functions of personages, but the interaction of these two functions is only one case of a larger field of possible interactions that often has little or nothing to do with notions of character at all. Thus, as the tenth rubric lays them out, we can find in the triptychs such interactions as vertical-horizontal, descent-rise, diastole-systole, naked-clothed, augmentation-diminution, and so on. Deleuze even notes that the prostheses, mutilations, and transformations that the body undergoes in Bacon's paintings are best read not as a sign of the horrors that flesh can undergo, but as elements that also allow variations into the painting so that the figure can be endlessly changing, even in its very shape and comportment.

No single value system—for example, any sort of moral judgment—could ever hope to lord over all these possibilities of vibratory, rhythmic transformation. Deleuze's approach is, first of all, not a Derridean deconstruction in which a hierarchy of terms would be upset by parodic inversion; it is not a question, for example, of showing that the passive is really the active and vice versa, but of showing that the very description of either of these poles according to peremptory valuations is inappropriate. Although Deleuze is constrained by the limits of language to name the two sides of a relation, he seems concerned to emphasize that all such namings are arbitrary impositions whose fictionality has to be insisted upon: "In fact, one cannot identify descent-rise and contraction-dilation, systole-diastole; for example, a falling apart is also a descent and also a dilation and an expansion, but there is also contraction in a falling apart" (p. 53).

But for all the freedom that inheres in this open and nonhierarchical combination of elements *within* the space of the tableaus, artists themselves are not in a position of pure spontaneous freedom *before* their tableaus. In rubric 11, "The Painting Before Being Painted," Deleuze examines how even the empty space of the white canvas is, in a certain sense, already filled up before the painter even begins to work. On the one hand, as earlier rubrics have shown, no painter ever works apart from a tradition, a heritage, an anxiety of influence. On the other hand, in a much more negative direction, the painter lives in a world overrun by representations, by figurations, and there can be no pure beginning, no innocent act of putting brush to canvas.

Here, as I noted earlier, Deleuze's analysis becomes directly sociological as he confronts a modern society dominated by everyday signs and images, and more than in any other section, his language becomes energetic, passionate in its condemnation:

> We are besieged by photos which are illustrations, newspapers which are narrations, cinema-images, tele-images . . . Here there is an experience which is very important for the painter: a whole category of things that one can term "clichés" already occupy the canvas, even before beginning. It is dramatic . . . Clichés, clichés! One can't say that the situation has gotten any better since Cézanne (pp. 57–58).

Deleuze plays on the double meaning of *cliché* which, in French, indicates both a stereotyped thinking and a snapshot (the link being that both are born out of an instantaneous act that requires little effort and that results in a freezing of reality into a reified image). The photograph is a particularly dangerous form of short-circuited thinking and representation, since its chemically based realism gives it an air of authenticity, of innocent directness, that anchors and supports all its stereotyping (a point central to Roland Barthes's thinking on photographic messages). For Bacon, this is both the problem and challenge of photography. As Deleuze puts it, "Bacon scarcely believes [in the aesthetic pretension of photography] since he thinks that the photo tends to crush sensation onto a single level and is powerless to put into sensation the difference of constitutive levels" (p. 59).

Throughout *Logique*, Deleuze, while avoiding a pure structuralism, has nonetheless imagined that aesthetic sensation always derives from the encounter of several elements, rather than the welling up of force inside a single thing. But in throwing attention back onto a world imaged therein, the photo unifies and robs itself of permutational possibilities. For Deleuze, photography can only become a complicated art in exceptional cases (he cites Muybridge's motion studies and, like Barthes, Eisenstein's photograms).

As Deleuze sees it, Bacon's painting starts always already with a realization that such painting has to exist in a world filled with photographic clichés. While "Bacon does not pretend to dictate universal solutions" (p. 62), his sense that photography's danger comes from a freezing that occurs automatically (as in the Kodak phrase cited by Susan Sontag: "You push the button, we do the rest") leads him to a very precise painterly practice. This practice, Deleuze notes, is that of trying to bring "chance" [*hasard*] back into the act of painting. Between the snapping of the camera button and the producing of the cliché, little but probability intervenes. Still, the painter can break down this automaticity:

> [Bacon will often] quickly make "free marks" in the interior of the painted image, in order to destroy the nascent figuration of it . . . The problem of the painter is not to enter into the canvas, because he is there already (prepictorial task), but to leave it, and by doing so to leave the cliché, leave probability (pictorial task). It is the manual marks of chance that will give him this possibility (pp. 60–61).

And even more, the very fact that the painter does this manually—that Bacon reacts to the automaticity of the camera with the physical activity of emphatic deformation—means that, again, Deleuze is able to treat the artist as cultural *worker*. Art is not spontaneity, but production, "manual labor" (p. 63, in the last line of the rubric).

In this respect, Bacon's practice of manual deformation can be specified and distinguished from other tactics of defiguration. Deleuze stakes out two in the twelfth rubric, "The Diagram": abstraction and action painting. In the case of abstraction (Deleuze is thinking of that geometric abstractionism characteristic of a Mondrian or a Kandinsky), the work of the hand is subordinate to a higher goal, an ulterior meaning. Through the effect of various binary codes that take over the painting (for example, horizontal lines versus vertical ones), the painting becomes a path to a spiritual energy. The modulated work of the hand is recoded in precise, rationalized terms (sharp lines, rectangles, and so on). In Deleuze's reading, "abstract forms belong to a purely optical new space that doesn't have to be subordinate to manual or tactile elements . . . abstract painting elaborates less a diagram than a symbolic *code* based on major formal oppositions" (p. 67).

In the case of abstract expressionism and action painting, there is certainly much emphasis on the hand, on the here-and-now conditions by which the painter splashes paint onto the surface of the work. There is "the extension of a manual power, 'all over' [English in the original], from one end of the painting to the other" (p. 69). But this rendering tactile of the surface of the painting is so complete and extreme that paradoxically (a paradox that the abstract expressionists are not always aware of, as their own pronouncements suggest) optical sensation is diffused, confused, lost:

> These [the elements of the painting] are no longer tactile referents of vision but, because it is the manual space of what is seen, it is a violence done to the eye . . . Bacon is not attracted by abstract expressionism, by the power and mystery of the contourless line. This is because here, the diagram has taken over the whole painting, he says, and because its proliferation has created a veritable "mess" (*gachis*) . . . Sensation is achieved but remains in an irremediably confused state (pp. 69–71).

Against rationalized coding, and against contourless cacophony, Bacon will follow a third path in which the cliché remains but is deformed through localized operations:

> [T]he precision of sensation, the clearness of the Figure, the rigour of the contour continue to act underneath the smearing or the strokes that don't erase them but, rather, give them a power of vibration or illocalization (the mouth that smiles or cries). And Bacon's ulterior period will return to a localization of strokes in random and brushed over zones (p. 71).

Bacon's particular path is given its most theoretical discussion in rubric 13, "Analogy," one of the most important sections of the book—important less perhaps for what it says about Bacon specifically than for its reiteration of arguments that have been central to Deleuze's philosophy of art throughout his career. Deleuze intends the section's title to refer less to any sort of correspondence theory of art than to the linguistic distinction of digital and analogical communication (as in Bateson, whose sense that certain forms of communication, such as that of the schizophrenic, do not follow the sharp digital distinctions of officialized languages has been decisive for Deleuze). Earlier, I referred to certain operations of *Logique de la sensation*—especially its treatment of Bacon's paintings as sources of permutations—as quasi-structuralist, but the thirteenth rubric clarifies the necessary limitations of such an image of Deleuze. Structural linguistics would be the province of an approach based on the isolation of fully discrete units that can enter into conflict with other units (for example, Saussure's phonemes, whose mutually exclusive oppositions create the meanings of words) but can only do so sharply, with no blurring or intermixing between them. Not at all setting out to avoid a linguistics or a semiotics, Deleuze nonetheless wants to create a theory of communication that would respect *gradations* of signification, that would not limit meaning to the rigorous opposition of totally differentiated bits of language. The procedure is quite explicit in the cinema books, where Deleuze opposes the dominant semiotics of film (that is, Metzian semiotics—a structural semiotics that searches for the large and discrete unities of film) with fluid semiotics concerned less with distinct elements than with signifying tonalities or graded shifts. To take just one example, standard semiotics of film argues that film has trouble dealing with tense (since the image appears in the present even if it is a representation of the past) and can only really achieve the representation of temporality through sharp, discrete oppositions of images (for example, the cut to a flashback that juxtaposes one image to another creates a binarism of past and present). For Deleuze however, especially in *L'image-temps*, the image itself can vibrate with the layers of temporality (as in the rich images of Welles or Mankiewicz); the image is itself not a single unit, but a graded richness, resonant with the modulations of past, present, and future.

"Modulation" is a key term here: Deleuze wants a semiotics attuned to the indiscrete variation, the tonal shift, the imprecise gradation. In this respect, Bacon's smears that defigure a representation but do so by transition, by a slow melting away of the body, are exemplary forms of painterly modulation.

> One can ask if painting hasn't always been the analogical language par excellence . . . In fact, painting as analogical language [as in Bacon] has three dimensions: *planes*, the connection or junction of planes (and first of all of vertical and horizontal planes) that replace perspective; *color*, the modulation of color which tends to suppress relations of value, chiaroscuro and the contrast of shadow and light; the *body*, mass and the disposition of the body which overflow the organism and break down the relation of form and content (pp. 74, 76–77).

In the tradition of Cézanne, Bacon's painting is not an encoder of reality (in the sense of the linguistic code as rigorous structuring), but a modulator of it.

The effort in these later rubrics to outline a taxonomy of languages, more particularly, of artistic languages, has led to less and less reference on Deleuze's part to Bacon's specific version of artistic language: indeed, the later rubrics are immediately distinguishable by their increased length (as if the general theorization of art requires more pages) and by the gradual dropping away of the marginal numbers keyed to the images in the pictures volume (as if the general theory required only minimal grounding in specific cases). It might seem that Deleuze has abandoned Bacon, but the title of rubric 14 makes clear that Deleuze's approach to the relations of the individual artist and the overall movement of art history is a dialectical one: "Every painter sums up [or "takes up": *résume*] in his own way the history of painting." Indeed, if earlier I noted that the first sections of *Logique*, with their references to Bacon's own pronouncements in interviews, seemed to invest in a romanticism of the individual artist, and if the later sections seem to deal more with the traditions of art and the pressures confronting art— the painting before being painted—Deleuze's approach finally seems to be one of mediation, an attempt to argue that art history is both about logics of history and about individual praxes in art. Paraphrasing Sartre from *Questions de méthode*, we might say that for Deleuze, Francis Bacon is an important modern painter, but not every important modern painter is Francis Bacon. As I said earlier, the painter is not a pure spontaneity, but a situated being who always works in relation to an already done—for example, to that coagulated antihistory that Sartre refers to as the *practico-inerte*.

If I mention Sartre, it is because he undoubtedly went the farthest of modern French thinkers in trying to think the personal career as a replaying of history. For all our clichéd attempts to imagine Sartrean Marxism in opposition to structuralism and poststructuralism (an attempt, to be sure, that Sartre himself engaged in), Sartre's influence can be felt in *Logique*'s desire to deal with the whole of artistic tradition and, at the same time, with one individual figure's assumption of that tradition; indeed, in *Logique*, Deleuze makes explicit use of *L'Etre et le Néant*[7] and *L'Idiot de la famille*[8], Sartre's masterwork of existential biography. In Sartre's terms, the individual is to be thought of as a concrete universal (see, for example, *Qu'est-ce que la littérature?*) or a universal singular (as he puts it in *Critique de la raison dialectique*). Each individual is not only in history, but insofar as he/she takes identity from all that history has been, each individual is also a full summation of history, a total incarnation of it, even as he/she is this history in irreproducibly personal ways.

No one else is Francis Bacon—there is an irreducible specificity to his being-in-the-world—but as with every other artist, one can read off of Bacon's work the totality of art history, a totality his work endlessly retotalizes and projects toward the future. "It is no longer just Bacon but the whole of Occidental art history that is in question," as the fourteenth rubric puts it (p. 80).

The dialectic of universal and singular is given immediate representation by the juxtaposition of rubrics 14 and 15. On the one hand, the fourteenth rubric sets out to define the traditions, the situations, that each and every artist confronts by the very fact of being an artist. Ranging through Egyptian, Greek, Christian, and modern art, Deleuze constructs a taxonomy of possibilities of figuration and defiguration around such options as essential/accidental, haptic/optic, light/shadow, color/light, figure/narrative, a whole range of "new and complex combinations or correlations" (p. 83).

On the other hand, the fifteenth rubric, "*La traversée de Bacon*," insists on the specificity and individuality of Bacon's particular assumption of artistic tradition. To take just one example, the fourteenth rubric borrows from Alois Riegl to define the contribution of Egyptian art as a haptic aesthetic based on the flattening of space in the bas-relief; the rendering frontal of this space; the simultaneous distinguishing and unifying of foreground and background by contour; the consequent establishing of space as essential, an enclosed unity impervious to accident; the rendering of space as flat geometric plane; and, most important, the figuring of human and animal alike as perfect, essential geometric forms. So the fifteenth rubric, in both continuity and contrast, treats Bacon as an inheritor of the Egyptian tradition who brings to the tradition important and inescapable modifications. For instance, if the geometrization of space flattens space and renders it tactile in a way that tempts Bacon dearly, at the same time Egyptian art essentializes space (and represents objects such as Man) in a way that Bacon can only abhor:

> One could say that Bacon is first of all an Egyptian . . . representation: foreground and background, connected to one another by contour, are on the same close haptic plane of vision—but here already an important difference insinuates itself into the Egyptian world, like a first catastrophe: the foreground form falls, inseparable from a plunging (*chute*). The foreground form is no longer essence; it has become accident, Man is an accident (p. 87).

Most of all, Deleuze finds a specificity of Bacon in the ways he deals with traditions of color passed down from Cézanne, and from Gauguin, and Van Gogh. If Egyptian art derives its strongest effects from the geometry of lines and contours, another tradition finds its sensations in modulations of color—color not as sharp opposition, but as undulating oscillation or gradation, or analogical (rather than digital) variation: "It is color, it is relations of color that constitute a haptic world and meaning, as a function of hot and cold, of expansion and contraction" (p. 88).

Distinguished from geometric tradition, colorist approaches are also distinguished from those in which the modulation of *light* is the dominant practice: "Light is time, but space is color. One terms 'colorists' those painters who tend to substitute for relations of value [as in the handling of light] relations of tonality, and who tend to 'render' not only form, but also light and shadow and time by the pure relations of color" (p. 89). In other words, the colorists can do in their own way what the artists of light do. But as Deleuze emphasizes, to say this is not to value one tradition over another: "Certainly, it is not a question of a better solution, but of a tendency that traverses painting and leaves behind characteristic masterpieces, distinct from those of other tendencies" (p. 89).

Within colorism, several subtendencies are visible, beginning with the Cézannean tradition: "Modulation by pure distinctive strokes and following the order of the spectrum was the specifically Cézannean invention for achieving the haptic sense of color." But for Deleuze, this tendency runs several risks: for example, beyond "the danger of reconstituting a code" (p. 90), there is also the danger of the background becoming so solid that it enters into no play of modulation with the foreground forms, "as if the singularity of the body detached itself from a uniform, indifferent, abstract flat domain" (p. 90). Yet there is possible a different colorist modulation that separates itself off from Cézanne's options; here the separation of flat background and foreground figure is combatted by, on the one hand, a vivid tone and saturation in the background that gives it not only the quality of "passage" from one color to another, but of an overall sense of movement, transformation and modulation; and, on the other hand, "broken tones for the foreground form which construct another sort of passage in which the color seems to cook and come out of a fire" (p. 90).

It is in this post-Cézanne modernity that Bacon's specificity is to be found: "The 'modern portrait' would be color and broken tones, in contrast with the classic portrait which is light and blended colors . . . Bacon is one of the great colorists since Van Gogh and Gauguin" (p. 91).

Devoting the sixteenth rubric to a "Note on Color," Deleuze argues that color is the ultimate force of permutation, the prime modulator, in Bacon's artistic practice. Having in early sections suggested that Bacon operates his permutation around three strategic elements—structure, figure, contour—Deleuze now argues that all three are little more than pieces of a larger permutational or modulatory assemblage governed by the vibratory powers of color: "*all three converge toward color, in color.* And it is modulation—that is, the relations of color—that explains simultaneously the unity of the whole, the repartition of each element, and the manner in which each acts in the others" (p. 93; Deleuze's emphasis).

For example, if one wonders how the background surface can form a structure or armature for the whole of the painting, the answer is in the handling of color. Either there is an internal modulation within the surface through a play of color values, or, more commonly, there are several background surfaces, each one of which enters into modulation with the rest. And even here, several variations are possible: one surface can be divided up into solidly distinguishable subsurfaces ("separate surfaces with different intensities or even different colors" [p. 94]); any one surface can be delimited by the surface of another color that frames it, cuts it off, surrounds it, and so on; or, as is often the case, a band of another color can cut across the colored surface.

If color modulates the background surface in these ways, it also operates its effects on the foreground figure. Deleuze notes how the primacy of blue and red in Bacon's faces serves as a reminder of the fleshy, meaty aspect of the face, but in this way the colors open up the figure to temporality, becoming flesh in mutation. As Deleuze puts it, "*color-structure* gives way to *color-force*; because each dominant, each broken tone indicates the immediate exercise of a force upon a corresponding zone of the body or the head, it renders force immediately visible" (p. 90; Deleuze's emphasis).

Even contour, which Deleuze earlier has treated as an effect of lines and shapes within shapes, is now discussed as an aftereffect of plays of color. Color is clearly the generative matrix of Bacon's modern art:

> Colorism (modulation) does not consist only of relations of hot and cold, of expansion and contraction, that vary in relation to the considered colors. It consists also of the regimes of color, of the connections between the regimes, of the accords between pure tones and broken tones. What one calls haptic vision is precisely this sense of colors (pp. 96–97).

Borrowing from Riegl, Deleuze refers to Bacon's logic of sensation as *haptic* to emphasize that it is simultaneously optical and manual, an art that overcomes divisions of spiritual and material. If Deleuze has attempted throughout *Logique de la sensation* to avoid valuative hierarchies that promote one term (usually a supposedly less carnal one) over another, the last rubric, "The Eye and the Hand," brings this antijudgmental project to its extreme point:

> To characterize the connection of eye and hand, it is certainly not enough to say that the eye is infinitely richer, and passes through dynamic tensions, logical reversals, organic exchanges and vicariances . . . We will speak of the *haptic* each time there is no longer strict subordination in one direction or the other . . . but when sight discovers in itself a function of touching that belongs to it and to it alone and which is independent of its optical function (p. 99).

In the case of Bacon, Deleuze suggests that his particular mode of bringing the manual into the optical is by means of a gradual injection, dramatized by the sweep of the hand, the stroke, the smear that defigures the figure and opens it up analogically to a whole of possible other representations. Deleuze refers twice to this process as an "injection"—a "drop-by-drop," a "coagulation," an "evolution," "as if one passed gradually from the hand to the haptic eye, from the manual diagram to the haptic vision" (p. 102). The haptic then, as Deleuze tells us in the last lines of *Logique*, is the surpassing (*dépassement*, the word used in French to translate the Hegelian *Aufhebung*) of hand and eye into a higher logic—that of the haptic, a singular logic not of sensations, but of sensation in and of itself.

In his cinema books, Deleuze refers to the work on the cinematic signifier by Jean-Luc Godard as a "pedagogy of the image," in which the paring down of the image, or, conversely, the rendering complex of the image, offers an instruction in seeing things and their representations alike in new ways. Godard is treated as a sort of scientist of imagery for whom films become virtual laboratory experiments inquiring into the power and play of images. Deleuze's general desire is to treat artists as workers (figures of production in the sense of *L'Anti-Oedipe*) and even as thinkers or conceptualists, not unlike thinkers or conceptualists in allied fields (such as philosophy, which generally operates on ideas rather than images). But in this respect, we might say that *Logique de la sensation* is Deleuze's own "pedagogy of the image," constructing for us the representation of a painterly practice that deforms the world to make us see anew. The project might seem to have parallels with that of the Russian formalists of the 1920s, for whom art was to serve to defamiliarize things rendered invisible by our habit, our taking for granted of them. Like the formalists, Deleuze wants to cut through the reifications of cliché and stereotype and habit to regain the intensity of a perception. There is undoubtedly a romanticism here, a longing for a purity of force stultified by modern living. But where the formalists targeted a utilitarian revolutionary society that in its drive to modernize determined that things were used as means to pragmatic ends and not appreciated aesthetically in and of themselves, Deleuze is writing in a very different historical context, with different historical targets. True, utilitarian culture comes in for its own critique—as in the Kafka book where the practice of minor language has to be directed to a large degree against the pragmatic language of bureaucracy (the bureaucracy of governments, but also of the large firm such as the one that Kafka himself works for)—but more often Deleuze's context is that of our contemporary society of consumption. This society has a place for images; indeed, almost more than anything else, it seems voraciously to need to consume images. But it is precisely this turning of the image into an easily ingested thing—for example, the photographic cliché, in which the seeing goes too quickly past the photo to a represented world—that Deleuze wants to defamiliarize. For all its concentration on the details of the artistic work of a single figure, *Logique de la sensation* may also be one of Gilles Deleuze's most general books, offering new insights into the possibilities of art in our society of the spectacle.

Notes

1. Patrick Vauday, review of *Logique de la sensation,* in *Critique* no. 426 (1982); Christine Buci-Glucksmann, "Le plissé baroque de la peinture," in *Magazine littéraire* no. 257 (September 1988). References to Gilles Deleuze, *Logique de la sensation* (Paris: Editions de la différence, 1981) will be given in the text.

2. Donald Miller, Art Column, *Pittsburgh Post-Gazette,* 6 October 1990: p. 16.

3. *Cinéma 1: L'image-mouvement* (Paris: Éditions de Minuit, 1983); *Cinéma 2: L'image-temps* (Paris: Éditions de Minuit, 1985).

4. Raymond Bellour, "The Unattainable Text," in *Screen* 16, no. 3 (1975).

5. Dana Polan, "Powers of Vision, Visions of Power," *Camera Obscura* 18 (September 1988).

6. Erwin Panofsky, *Gothic Architecture and Scholasticism* (Latrobe, PA: Archabbey Press, 1951).

7. Jean-Paul Sartre, *L'Être et le néant: Essai d'ontologie phénoménologique* (Paris: Gallimard, 1943).

8. *L'Idiot de la famille: Gustave Flaubert de 1821–1852* (Paris: Gallimard, 1971–72).

13

The Cinema,
Reader of Gilles Deleuze

Marie-Claire Ropars-Wuilleumier

IN THE PAGES that follow one should not look for a systematic account of the two books that the cinema led Gilles Deleuze to write.[1] In the form of organization they adopt—that of nonlinearity—and in the conceptual order they engage—that of divided thought—the two books defy any synthesis other than a direct one. And even this sort of synthesis might betray an exposition that takes the form of becoming. It seems much more in keeping with the spirit of this work, then, to divert its course and even its discursive cohesiveness and instead to outline several theoretical options and points of uncertainty whereby a reflection on the cinema becomes a philosopher's machine for reflection.

Indeed, the force of this work lies in its explicit decision to adopt a line of research that, far from shutting itself within cinematic space, would instead project transversely those concepts that the cinema has helped to establish. Rendered explicit at the end of the second volume, this approach is in fact in operation throughout the whole of the work: It is neither a question of applying a philosophical theory to cinema, nor even of constructing a new theory for the cinema, but rather of thinking with this object, working at one and the same time in and outside its field. We need to acknowledge all the implications of this limit position, characteristic of Deleuze's numerous works, concerning his choice of object and what the choice facilitates: The cinema, like any intelligible system, will be capable of intervening as an accelerator of reflection, even though this reflection does not pretend to derive the substance of its thought from the cinema alone.

Thus positioning himself between philosophy and cinema, Deleuze constructs two parameters for the filmic image—movement and time, or rather time through movement—but only in order to read them through Bergson while rereading Bergson alongside them. Like the world, the cinema

255

is Bergsonian, in spite of what Bergson himself said, because it reactivates the concept of duration. Here, matter (which is image-movement) changes into memory (thus, into image-time), and the present, never identical to itself, is doubled with the virtual image of the past it will become. The consequences of Deleuze's reading are significant for the theorization of cinema, which all too often privileges material over process. The cinema is time, the image is only a movement-image; the cinematic present does not exist in itself. Deleuze articulates these indispensable formulations in terms of a specifically philosophical trajectory; going beyond Bergson (who, in being applied to film, can be pulled away from depth psychology and turned to the very perception of things), it is to Nietzsche that Deleuze intends to graft the cinema, a Nietzsche for whom the circular becoming of time precipitates (as it does in modern cinema) short-circuits, bifurcations, detours, and irrational divisions, where the notion of intensity is substituted for that of truth.

The stakes, thus conceived, are extensive: the cinema operationalizes the image of an open totality, at once moving and nonorientable, where the temporality that envelops us offers itself in its doubly contradictory dimension—incessant flux and instantaneous disjunction. But in joining Nietzsche and Bergson cinematically, Deleuze in fact makes a new connection in his own approach. That paradoxical time legible in the cinema of modernity—incommensurable moments in Robbe-Grillet, undecidable memories of Resnais, the serialized instants of Godard, crystalline amnesia according to Welles—returns to a "logic of sense" (*logique du sens*) that fifteen years earlier Deleuze had charted in Lewis Carroll as the logic of paradox.[2] Sense confirms itself only in the experience of nonsense, because it expresses itself only in a language that, while speaking, runs after the sense of what it says.

Here, Deleuze appears to apply his notion of the paradoxical constitution of sense in relation to another mode of expression; the image takes the place of the sign, and time is serialized in the manner of the discourse of the song of the White Knight.[3] The question that then arises—and which Deleuze himself does not ask, at least not explicitly—would involve cinema's specific role in thinking through the relations between sense and language. Deleuze's emphasis on time and his account of the multiple forms of dissociation that time mobilizes project a more focused analysis, where the heterogeneity of cinema (the complexity of its signifying processes) leads to a general theoretical investigation: How does cinematic language intervene in the paradox of language? In what ways, or through what sorts of operations on signs, does the cinema reactivate the trajectory of modern thought that runs from Nietzsche to Blanchot in the quest for a syntax that neutralizes the quotidian uses of speech? Deleuze refuses to formulate these questions explicitly and takes a rigorously antilinguistic point of view on the cinema. And if he reproaches Metzian semiotics for substituting statements (*énoncé*) and syntagms for the plastic mass of visual material, his critique is not aimed at semiotic investigation per se, but, more radically, at the Saussurean conception of language where the signifier always ends up changing into the signified. For Deleuze, then, to work with the cinema means turning to the prelinguistic, to a material which bears, without expressing it, that which a language can express (*sans l'énoncer l'énoncable d'une langue*) prior to all processes of signification. This perspective would be productive if it led to the examination in each enunciation, even when materialized in linguistic forms, of the activity of withdrawal or overflow that transports enunciation beyond the expression (*énoncé*) of sense. But in deciding to oppose the plenitude of the image, asignifying and asyntactic, to every operation of a signifying nature, Deleuze chooses another option. Initially aesthetic, Deleuze's project can only become analytic by resorting to a semiotic model where all signs are formed and conceptualized on the basis of the image alone. In choosing Peirce against Metz, Deleuze thus cedes to the appeal of sight, which rules over the dispersion of all filmic signals, including the sonoral.[4] But, at the same time, he commits himself to the exigencies of classification, where the goal is not to question the multiple connections of the linguistic and the visual, but rather to assemble, classify, and totalize under the sign of the image, even if a mobile one, the ensemble of filmic figures by inscribing there the ensemble of films.

This reconciliation of the Peircean logic of exhaustive cataloguing and the Nietzschean logic of boundless paradox is accomplished only with difficulty. A double enterprise—classification, on the one hand, and displacement, on the other—inscribes Deleuze's thought in a contradictoriness witnessed by the division of the work into two volumes. Up to now, I have privileged the analyses in the second volume, i.e., those which examine the paradox of time in modern cinema. But referring explicitly to Peirce, the first volume intends to recover the different types of Peircean signs from the various components of classical cinema. Thus, a fissure (simultaneously aesthetic and historical) is described that around 1950 divides an "organic" cinema (whose temporality remains governed by the movement of action and the linear development of narrative) from a "crystalline" cinema (where time offers itself up directly to thought in the form of demultiplication and serialization).[5] Not only is Deleuze forced in the second volume to give up his Peircean models with respect to this current of modernity, but the difficulties of his division between classical and modern oblige him to return (in terms of fragmentary modernity) to auteurs like Bresson or Buñuel, who in the first volume had been analyzed in terms of classical narrativity.

More generally, the very foundations of the first volume tumble down in the second: The first volume proceeds by means of categories leading to traditional divisions in the history of cinema, while the second proceeds by operations that void the traditionally established typologies. Predictably, the point of greatest conflict involves the question of montage. More precisely, Eisenstein's conflictual hypotheses are treated in terms of organic synthesis in volume one, and are necessarily reexamined in volume two, where it becomes difficult to deal with visual breaks and audiovisual permutations without referring them to a problematic of discontinuity and disconnection. But it is not so much to montage as a syntax that Deleuze refers; the attraction and the limits of his analyses derive from his insistence on restoring to the perceptual continuum—whether optical or sonorous—the activity of crystallization or dissociation that montage makes readable in filmic modernity. Whether it is a question of the body or the brain, of memories or faces, of earth or voice, it is to matter, visible and in movement, that Deleuze obstinately pays the tribute of intelligibility. And filmic mass—this unexpressed expressible (*énoncable-nonénoncé*) of a language without signs—is transformed by Deleuze into a kind of speech (*parole*) that never stops collecting, citing, situating, and repositing, in short, which never stops expressing and enumerating that which is innumerable and unnameable in the cinema.

The problematic dichotomy of classical and modern, of the organic and the crystalline, of the Open (in Rike's terms) and of the Outside (in Blanchot's terms), is thus affirmed without accounting for the contradictions it induces or the questions it inspires concerning the traditional historical periodization of an art. And if Deleuze attributes this fracture to the cinema, it is to cinema conceived of as a totality where the most contradictory currents in its history would be united without conflict in their essence. The word "Whole" (*le Tout*) is without doubt one of the most recurrent in Deleuze's work. Cinematic totalization, even if contradictory, seems to replace here the impossible ensemble that the logic of sense inscribed within the heart of thought: that the totality of the seventh art form could well be open-ended, divided, dissociated, disjunctive; that analysis could distinguish, even while linking them, Renoir and Fellini, Kubrick and Resnais, Duras and Straub, Warhol and Garrel. What is essential is that the cinema, just like the world, comprehends and reconciles them all in a space where matter offers itself to mind in order to contemplate the unthinkable of thought.

One can discern here, beyond all the ambiguities and hesitations that a work of this scope admits, a more radical tension concerning the bet Deleuze made in playing the cinema. On the one hand, the cinema intervenes as a critical analyzer, capable of crystallizing the stakes of a conceptual modernity where the power of the false renders as unrealizable the distinctiveness of the categories of true and false, real and imaginary, which form the basis of classical philosophy. In this, Deleuze's recourse to cinema extends the attentiveness of Nietzsche or Klossowski, Lewis Carroll or Borges, which multiplies in time and in space the paradoxical game of a unity that is not one. But on the other hand, through Deleuze's filmic incantation there can be heard the echo of a demand for love that does not come from love for film alone. The cinema, Deleuze tells us, is a form of "catholicity" (Deleuze 1983, pp. 222–223) that, insofar as it is universal, gathers up everything (*tout*), accepts everything (*tout*), and reconciles us with the whole of everything (*le tout*). If the Bergsonian universe can be conceived in terms of a cinematic model— Deleuze's initial proposition—this is first of all because the cinema aids us in recognizing the world and living with it. And this is his ultimate proposition: This living takes place within the realm of belief, not that of certitude, but rather a form of living guided by the will for "redemption," where the wholeness (*le tout*) of the aesthetic would respond to the nothingness of the ethical. A rupture between man and the world has been carried out, but the cinema offers a mirror where this rupture can be read, and in being read, is sutured. Not a reconciliation, but a conciliation, is offered by film, which negotiates an exchange between the image and the real. This second voice in Deleuze comes to the surface here and there in a few phrases. But the general tone of his text remains a theoretical speculation where personal propositions melt, through the effects of free indirect discourse, into propositions determined by films, by all the films which make up the whole (*le tout*) of cinema.

To speak with the cinema: no doubt this would constitute the median line where, without blurring, the exigencies of analysis and the quest for mediation would intersect. But no word can be the first on the matter. Deleuze's final decision (and by no means his least interesting) consists of using as the materials for his analysis nothing but analyses that have already been completed, whose authors and bibliographic references he scrupulously notes. This is neither a form of modesty nor a declaration of weakness on Deleuze's part. This practice of reference, which is new in Deleuze, seems first of all attributable to the cinema itself, whose singularity derives only from what it accomplishes by transforming itself into words. But more radically, this "second-hand" tactic responds to Deleuze's desire to break theoretically with the empire of the sign and with the exact coincidence of signifier and signified.[6] By manipulating fragments that already have an established meaning—hypotheses, ideas, or viewpoints inspired by screening films— Deleuze makes it possible for himself to put them into movement, to make their meanings circulate, and to break their initial meanings by inscribing them into his own system of thought. The signifieds he collects thus change into the signifiers of another argument, which, without betraying them, assigns them a new place and function because of the way he opens up cinema to philosophy. This process is of interest in that it can consume any bit of writing. Taking its material from everywhere, it modifies this material and offers it to a new theorization, reminding us, as if there were need for this, that the analysis of films is not the ultimate goal of a reflection on cinema. But a price is exacted for such circumspect reading: By discarding every study of a semiological or textual sort, Deleuze limits his corpus to the domain of auteurs, whose affects and forms focus this theoretical venture. Certainly, it is by means of these auteurs that Deleuze constructs his principal figure, the crystal where time scintillates. But positing a theory of space-time does not prevent a thematic anchoring of the examples that sustain his theory. This return of a localized signified in the form of auteurs, more or less bothersome depending on the case, sometimes blocks the deployment of a transversal thought where the cinema conceives itself in formulating the historical and conceptual problems that it poses to understanding. Without doubt, this indicates a cinephilic connivance that nonetheless sustains Deleuze's aesthetic project: The love of signs (in the semiotic and not the linguistic sense of the word)[7] fuels a love of cinema, defined as a cinema of auteurs. Surreptitiously, the auteur is rendered here as facilitating a connection: Even while making analysis invoke its most abstract directions, at the same time each auteur's name inscribes, through an affect of memory, the trace of a presence that the cinema indefatigably renews.

It is the ultimate detour of a text in search of its end to furnish a summation where it promised a system. This selective synthesis would risk prevailing over the recognition of disjunction if, in a final reversal, it did not finally locate itself in a "synthetic" image of cinema (*l'image d'un cinéma synthétiseur*). A veritable "spiritual automaton" (Deleuze 1983, p. 343), connecting man to machine, blends contradictions and materializes the dream of a world where disjunctions communicate and where fusion operates within rupture. Here, we need to reread the last sentence of *Logique du sens* (in Deleuze 1983, p. 290). Beyond paradox, where the equivocation of language always speaks, an instantaneous and dazzling event pursues itself—that event when the univocality of sense suddenly emerges from a poetry freed of figures, maintaining the trace of the deepest sonorities, primary and adjacent to language. This ephemeral instant, when sense and being coincide, belongs to the cinema as an art of the figure, in that cinema restores the possibility of making this instant coexist with the awareness of paradox. By means of an impossible taxonomy of cinema, it is the integer (*intégrale*) of these fragments that makes itself heard: a sum of instances transformed into essences, where, in Deleuze's reading, the cinema answers to the nostalgia of a poetry without writing.

—*Translated by Dana Polan*

Notes

1. *Cinéma 1, L'image mouvement* and *Cinéma 2, L'image temps* (Paris: Minuit, 1983 and 1985, respectively). [Page references to the first volume are to the English language edition; references to the second volume are to the French edition. —Trans.]

2. In Gilles Deleuze, *Logique du sens* (Paris: Minuit, 1969).

3. *Logique du sens*, Fifth Series, pp. 41–49. In order to comment on the paradox of a regression to infinity, Deleuze refers to a dialogue between Alice and a knight about the name of a song in *Through the Looking Glass* (New York: Random House, 1946), pp. 131–136.

4. Deleuze explains his choice in chapter 12 of *Cinéma 1* and chapter 2 of *Cinéma 2*. He uses the collection of Peirce's writings presented by G. Deledalle, *Charles S. Peirce, Écrits sur le signe* (Paris: Seuil, 1978).

5. On the opposition of these two regimes, see the beginning of chapter 6 in *Cinéma 2*.

6. In the sense that Antoine Compagnon gives to this idea in *La seconde main, ou le travail de la citation* (Paris: Seuil, 1979).

7. See Gilles Deleuze, "Sur le régime cristallin," *Hors cadre* 4 (1986).

VI. Lines of Flight

14

Cartography of the Year 1000: Variations on *A Thousand Plateaus*

Jean-Clet Martin

1. Kyrielles

THE MONASTIC ORDER is inseparable from an order of somber light, driven wild by blue hues and red pillars. Their embossed gold succeeds in pushing the whispering darkness back toward the terrible weight of a blind sky. In this dark space, where light diffuses itself from the inside, thought drones out its war chant, marking thereby the dazzling intermittencies of an outside without measure. Cold and deep, a crypt closes upon its black ink, like an egg run through by a fragile limestone that the most external forces make indestructible. Above, the heavy carapace of a domed basilica traversed by an imperceptible clarity is absorbed in the acoustic power of the edifice. Two noncentered hemispheres intersect and create a two-headed monster, growing from the middle, at the place where, between crypt and basilica, a membrane softly forms a curve and struggles to gain height across the length of a double itinerant line marked with aleatory stations and disparate sanctuaries connected on the basis of irrational links. On top of the crypt, the dome struggles and slowly traces a passage toward the edifice above. Between the monastery and the hypogeum, as Georges Duby observes, there is experimentation going on, with a new model of construction.[1] On the median line that separates the two hemispheres, the technique of the dome is being developed, and a very special space is opening up. The disparate parts of this space intersect and fit each other according to an overlapping of perspectives that makes them indiscernible and totally incommensurable. This is the monastic space, capable of engendering things from the middle, across the length of an intermediary membrane on either side of which things begin to arch, and diverging ambulatories find their own modulations.

265

The force of the monastic art is expressed in the discovery of this space of overlap and this line of experimentation. With them, incompatible wholes begin to coexist; no centers of resonance ever emerge on this vector capable of absorbing the disparity of places in a perfectly homogeneous totality. As the basilica multiplies the chapels on its periphery and assembles a multiplicity of level, the church proliferates into several abodes and incorporates more and more floors. The diagonal that allows the church to do this is capable of bringing together heterogeneous dimensions without reducing them to unity. At every level of the building, the distribution of singularities changes the rules; from top to bottom, an intensive line is deployed that cannot be subdivided into levels without changing its nature at every step of its division. From the dome above to the square below, from the chancel to the underground crypt, a fall of intensity is initiated that liberates, with every step, other dynamic spaces and brings about dissimilar worlds, disparate orders of light, as well as differentiated figural complexes with irreducible faunas and floras on their surfaces. This is a veritable patchwork, which brings together elements snatched from Roman ruins, barbarian embroideries, curtains made of Byzantine silk, demonic effigies. Between the crypt and its sarcophagi, the chancel and its altars, the rules of distribution and dispersion change nature, without any law or superior principle being capable of legislating and extending its homogeneous jurisdiction over them. In every level of the monastic edifice, we encounter the problem that Romanesque architecture tries to solve.

Deleuze's entire philosophy constantly reminds us that a problem constitutes a multiplicity or a distribution of singularities in the vicinity of which curves and diagrams are determined, nonactual and yet real. Albert Lautman, in his theory of differential equations, liked to distinguish between two totally distinct and yet complementary realities: on the one hand, the distribution of singular points inside a vectorial field as the locus of problems, and on the other, the form of integral curves in their vicinity as cases of the solution.[2] From this point of view, a problem is able to receive a variety of solutions, an outline of which may be traced by a diagram. In mathematics, for example, we can divide a straight line in many ways. To determine this procedure, together with its variables, is, in fact, to constitute a diagram. Now, sectioning a straight line defines a problem, because one can divide it in a lot of ways, and one must choose among them. However, drawing a right angle inside a half circle is a simple theorem, because within the half circle every angle is a right angle. But, on the other hand, drawing an equilateral triangle inside a circle defines a problem, because this operation requires a choice for which there is no theorem. This is why Deleuze speaks of the problem as a choice for which no theorem is available.[3] To find the dimension of the problem is to engage, in a certain fashion, in becoming-idiot, in the sense in which Clément Rosset defines "idiocy," that is, as the site of the singular.[4] To confront a problem is to get tangled up in singularities in order to disentangle arabesques, through a strange choice that necessarily transcends all constituted knowledges (*savoirs*).

A wild light inhabits the monastic art as it chooses a single material for the entire construction. It is indeed a singular and eccentric choice that gives up the wooden frame for the dome of stones. This art, which is a little mad as it opts for one and only one material, casts its immoderate dice and generates a problem that no previous knowledge or theorematic formalization can resolve. The builders of cathedrals are grand visionaries who search for the conditions of a problem buried deeper than all available knowledge. From this perspective, one must welcome Duby's observation, which identifies as "hesitant experience" and "happy improvisations" the processes of monastic art, which go on "without rules, compass or plan."[5]

Indeed, as we move from the wooden structure to the domes of stone, the outlines of the diagram change and begin to determine a different dispersion of singularities and different characteristics of expression, which now constrain the artisan. It is also the case that the development of the dome cannot be separated from the social movement and the transformation of speed-vectors that continually agitate the Europe of the year one thousand. From this point of view, peregrinations and crusades determine changes of itineraries, halts, and deviations, which are related to technical innovations; they also determine mutations of forms that participate in the same movement of deterritorialization.[6] The necessity of offering hospitality to the hordes of itinerants opens the monastery wide and causes lines to flee in all directions and to intersect in diagonal ribs. It is inane, therefore, to believe that the Gothic is the mere flight away from the dark cloisters sheltering the remains of unknown sepulchers. Monastic art is already carried on a Gothic wave; demanding more light, it does not give up its association with the psalmodic model: As a result, it forms an original (*inédit*) assemblage.[7] Jacques Chailley's definition of the choral permits the best possible understanding of the psalmody: "It is a kind of first matter serving in the elaboration of many different forms whose traditional character has determined a style."[8] Psalmody, with its fluid outline, is a pure, dynamic material, a variable flow of acoustic singularities, the essence of which is modulation. The modulation of the plain chant traces a continuous, nonmetric, and antiphonic line, the division of which determines a radical change in tone, accent, intensity, and pitch in the emission of singularities.

Psalmody has no regular cutouts; rather it takes the appearance of a nonmeasured musical time. Released like a brutal and violent war chant, the choral is the line of a murderous confrontation between the regular and the singular; it is the intensive line, every break of which ends up in improvised tonic accents. The repetitiveness of psalmody must not be confused with the division of time in homogeneous segments or with the isochronous recurrence of identical elements. Psalmodic repetition is modulation and the division of the pitch of the emission, so that tonic and intensive values bring about dissymmetries and incommensurabilities in durations, which latter, from a metric point of view, are in fact equal. Repetition, from the architectural point of view, inscribes itself inside a dynamic and heterogeneous space, between ambulatories and sanctuaries. As for psalmodic repetition, it is a kyrielle able to emit tonic accents. As Deleuze remarks, these accents are repeated in unequal intervals, creating remarkable points whose nature is unequal and heterogeneous.[9] Hence, the diagram that corresponds to the monastic problem stirs up singularities. In their vicinity, melodic curves, diverging telluric waves, intensive lines, and crisscrossing scalar assemblages are determined according to the world's irreducible levels: We are faced with a veritable intensive, monophonic, and monochromatic cascade. This is a cascade similar to the one that Duby reveals in a convincing analysis in which the entire stirring power of the diagram becomes visible as it cuts across music, acoustics, mathematics, and architecture, and follows the altogether different rhythms of a univocal plane of consistency.

The ecclesiastical Romanesque, according to Duby, is both an equation and a fugue. Its architect, the "worshipping psalmist" is a pure visionary able to compose psalmodic assemblages and networks of intertwined numerical relations. Duby thinks that the transversal relation between equation and fugue is a trap set up to capture the human mind and to carry it as far as the unknown. We think, on the contrary, that it is a problem binding us to a line of flight and a molecular becoming, tearing us to pieces and dragging us along toward the four corners of the horizon where winds, rivers, sky, and earth ring out in many harmonies.[10] It cannot therefore be contested that Romanesque architecture denotes all at once secrecy, white magic, and aesthetics: "[I]t occurred to some, very pure and striving hard to pierce the mysteries and to enter unknown, fascinating and frightening territories, that they may very well exist beyond what the human senses and reason are able to grasp." It is to these territories that a minor science belongs—a science that Deleuze aptly calls "itinerant" and "nomad."

Monastic art should not be envisaged as a mere mutation in the static relation form-matter: What Deleuze attributes to the gothic, we must also attribute to the secret labor of the dome, between crypt and basilica. Upon this median line, Deleuze's entire philosophy comes alive. For the extrinsic relation form-matter, which characterizes the Romanesque in a strict sense, the monastic art of the year one thousand substitutes an intermediary space and some sort of dynamics between material and forces.[11]

Geometry, as a royal science, moves to a complete determination of matter and imposes upon all its forces a constraining flow; it is a punctual system, traced from one point to another according to a theorem. As always, matter constitutes an amorphous receptacle to which the form, as pure act, proposes and imposes its extrinsic quiddity and its a priori definable essence, separated from the accidental individuation of matter. Far from the monastery, rigorous geometry eliminates all material accidents for the sake of a totality capable of offsetting pernicious effects. Points everywhere are offered as ends of trajectories, lines, and curves, and they, through a transcendental regulative principle, control the itinerary. For all these reasons, as we can see, it is impossible to bring monastic art under the strict category of the Romanesque, because, as the analyses of Duby underscore, this art is never the offspring of rigorous geometry. Monastic art is the art of the problem, of the protogeometric choice, of a groping experience struggling to follow the heterogeneous bifurcations of the lines of material forces among which the monsters display a universal splashing. The proliferation on the narthex of embryonic animal forms that are alien to all classifications according to genus and species aptly testifies to this art of the problem; it also testifies to its ability to reveal the individuation of the living according to the distribution of all preindividual singularities upon one, and only one, plane of consistency. In the figures of the narthex, and tied to the constraints of the Christian eschatology, we find the demonic growth of a series of monsters that remain alien to all taxonomies.

This larval swarming, which is present in all categories, defines the conditions of a static genesis causing the bifurcation of the species under consideration. The monstrosity of the monastic narthex mobilizes a diverging anexact form capable of biting into every type of the living, the way that an embryo experiments with the distribution of singularities according to a diagram where the limits of a natural specification are obliterated. To the fundamental disparity of the monster that grows in the middle of all biological classes, there corresponds a vague essence that straddles over all constituted genres and every life-form in order to constitute life as a problem. Sculpture, on its own line, joins the problem out of which all monastic diagrams are born according to differentiated thresholds, and encounters, in its extreme points, the architectural diagram.

Monastic architecture must, in fact, be carried along by the material on which it is inscribed; it must take account of all the accidents of matter and coordinate its own movement with the forces of the material utilized. The wooden structure and the dome of stones cannot be bent in the same manner due to very essential reasons touching on a vague essentiality that has nothing to do with the ruinous distinctions of hylomorphism and its beneficiary royal, euclidean geometry. The essence of matter is the vague essence that makes disjunctions and bifurcations of the lines of force coexist like the divergences of an umbel. The forms "umbel" and "lens" denote with accuracy the sort of definition that Husserl gives to the vague or fluid essences that, in their fields of extension, differ from the frozen exactness of ideal concepts and genres.[12] Vague essences, Deleuze writes, are not the foundations of theorematic geometry; they designate instead the place of a constant approximation of a limit and a space of rhizomatic overlappings. Straddling several categorical registers, vague essences point at the anexact form of the disparate, vagabond, and nomad essence.[13] The internal structure of matter and its ability to be placed in variation totally transcend the hylomorphic model, just as, from another point of view, crusades and psalmody escape the state apparatus and the pontifical organization.[14] All the vagabond movements, susceptible to following the lines of force of the material and obliged to take into account the chances and the singularities of a vector field, define curves that are not easily submitted to the demands of a theorematic form, external to an allegedly amorphous space and to neutral matter. Saint Bernard was not fooled when he condemned, as heretical, the exuberance of Cluny. Cluny names the place of a protogeometry that escapes hylomorphism. It is an art of pure treason. This approximate geometry, with its vague essences, is characterized by the heretic usage to which it submits equations. Instead of being transcendent and distant forces for the organization of matter, its equations are the result of the superior art of the problem and of the force lines of the material itself. We are, therefore, faced with an ambulatory and itinerant science capable of coming to terms, blow by blow, with the singularities and traits of the expressions of the material that run along its dynamic lines. Theorematic science, on the other hand, under the representative demand to reproduce the model, could not have supported the discovery of techniques essential for the development of the dome. From the wooden structure to the dome, the nature of the diagram changes and, as it does, the insufficiency of theorems becomes more evident. The size of the wood, its veins and flexibility, cannot be compared to the size of stone, its veins, resistance, and rigidity. As we move from one register to another, singularities change; they display a dynamic, disjunctive, and diverging space and mobilize a set of variables that are apportioned according to different rules of distribution.

Hence, the determination of the monastic art as a problem is the following: a system of singularities corresponds to a variety of differential variations. The singularities are capable of being actualized according to diverging lines of realization, like a Lautman scheme that can distinguish between the distribution of singularities inside a vector field and the form that integral curves take in their vicinity. We find, therefore, a group of singularities admitting a determined number of virtual relations: The wooden structure and the dome, each in its own way, is an actualization and a differentiation. In order to be precise, we must say that, as we move from wood to stone, the problem stays the same but the diagram varies. We find, somehow, a group of determinable singularities distributed in a vector field that includes a determined number of differential relations. With respect to the latter, the usage of the dome and of the wooden structure represent, each in its way, an actualized determination and, in relation to the problem under consideration, an effective variable. From the wooden construction to the dome, we are able to count a number of singularities in the vicinity of which the dynamic formation of a space and the differential determination of an intensive line of force are actualized. One could therefore say, with justification, that the dome and the wooden structure are the realizations of a group of singularities that could also be actualized in other differential relations, in other intensive series, which would preexist, somehow, their actualization. In other words, neither the dome nor the wooden structure exhaust the potentialities of the monastic problem. In the directional space of the monastery, there is only one flow of matter-movement that encompasses all the differential relations of preindividual singularities. This continuous flow, which bears the singularities, can be actualized in a determined number of variables, to the extent that every singularity can be extended in all directions until it reaches another singularity and can form converging assemblages and differentiated series. It follows that as soon as the singularities are no longer compatible, as soon as they are no longer extended according to compossible vicinities, they begin to form diverging series, irreducible dynamic species, and lines of bifurcation. From this point of view, wooden structure and dome denote diverging assemblages able to make given singularities converge around a determined series.[15]

At this point, the entire extrinsic distinction between matter and form may be challenged. There is not—nor can there be—any amorphous matter or separate form; instead, we must think of the material as a vein, animated from the inside, or as matter-energy in continuous variation. Upon this basis, a multiplicity of virtually coexisting singularities is actualized according to the immanent plan that the artisan must follow. In other words, the preindividual space where the vague essences bifurcate constitutes a modular zone, which is intermediary between matter and form. In it, all coexisting combinations, in a creative throw of the dice, release their singularities in all directions as in countless, diverging arabesques. To follow the intensive modulations of a unique material in its intensive journey, rather than imposing a transcendent form on matter; to be involved in an itinerant process; to be distributed in space according to an upward fall, along a line of variable speeds—these are the wanderings of a nomad science. Straddling all the diverging series, in between all the dynamic spaces that coexist virtually, like a demon, man of music and man of war, artisan and geometer, the architect chants his kyrielles and draws a mobile diagonal across a vectorial field with countless curves. The worshipping psalmist breaks into his war chant and, with his terrible hands, from the depths of the crypt, causes to be cast an enormous throw of the dice, which then rolls with multiple echoes across thresholds of incompossible colliding worlds.

2. Cryptics

In relation to the arts of construction, the force of Deleuze's analyses is manifested in the strict correlation that they establish between the mutation of the architectural diagram and the mutation of the corresponding social formations. In fact, we find in Deleuze two organizations of the social field and two politics, the *compars* and the *dispars,* characterized by the spread of the smooth space and the organization of a striated space, respectively.[16] From the relation between the two spaces there emerges a multilinear block where monastic architecture and the peregrination characteristic of the Middle Ages intersect. In the last analysis, between the space of the production of the architectural mutations and the direction of a space defining the vectorial space of Europe during the year one thousand, there is consistency and abstract machinic assemblage, despite the fact that these two determine different concrete arrangements. In order to reach the plane of consistency, which, for convenience's sake, we call "cryptics," we must ride this absolute line of deterritorialization, which is capable of bringing about the consistency of the most diverging longitudes and latitudes.

In the secret piles of broken relics and incommensurable ossuaries, in the labyrinth of partial and incommensurable objects that a crypt flimsily assembles, our most stubborn convictions and obstinate certainties reach an inexpungeable gaiety that shakes off their calm assurance and premature authority. The fragmented humor by means of which our crypts disorganize the *compars* space of the *sensus communis,* in order to garner a collection without a guiding thread, finds its most joyful expression in a beautiful text of Umberto Eco, which, complacently, takes us to the depths of a sanctuary filled with objects of a strange variety. This text deserves to be reproduced in its entirety:

There was, in a case of aquamarine, a nail of the cross. In an ampoule, lying on a cushion of little withered roses, there was a portion of the crown of thorns; and in another box, again on a blanket of dried flowers, a yellowed shred of the tablecloth from the last supper. And then there was the purse of Saint Matthew, of silver links; and in a cylinder, bound by a violet ribbon eaten by time and sealed with gold, a bone from Saint Anne's arm. I saw, wonder of wonders, under a glass bell, on a red cushion embroidered with pearls, a piece of the manger of Bethlehem, and a hand's length of the purple tunic of Saint John the Evangelist, two links of the chains that bound the ankles of the apostle Peter in Rome, the skull of Saint Adalbert, the sword of Saint Stephen, a tibia of Saint Margaret, a finger of Saint Vitalis, a rib of Saint Sophia, the chin of Saint Eobanus, the upper part of Saint Chrysostom's shoulder blade, the engagement ring of Saint Joseph, a tooth of the Baptist, Moses's rod, a tattered scrap of very fine lace from the Virgin Mary's wedding dress.[17]

All these futile and yet venerable objects make a strange collection whose principle—truth to tell—is not immediately visible, being in this sense comparable to Borges's Chinese bestiary explored by Foucault in the context of heterotopy.[18] Plunged in the most blinding obscurity, the arrangement that made possible this display of fragments remains very problematic. As the common space of all encounters, the notion "support" remains the familiar pedestal of all Western existence, the space of similarities; the table of analogical judgments, categories, and multiplications; and the horizon for the display of the play of resemblances. But, on the other hand, the enumeration of the fragments directly challenges the thought of support and destabilizes the power of identities to the profit of a radical exploding of the aggregate and of a totally inordinate relation between support and driving force, figure and speed. There is no hidden sense, therefore, dissimulated behind the appearances, waiting to be exhumed from its founding retreat. Nor is there, up high, a totality able to seal off the collection. On the contrary, this heteroclite retinue of relics, with its aleatory distribution, does not lack (literally) anything; it rather deploys a plane of consistency that is very different both from the euphoria of the support and from its triumphal relief. Neither concealed depth nor final overhang, the humor of such an arrangement has at its disposal only a secret platitude on the basis of which it distributes its singularities in the disparate space of the crypt. One could say that Eco's description joins a curve in the vicinity of many and different singularities, according to the very special logic that Foucault and Deleuze found to be present in the formation statements. A statement is a discursive formation cutting through many levels and orders; it is a multiplicity that escapes structural normalization and hermeneutic interpretation. Although it may be a secret, it does not have a hidden sense, even if this sense is not immediately visible. This is the reason why it needs a particular handling—archaeological, topological, and problematic.[19] Eco's description may be compared to a statement to the extent that the aleatory series of relics maintains a number of propositions that are chosen around a function—not a category. Among fabrics, bones, jewels, and other objects, this text weaves a diagonal that gives them consistency without reducing the latter to a categorical unity. There is no hidden principle to find behind this description that would be a rule for the production of discourse, because the latter is assembled around a pure primitive function that cuts across heterogeneous orders, disparate structures, and irreducible classes of objects. Eco's statement defines a multiplicity, an emission of singularities, which looks like a curve as it passes in the multiplicity's vicinity in the form of a derived function. Eco's description forms a statement and refers immediately to a corresponding state of affairs or to a nondiscursive reality upon which it legislates. It refers to an order of visibility and to a set of autonomous practices that constitute a multiplicity and give rise to pragmatics and semantics, for linguistics is not enough to account for it. For the time being, we do not wish to thematize this problematic relation between statement and visibility, form of content and form of expression. It is enough to observe the two aspects of the assemblage (statement-state of affairs) and to indicate how the collection of singular fragments is translated into positions of derived subjects: saints, apostles, monarchs, and so on.

As we saw already, the basilica-crypt monolith forms two hemispheres with an intermediary membrane running through them as if they were a brain. The crypt, dug out from the bare rock, has expressive qualities very different from the qualities of the superimposed building, which is put together stone by stone. Here, on a fork or a bifurcation, two worlds coexist, and a universe of incompossibilities develops inside the monastic space. The world of the crypt and the world of the basilica deploy their own diverging ambulatories. Along these incompatible itineraries, the movement of the world traces the dance of the pilgrims, linking together the different sanctuaries like so many views of a kaleidoscope agitated according to various speeds and slownesses. Duby correctly states that "the liturgy unveils itself like a slow, majestic rondo, along the nave and the ambulatories, around the sacrificial stone, between the stones of the walls and under the stones of the dome."[20] Along this intensive path of the dance, there are as many worlds as there are pauses and rests. On each step of the rondo, worlds begin to swarm about. Thus, as Deleuze emphasizes, the dance traces a line of transition from one world to another, a veritable break in and an exploration of worlds, each one of which is closed onto itself.[21] All the sanctuaries alongside the nave refer to independent worlds, which are animated by the dance of the pilgrims and interconnected according to variable speeds and itineraries. We could then say that the indiscernible ambulatories of the crypt and the basilica form waves of fibers and world-movements on the trajectory of which the pilgrim is placed into orbit and made to trace the steps of a catatonic dance. The basilica, therefore, defines a world where disparate sanctuaries are piled up; as for the crypt, it marks the birth of an exploded ossuary, with disseminated fragments and harlequinlike sepulchers. In it, relics are distributed like the molecules of an excited brain. One can think of the crypt's ossuary as "fragments which have been soldered back again." The distribution of these fragments takes place according to a schema that is comparable to Clarkon's chains; that is, to chains of neurons carrying semidependent singularities in a way that differs from strictly determined sequences or from totally undetermined linkages. In other words, the schema is that of a semialeatory process situated between chance and necessity. Instead of tracing a homogeneous line with the usual isometric recurrence of identical sequences, the sequence of relics fluctuates on a network of multiple lines that overlap and intersect at junctions and interchanges. In these interchanges and junctions, independent lines meet, like unpredictable occurrences, which are necessary despite the fact that they are traversed by series that are not themselves determined (the encounter of independent series).

Thus we must rethink the crypt as a space that cuts across a great many structures or as a space of dispersion including a great many wholes and honeycombed reliquaries with many incongruous compartments. Think, for example, of the collective staurotheques of the church of Saint Mathias or of the dome of Saint George, where upon one and the same stage incommensurable particles coexist.[22] In general, the receptacle of these reliquaries assumes the form of a double cross. Arranged symmetrically in two sets, the display boxes permit the inspection of relics and of authentic parchments bearing the names of individual saints. Every protective cover is framed by gold and ivory in order to prevent the overlapping of display boxes. This pile of hermetic frames fits snugly inside another encompassing frame, and it is here, in the form of a cross, that the four branches of the tree of life are determined according to an orthonomous play of frames that separates territories and attributes to each saint the part that belongs to him or her. We are confronted by a system of predetermined places capable of making a swarm of saints coexist peacefully: Saints Lorains, Mathias, Euchairius, or, even, Abbot Jacobus and Friar Isenbrandus, the donors of the staurotheque. This is indeed a curious machine, with its sign and display regimes, and we cannot really see the totality of practices and forces that it encounters. And yet something does not run smoothly; the pacific structure of the double axis is not successful; it turns sour and is spoiled as if by an inappropriate seasoning. The tree of life, the sedentary distribution trying to work out the double articulation of the true cross, suddenly fails. Indexing the face and the need to comply with the pontifical will concerning the reliquaries are entirely bypassed by the bedeviled work of the goldsmiths. Here again, a different dance rumbles underneath the sedentary distributions—an entire rhizome that, ever since the Scythians, spreads and runs through reliquary art.[23]

In fact, one cannot fail to notice the heterotopic character of these collective reliquaries—veritable sealed boxes—whose common base literally implodes as it organizes the spaces of encounters and proximities. That monstrosity characterizes reliquaries is due to the fact that the relation of our faculties to an object presumed to be the same is, in this case, destroyed: common names fritter away under the extraordinary humor that Eco, in his way, retrieves. In this sense, the collective reliquary hides no contradiction that an amiable process of dialectical reconciliation could overcome. It develops, instead, degrees of humor that assign to each thing its place and its usage along a schizophrenic path. No common sense ever achieves here the establishment of hierarchies through the attribution of a transcendental subject or of an object taking the form of the same. Fragrances of sainthood, display cases, and sacred adorations are deployed around inorganic reliquaries of irreducible dimensions, inside a miraculating and peregrinating body without organs, which differs from itself as much as a stretched chord differs with each new degree of tension—discordant harmony of all faculties and division of the indivisible. We are therefore faced with a double reliquary order, the organic and the inorganic. We have, first of all, a symmetrical and arborescent distribution traversed by the true cross, apportioning territories and attributing parts: a sedentary distribution. But at the edge of this organic system, one can get a glimpse of a nomadic distribution of sealed boxes communicating according to the greatest possible distance: a transversal connection of fragments. Two senses of "synthesis" are present: According to the first, fixed subjects and stable signs—Saint Mathias and his emblem; Saint Euchairius and his symbol—are distributed within a system of homogeneous sites, which is then overcoded by a transcendent principle of distribution. But according to the second, the whole is, in fact, molecularized; like a fragrance of sainthood rising to the surface, it passes through all the barriers of an aleatory and inorganic itinerary, which cannot be reduced to the homogeneous structures of the whole. It forms a wild arabesque that straddles all sealed boxes, encompasses incompossible worlds, and causes a multiplicity of discordant faculties to cohere on the impersonal and the subjective line of a saraband or farandole. The power of the disjunctive synthesis is indeed here: it affirms separate terms across their distances and in all their difference as a set of fragments beating time according to different rhythms, as they turn and begin to diverge, without limiting or excluding one another. From this point of view the art of the goldsmith does not eliminate the disjunctions by identifying the contradictions; on the contrary, it affirms all the distances between the sealed boxes on an indivisible curve, as it lines up fragments, one at the end of the other, like the two extremities of a segment within a space that cannot be decomposed.[24] From this point of view, relics designate the pieces of a puzzle the solution to which has been destroyed by the affirmation of all distances: heterotopia. But across these distances, the goldsmith weaves his web and releases folds and false agreements, as he machines a heterogeneous system marked by inorganic unity. The many relics have, in fact, a unity, the way that a cloud of insects has a unity; in it each volatile particle evolves, and conserves all along without any center of gravity, the greatest possible distances from all the other particles. The collective reliquary thus stands for a veritable multiplicity, for a war machine that fights against the power apparatuses expressed in the double axis of the sedentary distribution.

If Duby has tried, in his own way, to define psalmody as a war chant,[25] Deleuze, from another point of view, has conceived of metallurgy as a weapon and as a movement of decoding that brings about a terrible war machine.[26] According to Deleuze, the weapon establishes an essential relation between jewelry and nomad art. According to Duby, there is a close relationship between the art of the steppes and the art of relics, for in the art of relics we find, once again, the aggressiveness of engraving, of the fibula and the arabesque, which turns living forms into abstractions and extracts from them an inorganic dimension.[27] In fact, fibulas, golden plates, and the jewels that decorate the reliquary cannot but confirm its mobile (*meuble*) nature, because to the extent that it moves and changes places, they belong to its texture: they are the traces of many faces and the umbels of diverging rays. Reliquary cases and the collective staurotheques are dispersed throughout Europe according to a continuous migration. Inlaid jewels initiate trajectories of pure speed and scintillate in every direction, creating thereby a system of interstices capable of smashing to pieces the very idea of a substrate. Thus, as Deleuze shows conclusively, metallurgy escapes the form-matter relationship for the sake of the motif-support interstice, where the earth is only a ground, or even better, where there is no more ground at all, for the substrate is now as mobile as the motif: emerging from the background, sidestepping foundations, growing into a smooth space. The support here has nothing to do with the subjacence of a substrate; it develops, instead, a field of mobile vectors. Boxes and reliquaries are supports only on the condition that they are mobile pieces of furniture (*meuble*), vector-speeds, or vectors of deterritorialization. As such they cause the generalized flight of ecclesiastical power as they carry it along a line of war where sedentary coordinates give way and leave behind a great number of packs.

3. From Ossuaries to Packs

There are fragments and there are fragments. What characterizes, in a very general way, the fragment is that it denotes a certain incompleteness. Splinter or remains, it is the supplement of a totality often unassignable, always drawn into itself and inaccessible. From this point of view, it is toward the lack of an unconditioned totality that the fragment obstinately gravitates, and this adequately defines the concealed essence of the fragment. This is why the Greek soul, expressed in fragments and tatters, is already inscribed in the reactive desire to fill the lack, through the restitution of the lost unity. But it is obvious that, in the monastic art of the year one thousand, the relation between fragment and whole begins to sketch out different itineraries:

> When a part is valid for itself, when a fragment speaks in itself, when a sign appears, it may be in two very different fashions: either because it permits us to divine the whole from which it is taken, to reconstitute the organism or the statue to which it belongs, and to seek out the other part which belongs to it—or else, on the contrary, because there is no other part which corresponds to it, no totality into which it can enter, no unity from which it is torn and to which it can be restored.[28]

It is at this precise point that the entire theory of the support and of the totalizing relief finds itself defused to the advantage of a logic of multiplicities. Multiplicities can be conceived only when the dimension of foundations is removed and subtracted according to a value defined by the $n-1$.[29] We cannot think about multiplicities except by subtracting from them the unity that allegedly grants them their origin. A multiplicity never denotes a simple multiple of the one; rather it is a variety from which unity has been removed. In this removal, the relation of the one to the multiple is no longer pertinent. But we must, at all costs, stop conceiving this removal and subtraction of unity as simply the labor of the negative. The question is not merely how to transcend the one as support, or how to gather again the multiple under an identical principle in order to negate them in a dialectical fashion. The question is, rather, how to begin to think again, without a stable support or invariable principle, as we learn how to assemble sign-regimes and states of affairs upon the flat dimension of a plane of consistency. There is not, nor can there be, a hidden principle or a transcending form capable of overcoding words and things. But this double negation must not be conceived on the model of a negative ontology. We do not say what the multiplicity is not; we must, on the contrary, say that n−1 is the formula that affirms the being of differences—a very positive formula that does not necessarily signify the power of the verb "to be." The multiplicity is the affirmation of all differences inside the dimension n−1, and, as such, it privileges the disjunctive conjunction as the realm of interstices, to the detriment of the verb "to be." In short, the collective and asubjective reliquary allows us to thematize the affirmation of all impersonal fragments.

The fact that in the case of the reliquary we do not discover a totality underlying the work of fragmentation means that this substance is indeed missing, not in the sense of lacking, but rather "missing" in a very positive way. Not only is the receptacle of the staurotheque irreducible to the idea of the support, not only is it extremely mobile, but it is also run through by motif-speeds, by traits of expression and distances, which, being themselves mobile, render unthinkable every organic unity: jewels, enamels, fibulas, and buckles display their piercing light rays as a cloud of luminous stars, a veritable swarm of shiny points turning around themselves, like a volatile whole. From time to time, a bone, a skull, or a tooth comes to punctuate this ballet of mobile singularities. The fact is that these fragments can never be conceived on the basis of a lost unity or a concealed totality. In the n−1 eclipses of the Middle Ages, the somber whole of the organic unity is subtracted from the relics. The tibia of Saint Margarite and the lower jaw of Saint Eobanus find their own proper value on the condition that organic unity retreats. In fact, all these relics denote perfectly autonomous elements, with no link to the whole from which they were removed. Here, the power of a nonorganic life begins to beat according to disparate rhythms. It is the power of a life liberated from the constraints of unity, totality, and organic purposiveness—dust of stars and solar singularities. A very special mode of individuation occurs in the form of the anexact ossuary. As Deleuze indicates so well, "a bone or a skull is never alone. Bones are a multiplicity."[30] Each of these elements ties up to the next in an unqualifiable distance and a monstrous proximity. There is no unity shared by all to make organic the growth of an ossuary, but only monstrous and devious links relating the bones to each other, without ever forming a whole. And yet, this disjunctive synthesis brings about life, albeit a life that does not pass through contradiction—the motor engine of dialectics. This is a life with animated interstices contracting, dilating, and dividing in a myriad of shapes, as in a kaleidoscope that someone has shaken. Here, fragments liberate themselves from organic constraints and make up singularities in the vicinity of which a continuous arabesque is deployed, capable of connecting them again, in a semialeatory farandole. A host of relics is animated and comes alive the way that dancers do as they form, in variable interstices, one single figure and motif. Each one of their jolts separates them and liberates new and different structures. We must, therefore, conceive the atomized bodies of the saints as germs of a new life, as seeds that have burst through the pavement—seeds of light and dancing particles of dust. This inorganic life, which spreads along the interstices, is not actualized only in the case of the crypt. It is also expressed inside sign-regimes marked by a particular proper name—the name of a saint with frightful, incorporeal effects.

Sign-regimes are everywhere; signifying sign-regimes have no privilege. Together with Deleuze, we will retain two, the despotic and the passional: a semiotic system of cheating and a semiotic system of betrayal, two quite different modes of incorpeal transformation. Around the year one thousand, it is the pontifical authority that best actualizes the despotic regime. This sign-regime, with the pope at its center, succeeds in making all European holy places converge and resonate around Rome. The papal despotism is a center of significance whose radiance causes the stratification of all barbaric invasions. It also brings about the reterritorialization of every speed-vector and every celerity upon a church whose concentric circles have the pontifical seat for center, and have a host of sanguinary evangelists leaping from one circle to the next. The despotic center of significance, with its order words and pontifical bulls, spreads over all Europe its own net of stratification, like a punctual system whose points converge around a central knot. The relation between church and barbarians, and the reterritorialization that results from it, along with the Church's God and its hell, mark the spot of an unclean betrayal. Every discourse whose function it is to convert the invaders testifies to betrayal. Becoming Christian is the index of an incorporeal transformation, attributable to things and bodies without belonging to them. It is the sign-regime that turns us into damned souls. Nevertheless, the sign-regime, which expresses the act of condemnation and the attribution of sin, despite the fact that it reterritorializes, may, in many respects, include a germ of deterritorialization in relation to the states of affairs that we are discussing. Of course, Rome sends its missionaries everywhere, loaded with restraining order words and apocalyptic faces capable of creating black holes and endowing with purpose all movements and all migrations from one point to another. The actions of Boniface constitute an excellent example. Under his leadership, "spurious priests, fornicating deacons and bad bishops were all removed. The calibre of the clergy was better controlled by insisting that future priests take an examination in the Holy Scriptures. The bishops were ordered to supervise their dioceses more closely."[31]

The work of Boniface mobilizes a paranoiac-despotic sign-regime that, from the pope to the archbishops, from the archbishops to the bishops, and from the bishops to the priests, succeeds in maintaining absolute unity. To survey and to control—through the establishment of places of worship—instruction and formation, knowledge and power, represent, along with the institution of confession, the primary tasks of the Church. As a consequence, all these black holes begin to resonate under the same melodic name. But in order to bring about this harmony it is necessary to make the pontifical efficacy clear, and the supremacy of the Christian God visible, through a massive recourse to miracles. We must make people see that a God who dies on the cross is not a sign of powerlessness and, by transforming this weakness into force, show that this apparent death is not the last one, that there are plenty of other dreadful, atrocious, and eternal sufferings. Around this reactive conversion is deployed the scene of a despotic, discursive formation, along with the spectacular dimension of the corresponding sign-regime; in other words, an entire symbolics able to open up the space of Christian visibility.

This entire stage is the space of a foul betrayal and the repugnant spectacle of a perversion by means of which, at last, the vanquished take their revenge and make palpable the victory of the reactive forces. It is the domination of an insidious sickness that will climax in the form of nihilism; later on, it will be diagnosed by Nietzsche. Faceness is the name of this visibility. The face is the icon that characterizes the signifying regime, and its space of presentation and exposure, through which humans will be forced to create a memory. As Deleuze observes, face, lie, and treachery constitute the body of this regime upon whose surface order words become legible. Such a semiotics is, of course, inscribed on other faces, as well, like a branding or tattooing operation; it is readable on the horrified faces of those who are tortured, on the strident grimaces of faces undone by fright, and on the sputtering and crackling of the skin that decomposes in the heat of the scaffold. It is the face of the tortured that the despotic regime invents in order to block every line of flight and every deterritorialization, or in order to turn people's instincts against themselves. This semiotics, along with the corresponding traits of faceness, includes a line of flight and a point of deterritorialization, although this point is always affected by a negative value, transformed into memory, and coded according to the logic of the scapegoat. Heretical experience is, in this respect, paradigmatic, since it reveals a gap, a deviation from the center of despotic significance. This gap is constantly enlarged for the sole purpose of being filled and of endowing the entropic sign-regime with more signifiers. The heretical deviation can be inscribed only inside an already constituted semiotic order. Whatever it timidly unravels, it puts back together in a better way—in its own wake—and this is the mark of every transgression. But if the despotic sign-regime, along with its faceness, succeeds in locking up exits, it does not, by itself, dominate the entire play of assemblages. An assemblage has no closure; it is always inside a system of thresholds and multilinear breaks, even if it allows itself to be stratified by an arborescent, punctual system. There is no reason, according to Deleuze, to identify a civilization, an epoch, or the history of a people with the radiation of an exclusive semiotic system, the way that Heidegger does: "There is such mixture within the same period or the same people that we can say no more than that a given people, language or period assures the relative dominance of a certain regime. Perhaps all semiotics are mixed and not only combine with various forms of content but also combine different regimes of signs."[32]

From this point of view, the idea of the closure of a system by a dominant regime with unlimited powers of reappropriation makes no sense, because every system is multilinear and in perpetual heterogeneity. We cannot go beyond a sign-regime, because it is inscribed inside a heterogenesis that causes it to flee through thresholds and breaks; a sign-regime is an assemblage of recombined fragments. The question, then, is how to prepare a map of sign-regimes, a veritable topology, which would have, for a given epoch, all sorts of longitudes and latitudes: how to compose a multilinear whole with entrances and exits that can be modulated in different ways so that no "ontotheology" can ever reproduce it ahead of its time or determine it a priori toward a tragic end?

To create the map of the year one thousand is to trace three lines, at least, capable of intersecting one another in always new assemblages; it is to construct, as a primitive function, a problematic and diagrammatic dimension, and, as a derivative function, a concrete dimension of assemblages. Among derivative functions, we place a line of hard segmentarity—the face of the despot and his order words—together with a line of supple segmentarity—which has different forms of expression and content: here belongs, for example, the proper name of the saint or of the relic. But there is also a third line, a primitive function this time, and the median vector of pure deterritorialization that carries along in its presence everything between crypt and basilica, form and matter, disparate sanctuaries and fragmented ossuaries, motif and support. It carries them along according to an aparallel becoming in the trajectory of which pure, preindividual singularities collide. With the line of hard segmentarity, which joins together order words and despotic faces, we must associate another line, which connects proper names and relics, passional, subjective regimes, and reliquary displays. Many segments make up this supple line, which crosses thresholds as diverse as those of architecture, geometry, dance, and metallurgy. It has points of subjectivization different from those of the first line; in relation to them, a relic, as a form of content, is linked up with a proper name of a saint, as a form of expression. There is a proliferation of singularities and a diffusion of proper names on this supple line; pontifical despotism can no longer force them to converge. Here, the saint replaces the priest as the pope's subject, and succeeds in placing all order words in continuous variation. The saint deploys, therefore, an incorporeal transformation that differs from Christianity and represents a miraculating dimension of pure betrayal. Between the two, the line of absolute deterritorialization traces a zigzag from which there emerges the hordes and the packs of pilgrims. This is the line of crusades causing, under the constraints of peregrination, all sorts of mutations: architectural, scientific, and political, to name only a few. The line of pure betrayal carries the hard segmentarity of the despotic regime and the supple line of the passional regime along a vector of intensive speed. These lines cannot be subdivided without changing nature. Thus, as it tries to regulate migratory movements, the Church is deterritorialized and barbarized, whereas, at the same time, the passional system, with its relics and its proper names, migrates in all directions, despite the fact that, from time to time, it is reterritorialized upon pontifical order words. This block of becoming, with its geohistorical lines, traces a map and a topography without hidden significations or transcendent purposiveness, and turns history into heterogeneous static genesis—a topological mutation instead of an ontological sending off (*envoi*) with a closed destination.

In this respect, the art of the relics and the use of proper names are paradigmatic: they escape, one way or another, the signifying demands of the despotic sign-regime. This art, as Duby remarks, could cause a lot of shock. The most learned men of the Church were frequently surprised by the proliferation of reliquaries in the form of inorganic bodies, and by the throngs of people fascinated by these simulacra.[33] Daniel-Rops openly revolts against such barbaric practices, which, thanks to their assimilation by the Church, drag it endlessly on a line of increasing barbarism: "In the Dark Ages there was the danger that Christianity might succumb to the general 'barbarization,' that instead of elevating the newly baptized, it might slip into violence and vice along with them."[34] Double now is the risk of gliding upon a smooth space. There is, first of all, an entire series of pagan practices of Germanic background around which Christian temples are erected; they, in various forms, work through the new cult. On the other hand, peregrination and the taste for migration, although present already in the Jewish culture, will come to know a formidable explosion on the occasion of the Christian reterritorialization, and the Church will find it very difficult to contain this wild errance. Mobile and diffuse groups are constituted; immense human tides, with their knights, monks, outlaws, troubadours, and jugglers, begin to deviate following a clinamen where the flesh rises to the surface in a huge mixture of bodies and in swirling fluxes that bend, intersect, and extend themselves in all directions according to diverse longitudes and latitudes. The Europe of the Middle Ages is best defined as a pure field of vectors from which packs spring up, on the basis of a very supple mode of individuation. The latter disrupts the link of baptism along a curve, or a continuous ballad, capable of integrating the most different practices and of forming thereby hordes with fluid outlines growing by the edges laterally. All these packs of fornicating brothers, bandits, heretics, and artisans form an arabesque slope, whose interval in relation to the tangent assumes, at every step, the name of a saint. Inside these packs, every saint's proper name takes the appearance of a particular curve, and the pontifical order words disintegrate, affected by a continuous decline. This is what causes the official language of the Church to flee in the direction of an intensive bilingualism: "The invaders picked up Latin and began to speak it, but what dreadful Latin it was! It was the low Latin of the common people . . . A vulgar tongue emerged which simplified the vocabulary, replacing proper words with popular slang expressions, eliminating the classical adverbs and substituting others formed by adding the ending 'ment' to the adjective, using 'de' and 'ad' instead of case endings, and turning syntax topsyturvy."[35] In short, in this continuous atomization, the pontifical and imperial language begins to stutter; it follows a line of minorizing translation that links, in an aparallel way, the deterritorialization of Latin to the expropriation of Germanism. This evolution carries along the dominant language and its order words in the direction of singular becomings.

To this deterritorialization of people and languages, the pontifical power will react in many ways: through the enactment of indulgences and offerings of forgiveness it will institute a system of jubilees capable of giving a purpose to the movements of peregrination, and of fixing goals that fit the correct jurisdiction. This, in turn, will introduce to the molecular space turbulence and deviations. Looking for ways to reterritorialize the pilgrimage, the Church will gradually, and by means of a system of rewards and penalties, replace geographic displacements with the practice of flagellation as a sedentary penitence. It is true that, contrary to all expectations, this practice will form, around the fifteenth century, a new geography, a new type of becoming, and a new body without organs. But, in the meantime, we witness a veritable inflation of jubilees, under the impulse of a growing deterritorialization. By means of these jubilees, pontifical power reaffirms its authority and succeeds in striating the rhizome. By such means, we see the face of the pope replace the face of Saint Peter and become the center toward which those who travel to Rome[36] converge, without ceasing to be reterritorialized upon the name of the saint. The legalization of the pilgrims' movement, therefore, initially requires that deviations be given a purpose and be reindexed upon the face of the pope, where the jubilees succeed in taking shape. But it also requires that the peregrination be integrated in a trajectory that is controlled by hospices empowered to deliver the certificates appropriate to the prescribed punishment. Fixed itineraries and straight lines dotted with stations of hospitality regulated by extremely rigorous codes replace the old, wild migrations. Hence, on every kind of pilgrim a particular juridical status is imposed, fixing the order of symbols and emblems, as well as the nature of the uniform. But under this strict and constraining jurisdiction, the knots never cease to be undone and to form an enormous war machine liberating a formidable charge of nomadism, doubling up every migrant with a nomad potential on a line of absolute deviation.[37]

Between the states of affairs that we discussed (sanctuaries, reliquaries, hospices, and pilgrims) and the corresponding sign-regimes (juridical codes for pilgrims, jubilees, indulgences, insignia, and prayers)—between form of content and form of expression—an incorporeal event is counteractualized. It traces a line of flight where the marchers of God rush on, according to variable speeds and intensities or longitudes and latitudes. In the crossroads of the latter pairing, packs of traitors surge up and the Church, despite its efforts, cannot integrate them into the triangle: Rome, Jerusalem, Saint Jacques de Compostelle. Everywhere, new hordes, with their own relics and their own proper names, begin to betray: Saint Roch against the pest; Saint Blaise against sore throats; Saint Matthew against dementia . . .[38] In certain regions, illnesses assume the name of the saint specialized in their cure. Proper names and relics designate a real war machine, with verbs like "to peregrinate," "to decline," "to miraculate" used to express its effects. Under those infinitives, all the pontifical faces and bulls start to skid, carried along by an arrangement of becoming capable of bringing about a sign-regime and a very particular mixture of bodies. Fistula becomes the illness of Saint Fiacre; epilepsy, the illness of Saint John; scabies, the illness of Saint Meon; the gout, the illness of Saint Maurus. At the same time, and following an incorporeal transformation, all these names become the names of lands—splinters of disparate worlds without relations—and are taken up in a ballad that recombines them upon a cryptic plane of consistency. For all these reasons, a saint's personal history and the faces that the Church tries to symbolize on its reliquaries end up as mere copies of an empirical dimension that cannot but dissolve, as an abstract machine carries it along. This machine is capable of placing, in a continuous variation, architecture, metallurgy, and all discursive formations, according to a line of crusades where packs and ossuaries swarm into infinity.

From architecture to psalmody, from psalmody to relics, and from relics to peregrination, an abstract machine is outlined, without any hidden support or principal overhang, and it develops its concrete differentiated assemblages according to the flat dimension of continuous multiplicities (n–1). Here, I have joined together these multiplicities on a map of the year one thousand, as in a rhizosphere with fluid coordinates, oriented toward diverging thresholds, translated into irreducible proper names, and placed in variation through illimitative verbs of becoming. In this context, I have looked for aesthetic thresholds able to mobilize knowledge (*savoir*) in a direction different from the scientific, in order to translate an architectural work into the problematic terms to which it belongs. I would have liked to develop more than I did the other thresholds—ethical, juridical, political—tied to different discursive practices, and to follow as a nomad "that foreign land where a literary form, a scientific proposition, a common phrase, a schizophrenic piece of non-sense and so on are also statements, but lack a common denominator and cannot be reduced or made equivalent in any discursive way."[39] It is inside this directional space and in continuous transformation that I would have liked to forge my concepts, like an itinerant artisan, with all the tact required by the material-force and support-motif complex, cleansed of their constraining theorems. I would then be able to follow the intensive lines of flight and to allow our vague essence to wander (*errer*) in every course (*parcours*) and every discourse. Perhaps we must, henceforth, learn to decline (*décliner*) all this, simultaneously, with an overgrown ear, on the trajectories of a nomadic philosophy.

—*Translated by Constantin V. Boundas*

Notes

1. Georges Duby, *L'Europe du Moyen-Age* (Paris: Champs Flammarion, 1984), p. 50, and *Saint Bernard: L'art cistercien* (Paris: Champs Flammarion, 1979), p. 45.

2. Albert Lautman, *Le Problème du temps* (Paris: Hermann, 1946), p. 41.

3. Gilles Deleuze, *Cinema 2, The Time-Image*, trans. Hugh Tomlinson and Robert Galeta (London: Athlone, 1989), p. 177.

4. Clément Rosset, *Le Réel: Traité de l'idiotie* (Paris: Les Editions de Minuit, 1977).

5. *Saint Bernard. L'art cistercien*, p. 155.

6. Deleuze and Guattari's decisive analysis spread over the entire "Treatise on Nomadology" in *Capitalism and Schizophrenia*, vol. 2, *A Thousand Plateaus*, trans. Brian Massumi (Minneapolis, University of Minnesota Press, 1987) and the book of Paul Alphandéry, *La chretienté et l'idée de croisade (Paris:* Albin Michel, 1954).

7. Elie Faure, *L'Art medieval* (Paris: Folio/Essais, 1985), pp. 253–257.

8. *Encyclopedia Universalis,* vol. 4 (Paris: Editions Encyclopedia Universalis, 1985), p. 984. See also Jacques Chailley, *Le musique medievale* (Paris, 1951).

9. Gilles Deleuze, *Différence et répétition* (Paris: Presses Universitaires de France, 1968), p. 33. On ritornello and deterritorialization, see *A Thousand Plateaus*, chapter 11.

10. *L'Europe du Moyen-Age*, pp. 53–55.

11. *A Thousand Plateaus*, pp. 364–365.

12. Edmund Husserl, *Ideas: General Introduction to Pure Phenomenology*, trans. W. R. Boyce Gibson (New York: Collier, 1962), p. 74. See also *On the Origin of Geometry*.

13. *A Thousand Plateaus*, pp. 367–368, 407.

14. On the relation between psalmody and war chant, see *Saint Bernard: L'Art cistercien*, pp. 42–43.

15. Deleuze makes use of the same procedure of differentiation with respect to the ironsword and the cast steel saber; see *A Thousand Plateaus*, pp. 404–407.

16. *A Thousand Plateaus*, pp. 369–370.

17. Umberto Eco, *The Name of the Rose*, trans. William Weaver (New York: Warner Books, 1984), pp. 512–513.

18. Michel Foucault, *The Order of Things: An Archaeology of the Human Sciences* (New York: Random House, 1970), preface.

19. Michel Foucault, *The Archaeology of Knowledge and the Discourse on Language*, trans. A. M. Sheridan Smith (New York: Harper, 1972). See also Gilles Deleuze, *Foucault*, trans. Sean Hand (Minneapolis: University of Minnesota Press, 1988), pp. 13–14.

20. *L'Europe du Moyen-Age*, p. 51.

21. *Cinema 2*, pp. 63–64.

22. M. M. Gothier, *Les routes de la foi* (Paris: Bibliothèque des Arts), pp. 68 and 72.

23. On the relationship between this art and the Scythians, see Henri Daniel-Rops, *L'Eglise des temps barbares* (Paris: Fayard, 1950), p. 371. See also *Saint Bernard: L'Art cistercien*, p. 50.

24. On disjunctive logic, see Gilles Deleuze and Felix Guattari, *Capitalism and Schizophrenia*, vol. 1, *Anti-Oedipus*, trans. Robert Hurley, Mark Seem, and Helen R. Lane (New York: Viking Press, 1977), pp. 68–84.

25. *Saint Bernard: L'Art cistercien*, pp. 42–43.

26. *A Thousand Plateaus*, pp. 400–402.

27. *Saint Bernard: L'Art cistercien*, p. 50.

28. Gilles Deleuze, *Proust and Signs*, trans. R. Howard (New York: George Braziller, 1972), p. 100.

29. *A Thousand Plateaus*, p. 21.

30. *A Thousand Plateaus*, p. 30.

31. Henri Daniel-Rops, *The Church in the Dark Ages*, trans. Audrey Butler (New York: Dutton, 1959), p. 383.

32. *A Thousand Plateaus*, p. 119.

33. *L'Europe du Moyen-Age*, p. 59.

34. *The Church in the Dark Ages*, p. 377.

35. *The Church in the Dark Ages*, p. 330.

36. "*Romieux*": pilgrims going to Rome.

37. *A Thousand Plateaus*, pp. 383–384.

38. P. A. Segal, *Les marcheurs de Dieu* (Paris: A. Colin, 1974), p. 35.

39. *Foucault*, p. 20.

15

The Society of Dismembered Body Parts
Alphonso Lingis

for Steve Hornibrook

THE NOTION OF SOCIETIES formed by contract posits law as the transcendent, universally valid, and transtemporal horizon of the contents of contracts. The notion of contract posits individuals as autonomous agents, individuals individuated as seats of understanding and will.

Our culture also maintains the image of a social body, as a multiplicity of individuals integrated as so many functions of an organism. The body writ small that serves as the analogon for societies consists of a set of parts and organs defined by their functions, which are fixed and complementary with one another.

Recent structuralism identified the social fabric with the system regulating the exchange of words, women, goods, and services. Ferdinand de Saussure's linguistics had separated the value of terms from their meanings: to consider the meaning of a term is to consider the way it designates its referent; to consider the value of a term is to consider the other terms that can substitute for it. It was this view of language as an economic system, a field of circulation of terms bearing messages, that made it possible to view the kinship structures that determine the division of tasks and of power in tribal societies as rules made by men for the distribution and exchange of women. The icons and practices of power, ritual, ceremony, religion, myths, and ideologies will also be envisioned as structured fields for the circulation of different kinds of values.

In the exchangist model, the terms of the social field are not simply individuals, the personas presupposed by the social contract theory. It is fundamental to the exchangist model that the terms be susceptible to several uses, be interchangeable. It is this feature that makes it incompatible with the old organic image of society, which depicted society as an integrated hierarchy of terms defined by their functions.

Gilles Deleuze and Félix Guattari's *Anti-Oedipus*[1] offers a new mapping of the libidinal body—the libidinal body of the primary process—which will serve to guide what the theorists have to say about societies. If, when we envision our bodies as organisms, we envision them as integrated sets of functions, the libidinal body being depicted in Deleuze and Guattari is not such an organism; it is the anorganic body, the orgasmic body. What we usually call the body as organism is the body of secondary process libido, the oedipalized body.

An anorganic body is not defined by its constitutive organization, but by its states. *Anti-Oedipus* distinguishes different states of the body. From birth, the orifices couple on to organs they find contiguous with them, and draw in nutritive flows. With the forces of its own strong jowls the infantile mouth draws in the milk, along with gulps of air and warmth. These forces produce plenitude, satisfaction, and contentment, which is not simply an affect shimmering over the inner content. For contentment is itself a force; the infantile body closes its orifices, curls up upon itself, closes its eyes and ears to outside fluxes, makes itself an anorganic plenum—a "body without organs," in Artaud's expression. This undifferentiated and closed plenum produces and reproduces itself; Deleuze and Guattari identify the id, and the primary repression that produces the id, with this state of the body. Its contentment is a primary mode of death drive, which is not a compulsion to disintegrate into the quiescence of the inert, but a primary catatonia.

Freud discerned libidinous pleasure already in the slavering and drooling with which the infant, over and beyond contentment, spreads a surface of pleasure. Every organ-coupling can, by an anaclitic deviation, be turned to the excess production of erotogenic surfaces; the mouth can draw in the nutrients but also slaver and drool, google and babble; the anus can release the excrement but also spread it in a surface of warm pleasure. The pleasure surfaces that are thus extended are surfaces of contact, indiscernibly infantile face and maternal breast, infant cheeks and blanket. Here the organs figure not as orifices leading into the inner functional body, but as productive apparatuses attached to the surfaces of the closed plenum of the body, functioning polymorphously perversely to extend pleasure surfaces. The surfaces are surfaces of sensuality, surfaces not of contentment, but of what Freud called excitations, freely mobile excitations. Flows of energy that irradiate, condense, intersect, build, ripple. Excitations are not properly "sensations," that is, sense data, givens of meaning and orientation, or information bits to be fed into the inner functional body. They are contact phenomena and reveal the other as the convex reveals the concave face of a surface. The infant extends its surplus energies in extending surfaces, discovers the plea-sures of surfaces, discovers the pleasures of having surfaces, of being outside, being born. This extension of the pleasure surfaces to which life attaches itself blocks the compulsion to return to the womb, the primary death drive.

These freely mobile excitations converge, affect themselves with their own intensities, discharge in eddies of egoism. Nomadic, multiple, ephemeral surface egos, where surplus energies are consumed in pleasure, eddies of egoism that consume themselves.

The infant contented—mouth, eyes, ears, fists closed—gives us the very image of the anorganic plenum to which the organs are attached, the "body without organs." Freud even reduced a great deal of the charm of babies to our fascination with the image of narcissism, of closed individuality. Yet the infantile body is anything but a separate substance. From the first it is in symbiosis with mother, earth mother, and earth; in symbiosis with mother, who is harassed, preoccupied, weighed down with the weight of the world—the social, imperial world. The closed plenum upon which organs are attached, producing surface effects, pleasure surfaces, and eddies of egoism, reduces to the individual mass of the body only in the discourse and practices of our epoch. That the closed plenum upon which our organs are attached is identified with the mass of our own individual bodies is the residue of a historical process of deterritorialization, abstraction, formalization.

The Deleuze-Guattari analysis distinguishes productive apparatuses, "machines" or engines where energy is produced, reproduced, distributed, consumed. Genetics places, at the point of origin of living systems in the nonliving, the maintenance of codes—the DNA and RNA molecules. If vital systems can be called "machines," it is because their operations are not simply random; they are coded, or, rather, are loci where coding forms and maintains itself.

For Deleuze and Guattari the question of the nature of the social system or structure or fabric is formulated as a question of code. "Society is not first of all a milieu for exchange where the essential would be to circulate or to cause to circulate, but rather a socius of inscription where the essential thing is to mark and to be marked" (p. 142). The social machinery operates essen-tially to record, channel, regulate the coded flows of libidinal energies. Three different kinds of codings determine the socius as the body of the earth (in nomadic societies), as the body of the despot (in imperial societies), and as the body of capital (in capitalist societies).

Savage societies—nomadic, hunter-gatherer societies—subdivide the people, but not the territory. The earth is the body without organs, the undi-vided plenum upon which the productive machinery, the organs of men, are attached; societies are territorial or terrestrial. Men are not viewed or treated as disconnected, separated, from the earth, as sovereign lords of the earth. Savages therefore do not experience human bodies as integral, whole units. The organs and limbs, experienced as productive of substances, flows, and energies, are experienced not as integrated into one another, but as separately attached to the earth.

An individual does not enter the society by assuming civic rights and responsibilities, as a juridical person. An individual does not enter the society by taking up a post in the distribution of tasks that the society has organized, by fulfilling a productive or defensive role. In nomadic societies pretty much every individual performs the whole gamut of tasks; an individual enters the society by initiation. In the initiation ceremonies he will be marked; more exactly, energy-productive organs and limbs will be separately marked. He will be tattooed, scarified, perforated, circumcised, subincised, clitoridectomized. Among the Lani of Irian Jaya, the eagle people perforate the ears of the initiate and insert into them the plumes of eagles, marking his belonging to the high crags where the eagles dwell; among the Kapuaku the initiated will have the septum of their nostrils perforated and the tusks of wild boars inserted, marking their belonging to the dense forest; among the Azmat the initiated will have the ridges of their ears perforated and the teeth of crocodiles inserted, marking their belonging to the swamps and rivers; among the Australian aborigines men at initiation will have the opening of their penis cut back, in monthly operations, until it is open to the root, so that they will urinate stooping like women, marking their belonging to the fertile body of maternal earth. Myths tell of these couplings, these marked and separate productive organs and limbs, and their attachment to the earth: Parvati is dismembered, and her body parts fall to the earth; at Varanasi her vulva falls and, attached to the Ganga, forms a whirlpool; at Rishikesh her eyes fall and form lakes in the Himalayan clefts; at Brindabar her breasts fall and form mountains on the plains. The marked penis of Shiva falls to the earth, forming lingam, stalactites, and outcroppings in rivers, in caves, in high mountains.

It is by attaching the impulsive organs of the bodies of the clan to the earth that the social body constitutes itself. Primitive societies are not constituted by a pact among its members, but by an attachment to the earth; the tribe is a group that inhabits, and that hunts and gathers together on, the productive surface of the earth that is not divided and parceled out among them. It is in being marked—in being tattooed, scarified, circumcised, subincised—that these men constitute a society, a social body or socius.

This conception Deleuze and Guattari direct against the exchangist conception of society, such as that presupposed by Claude Lévi-Strauss. Society is not a network that gets elaborated in the measure that individuals exchange women, goods, services, and messages with one another, and, in the delay between giving and receiving, contract obligations that are represented by claims. In primitive society I do not have relationships only with those individuals with whom I have exchanged women or goods. I may owe no one anything, but when the clan goes on a hunt, is attacked by wild beasts or human enemies, or pulls up its camp and moves elsewhere, I who live in this area, who have been marked with the tattoo of the leopard people or wear in my perforated septum the tusks of wild boars, have obligations to all those who are so marked. It may well be that I will suffer loss without getting the equivalent in return from the others, or even that I will risk or lose my life. The original obligation, the original debt, is not something contracted personally, when I received something in a transaction in which I agreed to give the equivalent in return. The original subject of obligation is not the persona, the subject as an autonomous and independent agent of initiatives; it is my body, more exactly, my productive body parts, which have been incorporated into the social code by being marked, inscribed, incised, circumcised, subincised, scarified, tattooed. When danger threatens the group, all those who by initiation have been marked with the sign of the boar are obliged to lend their arms to the task. When the group needs to reproduce, and approaches another moiety during the annual betrothal feast, all women who have been clitoridectomized are obliged to bring their reproductive bodies to the feast and accept a man of the other moiety.

Savages do not belong to society as persons, individuals, juridic subjects, but as organs attached to the full body of the earth. The society is the marking of this attachment. The multiplicity of the attached organs extends a productive surface. Deleuze and Guattari do not conceive of the social bond between individuals to be formed by each legislating for the others, nor do they take it to be formed by contracts among individuals who exchange words, women, goods, and services. They conceive it not as a contract nor as an exchange, but as couplings. Couplings not of individuals, but of organs.

Savage society is constituted by the coupling of voice with hearing: Primitive cultures are epic, narrative, oral cultures. In New Guinea, the hunter-gatherer societies, divided into seven hundred mutually incomprehensible languages (fully a third of the languages of humanity) have never engaged in any empire-building. They have no hereditary or elected chiefs. Most of these societies are head-hunting societies. Head-hunting is not war; neither territory, nor booty, nor women are captured in their battles. Rather, each young man seeks out the most brave and the most spectacular warrior on the field to kill, in order to cannibalize his body so as to interiorize his spirit. Men who have killed more than one are not respected and do not gain power over the group; they are regarded as twisted killers. Big men are big by virtue of two things: The power of language, and the capacity to organize feasts in which the people assemble, reaffirm their bonds, and communicate with distant peoples. They have astonishing memories and linguistic capabilities; they are capable of telling their ancestries back dozens of generations, capable of recalling and retelling in captivating ways the history of the people, its luck and its feasts, its heroisms and its ordeals. It is especially this power to hold an audience spellbound long nights that constitutes their prestige. The languages themselves are extraordinarily difficult to learn; not only is their grammar extremely complex, but they have developed great elaborations of ceremonious, poetic, and epic styles.

A second coupling is that of hand with surfaces of inscription. Primitive societies are not manufacturing, but graphic societies. They inscribe the earth with their paths, their dances; they inscribe the walls of their caves or huts; they inscribe their bodies. Savages do not so much build things, shelters and monuments, as do handcraft; they develop not architectural powers, but manual dexterity. They cut twigs to mark their paths, carve tools, weave baskets and clothing. The markings made do not express ideas, but reveal the dexterity of hands. The inscription is not related to the voice; they develop no alphabet or ideograms. Hands learn skills not by having explained to them the meaning and the methods of handling and manipulating, not by being shown the diagram or the model, but instead by immediate induction: the hands of the child imitate the movements of hands of the men and women. One learns to throw the boomerang by throwing it oneself in the company of the skilled. Like in Zen archery, there are no manuals, no discussions with the master: the master holds and tightens and his bow; one does the same, again and again.

A third coupling is that of eye with pain. The pain inflicted, in the initiation rites, is public, theatrical: one watches, the eye does not circumscribe, survey, comprehend; it winces, it senses the pain. As the young Maasai maiden is being scarified, the thorn inserted again and again to raise scars in regular patterns across her back, down her thighs, all afternoon, the others watch, eyes like flies feasting on the pain.

Savage inscription cuts into living flesh; the markings, perforations, inscriptions, incisions, circumcisions, subincisions, clitoridectomies are painful. Savage societies are machines of cruelty. The pain is by no means minimized; initiation rites redouble the pain, include gratuitous fastings, long incarcerations in dark men's houses, beatings, bleedings. Infections, deaths occur. The markings are done in long public feasts. It is clear that there is a collective pleasure in this savagery, this cruelty that so revolts us, and that also excites us, childhood readers of *National Geographic*, colonialists, missionaries, who soon indulge our own cruelties, unleashing upon the savages insults, beatings, hard labor, enslavement. Those who live long among savages soon acquire cruel habits. I remember spending a week with a missionary, a member of the order of Saint Francis, who had been in Irian Jaya for twenty-seven years, and helping him each morning in the clinic he had set up and personally staffed. I was surprised, then intrigued, then revolted by the roughness with which he tore off bandages, by the extra touch of cruelty with which he manhandled and jabbed children while vaccinating them. Those he baptized—initiated into his parish—were also perforated, scarred, marked.

Nietzsche, in the second essay of *The Genealogy of Morals,* speaks of the excitant that pain is for the spectator. When one lies with the sick one, the suffering and the moanings invade the space, invade one's own body, depress and devitalize in the contagion of suffering. But when one actively inflicts pain, on oneself or on others, there is excitement and jubilation in the spectacle of the pain. The eye is a crystal ball, where the pain suffered is transfigured into pleasure received.

Nietzsche observes that the one who is cheated by another who owed him some commodity or service is satisfied, not when justice intervenes and forces the debtor to bring what he owed, but when justice punishes the debtor. What is this? Nietzsche asks. How is it that the creditor could accept the transaction contracted for as fulfilled when the goods were not delivered but the debtor suffered? How can pain be some kind of payment? It is that the original social contract was not for goods and services but for the pleasure of those goods and services. It is that the spectacle of the pain of another can be a pleasure equivalent to the pleasure in those goods and services.

But the original marking is not the result of transactions between individuals freely entered into by which one becomes creditor and the other debtor, a marking that will be effaced when the goods contracted for are delivered. The prime marking, the prime coding, is the socialization itself, which isolates the productive organs of the body and codes their coupling with the body of the earth: the tattooing, scarifying, circumcising, subincising, clitoridectomizing. These markings sear with pain. Nietzsche does not go far enough, when he says that these brandings serve to mark the memory—or to create a memory—with a few "Thou shalt nots." The rites in which they are inflicted are public rites, festive occasions in which the clan affirms its unity. They are destined for the eyes that watch, and that derive from them from the start the surplus value of pleasure. It is not originally a pleasure owed them, contracted for; it is the original surplus value that the socialization itself generates. It is only afterward that one so marked will enter into limited transactions with other members of the group, will deliberately and on his own contract debts that he will pay or not pay, and if he does not pay, he will have to give his creditors the pleasure of seeing him suffer.

The markings with which savage societies record, channel, regulate the coded flows of the energies produced in the couplings are not *read*. Savage inscriptions are not signs that refer to concepts; they are diagrams and paths for the hand. The leopard footprint one sees on the path does not refer to the name and notion of leopard, but links up directly with the leopard itself. The leopard claw-print that one sees inscribed by human hand on the path or on the body of the initiate does not refer to the voice that utters the name "leopard" and conceives the meaning of that name; it directly designates the leopard itself. The eye does not read this sign; it sees the mark of the beast; it winces; it senses the pain. But now it is the leopard itself that functions as a sign. One takes those marked with the mark of the leopard to be a tribe, a society. (I remember visiting a mine on the Arctic Ocean at the border between Finland and the Soviet Union; the young miner who showed me the mine put out every cigarette he smoked on his hand, which was covered with scar tissue. Then I saw that the other young miners all had the backs of their hands covered with scar tissue. When I saw the scars, I did not read them as marks of words that could be pronounced, like tattoos where one can read things—"47th battalion, Nam"—rather, when my eye fell on them it flinched, seeing the burning cigarette being crushed and sensing the pain. And it is this burning cigarette I took to be a sign of the fiery and defiant young men who had come from the south and gone there, to the mines on the brink of the Arctic Ocean, and whose branding of their own hands functioned as a seal of their fraternity. The eye does not read the meaning in a sign; it *jumps* from the mark to the pain and the burning cigarette, and then jumps to the fraternity signaled by the burning cigarettes.)

Savage societies are transformed or incorporated into barbarian societies, sedentary and imperial, by a change in the nature of the codings. By an overcoding, all the lines of filiation and alliance are made to converge upon the body of the despot. As the productive organs are attached to the closed plenum of the body of the despot, they are detached from the earth, deterritorialized.

Barbarian societies are also characterized by a change in the couplings of the organs that extend the productive surface of the social order. The hand is coupled onto a graphics that is aligned with the voice. The coupling of voice with hearing through the intermediary of writing produces wholly new effects. The eye is uncoupled from pain, anesthetized. Writing begins with empires.[2] It is contrived for use in imperial legislation, in a bureaucracy, for accounting, for the collection of taxes, for the constitution of the state monopoly, for imperial justice, for historiography. But also it contains within itself a transcendent and despotic law. Savages possess extraordinary manual virtuosity; they do not lack writing for lack of manual dexterity. Writing is produced when graphics are coupled with the voice to become signs of words spoken.

The graphics now do not, as in a claw mark incised on the back of the Yoruba initiate that invites the hand to gingerly feel it, serve as grooves for the movement of hand and body. The graphics are destined for tablets, stones, books; destined to be indefinitely reproduced on more tablets (the textbook explained in the classroom is copied by students in notebooks, recopied by students in bluebooks at the end of the term, recopied later by graduates for articles to be published on more paper). When the savage eye saw the claw-mark cut into the white bark of the birch tree, it winced; it felt the wound of the tissue and the sap of the tree and jumped to the wound on the flesh and the blood of the Yoruba initiate. Now the eye no longer winces when it sees the mark; it does not see the incision with which the pen or the printer has cut into the white surface of the paper. The eye has lost the ability to see the cut, the incision, the wound; it passes lightly over the page, not seeing, not sensing the tissue of the paper at all, but seeing the words as though they were flat patterns suspended in a neutral emptiness. The eye is no longer active, palpating the pain, jumping to the leopard; it is now passive before the flow of abstract patterns passing across it.

Writing is graphics now coupled with the spoken word, but in this coupling the voice is transformed. The voice in its savage relation with hearing exists in a reciprocal relation: the voice speaks; the other hears and answers. The movement is a zigzag from one to the other, and it is broken by pauses, by silences. The voice that is now written has been linearized. The words no longer exist here, in this place, between these two savages stationed on the earth in front of one another; they now exist in a linear progression that has been deterritorialized. When I read, on paper, the lines, "The citizens of New Spain are hereby taxed five gold pesos each per year," all sense of a spot on the earth where these words were uttered is lost; I am not referred to that place, but rather to the meanings of these signs, which exist transtemporally and transspatially. The meanings are there wherever the text is read or recalled; the voice of the speaker does not echo in them. Writing is a form of graphics, Deleuze and Guattari say, that is aligned with the voice, but also supplants the voice. When I come upon the lines, "When noble metals are roasted, phlogiston is released," it would be pointless for me to strain to hear the voice that uttered them. It is in reading on down the lines that I will discover that phlogiston was a concept of ancient chemistry and will determine the meaning of "noble metals" from the lines of writing that contrast the expression "noble metals" with that of "base metals."

Now the voice no longer resonates, chants, invokes, calls forth; one hears only the voice of a law that orders one to move on down the line. Writing remains aligned by the voice—now a mute, impersonal, remote voice. A transcendent voice detaches itself from the whole of discourse and detaches the resonances from words. The voice is there only as that which once decreed that this inscription means this concept, that decrees that one must no longer settle on the resonance of any sensuous sound but take it as but a sign that refers to other signs. To hear the message, the meaning, one must subject oneself to the law: the phonetic, taxonomical, syntactical, semantical laws of significant language, which are conventional, laid down by decree, by another law that regulates the meaning of language because it regulates the whole of society. To subject oneself to the law of written language is to subject oneself to the one law of the one language of the empire.

When Siegfried, in the Enchanted Forest, hears the murmurs of the trees, he hears their individual substance and tensions and flexions that are being plucked by the wind and resounding. Through the sound and in them, he encounters the inner substances of the trees themselves. Then he drinks the magic potion brought to him by the bird descended from on high, from the throne of Wotan the law-giver, and, suddenly, he hears what they mean. He no longer hears the trees resounding; he hears a message: the warning that Alberich has bewitched him and is waiting to kill him.

You can wander the high Andes and, by night, hear the murmurs of the people around the fire, hear their Quechua tongue without understanding it, hear the light, subtle, supple tripping of their sounds, hear their intonations and their murmurs, hear it as the very resonance of their substance, their gentle, unassertive, vibrant, sensitive way of vocalizing together like gentle animals, quail foraging a field or muttering in a thicket for the night, vocalizing their togetherness. You can look at their inscriptions and see the letters *Saqsaywaman* and *intihuatana* carved in stone or staining the weathered boards of their homes, see these marks as incisions and stainings in the substance of the stone or wood, forming patterns with the cracks and fissures in the stone, the grain and diverse colors of the wood. But if you were to drink some magic potion, some cocktail of coca tea and whisky, and suddenly understood their language, and abruptly understood that they are speaking about "transporting cocaine into the hands of the Colombian agents," then abruptly you have subjected yourself to the codings of imperial society; you have suddenly related their sounds not to their own throats and substance but to the international code established by the reigning barbarian empire in Washington and Bonn and Tokyo, where cocaine means the same thing—crime—whenever, wherever it is spelled out; and you cannot detach this meaning from their murmurings around the fire without subjecting yourself to the decrees that fix the international imperial code. And you at the same time insert yourself in the code; you find yourself designated as a tourist, an observer and reporter for the empire, another plunderer bringing back to the imperial metropolis handcrafts and idols, souvenirs and memories, and field reports on the activities of the outlaws. If you want to speak of them murmuring together, without subjecting them and yourself to the law, if you want to speak a discourse of nomads and outlaws, if you want to tell of them speaking to you as outsiders, nomads and outlaws, you must never pronounce this word. But how then will others understand what you say—others who, like yourself, speak imperial English, which they have learned and continue to learn from the imperial media? At best you can speak of them in the imperial code, speak of them as cocaine traffickers and terrorists, in such a way the words begin to lose their consistency, become nonsensical, turn against the imperial grammar itself. You can try to make others conspirators who use the imperial formulas themselves as passwords by which the imperial discourse itself turns into babble and din.

Marx had spoken of the dismemberment of the human body in the social machinery of industrial capitalism. Laborers are coupled with the productive process only as hands that assemble on assembly lines, or as legs and backs that bear burdens, or as arms that stoke furnaces. It is only the hands and eyes of clerks in offices that are paid for. Soldiers are limbs connected to weapons, disconnected from brain and imagination. Foremen are eyes disconnected from heart. The capitalist is the calculating brain disconnected from the capitalist's own taste and caprice. The industrial enterprise is the whole body upon which these part-organs are attached.

Marxism invokes the missing whole organism, that of the species individual, to which the diverse limbs and organs, attached to the body of industry, would, in principle, belong. The revolution Marx envisions would bring about the social ownership of the productive enterprise and the individual ownership of the body-parts coupled onto that enterprise. But, in fact, capitalism itself invokes the private individual, owner of all his parts and members, motivated by self-interest, that is, interest in the consolidation and aggrandizement of the self as an integral whole. For the private ownership of productive enterprises, to which large numbers of limbs and members of others are coupled, invokes the subordination of the body of the productive enterprise to the integral body of the individual.

The private individual is constituted by a privatization of his organs, his productive engines. It is the social machine itself that privatizes the organs, decodes their couplings with their immediate objects, and makes their flows of substance and energies abstract. The first organ to undergo privatization, removal from the social field, was the anus. We have long since ceased to use it to make contact with the earth—joining our excrement with the humus, wiping our asses with leaves, peeing in puddles and streams. We have long since ceased attaching an anus to the full body of the emperor. In the Middle Ages theologians long debated whether Jesus had an anus; his priestly role, mediator between God and man, God-man, seemed to require an integral human body, but an anus seemed fundamentally contradictory to his role as transcendent word that inscribes the social coding on earth. Society decodes the flow of excrement, decrees that it cannot be spoken of, that meaning should not be sought in it. It becomes a pure residue, an abstract flow without significance, without coding. The first zone of privacy, of individu-ation, that is constituted in the core of the symbiotic world of the infant is his anus. One has to cover up one's anus, stop playing with it, stop playing with excrement, stop leaving traces of it in the living room. It is about this private part that the privacy of a whole individual is constituted. The notion of a private individual is that of a source of flows, of substances and fluids and energies, which are of themselves abstract, without social determination, without coding. Freud understood that the phallic phase follows the anal phase and builds on it: the pleasure that the boy feels in the hardening of his penis is felt as a prolongation outside of the pleasure he feels of a full bowel sliding outward. In the Oedipus complex, the boy will substitute for his real penis and this real pleasure the abstract pleasure of being a phallus and make himself into an ego, an ego posited over against others, making demands on others. The individual is identified with the phallus; the core of his status as a private individual lies in the identity of the phallus, which he can hide or reveal according to his own initiative. Deleuze and Guattari emphasize the decoded, deterritorialized nature of this phallic emanation. In primitive soci-eties the boy's first ejaculation and the girl's menarche are highly significant, coded, public events. In our societies the flows of pubescent semen and blood are decoded, deterritorialized, privatized; they are supposed to take place behind locked doors, at night. No one is supposed to see the evidence of wet dreams on the sheets. The privacy of the individual is constituted about these privatized organs and flows.

Marx conceptualized, as alienation, the dismemberment of the body whose productive parts and organs are attached to the full body of industry and invoked the idea of integral man, the man whose body parts would belong to himself. This notion of integral man, the species individual, has the status of a utopian concept. It would be necessary to show the constitution of this notion in the privatization of the individual about the privatization of his organs beginning with the anus. But then the utopian notion of integral man can no longer maintain the function Marxism allots to it: that of figuring as the benchmark that enables Marxism to criticize the social coding of capitalism, as well as that of barbarism and of savagery. For the notion of the integral man, the privatized body, is a moment of the capitalist coding.

The schizophrenic apocalypse Deleuze and Guattari envision on the horizon of capitalism would not bring together the body parts dispersed across the social field. It would rather free them for ever more diverse couplings with one another.

For the surface productive of the social is being extended, elaborated, transformed not simply by new laws being legislated, by new enterprises being launched for the international exchange of messages, digitally coded information, women, Filipino maids to England or Kuwait, goods, handguns, redeye or silkworm missiles, Korean Scuds to Iran, and Ukrainian plutonium to Japan, and the services of Singapore bankers, Tokyo stockbrokers, and Brussels consultant firms. The social body is being laid bare, laid out, laid, excited, metamorphosed when hands clasp in greeting and in understanding and in commitment and in sensuality and also in parting. When the ear put against the cellular receiver is in contact with a voice from any tribe and any continent. Where automated, robotized, cybernetically programmed industry detaches the hands from any craft, save that of touching buttons that project patterns on computer screens that vanish without leaving a trace. Where the eyes no longer feast on the pain of Iraqi soldiers buried in the sands or the unemployed and homeless in Rio and London and New York, but on pains more fascinating, more ravishing, incomparably more visible—those of *Basic Instinct* and *The Silence of the Lambs*. Where the hands of the medical technician implant the detached, marked, labeled fertilized egg of an upwardly mobile couple in the womb of an unemployed woman. Where eyes watch a CAT scan of a metastasizing cancer or the sonar probe of a pregnancy. Where the car on cruise control races the Los Angeles freeways, the hands free to dial the cellular phone, cut the lines of coke, or cock a handgun. Where the hearts, livers, kidneys of newly executed Chinese prisoners are rushed to clinics in Hong Kong, where ailing financiers and aging media superstars arrive by limousine. When hands holding a video camera connect with hands on batons beating the black legs of a speeding motorist. When hearts, livers, kidneys are being cut out of young black male corpses and transplanted into anesthetized bodies of CEOs and aging media superstars in exclusive clinics in Hollywood and Las Vegas. Where the cold hearts and annealed nerves of a few youths from despised peoples imprisoned by blockades hijack the most advanced marvels of supersonic jet technology, the most invincible smart weapons. When high school dropouts in Karachi insert viruses on computer disks that shut down the Pentagon. Where hands extend into Alaskan seas for oil-drenched seabirds. Where lips kiss the pain of the AIDS victim, where fingers close the eyes of the one whose agony has at length come to an end.

Notes

1. Gilles Deleuze and Félix Guattari, *Capitalism and Schizophrenia: Anti-Oedipus*, vol. 1, trans. Robert Hurley, Mark Seem, and Helen R. Lane (Minneapolis: University of Minnesota Press, 1983). All page references in the text refer to this volume.

2. What a strange thing writing is! It would seem that its apparition could not fail to determine profound changes in the conditions of existence of humanity, and that these transformations would have had to have been especially intellectual in nature. The possession of writing prodigiously multiplies the aptitude of men to preserve knowledge. We like to conceive of writing as an artificial memory, whose development should be accompanied with a better consciousness of the past, hence a greater capacity to organize the present and the future. After one eliminates all the criteria proposed to distinguish barbarism from civilization, one would like at least to retain this: the people with writing are capable of accumulating ancient acquisitions and progress more and more quickly toward the goal they have assigned themselves, while the peoples without writing, incapable of retaining the past beyond the fringe that individual memory suffices to fix, would remain prisoners of a fluctuating history which would always lack an origin and the durable consciousness of a project.

    And yet nothing of what we know of writing and its role in evolution justifies such a conception. One of the most creative phases of the history of humanity took place during the approach of the neolithic age, responsible for agriculture, the domestication of animals and other arts. To reach it, it was necessary that during millennia little human collectivities observed, experimented and transmitted the fruit of their reflections. This immense enterprise was carried on with a rigor and a continuity attested to by success, while writing was still unknown. If writing appeared between the fourth and third millennia before Christ, we must see in it an already distant (and no doubt indirect) result of the neolithic revolution, but nowise its condition. To what great innovation is it bound? On the plane of technology, we can cite hardly anything but architecture at this period. But the architecture of the Egyptians or the Sumerians was not superior to the works of certain Americans who were ignorant of writing at the time of the arrival of Cortez. Conversely, from the invention of writing up to the birth of modern science, the western world lived some 5000 years during which its knowledge fluctuated more than it was increased. It has often been remarked that between the kind of life of a Greek or Roman citizen and that of a European bourgeois of the 18th century, there was hardly much difference.

In the neolithic period, humanity took giant steps forward without the help of writing; with writing the historical civilizations of the West long stagnated. No doubt the scientific expansion of the 19th and 20th centuries would hardly be conceivable without writing. But this necessary condition is certainly not sufficient to explain it.

If we want to correlate the apparition of writing with certain characteristic traits of civilization, we have to look in another direction. The sole phenomenon that faithfully accompanied writing is the formation of cities and empires, that is, the integration into a political system of a considerable number of individuals and their hierarchization into castes and classes. Such is, in any case, the typical evolution we see from Egypt to China, the moment that writing begins: it appears to favorize the exploitation of men before it favorizes their illumination. This exploitation, which make it possible to assemble thousands of workers to yoke them to extenuating tasks, better accounts for the birth of architecture than does the direct relation envisioned a moment ago. If my hypothesis is correct, we have to admit that the primary function of written communication is to facilitate enslavement" (Claude Lévi-Strauss, *Tristes tropiques* [Paris: Plon, 1955], pp. 265–66).

Selected Critical References to Gilles Deleuze and His Works

Compiled by Timothy S. Murphy
with Constantin V. Boundas

I. Books and Articles on Deleuze

Abraham, Tomás. *Pensadores Bajos* (Sartre/Foucault/Deleuze). Buenos Aires: Catalogos Editora, 1987.

Adams, Hazard, and Leroy Searle, eds. *Critical Theory Since 1965*. Tallahassee: University Press of Florida, 1986. 283–285.

Adams, Joseph. *Yeats and the Masks of Syntax*. New York: Columbia University Press, 1984.

Agostini, Daniela de. Review of "Table ronde" from Cahiers Marcel Proust. *Studi francesi XIX* (1975): 388–389.

Alliez, Eric. "Ontologie et logographie: La pharmacie, Platon et le simulacre" in Barbara Cassin, ed., *Nos Grecs et leurs modernes: Les Stratégies contemporaines d'appropriation de l'Antiquité*. Paris: Seuil, 1992. 211–231.

———. *Les Temps capitaux tome 1: Récits de la conquête du temps*. Paris: Éditions du Cerf, 1991. Preface by Gilles Deleuze.

Alliez, Eric, and Michel Feher. "The Luster of Capital." Trans. by Alyson Waters. *Zone 1/2*: 315–359.

———. "Notes on the Sophisticated City." Trans. by David Beriss and Astrid Hustedt. *Zone 1/2*: 41–55.

Alzon, Claude. *Femme mythifiée, femme mystifiée*. Paris: Presses universitaires de France, 1978.

Anquetil, Gilles. "Mille idées courtes pour faire la peau aux longs concepts." *Nouvelles Littéraires* October 2–9 (1980).

Antonini, Antoine. Review of *Marcel Proust et le signes. Adam 349–351* (1971): 34–42.

Aron, Jean-Paul. "Mars 1972: l'Anti-Oedipe." *Les Modernes*. Paris: Éditions Gallimard, 1984.

Aronowitz, Stanley. "Anti-Oedipus and Molecular Politics." *New Political Science* 1:4 (Fall 1980): 19–24.

Arthur, Kateryna Olijnyk. "Between Literatures: Canada and Australia." *Ariel: A Review of International English Literature* 19:1 (Jan. 1988): 3–12.

Assad-Michail, Fawzia. "Mort de l'homme et subjectivité." *Revue de Métaphysique et de Morale* vol. 73 (1968): 430–61.

Aubral, François, and Xavier Delcourt. *Contre la nouvelle philosophie.* Paris: Gallimard, 1977.

Augé, Marc. *The Anthropological Circle: Symbol, Function, History.* Trans. by Martin Thom. (Cambridge: Cambridge University Press, 1982. Originally published as *Symbole, Fonction, Histoire.* Paris: Hachette, 1979.

Axelos, Kostas. "Sept questions d'un philosophe." *Le Monde,* 28 April 1972: 19.

Backès-Clément, Catherine. "Les petites filles." *L'Arc 49: Deleuze* (1972, revised 1980): 1–2.

Badiou, Alain. "Le flux et le parti (dans les marges de l'anti-oedipe)." *Théorie et politique 6* (March 1976), reprinted in *Cahiers Yenan 4: La situation actuelle sur le front de la philosophie.* Paris: Maspero, 1977: 24–41.

———. *Manifeste pour la philosophie.* Paris: Seuil, 1990.

———. Review of *Le Pli: Leibniz et le baroque. Annuaire Philosophique 1988–1989.* Paris: Éditions du Seuil, 1989: 161–184.

Barthelemy-Madaule, Madeleine. "Lire Bergson." *Les Études bergsonniennes VIII* (1968): 83–120.

Baudrillard, Jean. *Forget Foucault.* Trans. by Nicole Dufresne. New York: Semiotext(e), 1987. With "Forget Baudrillard", an interview with Sylvère Lotringer. Originally published as *Oublier Foucault.* Paris: Éditions Galilée, 1977.

Baugh, Bruce. "Deleuze and Empiricism." *The Journal of the British Society For Phenomenology* 24:1 (Jan. 1993): 15–31.

———. "Transcendental Empiricism. Deleuze's Response to Hegel." *Man and World* 25:2 (1992): 133–148.

Bell, William S. Review of Marcel Proust et les signes. *The French Review* XLVII (1973/1974): 1199–1200.

Belle, E. *Macht en Verlangen. Nietzsche en het Denken van Foucault, Deleuze en Guattari.* Nijmegen: Sun, 1981.

Bellour, Raymond. "Gilles Deleuze: Un philosophe nomade." *Magazine littéraire 257* (Sept. 1988): 14.

———. "Gais savoirs" in *Magazine littéraire 280* (Oct. 1991): 70–71.

Bellour, Raymond, Alison Rowe and Elisabeth Lyon. "The Film Stilled." *Camera Obscura* vol. 24 (Sept. 1990): 99–121.

Benoist, Jean-Marie. "L'Alphabet de formes de Gilles Deleuze." *Revue des deux mondes* (Dec. 1988): 216–220.

———. "Réponse à Gilles Deleuze sur les nouveaux philosophes: Avarices de la machine désir-ante ou avanies de la machine délirante?" *Le Monde aujourd'hui* July 3–4 (1977): 16.

———. *The Structural Revolution.* New York: St. Martin's Press, 1978. Translated by Arnold Pomerans and Robert Olorenshaw. Originally published as *La Révolution structurale.* Paris: Grasset, 1975.

Bensimon, Marc J. "Apocalypse Now or in the Magic Hole?" M. Chefdor, R. Quinones, and A. Wachtel, eds., *Modernism: Challenges and Perspectives.* Urbana: University of Illinois Press, 1986: 284–303.

Bensmaia, Réda. "Gilles Deleuze ou comment devenir un Stalker en philosophie?" *Lendemains* XIV:53 (1989): 7–8.

————. "L'Effet Kafka." *Lendemains* XIV:53 (1989): 63–71. Published in translation as "The Kafka Effect" as the preface to Deleuze and Guattari, *Kafka: Toward a Minor Literature.* Trans. Dana Polan. Minneapolis: University of Minnesota Press, 1986.

————. "Un philosophe au cinéma." *Magazine littéraire* 257 (Sept. 1988): 57–59.

Berçu, France. "Sed perseverare diabolicum." *L'Arc* 49: Deleuze (1972, revised 1980): 23–30.

Berger, Herman. "L'Anti-Oedipe." *Bijdragen ven het Institut voor Rechtsgeschiedenis der Rijks-univrsiteit te Utrecht,* vol. 46 (1985): 289–312.

Bersani, J., ed. *Les Critiques de notre temps et Proust.* Paris: Garnier-Frères, 1971: 147–158.

Bersani, Leo. *A Future for Astyanax: Character and Desire in Literature.* Boston: Little, Brown, 1976.

Bertrand, Pierre. *L'oubli: Révolution ou mort de l'histoire.* Paris: Presses universitaires de France, 1975.

Bianquis, Geneviève. "Nietzsche et la philosophie." *Bulletin de la société française d'études niet-zschéennes* 1963:2: 37.

Bindé, Jérôme. "Deleuze va au cinema." *Le Nouvel Observateur* 989 (Oct. 21, 1983).

Blincoe, Nicholas. "Deleuze and Masochism." *Pli: Deleuze and the Transcendental Unconscious.* Coventry: University of Warwick, 1992: 81–96.

Bogue, Ronald. *Deleuze and Guattari.* New York: Routledge, 1989. Contains extensive bibliography.

————. "Gilles Deleuze: Postmodern Philosopher?" *Criticism: A Quarterly for Literature and the Arts* XXXII:4 (fall 1990): 401–418.

————. "Rhizomusicosmology." *SubStance* XX:3 no. 66 (Winter 1991): 85–101.

————. "Word, Image and Sound: The Non-Representational Semiotics of Gilles Deleuze." *Mimesis in Contemporary Theory: An Interdisciplinary Approach.* Edited by Roland Bogue. Philadelphia: John Benjamins, 1991, volume 2: 77–97.

————. "The Aesthetics of Force." *The Journal of the British Society for Phenomenology* 24:1 (Jan. 1993): 56–65.

Bonilla, Luis. Review of *Proust y los signos. Estafeta literaria* 496 (July 15, 1972): 1016.

Bonitzer, Pascal. "Dictionnaire sans foi ni loi: Deleuze (Gilles)." *Cahiers du cinéma* 325 (June 1981): 115.

Bonnet, Henri. *Roman et poésie: essai su l'esthétique des genres.* Paris: Nizet, 1980.

————. "La tentative 'structuraliste' de Gilles Deleuze." *Bulletin de la Société des Amis de Marcel Proust et des Amis de Combray* 21 (1971): 1190–1200.

Bontemps, Jacques. "Le Philosope et le cinéma." *Le Matin* 25 October 1983: 29.

Bonzon, Sylvie. Review of *Différence et Répétition* by Gilles Deleuze. *Revue de Théologie et de Philosophie,* vol. 20 (1970): 247–48.

Borel, Jacques. "Notes sur l'imparfait proustien." *Critique,* 195 (Dec. 1971).

Boston, Richard. "No Sadist." *Times Literary Supplement,* August 6, 1971: 971.

————. "Ouch." *New Statesman,* vol. 81 (May 28, 1971): 743–44.

Botturi, Francesco. "Filosofia della in-differenza: Univocità e nichilismo in Deleuze." *Rivista di filosofia neo-scolastica* LXXVIII (1986): 545–576; LXXVIX (1987): 33–52.

Boundas, Constantin V. "Minoritarian Deconstruction and the Rhetoric of Nihilism." *Nietzsche and the Rhetoric of Nihilism,* Ed. Tom Darby, Bela Egyed and Ben Jones. Ottawa: Carleton University Press, 1989. 81–92.

————— . "Deleuze, Empiricism, and the Struggle for Subjectivity," translator's introduction to *Deleuze, Empiricism and Subjectivity: An Essay on Hume's Theory of Human Nature*. New York: Columbia University Press, 1991. 1–19.

————— . "Gilles Deleuze's Joyful Encounters." *Joyful Wisdom*, Ed. Marco Zlomislic, Gerard Grand and David Goicoechea. St. Catharines: Joyful Wisdom Publishing Ltd., 1991. 1–18

————— . "Gilles Deleuze: The Ethics of the Event." *Joyful Wisdom*, Ed. David Goicoechea and Marco Zlomislic: St. Catharines: Thought House, 1992. 169–99.

————— , Ed. *The Deleuze Reader*. New York: Columbia University Press, 1992.

————— . "The Foreclosure of the Other: From Sartre to Deleuze." *The Journal of the British Society for Phenomenlogy* 24:1 (Jan. 1993): 32–43.

————— , Ed. *The Journal of the British Society for Phenomenlogy* 24:1 (Jan. 1993). (Special issue on Gilles Deleuze.)

Bouscasse, Sylvie, and Denis Bourgeois, eds. *Faut-il brûler les nouveaux philosophes?* Paris: Nouvelles Éditions Oswald, 1978.

Boutang, Pierre. *Apocalypse du désir*. Paris: Grasset, 1979.

Bové, Paul. "The Foucault Phenomenon: The Problematics of Style," foreword to *Deleuze, Foucault*. Minneapolis: University of Minnesota Press, 1988. vii–xi.

Boyer, Philippe. *L'écarté(e) (fiction théorique)*. Paris: Seghers, 1973.

Boyne, Roy and Scott Lash. "Communicative Rationality and Desire." *Telos* no. 61: (1984): 152–58.

Brabant, G. P. "Masoch ou . . . masochisme?" *L'Inconscient* 6 (April–June 1968).

Brady, Patrick. *Marcel Proust*. Boston: Twayne, 1977.

Braidotti, Rosi. *Patterns of Dissonance*. New York: Routledge, 1991.

—————. "Discontinuing Becomings: Deleuze on the Becoming-Woman of Philosophy." *The Journal of the British Society for Phenomenology* 24:1 (Jan. 1993): 44–55.

Brede, Werner. "Anmerkungen zum 'Anti-Ödipus' von Deleuze/Guattari." *Psyche* vol. 33 (1979): 784–91

Brès, Yvon. "Oedipe ou Freud." *Revue Philosophique de la France et de l'Etranger* 163 (1973): 35–52.

Brinkley, R.A. and Robert Dyer. " . . . returns home (Mythologies, Dialectics, Structures): Disruptions." *Semiotext(e): Anti-Oedipus* vol. 2 no. 3 (1977): 159–171.

Bryant-Bertail, Sarah. "Kafka and the Dialectical Theater." *Journal of the Kafka Society of America* 12: 1–2 (1988): 19–26.

Buci-Glucksmann, Christine. "Le plissé baroque de la peinture." *Magazine littéraire* 257 (Sept. 1988): 54–56.

Burchell, Graham. "Introduction to Deleuze." *Economy and Society* 13:1 (1984): 43–51.

Bürger, Christa. "The Reality of 'Machines,' Notes on the Rhizome-Thinking of Deleuze and Guattari." *Telos* 64 (summer 1985): 33–44. Translated by Simon Srebrny.

Burnham, John C. "Psychotic Delusions as a Key to Historial Cultures. Tasmania 1830–1940." *Journal of Social History* 13:3 (Spring 1980): 368–83.

Busdon, Alessandr. "Lettura di Mille Plateaux." *Aut Aut* nos. 187–88 (1982): 137–51.

Butler, A. "New Film Histories and the Politics of Location." *Screen* 33:4 (Winter 1993): 413–26.

Butler, Judith P. "The Life and Death Struggle of Desire: Hegel and Contemporary Theory." *Subjects of Desire: Hegelian Reflections in Twentieth-Century France:* 175–238. New York: Columbia University Press, 1987.

Buydens, Mireille. *Sahara: L'esthétique de Gilles Deleuze.* (Paris: Vrin, 1990. Preface by Gilles Deleuze.

Cacciari, Massimo. "'Razionalità' e 'irrazionalità' nella critica del politico in Deleuze e Foucault." *Aut Aut* 161 (Sept.–Oct. 1977): 119–133.

Cadet, Valérie, and Josyane Savigneau. "En feuilletant mille deux cent cinquante numéros." *Le Monde des Livres* Mar. 20, 1992: IV–XX.

Callinicos, Alex. *Against Postmodernism: A Marxist Critique.* Cambridge: Polity Press, 1989.

——— . *Is There a Future for Marxism?* London: Macmillan Press, 1982.

Campbell, Lorna. "Anteros and Intensity." *Pli: Deleuze and the Transcendental Unconscious.* Coventry: University of Warwick, 1992: 97–104.

Campbell, Marion. *Lines of Flight.* Freemantle: Freemantle Arts Centre, 1985.

Canning, Peter M. "Fluidentity." *SubStance* XIII 3/4 (1984): 35–46.

Cantor, Jay. "Anti-Oedipus: Capitalism and Schizophrenia by Gilles Deleuze and Félix Guattari." *The New Republic, 24* Dec. 1977.

Caron, Didier. "Le Cinéma expérimental: une ignorance entretenue." *Critique* 469–470 (June–July 1986): 678–691.

Carusi, A. "The Productivity of the Zero Degree." *Journal of Literary Studies/Tydrkrif vir Literaturwetenska,* 2:1 (March 1986): 34–44.

Castel, Robert. *Le Psychanalysme.* Paris: Union générale d'éditions, 1976.

Chalumeau, Jean-Luc. *La Pensée en France: de Sartre à Foucault.* Paris: Fernand Nathan/Alliance Française, 1974.

——— . "L'agonie de la philosophic: Revanche de l'image." *Opus International* no. 50 (May 1974): 76–77.

Champagne, Roland. "A Schizoanalysis of Marcel: Gilles Deleuze's Critical Theories at Work." *Helicon* 2 (1975): 39–50.

Chapsal, Madeleine. Review of *Présentation de Sacher-Masoch. L'Express,* 1967.

Chasseguet-Smirgel, Janine, *et al.* eds. *Les chemins de l'Anti-Oedipe.* Toulouse: Edouard Privat, 1974. Includes the following: "Introduction" by Janine Chasseguet-Smirgel, 7–15; "Réflexions préliminaires" by Bela Grunberger, 17–19; "Freud, Abraham, Laios" by Alain Besançon, 23–38; "Chemins de l'"Oedipe a l'Anti-Oedipe" by Colette Chiland, 39–58; "Les auteurs de l'Anti-Oedipe, freudiens malgré eux" by Françoise Paramelle, 61–83; "Le flux et le reflux: critique de la notion de 'Schize' et non la 'Schize' comme critique de la raison" by Jean Gillibert, 87–98; "De la psychanalyse à l'anti-éducation" by Jean-Pierre Bigeault and Gilbert Terrier, 101–136; "L'Anti-Oedipe ou la destruction envieuse du sein" by Jean Bégoin, 139–158; "De la marque laissée sur la psychanalyse par ses origines" by Didier Anzieu, 159–169.

Chasseguet-Smirgel, Janine, and Bela Grunsberger, eds. *L'Oedipe un complexe universel* Paris: Tchou, 1977.

Châtelet, François. *Chronique des idées perdues.* Paris: Stock, 1977.

———— . "L'éloge d'un marxiste: Le combat d'un nouveau Lucrèce." *Le Monde 28* April 1972: 19.

Châtelet, François, Olivier Duhamel and Evelyne Pisier-Kouchner. *Histoire des idées politiques:* 277–78. Paris: Presses Universitaires de France, 1982.

Châtelet, François, and Evelyne Pisier-Kouchner. *Les Conceptions politiques du XXe siècle:* 944–962. Paris: Presses Universitaires de France, 1981.

Chen, K. H. "Post-Marxism: Between Beyond Critical Postmodernism and Cultural Studies." *Media, Culture and Society* 13:1 (1991): 35–51.

Chesneaux, J. "Guattari, Félix: obituary." *Quinzaine Littéraire* no. 608 (Sept. 16, 1992): 19–20.

Clair, Jean. "Les machines célibataires." in *Art International* (Switzerland) 19:9 (November 1975): 56–60.

Clastres, Pierre. *Society Against the State.* New York: Zone Books, 1987. Translated by Robert Hurley in collaboration with Abe Stein. Originally published as *Société contre l'état.* Paris: Éditions de Minuit, 1974.

Clément, Catherine. "L'incarnation fantasmatique." *Miroirs du sujet* 10/18, Paris: 1975: 163–182.

———— . "Sur Capitalisme et schizophrénie: Entretien avec Félix Guattari et Gilles Deleuze." *L'Arc* no. 49 (1972): 47–55.

———— . "Postface 1980: de L'Anti-Oedipe aux Mille Plateaux." *L'Arc 49: Deleuze* (1972, revised 1980): 94–98.

———— . "Entretien 1980." *L'Arc* no. 49 (1980): 99–102.

Clouscard, Michel. *Néo-Fascisme et idéologie du désir: Les Tartuffes de la révolution.* Paris: Denoël, 1973.

Cocking, J. M. Review of *Marcel Proust et les signes. French Studies* XXVI (1972): 474–476.

Colette, J. "A propos de Proust." *Revue nouvelle 42* (1965): 88–90.

Colombat, André Pierre. *Deleuze et la littérature.* Paris: Peter Lang, 1990.

———— . "Le Philosophe critique et poète: Deleuze, Foucault et l'oeuvre de Michaux." *French Forum* 16:2 (May 1991): 209–225.

———— . "La Princessse de Clèves et l'epouvantable." *Papers on French Seventeenth Century Literature* 17:33 (1990): 517–529.

———— . "A Thousand Trails to Work with Deleuze." *SubStance* XX:3 #66 (Winter 1991): 10–23.

———— . "Le Voyant et les enragés: Rimbaud, Deleuze et Mai 1968." *The French Review 63:5* (1990): 838–848.

Columbel, Jeannette. "La Psychanalyse en question." *Magazine littéraire* 67–68 (Sept. 1972): 46–47.

Comolli, Giampero. "Desiderio e bisogno. Note critiche a Lacan e Deleuze/Guattari." *Aut Aut* no. 139 (1974): 21–44.

Contat, Michel. "Il y a huit ans, l'"Anti-Oedipe." *Le Monde* 10 October 1980.

Cooper, David. "Guattari, et notre implication dans les luttes quotidiennes." *La Quinzaine littéraire* Feb. 1980.

Corradi, E. "Linee dell'antropologia di Deleuze-Guattari" in *Metafisica e Scienze dell'Uomo* vol. 1. ed. by D'Amore Benedetto and Angela Ales Bello: 671–76. Roma: Edizioni Borla, 1982.

Corradini, Domenico. "Il diritto tra metafisica e filosofia del desiderio." *Rivista Internazionale di Filosofia del Diritto* vol. 65 (1988): 625–712.

Crepu, M. "The Faceless Body." *Esprit* no. 2 (1982): 164–65.

Cressole, Michel. *Deleuze.* Paris: Éditions Universitaires, 1973. With a letter by Gilles Deleuze.

——— . "Deleuze, tu es bloqué, coincé." in *La Quinzaine littéraire* 161 (April 1, 1973): 16–17.

D., R.-P. "Dix ans de lecture. Philosophie: Mort et renouveau." *Le Monde* 25 Feb. 1973: 16–17.

Dadoun, Roger. "Les machines désirantes." *La Quinzaine littéraire* 142 (June 1–15, 1972): 19–20.

——— . "Le nouveau deleuze-et-guattari." *La Quinzaine littéraire 336* (Nov. 16, 1980).

Dallevacche, A. "Self Life and the Close-up as Feminine Space: Cavalier Therese." *Film Criticism* 17:1 (Fall 1992): 3–25.

Dallmayr, Fred. "Democracy and Post-Modernism." *Human Studies 10:1* (1987): 143–170.

D'Amico, Robert. "Introduction to the Foucault-Deleuze Discussion." *Telos* no. 16 (Summer 1973): 101–102.

———. "Desire and the Commodity Form." *Telos* 35 (Spring 1978): 88–122.

———. *Marx and Philosophy of Culture.* Gainesville: University Press of Florida, 1980.

Daney, Serge. *Ciné-Journal.* Paris: Cahiers du cinéma, 1986. Preface by Gilles Deleuze.

——— . Nos amies les images." *Libération, 3* October 1983: 31.

d'Arcy, Philippe. "Du côté de Gilles Deleuze." *Bulletin des Lettres* 36:372 (Nov. 15, 1975): 321–323.

Davis, Erik. "Professor of Desire: Gilles Deleuze at Work and Play." *The Village Voice Literary Supplement* 72 (March 1988): 19–20.

Davis, R. C. "Freud, Lacan, and the Subject of Cultural Studies." *College Literature* 18:2 (1991): 22–37.

Deano, Alfredo. Review of *Logica del sentido. Revista de Occident* XXXVI:108 (Mar. 1972): 435–438.

Decottignies, J. *L'Ecriture de la fiction: situation idéologique du roman.* Paris: Presses Universitaires de France, 1979.

De Dijn, H. "Spinoza en het Expressie-Probleem." *Tydschrift der Filosofie* vol. 31 (1969): 572–82.

Delacampagne, Christian. "Deleuze et Guattari dans leur machine délirante." *Le Monde,* 10 October 1980.

——— . "Derrida et Deleuze." *Le Monde,* 30 April 1976.

Delauney, Marc B. "Deleuze et Nietzsche ou l'inverse . . . " *Magazine littéraire* 257 (Sept. 1988): 44–46.

Delco di Bellinzona, Alessandro. "Deleuze: Dalla metafisica della copia alla teoria del simulacro." *Rivista di Estetica* 28:30 (1988): 54–63.

——— . *Filosofia della differenza: La critica del pensiero rappresentivo in Deleuze.* Locarno: Pedrazzini Ed., 1988.

Delcourt, Xavier. "Les filles de Chaos." *La Quinzaine littéraire* 585 (Sept. 16–30, 1991): 21–23.

————— . "Foucault, par Deleuze." *La Quinzaine littéraire* 470 (Sept. 16, 1986): 5–7.

————— . "La ligne baroque." *La Quinzaine littéraire* 516 (Sept. 1988).

Deligeorges, Stéphane. "Un passeport pour l'imagination philosophique." *Nouvelles Littéraires,* Oct. 2–9, (1980).

De Martelaere, Patricia. "Gilles Deleuze, interprète de Hume." *Revue philosophique de Louvain 82,* 4th series no. 54 (May 1984): 224–248.

Derrida, Jacques. "Introduction: Desistance," *Typography: Mimesis, Philosophy, Politics.* By Philippe Lacoue-Labarthe. Trans. Christopher Fynsk. Cambridge: Harvard University Press, 1989. 1–42.

————— . "Afterword: Toward an Ethic of Discussion." *Limited Inc..* Trans. Samuel Weber. Evanston: Northwestern University Press, 19—. 111–160.

————— . *Margins of Philosophy.* Trans. by Alan Bass. Chicago: University of Chicago Press, 1982. Originally published as *Marges de la philosophie.* Paris: Éditions de Minuit, 1972.

————— . "Nous autres Grecs." Ed. Barbara Cassin. *Nos Grecs et leurs moderne.:* Paris: Seuil, 1992. 251–276.

Descamps, Christian. *Les idées philosophiques contemporaines en France.* Paris: Bordas, 1986.

Descombes, Vincent. *Modern French Philosophy.* Trans. by L. Scott-Fox and J. M. Harding. Cambridge: Cambridge University Press, 1980. Originally published as *Le Même et l'Autre.* Paris: Éditions de Minuit, 1979.

Dews, Peter. "The 'New Philosophers' and the End of Leftism." *Radical Philosophy* no. 24 (1980): 2–11.

————— . "Power and Subjectivity in Foucault." *New Left Review* 144 (March–April 1984): 72–95.

Dicenso, J. Review of *Bergsonism. Journal of Religion* 70:1 (Jan. 1990): 139.

Di Domenico, G. *L'Uomo parallelo (Anti-Deleuze).* Brescia: Shakespeare and Co., 1978.

Dieckmann, Bernhard. "Der psychoanalytische und der organlose Körper." Ed. D. Kamper & C. Wulf. *Der andere Körper.* Berline: Verlag Mensch und Leben, 1984. 103–122.

Dionne, André. "Rhizome d'une performance: *Gilles Deleuze et la modernité* de Armand Guil-mette." *Lettres Québécoises* 38 (1985): 57.

Dolle, Jean-Paul. "Mille Plateaux pour combien de chemins?" *Magazine littéraire* 167 (Dec. 1980): 58–59.

—————. *Voie d'accès au plaisir (la Métaphysique).* Paris: Grasset 1974.

Domenach, J.-M. "Oedipe à l'usine." *Esprit* 40:12 (Dec. 1972): 856–865.

Donzelot, Jacques. "An Antisociology." *Semiotext(e): Anti-Oedipus* vol. 2 no. 3 (1977): 27–44. Translated by Mark Seem. Originally published as "Une anti-sociologie." *Esprit* (Dec. 1972).

————— . *The Policing of Families.* New York: Pantheon, 1979. Translated by Robert Hurley. Fore-word by Gilles Deleuze. Originally published as *La police des familles.* Paris: Éditions de Minuit, 1977.

Dosse, François. *Histoire du structuralisme tome 2: Le chant du cygne 1967 à nos jours.* Paris: Éditions la découverte, 1992.

Douglass, Paul. "Deleuze's Bergson: Bergson redux. Ed. F. Burwick and P. Douglass. *The Crisis in Modernism: Bergson and the Vitalist Controversy.* Cambridge: Cambridge University Press, 1992.

———. "Deleuze and the Endurance of Bergson." *Thought* 67:264 (March 1992): 47–61.

Droit, Roger-Pol. "La création des concepts." *Le Monde* 13 Sept. 1991: 4–10.

———. "Un livre de Gilles Deleuze: la cohérence totale de Michel Foucault: Foucault, Deleuze et la pensée du dehors." *Le Monde* 5 Sept. 1986: 1, 13.

———. "Leibniz selon Deleuze." *Le Monde* 9 Sept. 1988.

———. "Review of *Kafka: pour une littérature mineure. Le Monde* 1975.

Dubost, Jean-Pierre. "Nomaden gegen Monaden: Deleuze und die literarische Kriegsmachine." *Lendemains* XIV:53 (1989): 18–25.

Dulac, Philippe. "Gilles Deleuze et Félix Guattari: *Mille Plateaux." Nouvelle Revue Française* 337 (Feb. 1981): 122–125.

Dumery, H. "Schizophrénie et schizo-analyse." *Encyclopaedia Universalis* vol. 14. Paris: Encyclopaedia Universalis, 1975. 735–736.

Dumoncel, Jean-Claude. "Deleuze, Platon et les poètes." *Poétique: Revue de Théorie et d'Analyse litteraires* 15:59 (Sept. 1984): 369–387.

Dumoilié, Camille. *Nietzsche et Artaud: pour une éthique de la cruauté.* Paris: Presses universitaires de France, 1992.

Duvignaud, J. Review of *Marcel Proust et les signes. Nouvelle revue française* 24 (1964): 907–909.

Eco, Umberto. "Soyez tranquilles, je ne me suiciderai pas." Ed. F. Calvi, *Italie '77: le "Mouvement," les intellectuels.* Paris: Seuil, 1977. Reprinted from *L'Espresso* (Italy), May 1, 1977.

Eizykman, B. "Robida le 'Vingtième Siècle'." *Romantisme* 22:76 (1992): 121–30.

Engels, Pascal. Review of *Qu'est-ce que la philosophie? Lettres philosophiques* 4 (1992).

Eribon, Didier. "Foucault vivant." *Le Nouvel Observateur 1138.* 4 Sept. 1986: 64–65.

———. *Michel Foucault (1926–1984).* Paris: Flammarion, 1989. English translation by Betsy Wing. Cambridge: Harvard University Press, 1991.

———. "La Philo sabre au clair." *Le Nouvel Observateur* 12–18 Sept. 1991.

———. Review of Cinéma-2: L'Image-temps. *Le Nouvel Observateur* 1985.

Erickson, J. D. "Kateb-Yacine 'Nedjma': A Dialogue of Difference." *SubStance* no. 69 (1992): 30–45.

Escapo, Ernesto. Review of *Presentación de Sacher-Masoch. Estafeta literaria* 553 (Dec. 1, 1974): 1932.

Ewald, François. "Foucault, Deleuze: un dialogue fécond et interrompu." *Magazine littéraire 257* (Sept. 1988): 48.

———. "Gilles Deleuze: Foucault." *Magazine littéraire, 233* (Sept. 1986): 83–84.

———. "Hommage a François Chatelet." *Magazine littéraire 257* (Sept. 1988): 43.

———. Note on Deleuze. *Magazine littéraire* 298 (April 1992): 20.

———. "La schizo-analyse." *Magazine littéraire* 257 (Sept. 1988): 52–53.

Fagès, J.-B. *Histoire de la psychanalyse après Freud.* Toulouse: Privat, 1976.

Fay, Bernard. "A la recherche du soldat perdu." *Les Précieux.* Paris: 1966. 83–110.

Federman, Raymond. Review of *Marcel Proust et les signes. The French Review* 40:1 (Oct. 1966): 151–153.

Fedida, Pierre. "Le philosophe et sa peau." *L'Arc 49: Deleuze* (1972, revised 1980): 61–69.

——— . *Le Concept et la violence*. Paris: Union général d'editions, 1977.

Ferguson, K. E. "Political Feminism and Deconstruction Theories." *Argument* 34:6 (1992): 873–85.

Ferraris, Maurizio. 'Deleuze. Critica, affirmatività, sperimentazione." *Aut Aut* nos. 187–88 (1982): 123–36.

Ferraris, Maurizio and Daniela de Agostini. "Proust, Deleuze et la répétition: Notes sur les niveaux narratifs d'A la recherche du temps perdu." *Littérature* VIII:32 (Dec. 1978): 66–85.

Ferry, Luc and Alain Renaut. "Foucault et Deleuze: le vitalisme contre le droit" in L. Ferry and A. Renaut, *68–86. Itinéraires de l'individu*. Paris: Gallimard, 1987. 75–108.

Forrester, John. "The Coming of the Nomads." *TLS 4083* (July 31, 1981): 765.

Foss, Paul. "Entr'acte: A Slim Note." Ed. P. Botsman. *Theoretical Strategies*. Sydney: Local Consumption, 1982: 183–187.

Foucault, Michel. "Ariane s'est pendue." *Le Nouvel Observateur* 31 March 1969: 36–37.

——— . *Discipline and Punish: The Birth of the Prison*. Trans. Alan Sheridan. New York: Vintage, 1977. Originally published as *Surveiller et punir: Naissance de la prison*. Paris: Editions Gallimard, 1975.

——— . "How much Does it Cost for Reason to Tell the Truth?" *Foucault Live:* Interviews 1966–1984. Trans. Mia Foret and Marion Martius. Ed. Sylvère Lotringer. New York: *Semiotext(e)*, (1989): 233–256. The same interview is translated as "Critical Theory/ Intellectual History." *Politics, Philosophy, Culture: Interviews and Other Writings 1977–1984*. New York: Routledge, 1988 by Jeremy Harding and edited by Lawrence Kritzman. Originally published in *Spuren*.

——— . "Michel Foucault et Gilles Deleuze veulent rendre à Nietzsche son vrai visage." *Le Figaro Littéraire* 15 Sept. 1966: 7.

——— . "Preface" to the English-language edition of *Deleuze and Guattari, Anti-Oedipus*. Trans. Robert Hurley, Mark Seem and Helen R. Lane. New York: Viking Press, 1977. Reprinted by the University of Minnesota Press (Minneapolis: 1983). xi–xiv.

——— . "Theatrum Philosophicum." *Language, Counter-Memory, Practice: Selected Essays and Interviews*. Ithaca: Cornell University Press, 1977. Translated by Donald Bouchard and Sherry Simon. Edited by Donald Bouchard. Originally published in *Critique, 282* (1970).

——— . "Two Lectures." *Power/Knowledge: Selected Interviews and Other Writings 1972–1977*. Trans. Colin Gordon, Leo Marshall, John Mepham and Kate Soper. Ed. Colin Gordon. New York: Pantheon, 1980. Originally published in *Microfisica del Potere* (Turin: 1977).

——— . "La vérité et les formes juridiques." *Chimères 10* (Winter 1990–1991): 9–28.

Fourquet, François. Recherches 46: *L'Accumulation du pouvoir, ou le désir d'état: Synthèse des recherches du Cerfi de 1970 à 1981*. (Paris: Recherches, 1982).

Frank, Manfred. *What is Neostructuralism?* Trans. Sabine Wilke and Richard T. Gray. Minneapolis: University of Minnesota Press, 1989. Originally published as *Was ist Neostrukturalismus?* Frankfurt: Suhrkamp Verlag, 1984.

——— . "The World as Will and Representation: Deleuze's and Guattari's Critique of Capitalism as Schizo-analysis and Schizo-Discourse." Trans. David Berger. *Telos 57* (Fall 1983): 166–176.

Fremont, Christiane. "Complication et singularité." *Revue de Métaphysique et de Morale* 1991:1: 105–120.

Fuller, Jack. "Distillations: A Premonitory Reading of Deleuze." *Le Pli: Deleuze and the Transcendental Unconscious*. Coventry: University of Warwick, 1992. 159–73.

Furtos, J. and R. R. Roussillon. "L'Anti-Oedipe: Essai d'explication." *Esprit* 40:12 (Dec. 1972): 817–834.

Gandillac, Maurice de. "Vers une schizo-analyse?" *L'Arc 49: Deleuze* (1972, revised 1980): 56–60.

Garcia, L. Germán, with Graciela Aonsio, Vera Gorali, Sergio Larsstuen and Anibal Leserre. "L'Anti-Oedipe, periphrases et paraphrases." *Clinique différentielle des psychoses: Rapports de la Rencontre Internationale 1988 du Champ Freudien à Buenos Aires*. Paris: Navarin Editeur, 1988. 122–132.

Gardair, Jean-Michel. "La machine litteraire." *Paragones 260* (Oct 1971): 136–140.

Gattinara, Enrico Castelli. Review of Foucault. *Aut Aut* 220–221 (July–Oct. 1987): 181–185.

Gelder, J. "Robert Cremean. His Sculpture Sanctuary in Tomales, California." *Revue d'Esthétique*, no. 21 (1992): 152–62.

Gentis, R. "Guattari, Félix: Obituary." *Quinzaine Littéraire* no. 608 (Sept. 16, 1992): 19.

Gieri, M. "Character and Discourse from Pirandello to Fellini: Defining a Counter-tradition in an Italian Context." *Quaderni d'Italianistica* 13:1 (1992): 43–55.

Gil, José. *Fernando Pessoa ou Métaphysique des sensations*. Paris: Éditions de la Différence, 1988.

——— . *Métamorphoses du corps*. Paris: Éditions de la Différence, 1985.

Gilman, S. L. Book review of *A Thousand Plateaux: Capitalism and Schizophrenia. Journal of Interdisciplinary History* 19:4 (1989): 657–59.

Girard, René. "Delirium as System." *To Double Business Bound*. Trans. Paisley N. Livingston and Tobin Siebers. (Baltimore: Johns Hopkins University Press, 1978. 84–120. Originally published as "Systeme du delire" in *Critique* 28 (Nov. 1972).

Glaudes, Pierre. "Du sant, de la douleur, et des larmes . . . : Lecture du Désespéré de Leon Bloy à la lumière de Sacher-Masoch." *Romantisme: Revue du Dix-Neuvième Siècle* 15:48 (1985): 47–61.

Glucksmann, André. "Préméditations Nietzschéennes." *Critique* 213 (Feb. 1965): 125–144.

Gobard, Henri. *L'Aliénation linguistique*. Paris: Flammarion, 1876. Preface by Gilles Deleuze.

Goffey, Andrew. "The Cruelty of the (neo-) Baroque." *Le Pli: Deleuze and the Transcendental Unconscious*. Coventry, University of Warwick, 1992. 67–79.

Goncalves, A. J. "Cabraldemeloneto, Joad and Modernity." *World Literature Today* 66:4 (Fall 1992): 639–43.

Gordon, Colin. "The Subtracting Machine." *I and C* 8 (1981): 27–40.

Grant, Iain Hamilton. "Energumen Critique" in *Pli: Deleuze and the Transcendental Unconscious*: Coventry: University of Warwick, 1992. 25–40.

Green, André. "La reponse d'un psychanalyste: A quoi ça sert?" *Le Monde* 28 April 1972: 19.

Greene, Naomi. "Deadley Statues: Eros in the Films of Jean Cocteau." *The French Review* 61:6 (May 1988): pp. 890–898.

Greisch, Jean. "Les Métamorphoses de la narrativité: Le récit de fiction selon Paul Ricoeur et le cinéma selon Gilles Deleuze." *Revue des Sciences philosophiques et théologiques* 69:1 (Jan. 1985): 87–100.

——— . "Le Temps bifurqué." *Revue des sciences philosophiques et théologiques* 70 (1986): 419–437.

Grimpe, Gabriele, K. Tholen-Struthoff and G. C. Tholen. "Die politische Ökonomie der Libido: zur Konzeption von Gesellschafts—und Wunschmaschine im Anti-Ödipus von Deleuze/Guattari." *Konkursbuch* I (Tubingen 1978). 201–217.

Grimshaw, Therese. "Linguistics as an Indiscipline: Deleuze and Guattari's Pragmatics." *SubStance* 20:3 66 (Winter 1991): 36–54.

Grisoni, Dominique. "Années soixantes: la critique des philosophes." *Magazine littéraire* 192 (Feb. 1983): 43–44.

————, Ed. *Les Dieux dans la cuisine: 20 ans de philosophie en France*. Paris: Aubier, 1978.

————. "Onamatopées du désir." *Magazine littéraire* 127–128 (Sept. 1977). Reprinted in Grisoni, ed., *Les Dieux dans la cuisine*. Paris: Aubier, 1978. Translated as "Onamatopoeia of Desire" in Ed. P. Botsman, *Theoretical Strategies*. Sydney: Local Consumption, 1982. 169–182.

————. "les vingt idéologues d'aujourd'hui." *Magazine littéraire* 239–240 (Mar. 1987): 98–102.

Grossberg, Lawrence. "Does Communication Theory Need Intersubjectivity? Toward an Immanent Philosophy of Interpersonal Relations." Ed. M. Burgoon, *Communications Yearbook* 6. Beverly Hills: Sage, 1982.

————. "Experience, signification, and reality: The boundaries of cultural semiotics." *Semiotica* 41:1/4 (1982): 73–106.

————. "Cultural Studies in New Worlds" in *Critical Studies in Mass Communication* 10:1 (March 1993): 1–22.

Guattari, Félix. *Les Années d'Hiver: 1980–1985*. Paris: Barrault, 1986.

————. "Au-delà du retour à zero." *Futur antérieur* 4 (Winter 1990): 95–103.

————. *Cartographies schizoanalytiques*. Paris: Éditions Galilée, 1989.

————. *Chaosmose*. Paris: Éditions Galilée, 1992.

————. "Chapitre 1: La ville-ordinateur" (entretien). Ed. F. Fourquet and L. Murard, *Les équipements de pouvoir* (*Recherches* 13 [Dec. 1973]. Paris: 10/18, 1976. 39–47.

————. "Chapitre IV: Formation des équipements collectifs" (entretien) Ed. F. Fourquet and L. Murard, *Les équipements de pouvoir* (*Recherches* 13 [Dec. 1973]). Paris: 10/18, 1976. 161–195.

————. "Cinematic Desiring-Machines." Trans. Jon Anderson and Gary Hentzi. *Critical Texts* 3:1 (autumn 1985): 3–9.

————. "Everybody Wants to be a Fascist." Trans. Suzanne Fletcher. *Semiotext(e): Anti-Oedipus* 2:3 (1977): 86–98. Originally published in *La Revolution moleculaire*. Paris: 10/18, 1980.

————. "Freudo-Marxism." Trans.Janis Forman. *Semiotext(e): Anti-Oedipus* 2:3 (1977): 73–75.

————. "I Have Even Met Happy Travelos." Trans. Rachel McComas. *Semiotext(e): Polysexuality* 4:1 (1981): 80–81. Originally published in *La Révolution moléculaire*. Paris: 10/18, 1980.

————. *L'inconscient machinique: Essais de schizo-analyse*. Fontenay-sous-Bois: Recherches, 1979.

————. Interview in *Diacritics* IV:3 (Fall 1974): pp. 38–41. Translated by Mark Seem.

————. "A Liberation of Desire." Trans. G. Stambolian. *Homosexualities and French Literature: Cultural Contexts/Critical Texts*. Ed. G. Stambolian and E. Marks. Ithaca: Cornell University Press. 56–69.

————. *Molecular Revolution: Psychiatry and Politics.* Trans. Rosemary Sheed. New York: Penguin, 1984. Sections originally published in *La Révolution moléculaire*. Paris: 10/18, 1980.

————. "The New Alliance." Trans. Arthur Evans and John Johnston. *Impulse* 10:2 (Winter 1982): 41–44.

————. *Psychanalyse et transversalité: Essais d'analyse institutionnelle.* Paris: Maspero, 1974. Preface by Gilles Deleuze.

————. "Psychoanalysis and Schizoanalysis." Trans. Janis Forman. *Semiotext(e): Anti-Oedipus* 2:3 (1977): 77–85. Originally published in *La Révolution moléculaire*. Paris: 10/18, 1980.

————. "Revolution and Desire." *State and Mind* 6:4/7:1 (Summer/Fall 1978): 53–57.

————. *La révolution moléculaire.* Fontenay-sous-Bois: *Recherches,* 1977; 2nd ed. Paris 10/18, 1980. Second edition is condensed and augmented.

————. "La Schizoanalyse." *L'Esprit createur* 26:4 (Winter 1986): 6–15.

————. "L'Impasse post-moderne." *La Quinzaire Littéraire* no. 456, (1–15 February, 1986): 21.

————. Les Schizoanalyses." *Chimères* 1 (Spring 1987).

————. "Sémiologies signifiantes et sémiologics asignifiantes." *Psychanalyse et sémiotique: Actes du colloque de Milan.* Paris: 10/18, 1975. 151–163.

————. *Les Trois Écologies.* Paris: Éditions Galilée, 1989.

————. "Ritornellos and Existential Affects." *Discourse: Journal for Theoretical Studies in Media and Culture* 12:2 (1990): 66–81.

Guattari, Félix and Toni Negri. *Les nouveaux espaces de liberté.* Paris: Dominique Bedou, 1985. Partially translated as *Communists Like Us: New Spaces of Liberty, New Lines of Alliance.* New York: Semiotext(e), 1990, by Michael Ryan, with a new postscript by Toni Negri.

Guattari, Félix, Jean Oury and François Tosquelles. *Pratique de l'institutionnel et politique.* Vigneux: Matrice Éditions, 1985.

Guilmette, Armand. *Gilles Deleuze et la modernité.* Trois-Rivieres, Quebec: Éditions du Zephyr, 1984.

————. "Le Mouvement du texte hors des formes: Passacaille et Un Testament bizarre' *Études littéraires* 19:3 (Winter 1986–1987): 63–80.

Hand, Sean. "Translating Theory, or the Difference Between Deleuze and Foucault." Introduction to Deleuze, *Foucault.* Minneapolis: University of Minnesota Press, 1988. xli–xliv.

Hans, James S. *The Play of the World.* Amherst: University of Massachusetts Press, 1981.

Harland, Richard. "More Post-Structuralists." *Superstructuralism.* New York: Methuen, 1987. 167–183.

Hardt, H. "Authenticity, Communication and Critical Theory." *Critical Studies in Mass Communication* 10:1 (March 1993): 49–69.

Hardt, Michael. "L'art de l'organisation: agencements ontologiques et agencements politiques chez Spinoza." *Futur Anterieur* 7 (Autumn 1991): 118–143.

————. *Gilles Deleuze: An Apprenticeship in Philosophy.* Minneapolis: University of Minnesota Press, 1992.

————. "La Renaissance hégélienne américaine et l'intériorisation de conflit." *Futur antérieur* 2 (Spring 1990): 133–146.

Hassan, Ihab. "Parabiography: The Varieties of Critical Experience." *Georgia Review* XXXIV:3 (Fall 1980): 593–612.

Hasumi, Shigehiko. *Foucault, Deleuze, Derrida.* Japan: Asahi Shuppansha, 1978.

Heaton, John M. "Language Games, Expression and Desire in the Work of Deleuze." *The Journal of the British Society for Phenomenology* 24:1 (Jan. 1993): 77–87.

Heinz, Rudolf and G. C. Tholen, eds., *Schizo-Schleichwege: Beiträge zum Anti-Ödipus.* Bremen: Impulse Verlag, no date.

Henning, B. "The World was Stone Cold: Basic Writings in an Urban University." *College English* 53:6 (1991): 674–85.

Hertz-Ohmes, Peter. "Serres and Deleuze: Hermes and Humour." *Canadian Review in Comparative Literature* 14:2 (June 1987): 239–250.

Hever, Hannan. "Hebrew in an Israeli Arab Hand: Six Miniatures on Anton Shammas's Arabesques." *Cultural Critique* 7 (fall 1987): 47–76.

Hicks, Emily D. "Deterritorialization and Border Writing." *Ethics/Aesthetics*, Ed. Robert Merrill. Washington: Maisonneuve, 1988. 47–58.

Hockmann, J. and A. André. "La comtesse du Regard: Essai de familialisme appliqué." *Esprit* no. 12 (1972): 886–909.

Hockney, David. "Images avec les Deux Yeux." *Chroniques de l'Art Vivant* no. 52 (Oct. 1975): 26–8.

Hocquenghem, Guy. *L'Après-Mai des faunes.* Paris: Grasset, 1974. Preface by Gilles Deleuze.

———. *Homosexual Desire.* Trans. Daniella Dangoor. London: Allison & Busby, 1978. Originally published as *La Désir homosexuel.* Paris: Éditions universitaires, 1972.

Hodge, Joanna. "Feminism and Postmodernism: Misleading Divisions Imposed by the Opposition between Modernism and Postmodernism." Ed. A. Benjamin. *The Problems of Modernity: Adorno and Benjamin.* London: Routledge, 1989. 86–111.

Holland, Eugene. "The Anti-Oedipus: Postmodernism in Theory, or the Post-Lacanian Historial Contextualization of Psychoanalysis." *Boundary* 2 14:1–2 (1985–1986).

———. "Deterritorializing 'Deterritorialization'—From the *Anti-Oedipus* to *A Thousand Plateaus* in *SubStance* 20:3 #66 (Winter 1991): 55–65.

———. "'Introduction to the Non-Fascist Life': Deleuze and Guattari's 'Revolutionary' Semiotics." *L'Esprit Createur* 27:2 (Summer 1987): 19–29.

———. "Schizoanalysis: The Postmodern Contextualization of Psychoanalysis." Ed. C. Nelson and L. Grossberg, *Marxism and the Interpretation of Culture.* Urbana: University of Illinois Press, 1988. 405–416.

———. "The Ideology of Lack in Lacanianism." *Ethics/Aesthetics* Ed. Robert Merrill:Washington: Maisonneuve, 1988. 59–69.

Hollier, Denis. "'Actions, no! Words, yes!'" Ed. Hollier, *A New History of French Literature.* Cambridge: Harvard University Press, 1989.

Hollington, Michael. Review of *Proust and Signs. Language and Style 11*:3 (Summer 1978): 190.

Holub, Robert C. "Trends in Literary Criticism Politicizing Post-Structuralism: French Theory and the Left in the Federal Republic and the United States." *The German Quarterly* 57:1 (Winter 1984).

Houde, Roland. "Lire et délire." *Dialogue* 11:1 (Mar. 1972): 78–85.

Houlgate, Steven. *Hegel, Nietzsche and the Criticism of Metaphysics*. Cambridge: Cambridge University Press, 1986.

Hurley, Robert. Preface to *Deleuze, Spinoza: Practical Philosophy*. San Francisco: City Lights, 1988. i–iii.

Innocenti, Giancarlo. *L'Immagine significante: Studio sull'emblematica cinquecentesca*. Padova: Liviana editrice, 1981.

Irigaray, Luce. "Questions." *This Sex Which is Not One*. Trans. Catherine Porter. Ithaca: Cornell Univeristy Press, 1985. Originally published in *Ce Sexe qui n'en est pas un*. Paris: Éditions de Minuit, 1978.

Jaccard, Roland. "Debat: L'Anti-Oedipe." *Le Monde*, 28 April 1972: 18.

———. "Être bête, c'est mal poser les problèmes." *Le Monde*, 28 April 1972: 18.

Jacob, André. "Sens, énoncé et communication." *L'Homme et la société* 14 (Oct.–Dec. 1969).

——— . "Langage et schizoanalyse." *Introduction à la philosophie du langage*. Paris: Gallimard, 1976.

Jambet, Christian. *Apologie de Platon: essais de métaphysique*. Paris: Grasset, 1976.

Jameson, Fredric. *Fables of Aggression: Wyndham Lewis, the Modernist as Fascist*. Berkeley: University of California Press, 1979.

——— . "Marxism and Historicism." *New Literary History* 11:1 (Autumn 1979).

——— . *The Political Unconscious: Narrative as a Socially Symbolic Act*. Ithaca: Cornell University Press, 1981.

JanMohamed, Abdul R. "The Nature and Context of Minority Discourse." *Cultural Critique* (Spring and Fall 1989).

Janowitz, Annie. "An Introduction to the Machinic Unconscious." *Tabloid: A Review of Mass Culture and Everyday Life* (Winter 1981).

Jardine, Alice A. *Gynesis: Configurations of Woman and Modernity*. Ithaca: Cornell University Press, 1985.

——— . "Women in Limbo: Deleuze and His Br(others)." *SubStance* 13:3/4 (1984): 46–60.

Jessua, Sylvie. "L'Inconscient est-il orphelin?" *Nouveaux Cahiers* 33 (1973):71–80.

Johnston, John. *Carnival of Repetition: Gaddis's The Recognitions and Postmodern Theory*. Philadelphia: University of Pennsylvania Press, 1990.

——— . "Pynchon's 'Zone': A Post-Modern Multiplicity." *Arizona Quarterly* 46:3 (Autumn 1990): 91–122.

Jones, Kathy. "Response to Lingis." *Pli: Deleuze and the Transcendental Unconscious*. Coventry: University of Warwick, 1992. 21–24.

Jouffroy, Alain. "Lyotard, le deleuzisme et la peinture." *Opus International* 48 (Jan. 1974): 93–94.

Joughin, Martin. Translator's preface to *Deleuze, Expressionism in Philosophy: Spinoza*. New York: Zone, 1990. 5–11.

Kaleka, Gérard. "Un Hegel philosophiquement barbu." *L'Arc* 49: *Deleuze* (1972, revised 1980): 39–44.

Kaplan, Caren. "Deterritorialization: The Rewriting of Home and Exile in Western Feminist Discourse." *Cultural Critique* 6 (Spring 1987): 187–98.

Kidder, Review of *Bergsonism. Review of Metaphysics* 43:1 (Sept. 1989): 152–154.

King, N. "Reading 'White Noise': Floating Remarks." *Critical Quarterly* 33:3 (1991): 66–83.

Kirby, D. Review of *Masochism. Virginia Quarterly Review* 66:4 (Fall 1990): 759–768.

Kirby, K. M. "The Personal and the Political: Rearticulating the Difference." *New Orleans Review* 19:2 (Summer 1992): 9–17.

Klingmann, Ulrich. "Problem und Problemlösung: Die Problematik der Schizo-Analyse am Beispiel Kafkas." *Neophilologus* 74:1 (Jan. 1990): 87–101.

Klossowski, Pierre. "Circulus vitiosus. Nietzsche aujourd'hui," *Intensités.* Paris: 10/18, 1973. 91–103.

————. "Digression à partir d'un portrait apocryphe." *L'Arc* 49: *Deleuze* (1972, revised 1980): 11–14.

————. *Nietzsche et le cercle vicieux.* Paris: Mercure de France, 1969.

————. "Roberte et Gulliver: Divertimento pour Gilles Deleuze." *L'Arc 49: Deleuze* (1972, revised 1980): 15–22. Reprinted separately by Fata Morgana.

Kohler, J. "Spiritualist Nomadism: Critical Observations on the Post-Structuralism of Gilles Deleuze." *Philosophisches Jahrbuch* 91:1 (1984): 158–75.

Koupermilk, Cyrille. "L'opinion d'un psychiatre: Un délire intelligent mais gratuit." *Le Monde, 28* April 1972: 19.

Kowsar, Mohammad. "Analytics of Schizophrenia: A Deleuze-Guattarian Consideration of Büchner's *Danton's Death* and *Weiss's* Marat/Sade." *Modern Drama* 27 (Sept. 1984): 361–381.

————. "Deleuze on theatre: a case study of Carmelo Bene's *Richard III." Theatre Journal* 38:1 (Mar. 1986): 19–33.

Kremer-Marietti, Angèle. "Différence et qualité." *Revue de Métaphysique et de Morale* 3 (1970): 339–349.

Kudszus, W. G. "Reflections on the Double Bind of Literature and Psychopathology." *SubStance* 20 (1978): 19–36.

Kulchyski, Peter. "Primitive Subversions, Totalization and Resistance in Native-Canadian Politics." *Cultural Critique* No. 21 (Spring 1992): 171–95.

Kurzweil, Edith. Book review of *Gilles Deleuze, Foucault* in *Contemporary Sociology. A Journal of Reviews* 18:3 (1989): 458–59.

Lacan, Jacques. *D'un AUTRE à l'autre* (unpublished typescript of Lacan's seminar for the academic year 1968–1969).

Lacoste, J. Review of *Pourparlers 1972–1990. La Quinzaine littéraire* 562 (Sept. 16, 1990): 7–8.

Lacroix, Jean. Review of *Différence et répétition. Le Monde,* June 15–16, 1969: 17.

Lamberti, Amato. "Il luogo de senso e o del discorso." *Altri Termini* new series 8 (June 1975): 63–85.

Land, Nick. "Making it with Death: Remarks on Thanatos and Desiring-Production." *The Journal of the British Society for Phenomenology* 24:1 (Jan. 1993): 66–76.

————. "Circuitries." *Pli: Deleuze and the Transcendental Unconscious.* Coventry: University of Warwick, 1992. 217–35.

Lange, Thomas. *Die Ordnung des Begehrens: Nietzscheanische Aspekte im philosophischen Werk von Gilles Deleuze*. Bielefeld: Aisthesis Verlag, 1989.

Laporte, Roger. "Gilles Deleuze et Félix Guattari: Capitalisme et schizophrénie: l'Anti-Oedipe." *Cahiers du chemin* 16 (Oct. 15, 1972): 95–111.

Larcher, P.-L. Review of *Marcel Proust et les signes*. *Bulletin de la Société des Amis de Marcel Proust et des Amis de Combray* 18 (1968): 780–781.

Lardreau, Guy and Christian Jambet. *L'Ange: Pour une cynégétique du semblant*. Paris: Grasset, 1976.

Laruelle, François. *Au-delà du principe de pouvoir*. Paris: Payot, 1978.

———. *Machines textuelles: Déconstruction et libido d'écriture*. Paris: Seuil, 1976.

———. "Comment 'sortir' de Heidegger et de la différence en général." *Exer Pat* nos. 3–4 (1982): 171–88.

———. "Marges et limites de la métaphysique." Ed. A. Jacob, *L'Univers Philosophique*. Paris: Presses universitaires de France, 1989. 71–80.

———. *Nietzsche contre Heidegger*. Paris: Payot, 1977.

———. *Les philosophies de la différence: introduction critique*. Paris: Presses universitaires de France, 1986.

———. *Le Principe de minorité*. Paris: Aubier Montaigne, 1981.

Lascault, G. "La diversité des récits érotiques." *Revue d'Esthétique* 21 (1968): 70–74.

Laveggi, Lucile. "Gilles Deleuze: Philosophe de la résistance." *Le Figaro* 17 (Sept. 1990).

Layoun, Mary. "The Strategy of Narrative Form." *Crit. Exchange* 22 (Spring 1987): 37–42.

Lebel, Robert. "Notes pour un post-Duchamp." *XXe Siecle* 36:42 (June 1974): 84–89.

Lecercle, Jean-Jacques. "The Misprision of Pragmatics: Conceptions of Language in Contemporary French Philosophy." Ed. A. P. Griffiths, *Contemporary French Philosophy*. Cambridge: Cambridge University Press, 1987: 21–40.

———. *Philosophy Through the Looking Glass*. La Salle: Open Court, 1985.

Lehmann, Hans-Thies. "Rhizom und Maschine: zu den Schriften von Gilles Deleuze und Félix Guattari." *Merkur* 38 (July 1984): 542–550.

Leigh, James A. "Deleuze, Nietzsche and the Eternal Return." *Philosophy Today* 22:3/4 (Fall 1978): 206–223.

Leitch, Vincent B. *Deconstructive Criticism: An Advanced Introduction*. New York: Columbia University Press, 1983.

Lemaitre, Monique J. "Territorialidad y transgresion en Gringo viejo de Carlos Fuentes." *Revista Iberoamericana* 53:141 (Oct.–Dec. 1987): 955–963.

Lenglet, Roger. "La cinésophie de Gilles Deleuze." *Revue d'Esthétique* 10 (1986): 185–195.

Leroy, Geraldi. "Différence et répétition par Gilles Deleuze." *Feuillets de l'Amitié Charles Peguy* 173 (Dec. 1971): 38–39.

Leutrat, Jean-Louis. "Deux temps, deux mouvements." *Lendemains* 14:53 (1989): 48–54.

Levoyer, Pascal and Philippe Encrenaz. "Politique de Deleuze." *Lendemains* 14:53 (1989): 35–47.

Lévy, Bernard-Henri. *Barbarism with a Human Face.* New York: Harper & Row, 1979. Trans. George Holoch. Originally published as *La Barbarie à visage humain* Paris: Grasset, 1977.

Lingis, Alphonso. "The Society of Dismembered Body Parts." *Pli: Deleuze and the Transcendental Unconscious:* Coventry: University of Warwick, 1992. 1–19.

———. *Deathbound Subjectivity.* Bloomington: Indiana University Press, 1989.

———. "Deleuze on a Deserted Island." H. Silverman, ed., *Philosophy and Non-Philosophy since Merleau-Ponty:* New York: Routledge, 1988. 152–173.

———. *Libido: The French Existentialist Theories.* Bloomington: Indiana University Press, 1985.

Little, K. Masochism, Spectacle and the Broken Mirror Clown Entree: A Note on the Anthropology of Performance in Postmodern Culture." *Cultural Anthropology* 8:1 (Feb. 1993): 117–29.

Losche, D. "Deus ex Machina." *Meanjin* 51:4 (Summer 1992): 691–700.

Lotringer, Sylvère. "The Fiction of Analysis." Trans. Daniel Moshenberg. *Semiotext(e) Anti-Oedipus* 2:3 (1977): 173–189.

———. "Libido Unbound: The Politics of 'Schizophrenia." *Semiotext(e): Anti-Oedipus* 2:3 (1977): 5–10.

Lovibond, S. "Feminism and Pragmatism: A Reply." *New Left Review* no. 193 (May–June 1992): 56–74.

Lyotard, Jean-François. "Conservation and Color." Trans. Geoffrey Bennington and Rachel Bowlby. *The Inhuman: Reflections on Time.* Stanford: Stanford University Press, 1991. Originally published as *L'Inhumain: Causeries sur le temps.* Paris: Galilée, 1988.

———. *Économie libidinale.* Paris: Éditions de Minuit, 1973.

———. "Energumen Capitalism." Trans. James Leigh. *Semiotext(e): Anti-Oedipus* 2:3 (1977): 11–26. Originally published as "Capitalisme énergumène." *Critique* 28 (Nov. 1972) and reprinted in *Des Dispositifs pulsionnels.* Paris: Christian Bourgois, 1975.

———. *Heidegger and "the jews."* Trans. Andreas Michel and Mark Roberts. Minneapolis: University of Minnesota Press, 1990. Originally published as *Heidegger et "les juifs."* Paris: Éditions Galilée, 1988.

———. "Answering the Question: What is Postmodernism?" *The Post-modern Condition: A Report on Knowledge.* Trans. Regis Durand. Minneapolis: University of Minnesota Press, 1984. Originally published as "Réponse à la question: qu'est-ce que le postmoderne?" *Critique* 419 (April 1982).

Macherey, Pierre. "Foucault avec Deleuze: Le retour éternel du vrai." *Revue de Synthèse* 108 (1987): 277–285.

———. "Penser dans Spinoza." *Magazine littéraire* 257 (Sept. 1988): 40–43.

Maggiori, Robert. "Une bombe sous la philosophie." *Libération* Sept. 12, 1991.

———. "Con Gilles Deleuze." *Alfabeta* 9:95 (April 1987): iii.

———. "Gilles Deleuze—Michel Foucault: une amitié philosophique." *Libération* (Sept. 1, 1986).

Mahon, M. "Michel Foucault: Archaeology, Enlightenment and Critique." *Human Studies* 16:1–2 (Apr. 1993): 129–41.

Maigueneau, D. "The Use of Maxims in Corneille Theater from the Viewpoint of Pragmatic Criticism." *Études littéraires* 25:1–2 (1992): 11–22.

Makropoulos, M. "Fragments pour une théorie de la nouvelle realité." *Cahiers Confrontation* no. 7 (1982): 85–96.

Maltzan, Carlotta von. "Masochismus und Macht in Klaus Manns *Mephisto: Roman einer Karriere.*" *Acta Germanica* supplement 1 (1990): 145–163.

Maniquis, Robert M. "Pascal's Bet, Totalities, and Guerilla Criticism." *Humanities in Society* 6:2–3 (Spring–Summer 1983).

Margolin, Jean-Claude. "Michel Cressole: Deleuze." *Revue de Synthèse* 73–74 (Jan.–June 1974): 101.

Marietti, Pierre-François. "Gilles Deleuze 1925–." D. Hiusman, ed., Dictionnaire des Philosophes. Paris: Presses universitaires de France, 1984. 693–696.

Martin, Jean-Clet. *Variations. La Philosophie de Gilles Deleuze.* Paris: Éditions Payot et Rivages, 1993.

Marzocco, Ottavio. "Deleuze, la topologia fine e le essenze vaghe." Filosofia dell' incommensurabile: Termi e metafore oltre-enclidee in Bachelard, Serres, Foucault, Deleuze, Virilio. Milano: Franco Angeli, 1989.

Massumi, Brian. "Deleuze and Guattari's Theories of the Group Subject, through a Reading of Corneille's *Le Cid.*" *Discours Social/Social Discourse: The International Research Papers in Comparative Literature* 1:4 (Winter 1988): 423–440.

———. "Realer than Real: The Simulacrum according to Deleuze and Guattari. *Copyright* (Fall 1987): 90–97.

———. Translator's introduction to Deleuze and Guattari, *A Thousand Plateaus: Capitalism and Schizophrenia.* Minneapolis: University of Minneaplis Press, 1987. xvi–xix.

———. *A User's Guide to Capitalism and Schizophrenia: Deviations from Deleuze and Guattari.* Cambridge: MIT Press, 1992.

———. "Everywhere you want to be: Introduction to Fear." *Pli: Deleuze and the Transcendental Unconscious.* Coventry: University of Warwick, 1992. 175–215

Massumi, Brian and Kenneth Dean. *First and Last Emperors: The Absolute State and the Body of the Despot.* New York: Automedia, 1992.

Mattei, Jean-Francois. *L'Etrangère et le simulacre.* Paris: Presses Universitaires de France, 1983.

Mauriac, Claude. "Du bon usage des machines deleuziennes." *Le Figaro littéraire* 1411 (June 2, 1973): 16.

———. "Défense et illustration de la littérature mineure." *Le Figaro littéraire* 1539 (Nov. 15, 1975): 13.

———. "La guêpe et l'orchidée." *Le Figaro littéraire* 1564 (May 8, 1976): 14.

———. "L'Oedipe mis en accusation." *Le Figaro littéraire* 1350 (April 1, 1972): 10.

———. "Proust métamorphose en arraignée." *Le Figaro littéraire* 1500 (Feb. 15, 1975): 17.

Mauzi, Robert. "Les complexes et les signes." *Critique* 225 (Feb. 1966): 155–171.

May, Todd G. "The Politics of Life in the Thought of Gilles Deleuze." *SubStance* 20:3 no. 66 (Winter 1991): 24–35.

————. "The System and its Fractures: Gilles Deleuze on Otherness." *The Journal of the British Society for Phenomenology* 24:1 (Jan. 1993): 3–14.

————. *Between Genealogy and Epistemology: Psychology, Politics and Knowledge in the Thought of Michel Foucault.* University Park: The Pennsylvania State University Press, 1993.

McGraw, B. R. Review of Marcel Proust et les signes. The French Review 50 (1976–1977): 774–775.

McHugh, Patrick. "Dialectics, Subjectivity and Foucault's Ethos of Modernity." Boundary 2 XVI:2,3 (Winter–Spring 1989): 91–108.

Meerbote, Ralf. "Deleuze on the Systematic Unity of the Critical Philosophy." *Kantstudien* 77 (1986): 347–354.

Megill, Allan. "Foucault, Structuralism and the Ends of History." *Journal of Modern History* 51:3 (Sept. 1979): 451–503.

Mehlman, Jeffrey. "Portnoy in Paris." *Diacritics* 11:4 (Winter 1972): 21–28.

Metzidakis, Stamos. "Contra Deleuze: towards a singular theory of reading." *Romantic Review* 76:3 (1985): 316–322.

————. *Repetition and Semiotics.* Birmingham: Summa Publications, 1985.

Michael, M. and A. Still. "A Resource for Resistance: Power-Knowledge and Affordance." *Theory and Society* 21:6 (Dec. 1992): 869–88.

Michael, M. and R. Grovewhite. "Talking about Talking about Nature: Nurturing Ecological Consciousness." *Environmental Ethics* 15:1 (Spring 1993): 33–47.

Mihailescu, Calin. "Corpus Epochalis: Mysticism, Body, History." *Surfaces* vol. 1, section 9 (Dec. 1991). Electronic publication.

Miyakawa, A. "Again, in Gilles Deleuze's Space: Shusaku Arakawa." *Mizue* (Japan) no. 842 (May 1975): 108–115.

Ms., L. "Foucault et Deleuze aux Cahiers." *Le Monde,* 3 Feb. 1977: 14.

Muecke, Stephen, "The Discourse of Nomadology: Phylums in Flux." *Art and Text* 14 (1984).

Murphy, J. W. and J. M. Choi. "Theatrical Justification for a Politics of Difference." *New Orleans Review* 19:2 (Summer 1992): 62–68.

Murphy, Timothy S. Entry on Gilles Deleuze in *Dictionary of Contemporary Criticism and Critical Terms.* Toronto: University of Toronto Press, forthcoming.

————. Review of *The Logic of Sense. The Jacaranda Review* 5:1 (Winter/ Spring 1991): 131–132.

————. "The Theater of (the Philosophy of) Cruelty in Gilles Deleuze's Difference and Repetition." *Pli: The University of Warwick Journal of Philosophy.* Coventry: University of Warwick, 1992. 105–35.

Nadeau, Maurice. "La machine 'Kafka'." *La Quinzaine littéraire* 210 (May 16–31, 1975): 3.

————. Se brancher sur la machine Deleuze." *La Quinzaine littéraire* 272 (Feb. 1978).

Negri, Antonio. *Marx Beyond Marx: Lessons on the Grundrisse.* South Hadley, MA: Bergin & Garvey, 1984; New York: Autonomedia, 1991. Trans. Harry Cleaver, Michael Ryan and Maurizio Viano. Edited by Jim Fleming. Originally published as Marx oltre Marx. Paris: Christian Bourgois, 1979.

———— . *The Politics of Subversion: A Manifesto for the Twenty-First Century.* Cambridge: Polity Press, 1989. Trans. James Newell. Introduction by Yann Moulier.

———— . Review of *Qu'est-ce que la philosophie? Futur antérieur* 8 (Winter 1991): 132–143.

———— . *Revolution Retrieved: Writings on Marx, Keynes, Capitalist Crisis and New Social Subjects 1967–1983.* London: Red Notes, 1988.

———— . *The Savage Anomaly: The Power of Spinoza's Metaphysics and Politics.* Trans. Michael Hardt. Minneapolis: University of Minnesota Press, 1991. Originally published as *L'anomalia selvaggia. Saggio su potere e potenza in Baruch Spinoza.* Milan: Faltrinelli, 1981. French translation contains a preface by Deleuze.

Norris, Christopher. *Spinoza and the Origins of Modern Critical Theory.* Oxford: Basil Blackwell, 1991.

Norton, Theodore Mills. "Lines of Flight: Gilles Deleuze, or political science fiction." *New Political Science* 15 (Summer 1986): 77–93.

Noyes, John. "The Capture of Space: An Episode in a Colonial Story by Hans Grimm." *Pretexts* 1:1 (Winter 1989): 52–63.

———— . "Deleuze liest Leopold von Sacher-Masoch: Zur Ambivalenz des literarischen Kanons." *Acta Germanica* supplement 1 (1990): 69–80.

Oittinen, V. "Deleuze und Spinoza: Ethik." *Deutschen Zeitschrift für Philosophie* 38:5 (1990): 470–93.

Olabuenaga, Alicia. "Gilles Deleuze: por una filosofia de la disolucion." *Revista de Occidente* 56 (1986): 27–34.

Oliva, A. B. and M. Bandine. "Roman Opalka: Work as Detail." *Data* No. 19 (Nov.–Dec. 1975): 40–46.

Olkowski, Dorothea. "Flows of Desire and the Body," in *Continental Philosophy* VI, *Philosophy and the Discourse of Desire,* Ed. H. J. Silverman, Albany: SUNY, 1991.

———— . "Monstrous Reflection: Sade and Masoch, Rewriting the History of Reason," *Crisis in Continental Philosophy, Selected Studies in Phenomenology and Existential Philosophy,* Ed. Arleen Dallery and Charles E. Scott, Albany: SUNY Press, 1990.

———— . "The Postmodern Dead-End, Minor Consensus on Race and Sexuality" in *Topoi* 12 (1993): 161–166.

———— . "Semiotics and Gilles Deleuze," *The Semiotic Web 1990,* Eds. Thomas A. Sebeok and Jean Umiker-Sebeok, Indiana University Press, 1990.

Onstenk, J. "De Politieke Machines van Let Verlangen over Deleuze en Guattari." *Krisis* vol. 2 (1981–82): 20–31.

Oppenheim, Lois. "The Philosopher and the Poet: Modes of Creation." *Denver Quarterly* 21:2 (Fall 1986): 160–170.

Palmero, P. "Empatia, Astrazione, Arte Ornamentale: Worringer, Jung ad 'Mille Plateaux'." *Rivista di Estetica* no. 12 (1982): 91–8.

Paradis, André. "Bernard-Henri Lévy: Le Mal radical ou la philosophie du désespoir." *Philosophiques* no. 10 (April 1983): 3–14.

Paradis, Bruno. "Cinema secondo Deleuze." *Alfabeta* 6:61 (June 1984): 34–35.

———— ."Le futur et l'epreuve de la pensée." *Lendemains* 14:53 (1989): 26–29.

————— . "Indetermination et mouvements de bifurcation chez Bergson." *Philosophie* 32 (Fall 1991).

————— . "Leibniz: un monde unique et relatif." *Magazine littéraire* 257 (Sept. 1988): 26–29.

Parrain-Vial, Jeanne. "La création dans la perspective structuraliste." *Diotima* no. 5 (1977): 182–89.

Pasqua, H. Review of *Leibniz et le baroque. Revue philosophique de Louvain* 87:75 (Aug. 1989): 537–538.

Passerone, Giorgio. "Il Bacon di Deleuze." *Alfabeta* 4:43 (Dec. 1982): 6–7.

————— . "Cinema secundo Deleuze." *Alfabeta* 6:61 (June 1984): 34–35.

————— . "Le dernier cours?" *Magazine littéraire* 257 (Sept. 1988): 35–37.

————— . *La Linea astratta: Pragmatica dello stile.* Milano: Edizioni Angelo Guerini, 1991. Preface by Gilles Deleuze.

Patton, Paul. "Conceptual Politics and the War-Machine in *Mille Plateaux*." *SubStance* 13:3/4 (1984): 61–80.

————— . "Deleuze and Guattari: Ethics and Post-Modernity." *Leftwright* 20 (1986): 24–32.

————— . "Marxism and Beyond: Strategies of Reterritorialization." C. Nelson and L. Grossberg, eds., *Marxism and the Interpretation of Culture.* Urbana: University of Illinois Press, 1988. 123–129.

————— . "Notes for a Glossary." *I and C* 8 (1981).

Pecora, Vincent P. "Adversarial Culture and the Fate of Dialectics." *Cultural Critique* 8 (Winter 1987–1988): 197–216.

————— . "Deleuze's Nietzsche and Post-Structuralist Thought." *SubStance* 48 (1986): 34–50.

————— . "Simulacral Economies." *Telos* 75 (Spring 1988): 125–140.

Pedulla, W., ed. *Nuovi filosofi letti e interpretati da Deleuze, Foucault, Debray, Sollers, Droit, Mauriac, Duverger, Castoriadis, Poulantzas, Morin, Ellenstein.* Cosenza: Lerici, 1978.

Penzo, M. *Tra Heidegger e Deleuze. Saggio sulla singolarità.* Venezia: Cluec, 1978.

Perez, Rolando. *On An(archy) and Schizoanalysis.* Brooklyn: Autonomedia, 1990.

Peyrol, Georges. "Le fascisme de la pomme de terre." *Cahiers Yenan* 4: La situation actuelle sur le front de la philosophie. Paris: Maspero, 1977. 42–52.

Piancioia, Cesare. *Filosofia e politica nel pensiero francese del dopoguerra.* Torino: Loescher, 1979.

Pierssens, Michael. "L'appareil sériel." La Critique générative. Paris: Seghers, 1973. 42–52

————— . "Gilles Deleuze: Diabolus in Semiotica." *Modern Language Notes* 96:4 (1975).

Pietz, William. "The Phonograph in Africa: International Phonocentrism from Stanley to Sarnoff." D. Attridge, R. Young and G. Bennington, eds., Post-Structuralism and the Question of History. Cambridge: Cambridge University Press, 1987. 263–285

Pividal, Raphaël. "Fondements et perspectives d'un critique: Psychanalyse, schizophrénie, capitalisme." *Le Monde,* April 28, 1972: 18.

Plant, Sadie. "Nomads and Revolutionaries." *The Journal of the British Society for Phenomenology* 24:1 (Jan. 1993): 88–101.

Plantier, Thérèse. *La discours du mâle, Logos Spermaticos.* Paris: Éditions Anthropos, 1980.

Pogliano, C. "Labyrinths in Science and Literature." *Belfagor* 47:6 (Nov. 20, 1992): 643–67.

Polan, Dana. "Cinéma 1: L'Image-mouvement." *Film Quarterly* 38:1 (1984): 50–52.

———— . Review of *Foucault. Camera Obscura* 18 (Sept. 1988): 106–119.

———— . Translator's introduction to Deleuze and Guattari, *Kafka: Toward a Minor Literature.* Minneapolis: University of Minnesota Press, 1986. xxii–xxix.

Poster, Mark. *Critical Theory of the Family.* New York: Seabury Press, 1978.

Prigogine, Ilya and Isabelle Stengers. *La Nouvelle alliance.* Paris: Gallimard, 1979; revised edition, 1986).

Prince, G. "Reviewing Narratology." *Comparative Literature* 44:4 (1992): 409–14.

Pucciarelli, Eugenio. "Dos actitudes frente al tiempo." *Cuad Filosof* no. 10 (1970): 7–48.

Purcell, J. "Bergson. Lacey A R." *Man and World* 26:1 (Jan. 1993): 103–108.

Quoniam, Thomas. Review of *Le Bergsonisme. Études philosophiques* 21 (1966): 545–546.

Rabant, Claude. "Sacher-Masoch ou l'echange fou." *Critique* 273 (Feb. 1970).

Racevskis, Karlis. Review of *Foucault. World Literature Today* 61 (1987): 603–604.

Raillard, Georges. "Un bon objet pour Gilles Deleuze." *La Quinzaine littéraire* 367 (March 16, 1982).

Rajchman, John. "Analysis in Power: A Few Foucauldian Theses." *Semiotext(e)* Anti-Oedipus 2:3 (1977): 45–58.

———— . "Crisis." *Representations* 28 (Fall 1989): 90–98.

———— . "Logique du sens, éthique de l'évènement." *Magazine littéraire* 257 (Sept. 1988): 37–39.

———— . *Philosophical Events: Essays of the Eighties.* New York: Columbia University Press, 1991.

Raulf, Ulrich. "Der nicht-ödipale Wunsch: Notizen zu Deleuze/Guattari: Anti-Ödipus."

D. Kamper, ed., Über die Wünsche. Munich: Carl Hanser Verlag, 1977. 64–81

Reader, Keith A. *Intellectuals and the Left in France since 1968.* London: Macmillan Press, 1987.

———— . "The Scene of Action is Different." *Retorts, Replies, Reviews, Reconsiderations.* .London: Society for Education in Film and Television, 1987. 98–102.

Regnault, François. "La vie philosophique." *Magazine littéraire* 257 (Sept. 1988): 30–35.

Rella, Franco. "Una Tomba per Edipo? Nota su Deleuze-Guattari." *Aut Aut* no. 144 (1974): 65–78.

———— . *Il Mito dell'altro: Lacan, Deleuze, Freud.* Milan: Feltrinelli, 1978.

Renza, Louis A. *"A White Heron" and the Question of Minor Literature.* Madison: University of Wisconsin Press, 1994.

Resch, Robert Paul. *Althusser and the Renewal of Marxist Social Theory.* Berkeley: University of California Press, 1992.

Restuccia, Frances L. "Deleuzean/Masochian Masochism in the Writing of James Joyce." *Novel: A Forum on Fiction* 18:2 (Winter 1985): 101–16.

———— . *Joyce and the Law of the Father.* New Haven: Yale University Press, 1989.

Restuccia, Maria Rosario. "Deleuze e Bergson." *Cannochiale* nos. 1–2 (1983): 167–71.

Richardson, Maurice. "Masochist's Honeymoon." *Observer* 9:379 (April 25, 1971): 33.

Rigal, Elisabeth. *Du strass sur un tombeau: Le Foucault de Gilles Deleuze.* Mauzerin: Trans-Europ-Repress, 1987.

Robinet, André. ed. *Doctrines et concepts 1937–1987: Cinquante ans de philosophie de langue française.* Paris: Vrin, 1988.

Robinson, Sally. "Misappropriations of the Feminine." *SubStance* 18:2 (#59, 1989): 48–70.

Rodowick, D. N. "Reading the Figural." *Camera Obscura* vol. 24 (Sept. 1990): 11–46.

Rogozinski, Jacob. "Defaillance (entre Nietzsche et Kant)." *Lendemains,* 14:53 (1989): 55–62.

——— . "La Fêlure de la pensée." *Magazine littéraire* 257 (Sept. 1988): 46–48.

Rolland de Renéville, Jacques. *Itinéraire du sens.* Paris: Presses Universitaires de France, 1982.

Ropars-Wuilleumier, Marie Claire. Review of *Cinéma-1* and *Cinéma-2. Camera Obscura* 18 (Sept. 1988): 120–126.

Rorty, Richard. "Unsoundness in Perspective." *The Times Literary Supplement* (June 17, 1983): 619.

Rosaldo, Renato. "Politics, Patriarchs and Laughter." *Cultural Critique* 6 (Spring 1987): 65–86.

Rose, Gillian. *Dialectic of Nihilism: Post-Structuralism and Law.* New York: Basil Blackwell, 1984.

Rosset, Clément. "Sécheresse de Deleuze." *L'Arc* 49: Deleuze (1972, revised 1980): 89–91.

Roth, Michael. *Knowing and History: Appropriations of Hegel in Twentieth-Century France.* Ithaca: Cornell University Press, 1988.

Roudinesco, Elisabeth. *Jacques Lacan & Co.* Chicago: University of Chicago Press, 1990. Translated with a foreword by Jeffrey Mehlman. Originally published as *Le Bataille de cent ans.* Paris: Seuil.

Roy, Claude. "De la musique avant toute chose." *Le Nouvel Observateur* 235 (May 12–18, 1969): 38–39.

Ruby, Christian. *Les Archipels de la différence: Foucault-Derrida-Deleuze-Lyotard.* Paris: Editions du Felin, 1989.

Rudnytsky, Peter L. *Freud and Oedipus.* New York: Columbia University Press, 1987.

Saalman, Dieter. "Guest Literature in the Federal Republic: German as a Means of Literary Articulation." *The Language Quarterly* 28:3–4 (Summer/Fall 1990): 70–80.

Salgas, Jean-Pierre. Presentation of Deleuze's *Foucault* together with an article by Xavier Delcourt. *La Quinzaine littéraire* 470 (Sept. 1986).

Santacroce, Alberto. "Kafka e il guico della Legge." *Deleuze* Cosenza: Edistampa-Edizioni Lerici, 1976.

Saper, Craig. "Electronic Media Studies: From Video Art to Artificial Invention." *SubStance* 20:3 #66 (Winter 1991): 114–134.

Scarpetta, Guy. "Kafka, pour une littérature mineure." *Tel Quel* 63 (Autumn 1975).

Scheepers, Monique. "Subjektivität und Politik." *Lendemains* 14:53 (1989): 30–34.

Schenkel, Lambert and Simon Joosten de Vries. *Umleitung oder: wie heisst Bruno mit Nachnamen?* Giessen: Germinal Verlag, 1989.

Schleicher, Helmut. "Gilles Deleuze-Félix Guattari." *Französische Literatur des 20, Jahrhunderts: Gestalten und Tendenzen, Zur Erinnerung an Ernst Robert Curtius.* Bonn: Bouvier, 1986. 110–125.

Schmid Noerr, Gunzelin. "Ethnologie des Unbewussten: Zum Anti-Ödipus: Capitalismus und Schizophrenie 1 von Gilles Deleuze und Félix Guattari." *Psyche* 33:12 (1979): 1149–1156.

Schmidt, Aurel. "Gilles Deleuze und Félix Guattari oder der Anti-Ödipus und die molekulare Revolution." J. Altwegg and A. Schmidt, *Französische Denker der Gegenwart: 20 Portraits.* Munchen: Beck, 1987.

Schmidt, D. J. Review of Kant's *Critical Philosophy. International Studies in Philosophy* 21:1 (1989): 74–75.

Seem, Mark D. "*Introduction to Deleuze and Guattari,*" *Anti-Oedipus: Capitalism and Schizophrenia.* Minneapolis: University of Minnesota Press, 1977, 1983. xiv–xxiv

———. "Liberation of Difference: Toward a Theory of Antiliterature." *New Literary History* V:1 (Autumn 1973): 119–133.

———. "To oedipalize or not to oedipalize, that is the question . . . " *SubStance* 11–12 (1975): 166–169.

Seglard, Dominique. "Bibliographie: L'Oeuvre de Deleuze." *Magazine littéraire* (Sept. 1988): 64–65.

Seguin, Louis. "Le retour du 'théore'." *La Quinzaine littéraire* 404 (Nov. 1, 1983): 5–6.

Sempé, Jean-Claude. "Le leurre et le simulacre." *L'Arc 49: Deleuze* (1972, revised 1980): 70–77.

Seval, Christian. "Who's who du savoir contemporain." *Magazine littéraire 200–201* (Dec. 1983): 59–73.

Sève, Lucien, ed. *Structuralisme et dialectique.* Paris: Éditions Sociales, 1984.

Shaviro, Steven. "A chacun ses sexes: Deleuze and Guattari's *Theory of Sexuality.*" *Discours Social/Social Discourse: The International Research Papers in Comparative Literature* 1:3 (Winter 1988): 287–299.

———. "'That Which is Always Beginning': Steven's Poetry of Affirmation." *PMLA* 100:2 (March 1985): 220–233.

Sirinelli, Jean-François. *Intellectuels et passions françaises: Manifestes et petitions au XXe siècle.* Paris: Fayard, 1990.

Sokel, Walter H. "Two Visions of 'Minority'' literature: Deleuze, Kafka, and the German-Jewish Enclave of Prague." *Council on National Literatures/World Report* 6:1–2 (Jan,–April 1983): 5–8.

Sollers, Philippe. "Gilles Deleuze: Proust et les signes." *Tel Quel* 19 (Autumn 1964): 94–95.

Spivak, Gayatri Chakravorty. "Can the Subaltern Speak?" C. Nelson and L. Grossberg, eds., *Marxism and the Interpretation of Culture.* Urbana: University of Illinois Press, 1988.

Spivak, Gayatri Chakravorty and Michael Ryan. "Anarchism Revisited: A New Philosophy." *Diacritics* 82 (Summer 1978): 66–79.

Stéphane, André. *L'Universe contestationnaire.* Paris: Payot, 1969.

———. "La fin d'un malentendu." *Contrepoint* 7–8 (1972).

Stack, G. J. Review of *Foucault. Review of Metaphysics* 43:3 (March 1990): 629.

Stivale, Charles J. "Bibliography: Gilles Deleuze, Félix Guattari." *SubStance* 13:3/4 (1984): 96–105.

———. "Deleuze and Guattari." *SubStance* 20:3 no. 66 (Winter 1991).

———. "Gilles Deleuze & Félix Guattari: Schizoanalysis and Literary Discourse." *SubStance* 29 (1981): 46–57.

———. "Introduction." *SubStance* 13:3/4 (1984): 3–6.

———. "Introduction: Actuality and Concepts." *SubStance* 20:3 no. 66 (Winter 1991): 3–9.

———. "The Literary Element in *Mille Plateaux:* The New Cartography of Deleuze and Guattari." *SubStance* 13:3/4 (1984): 20–34.

———. "Mille/Punks/Cyber/Plateaus: Science Fiction and Deleuzo-Guattarian 'Becomings.'" *SubStance* 20:3 no. 66 (Winter 1991): 66–84.

———. *Oeuvre de sentiment, oeuvre de combat: La Trilogie de Jules Valles.* Presses universitaires de Lyon, 1988.

Strawson, Galen. "You can't see the world for the trees." *TLS* 3978 (June 30, 1978): 737.

Studlar, Gaylyn. *In the Realm of Pleasure.* Urbana: University of Illinois Press, 1988.

———. "Masochism and the Perverse Pleasures of the Cinema." Ed. B. Nichols, *Movies and Methods II.* Berkeley: University of California Press, 1985. 602–621.

———. Review of *Cinema-1. Quarterly Review of Film and Video* 12:3 (1990): 103–106.

Surin, Kenneth. "The Undecidable and the Fugitive: *Mille Plateaux* and the State-Form." *SubStance* 20:3 no. 66 (Winter 1991): 102–113.

Taat, A. Mieke. "Les signes du feu." *L'Arc* 49: *Deleuze* (1972, revised 1980): 78–88.

Tadie, Y. D., ed. *Lectures de Proust* Paris: Armand Colin, 1971.. 183–190.

Tarter, J. "Baudrillard and the Problematics of Post-New Left Media Theory." *American Journal of Semiotics*, 8:4 (1991): 155–71.

Taureck, Bernard. Review of *Foucault. Prima Philosophia* 1 (1988): 93–95.

Theweleit, Klaus. *Male Fantasies I: Women, Floods, Bodies, History.* Trans. Stephen Conway in collaboration with Erica Carter and Chris Turner. Minneapolis: University of Minnesota Press, 1987. Originally published as *Männerphantasien 1: Frauen, Fluten, Körper, Geschichte.* Verlag Roter Stern, 1977.

———. *Male Fantasies: II: Male Bodies: Psychoanalyzing the White Terror.* Trans. Erica Carter and Chris Turner in collaboration with Stephen Conway. Minneapolis: University of Minnesota Press, 1989. Originally publihsed as *Männerphantasien 2: Zur Psychoanalyse des weissens Terrors.* Verlag Roter Stern, 1978.

Thiher, Allen. Review of *Cinéma 2: L'Image-temps. The French Review* 61:5 (April 1988): 821–822.

———. Review of *Foucault. The French Review* 61:2 (Dec. 1987): 300–301.

Tholen, Georg Christoph. "Die frohliche Funktionalismus." F. Guattari, *Schizo-analyse und Wunschenergie* Bielefeld: Vergal Impulse, no date. 4–26.

Tomlinson, Hugh. Translator's note in *Deleuze, Nietzsche and Philosophy.* New York: Columbia University Press, 1983. xv.

————. "Nietzsche on the Edge of Town: Deleuze and Reflexivity." *Exceedingly Nietzsche: Aspects of Contemporary Nietzschean Interpretation.* Ed. David Farrell Krell and David Wood. New York: Routledge, 1988. 150–63.

Tomlinson, Hugh and Robert Galeta. Translators' introduction to Deleuze, *Cinema 2: The Time-Image.* Minneapolis: University of Minnesota Press, 1989. xv–xviii.

Tomlinson, Hugh, Robert Galeta, Giorgio Passerone, Kuniichi Uno and Dana Polan. "Anti-Ödipus, Mill Mesetas . . . " *Magazine littéraire* 257 (Sept. 1988): 60–63.

Tomlinson, Hugh and Barbara Habberjam. Translators' introduction to Deleuze, *Bergsonism.* New York: Zone, 1988. 7–10.

————. Translators' introduction to Deleuze, *Cinema 1: The Movement-Image* Minneapolis: University of Minnesota Press, 1986. xi–xiii.

————. Translators' introduction to Deleuze, *Dialogues.* New York: Columbia University Press, 1987. xi–xiii.

————. Translators' introduction to Deleuze, *Kant's Critical Philosophy: The Doctrine of the Faculties.* Minneapolis: University of Minnesota Press, 1984. xv–xvi.

Toro, A. D. "Postmodernism and the Latin-American Narrative." *Revista Iberoamericana* 57:155 (1991): 441–67.

Toubiana, S. "Philosophical Concepts and Cinematography. A Conversation with Gilles Deleuze." *Cahiers du Cinéma* No. 380 (1986): 24–32.

Tournier, Michel. *The Wind Spirit: An Autobiography.* Trans. Arthur Goldhammer. Boston: Beacon Press, 1988. Originally published as *Le Vent paraclet.* Paris: Editions Gallimard, 1977.

Troisfontaines, Claude. "Dieu dans le premier livre de l'Ethique." *Revue Philosophique de Louvain* vol. 72 (1974): 467–81.

Tucker, Bernhard. "Palimpsest: Ein propadeutischer Versuch zur Geschichts- und Staats-philosophie des Anti-Ödipus." Ed. R. Heinz & G. C. Tholen, *Schizo-Scleichwege.* Bremen: Impulse Verlag, no. date.

Turgeon, "*What is Philosophy* by Gilles Deleuze and Félix Guattari." *Liberté* 34:2 (April 1992): 95–8.

Turkle, Sherry. *Psychoanalytic Politics: Freud's French Revolution.* Cambridge: MIT Press, 1978.

Vattimo, Gianni. *Il Soggetto e la Maschera: Nietzsche e il Problema della Liberazione.* Milan, 1974.

Vauday, Patrick. "Écrit à vue: Deleuze-Bacon." *Critique* 426 (Nov. 1982): 956–964.

Vigorelli, Amadeo. "Towards a Critique of the French Ideology." *Telos* 47 (Spring 1981): 190–197. Translated by Greg Ostrander.

Villani, Arnaud. "Deleuze et la philosophie microphysique." D. Janicaud, ed., *Philosophie contemporaine.* Paris: Belles Lettres, 1985: 45–74.

————. "Géographie physique de *Mille Plateaux.*" *Critique* 455 (April 1985): 331–347.

————. "Poststructuralist Alternatives to Deconstruction." Hugh Silverman and Gary Aylesworth, Eds., *The Textual Sublime: Deconstruction and Its Difference.* Albany: SUNY Press, 1990. 223–230.

Virmaux, Alain and Odette. *Artaud: un bilan critique.* Paris: Pierre Belfond, 1979.

Vizier, Alain. Review of *Foucault. Modern Language Notes* C11 (1987): 943–947.

Vuarnet, Jean-Noël. "Métamorphoses de Sophie." *L'Arc 49: Deleuze* (1972, revised 1980): 31–38.

Wahl, François. "Hors ou dans la philosophie?" *Michel Foucault philosophe.* Paris: Seuil, 1989. 85–100

Wahl, Jean. "Nietzsche et la philosophie." *Revue de Métaphysique et de Morale* 3 (July–Sept. 1963): 352–379.

Walsh, M. Review of *Masochism. Journal of Film and Video* 41:4 (Winter 1989): 84–87.

Wang, B. "On the Run: Crisis of Identity in V. Woolf's Mrs. Dalloway." *Modern Fiction Studies* 38:1 (Spring 1992): 177–91.

Wark, M. "After Literature: Culture, Policy, Theory and Beyond." *Meanjin* 51:4 (Summer 1992): 677–90.

Watte, Pierre. "Les avatars d'Oedipe-Roi." *Revue nouvelle* 62 (Jan.–June 1973): 556–566.

Weber, Samuel. *The Legend of Freud.* Minneapolis: University of Minnesota Press, 1982.

Weber, Sebastian. "Cinema von Gilles Deleuze." *Merkur* XLII (1988): 418–424.

Welchman, Alistair. "On the Matter of Chaos." *Pli: Deleuze and the Transcendental Unconscious.* Coventry: University of Warwick, 1992. 137–57.

Wetzel, Michael. "Mit 'Bewaffnetem Auge': Von der 'Phänomenologie des Geistes' zur 'Mikrophysik der Krafte'." Ed. R. Heinz & G. C. Tholen, *Schizo-Schleichwege.* Bremen: Impulse Verlag, no date.

Wilke, S. "The Role of Art in a Dialectic of Modernism and Postmodernism: The Theater of Heiner Muller." *Paragraph* 14:3 (Nov. 1991): 276–89.

Williams, James. "Monitoring vs Metaphysical Modeling: or How to Predict the Future of the Postmodern Condition." *Pli: Deleuze and the Transcendental Unconscious.* Coventry: University of Warwick, 1992. 41–65.

Wolfromm, J. D. "Les toiles du maître." *Magazine littéraire* 210 (Sept. 1984): 42.

Wolff, Francis. "Trios: Deleuze, Derrida, Foucault, historiens du platonisme." Barbara Cassin, ed., *Nos Grecs et leurs modernes: Les Stratégies contemporaines d'appropriation de l'Antiquité.* Paris: Seuil, 1992: 232–248.

Wood, David. *The Deconstruction of Time.* Atlantic Highlands, N.J.: Humanities Press, 1989.

Wright, Elizabeth. "Another Look at Lacan and Literary Criticism." *New Literary History* (Spring 1988): 617–627.

———. *Psychoanalytic Criticism: Theory in Practice.* New York: Methuen, 1984.

Wyschogrod, Edith. *Saints and Postmodernism.* Chicago: University of Chicago Press, 1990.

Zanini, Adelino. "La Pensée 'faible' entre être et différence: esquisse critique d'une éthique molle." *Futur antérieur, supplement: "Le Gai renoncement"* (1991): 107–114.

Zavadil, Alexandre. "Deleuze ou la mort en detail." *Lendemains* 14:53 (1989): 10–17.

Zehn Yahre Anti-Ödipus von Deleuze/Guattari. Dusseldorf: unpublished reader, 1984.

Zourabichvili, François. "Deleuze: le negatif destitué." *Magazine littéraire* 298 (April 1992): 85–87.

———. *Deleuze: Une philosophie de l'évènement.* Paris: Presses universitaires de France, forthcoming.

II. Special Journal Issues on Deleuze

Esprit 12 (1972). French

L'Arc 49: Deleuze (1972, revised 1980). French.

Semiotext(e): Anti-Oedipus 3:2 (1977). English.

SubStance XIII:3/4 (1984). English.

Revue de la pensée aujourd'hui 12:11 (no. 9, 1984). Japanese.

Magazine littéraire 257 (Sept. 1988). French.

Lendemains XIV:53 (1989). French and German.

SubStance XX:3 (no. 66, Winter 1991). English.

Pli: University of Warwick Journal of Philosophy (1992). English.

The Journal of the British Society for Phenomenology 24:1 (1993). English.

Agenda: Contemporary Art Magazine 33 (1993). English.

III. Theses and Dissertations on Deleuze

Aumetre, Jacques. "Deleuze ou la décapitalisation". Doctorat du troisième cycle 1977, Université de Paris l-Sorbonne.

Baker, Langton G. "La bête philosophe: French Nietzsche Reception". Doctorate of Philosophy in Philosophy, York University, 1990.

Barker, Stephen, F. "Articulation Etrangeté and Power: Aspects of Nietzsche in Theory and Practice". Doctorate of Philosophy in Comparative Literature, University of Arizona, 1987.

Boundas, Constantin V. "The Theory of Difference of Gilles Deleuze". Doctorate of Philosophy in Philosopy, Purdue University, 1985.

Brandt, Joan E. "The Problem of Discontinuity in Contemporary French Poetry and Theory". Doctorate of Philosophy in Romance Literature, University of California at Irvine, 1982.

Bryden, Mary. "'Another Like Herself'? Women in the Prose and Drama of Samuel Beckett". Doctorate of Philosophy in Romance Languages, University of Reading, 1990.

Cancino, Cesar. "Nietzsche, examen critique de la lecture de Gilles Deleuze". Université de Paris IV-Censier.

Chen, Kuan-Hsing. "History, Theory and Cultural Politics: Towards a Minor Discourse of Mass Media and Postmodernity". Doctorate of Philosophy in Mass Communications, University of Iowa, 1988.

Colombat, André Pierre. "Deleuze et la littérature". Doctorate of Philosophy in French Literature, Washington University, 1989.

Damon, Maria. "The Poetics of Marginality: 'Minority Discourse' in American Modernist Poetry". Doctorate of Philosophy in American Literature, Stanford University, 1988.

de Verneil, Marie C. "Apollinaire: Un reexamen du modernisme". Doctorate of Philosophy in Modern Literature, Catholic University of America, 1983.

Dienst, Richard W. "The Words of Television: Theories of Culture and Technology". Doctorate of Philosophy in Mass Communications, Duke University, 1991.

Dix, Douglas S. "The Text as War Machine: Writing to Destroy". Doctorate of Philosophy in English Literature, University of Washington, 1988.

Epps, Bradley S. "The Violence of the Letter: Oppression and Resistance in Juan Goytisolo". Doctorate of Philosophy in Comparative Literature, Brown University, 1989.

Epstein, Grace A. "Fluid Bodies: Narrative Disruption and Layering in Doris Lessing, Toni Morrison and Margaret Atwood". Doctorate of Philosophy in Women's Studies, Ohio State University, 1990.

Everett, Jay D. "Freud and du Prel: Psychoanalysis, Magic and Mediation". Doctorate of Philosophy in Philosophy, State University of New York at Stony Brook, 1989.

Gibbs, Jason M. "Prolongation in Order Determinate Music: Semblances". Doctorate of Philosophy in Music, University of Pittsburgh, 1989.

Gilliland, Gail. "A Poetics of Being Minor". Doctorate of Philosophy in Comparative Literature, University of Michigan, 1990.

Godorecci, Maurizio A. "La voce di fedele romani: Ombre e corpi nell'ottono-vecento italiano". Doctorate of Philosophy in Comparative Literature, New York University, 1990.

Guglielmo, Rebecca W. "The Prophetic Mode in Postmodern Fiction: From Pynchon to Rushdie". Doctorate of Philosophy in Comparative Literature, Indiana University, 1991.

Hardt, Michael. "The Art of Organization: Foundations of Political Ontology in Gilles Deleuze and Antonio Negri". Doctorate of Philosophy in Comparative Literature, University of Washington, 1991.

Harland, Richard. "Superstructuralism". Doctorate of Philosophy in Linguistics, University of New South Wales (Australia), 1986.

Hobbs, Claire. "Cutting Off the King's Head: Discourse and Subjection". Doctorate of Philosophy in Modern Literature, University of Essex, 1988.

Holland, Eugene W. "Toward a Redefinition of Masochism". Doctorate of Philosophy in Romance Literature, University of California at San Diego, 1982.

Infantino, Stephen C. "Proust and Photography: Studies in Single-Lens Reflexivity". Doctorate of Philosophy in Romance Literature, University of Southern California, 1986.

Izagirre, Josu Rekalde. "Una experimentacion en el campo del video-arte fundamentada en la nocion de transformacion temporali". Degree in Fine Arts, Universidad del Pais Vasco (Spain), 1989.

Jardine, Alice A. "Gynesis: Configurations of Woman in the Contemporary Imagination". Doctorate of Philosophy in Comparative Literature, Columbia University, 1982.

Johnston, John. "The Dialogic in William Gaddis's *The Recognitions*". Doctorate of Philosophy in American Literature, Columbia University, 1984.

Langsam, Hannah. "Proust: Literary Couturier". Doctorate of Philosophy in Romance Literature, Washington University, 1985.

Leroy, Fabrice I. "Le Vase clos Proustien". Doctorate of Philosophy in Romance Literature, The Louisiana State University, 1991.

Liao, Ping-Hui. "Inscription, Memory, Transgression: Sung-Yuan Poet-Painters". Doctorate of Philosophy in Comparative Literature, University of California at San Diego, 1987.

Lovett, Marilyn. "Fire in the Library: Paranoia and Schizophrenia as Models of Linguistic Crisis in Elias Canetti's *Die Blendung*". Doctorate of Philosophy in Comparative Literature, Indiana University, 1982.

Martin, Joel, W. "Cultural Hermeneutics on the Frontier: Colonialism and the Muscogulge Millenarian Revolt of 1813". Doctorate of Philosophy in Religion, Duke University, 1988.

Massumi, Brian. "Annotated Translation with Critical Introduction of *Mille Plateaux*". Doctorate of Philosophy in Romance Literature, Yale University, 1987.

McDonald, Kevin R. "Writing the Active: Nietzsche's Address to the Individual". Doctorate of Philosophy in Philosophy, State University of New York at Stony Brook, 1990.

McHugh, Patrick. "Culture and Masculinity: Critical Impasses in Twentieth Century Social Narrative and Discourse". Doctorate of Philosophy in Comparative Literature, State University of New York at Binghampton, 1988.

Melaver, Martin E. "The Resistance of Narrative". Doctorate of Philosophy in Comparative Literature, Harvard University, 1990.

Moore, George B. "Difference in Kind: The Origin of Gertrude Stein's Aesthetics in *The Making of Americans*. Doctorate of Philosophy in American Literature, University of Colorado at Boulder, 1990.

Murphy, Timothy. "Wising up the Marks: Politics Without Right in William S. Burroughs and Gilles Deleuze". Doctorate of Philosophy in English Literature, University of California at Los Angeles, 1993 (expected).

Meyerson, Gregory D. "The Dialectics of Defeat: Domination and Liberation in Contemporary Critical Theory". Doctorate of Philosophy in Philosophy, Northwestern University, 1989.

Nelson, Lycette. "Maurice Blanchet: The Fragment and the Whole" Doctorate of Philosophy in Comparative Literature, State University of New York at Buffalo, 1992.

Purcell, Jack A. "Heidegger's Early Ontology: Rethinking the Ground". Doctorate of Philosophy in Philosophy, Purdue University, 1989.

Richardson, Elizabeth M. "Mothers, Madams and 'Lady-like' Men: Femininity in *A la recherche du temps perdu*". Doctorate of Philosophy in Romance Literature, New York University, 1983.

Rosenberg, Martin E. "Being and Becoming: Physics, Hegemony, Art and the Nomad". Doctorate of Philosophy in English Literature, University of Michigan, 1990.

Sacca, Annalisa. "Signifying Simulacra". Doctorate of Philosophy in Romance Literature, New York University, 1990.

Scoggan, John W. "De(con)structive Poetics: Readings of Hilda Doolittle's *The War Trilogy*". Doctorate of Philosophy in Modern Literature, University of British Columbia, 1982.

Seem, Mark D. "The Logic of Power: An Essay on Gilles Deleuze, Michel Foucault and Félix Guattari". Doctorate of Philosophy in Philosopy, State University of New York at Buffalo, 1976.

Seelow, David D. "Radical Modernism and Sexuality: Freud, Reich, D. H. Lawrence". Doctorate of Philosophy in Comparative Literature, State University of New York at Stony Brook, 1990.

Stivale, Charles J. "Oeuvre de sentiment, oeuvre de combat: La trilogie Jacques Vingtras de Jules Valles". Doctorate of Philosophy in Modern Langauges, University of Illinois at Urbana, 1987.

Stone, Craig E. "Retaining Resemblance: Rietveld Represented". Masters Degree in Fine Arts, California State University at Long Beach, 1988.

Trezise, Thomas A. "Into the Breach: Samuel Beckett and the Ends of Literature". Doctorate of Philosophy in Romance Literature, Yale University, 1987.

Wenstrom, John D. "Modernist Irony: Frost, Eliot". Doctorate of Philosophy in Modern Literature, University of Minnesota, 1991.

Winchester, James J. "Nietzsche's Aesthetic Turn". Doctorate of Philosophy in Philosophy, Emory University, 1991.

Wood, Naomi J. "Better than Life: Death as a Developmental Trope in Nineteenth-Century British Children's Fiction". Doctorate of Philosophy in English Literature, Duke University, 1991.

Contributors

ALAIN BADIOU teaches at the Université de Paris VIII. He is the author of *Peut-on penser la politique* (Paris: Seuil, 1985), *L'être et l'évènement* (Paris: Seuil, 1988), and *Manifeste pour la philosophie* (Paris: Seuil, 1989).

RÉDA BENSMAIA teaches theory of literature, film and francophone literature in the French Studies Department at Brown University. He is the author of *The Barthes Effect: Introduction to the Reflective Text* (Minneapolis: University of Minnesota Press, 1987) and editor of a special issue of *Lendemains* on Gilles Deleuze. He has published widely on contemporary French and francophone literature, film theory, and cultural studies in *Iris, Hors-Cadre, Ciné-maction, Camera Obscura, Poétique, Yale French Studies, Substance,* etc. He is currently working on a study tentatively titled *The Return of Rhetoric: Literary Theory from Paulhan to de Man.*

CONSTANTIN V. BOUNDAS teaches Philosophy at Trent University, Ontario. He has written numerous essays on Deleuze and translated and edited *Logique du Sens* with Mark Lester and Charles Stivale (New York: Columbia University Press, 1990), translated *Empiricism and Subjectivity* (New York: Columbia University Press, 1991), and edited *The Deleuze Reader* (New York: Columbia Unversity Press, 1992).

ROSI BRAIDOTTI teaches in and chairs the Women's Studies Department in the arts faculty at the University of Utrecht in the Netherlands. She is the author of *Patterns of Dissonance* (New York: Routledge, 1991) and of articles on feminist philosophy and psychoanalysis. She is an advisor for the journals: *Différences, Les Cahiers du Grif, Women's Studies, International Forum,* and *Dutch Women's Studies Journal.* She is currently completing a study of Deleuze in a feminist perspective, which focuses on the female body, biotechnology, and the "monstrous other."

337

PETER CANNING teaches comparative literature at the University of Minnesota. He has published on Deleuze, Lacan, and Nietzsche. He is the author of "Fabulation of the Jews in Christian and Nazi History" (in *Copyright* no. 1) and "Transcendental Narcissism Meets the Multiplicity," in *Thinking Bodies* forthcoming from Stanford: Stanford University Press. He is currently working on a book on time and event.

GILLES DELEUZE taught philosophy at the Université de Paris VIII until his retirement in 1987. His most recent publications include *Qu'est-ce que la philosophie?* with Félix Guattari, (Paris: Minuit, 1991); *Pourparlers 1972-1990* (Paris: Minuit, 1990); *Le Pli: Leibniz et le Baroque* (Paris: Minuit, 1988); *Foucault*, trans. Sean Hand (Minneapolis: University of Minnesota Press, 1988); *Cinema 1: The Movement-Image*, trans. Hugh Tomlinson and Barbara Habberjam (Minneapolis: University of Minnesota Press, 1986); and *Cinema 2: The Time-Image*, trans. Hugh Tomlinson and Robert Galeta (Minneapolis: University of Minnesota Press, 1989).

ELIZABETH GROSZ teaches critical theory, philosophy, and women's studies at the University of Sydney, Australia. She is the author of *Sexual Subversions, Three French Feminists* (Sydney: Allen and Unwin, 1989) and *Jacques Lacan, A Feminist Introduction* (New York: Routledge, 1990). She has also edited a special issue of *Hypatia* on "Feminism and the Body."

ALPHONSO LINGIS teaches philosophy at Pennsylvania State University. He is the author of *Excesses: Eros and Culture*, (New York: SUNY, 1984), *Libido, The French Existential Theories* (Bloomington: Indiana University Press, 1985), *Phenomenological Explanations* (Boston: Hingham, MA, 1986), and *Deathbound Subjectivity* (Bloomington: Indiana University Press, 1989).

JEAN-CLET MARTIN is the author of *Variations: La philosophie de Gilles Deleuze* (Paris: Payot, 1993). He is completing a book on the Middle Ages and Romanesque art inspired by the methods of Foucault and Deleuze; he is also the editor of a forthcoming collection of essays on the work of Alain Badiou entitled *Une logique de l'évènement*.

TODD MAY teaches philosophy at Clemson University. He is the author of *Foucault: Between Genealogy and Epistemology* (University Park: Pennsylvania State University Press, 1993) and has published on post-structuralism and political thought.

DOROTHEA OLKOWSKI teaches philosophy and is director of the Women's Studies Department at the University of Colorado, Colorado Springs. She is series editor of "Theory, Culture and the Arts" for Humanities Press and is the author of articles on film theory, aesthetics, and semiotics. She is currently working on a book on representation and women and is co-editing (with James Morley) *Merleau-Ponty: Desires and Imaginings* and (with Kenneth Calhoon) *Beside Expressionism: New Histories of Early German Cinema.*

PAUL PATTON lectures in philosophy at the University of Sydney. He has published articles on various aspects of recent French philosophy, notably on Foucault and Deleuze. He has recently completed the translation of *Différence et Répétition* and has edited *Nietzsche, Feminism, and Political Theory.*

DANA POLAN is professor of English and film at the University of Pittsburgh. He is the author of *Power and Paranoia: History, Narrative and the American Cinema, 1940-1950* (New York: Columbia University Press, 1986), and *The Political Language of Film and the Avant-Garde* (Ann Arbor: UMI, 1985). He translated Deleuze and Guattari's *Kafka.* He is currently at work on a book on the public representation of academics.

MARIE-CLAIRE ROPARS-WUILLEUMIER is a film theorist whose essays appear frequently in *Littérature, Esprit, Poétique* and *Études littéraires.* She is the author of several books which include *La Politique du texte: enjeux sociocritiques* (Lille: Presses Universitaires de Lille, 1992), *Le texte divisé: essai sur l'écriture filmique* (Paris: PUF, 1981), *Octobre: écriture et idéologie* (with Pierre Sorlin and Michèle Lagny) (Paris: Albatros, 1976), and *De la littérature au cinéma: génèse d'une écriture* (Paris: Armand Colin, 1970).

Index

341